## 1989 Tax Rate Schedules

2

| If Taxable Income Is: | | Then the Gross Tax Payable Is: | | |
|---|---|---|---|---|
| Over | But not over | Amount | Plus (Percent) | Of the amount over: |

**Single Taxpayers (other than surviving spouses and heads of households)**

| Over | But not over | Amount | Plus (Percent) | Of the amount over: |
|---|---|---|---|---|
| $ –0– | $ 18,550 | $ –0– | 15 | $ –0– |
| 18,550 | 44,900 | 2,782.50 | 28 | 18,550 |
| 44,900 | 93,130 | 10,160.50 | 33 | 44,900 |
| 93,130 | | 26,076.40(a) | 28 | 93,130 |

**Married Individuals (and surviving spouses) Filing Joint Returns**

| Over | But not over | Amount | Plus (Percent) | Of the amount over: |
|---|---|---|---|---|
| $ –0– | $ 30,950 | $ –0– | 15 | $ –0– |
| 30,950 | 74,850 | 4,642.50 | 28 | 30,950 |
| 74,850 | 155,320 | 16,934.50 | 33 | 74,850 |
| 155,320 | | 43,489.60(b) | 28 | 155,320 |

**Heads of Households**

| Over | But not over | Amount | Plus (Percent) | Of the amount over: |
|---|---|---|---|---|
| $ –0– | $ 24,850 | $ –0– | 15 | $ –0– |
| 24,850 | 64,200 | 3,727.50 | 28 | 24,850 |
| 64,200 | 128,810 | 14,745.50 | 33 | 64,200 |
| 128,810 | | 36,066.80(c) | 28 | 128,810 |

**Married Individuals Filing Separate Returns**

| Over | But not over | Amount | Plus (Percent) | Of the amount over: |
|---|---|---|---|---|
| $ –0– | $ 15,475 | $ –0– | 15 | $ –0– |
| 15,475 | 37,425 | 2,321.25 | 28 | 15,475 |
| 37,425 | 117,895 | 8,467.25 | 33 | 37,425 |
| 117,895 | | 35,022.35(d) | 28 | 117,895 |

**Fiduciary Taxpayers**

| Over | But not over | Amount | Plus (Percent) | Of the amount over: |
|---|---|---|---|---|
| $ –0– | $ 5,200 | $ –0– | 15 | $ –0– |
| 5,200 | 13,500 | 780 | 28 | 5,200 |
| 13,500 | 27,020 | 3,104 | 33 | 13,500 |
| 27,020 | | –0– | 28 | –0– |

**Corporate Taxpayers**

| Over | But not over | Amount | Plus (Percent) | Of the amount over: |
|---|---|---|---|---|
| $ –0– | $ 50,000 | $ –0– | 15 | $ –0– |
| 50,000 | 75,000 | 7,500 | 25 | 50,000 |
| 75,000 | 100,000 | 13,750 | 34 | 75,000 |
| 100,000 | 335,000 | 22,250 | 39 | 100,000 |
| 335,000 | | –0– | 34 | –0– |

(a) PLUS the lesser of (1) 5% (taxable income *less* $93,130) or (2) 28% × (the total amount claimed for personal and dependent exemption deductions).

(b) PLUS the lesser of (1) 5% (taxable income *less* $155,320) or (2) 28% × (the total amount claimed for personal and dependent exemption deductions).

(c) PLUS the lesser of (1) 5% (taxable income *less* $128,810) or (2) 28% × (the total amount claimed for personal and dependent exemption deductions).

(d) PLUS the lesser of (1) 5% (taxable income *less* $117,895) or (2) 28% × (the total amount claimed for personal and dependent exemption deductions).

# Federal Taxes
# and Management Decisions

The Robert N. Anthony/Willard J. Graham Series in Accounting
Consulting Editor    Robert N. Anthony    Harvard University

# Federal Taxes and Management Decisions

**Ray M. Sommerfeld**
The James L. Bayless/Rauscher Pierce Refsnes, Inc.
Professor in Business Administration
The University of Texas at Austin

1989–90 Edition
**IRWIN**
Homewood, IL 60430
Boston, MA 02116

Sponsoring editor: Ron M. Regis
Project editor: Jean Roberts
Production manager: Irene H. Sotiroff
Compositor: Carlisle Communications, Ltd.
Typeface: 10/12 Palatino
Printer: R. R. Donnelley & Sons Company

LIBRARY OF CONGRESS

Library of Congress Cataloging-in-Publication Data

Sommerfeld, Ray M.
    Federal taxes and management decisions/Ray M. Sommerfeld—
1989-90 ed.
        p.    cm.
    Includes index.
    Irwin: ISBN 0-256-07252-3
    CFP: ISBN 0-256-07670-7
    1. Business enterprises—Taxation—UnitedStates. 2. Tax
planning—United States.   I. Title.
KF6450.S65 1989
343.7304—dc19                                                     88–23781
[347.3034]                                                        CIP

*Printed in the United States of America*

1 2 3 4 5 6 7 8 9 0 DO 5 4 3 2 1 0 9 8

*To Andrea and Kristin*

# Preface

This text is written for all students who need only to *recognize* the important tax consequences that attach to many common business transactions. This group includes most students of business administration enrolled in general management programs, especially those in M.B.A. programs. It may also include that majority of accounting and law students who do not intend to become tax specialists.

*Federal Taxes and Management Decisions* is pragmatic. It attempts to demonstrate how substantially different tax liabilities sometimes attach to nearly identical economic events. That knowledge explains why tax rules substantially alter human behavior at the individual and the business entity level, at least for those who understand the rules. The book constantly emphasizes practical results, giving little or no consideration to the intellectual, social, or political considerations inherent in those results.

Because of this emphasis, there is no necessity to discuss in detail every last-minute development in tax legislation and/or tax administration. Rather, this text will be revised or supplemented only as major new developments occur. As a general rule, entirely new editions will be prepared every other year; special supplements may be made available to those who adopt the text on an as-needed basis. The 1989–90 edition reflects the changes made in the law through September 1988.

Many chapters of this text are topical in nature and can therefore be read and understood independently. The only major exceptions are Chapters 2, 3, 4, 5, and 6. They should be read before any subsequent materials if the book is to be used as a primary text. Chapter 2 provides a broad review of some basic income tax propositions that are fundamental to the remainder of the book; I hope it will also clarify some common misconceptions. Chapter 3 explains which entities are required to report and pay taxes on their incomes. It also explains how the income earned by other entities is attributed to one of the taxable entities and the important differences in the tax rate schedules that are applied to each of the taxable entities. Chapter 4 explains why the careful selection of a business entity is so important to many tax plans. Chapter 5 introduces the reader to basic accounting methods and their significance in income taxation. Chapter 6 reviews the AMT (or alternative minimum tax) which effectively creates an alternative income tax system for many taxpayers.

The rules for the AMT are rather complex. Nevertheless they cannot be dismissed because they affect tax planning so frequently.

All other chapters—except 13 and 15, which deal with related problems—represent self-contained discussions of important tax-saving opportunities in specific though common business decisions. Chapter 13 describes some of the more common tax traps. It is as important for the potential entrepreneur to be aware of a tax trap as it is to be aware of common tax-saving opportunities. The final chapter describes the several events which collectively constitute the taxing process of taxing—the filing of returns, the audit selection procedures, the accompanying administrative reviews by the IRS, and possible litigation alternatives.

Chapter 15 also deals with the common problem of identifying qualified taxpayer assistance. In a very important sense, the tax responsibilities of the future business managers (to whom this book is addressed) end just where the tax expert's begin. It is assumed that no one would directly apply the ideas suggested here until a tax expert had been consulted. I hope this book may help the student distinguish between real tax experts and those who are only marginally qualified.

Finally, the reader should understand that the book is in no sense comprehensive. The provisions selected for discussion are those that contain the most tax significance in the most common transactions. In general these are income tax provisions, although a lesser emphasis is placed, in one chapter, on estate and gift tax considerations. The reason for this concentration of attention is explained by the fact that the federal income tax dominates the tax structure of the United States. By comparison, relatively little can be done by the taxpayer to modify nonincome tax liabilities. The only major exception involves the federal estate and gift taxes, which, as noted, are discussed in this text.

A special word of caution is appropriate for this 1989–90 edition. The 1986 tax law changes can only be described as massive. The many ways in which these changes will affect behavior will not be fully understood for several years. Thus, what appears in this edition are still only the more obvious implications for tax planning after the 1986 Act. All readers are urged to follow the business press for additional ideas that inevitably will be discovered in the coming months.

I would like to take this opportunity to thank the many students who have contributed so importantly to my own education. Their patience and assistance in bringing this project to fruition is deeply appreciated. I would also like to express my appreciation to those professors who have adopted prior editions of this text and, as a consequence of their experiences, made recommendations for its improvement.

The opinions expressed, of course, are mine alone and in no way represent an official position of the institution with which I am associated.

**Ray M. Sommerfeld**

# Contents

*Operating Losses. Employee Status. Gaining a Special Tax
Deduction. Disposition of a Business. Fluctuating Income.*
Special Considerations for Multinational Businesses:
*Unincorporated Businesses. Corporate Businesses.*

# Federal Taxes
# and Management Decisions

# CHAPTER 1

# An Introduction

Tax planning is a complex subject. That unfortunate conclusion does not mean, however, that the average person can never understand the fundamental concepts upon which successful tax plans are based. Rather, this complexity means that the average individual will have to be satisfied with understanding general rules and allow others who are more expert in tax matters to concern themselves with the details actually needed to implement many tax plans. Stated in another way, tax complexity means that the average U.S. citizen will have to be satisfied with a symptom-recognition level of knowledge.

The increasing dependence on symptom recognition combined with expert assistance is by no means unique to federal taxation. In the last few decades, virtually all Americans have come to rely upon expert assistance in fields as diverse as automobile mechanics and medicine. What is unusual in taxation is the relative scarcity of published materials that can be used as a general guide to overall tax planning. There are literally hundreds of books and articles published each year on tax subjects, but most of those are either written for the expert or concerned with only one aspect of tax planning. Unlike most of the other books, this one attempts to provide the reader with the broadest possible vista of tax-planning opportunities and tax traps. Simply stated, the goal of this book is symptom recognition—for those who either manage a business or control wealth—a tax equivalent of Dr. Spock's well-known book on pediatric medicine for parents. The tax-conscious businessperson and the expert tax adviser, working together, can very often significantly reduce the liability that otherwise would be payable.

Once each year the daily press dutifully reports the number of individual taxpayers who earned an income of $200,000 or more in the preceding year, but paid no taxes. That annual announcement triggers two basic emotions—namely, disgust for a tax system that allows such an occurrence and curiosity about how we might do the same. This book is intended to help you understand how and why a significant tax reduction may be possible for you. In all candor, you should understand that the probabilities of being able to reduce your own tax liability to zero are really very limited and not terribly important. What is far more important is that there are things you can do to reduce your tax liability substantially even though those actions will not reduce it to zero.

Headlines and political interest may focus on the few wealthy individuals who reduce their income tax to nothing; fortunately, real economic success is not so demanding.

Before we go further, the reader should understand that this book has limited immediate impact for the nonpropertied, salaried employee of a large corporation. The only reason for this neglect is the cold fact that relatively little can be done to save this person significant amounts of taxes. Our income tax bears most heavily upon wage and salary earners simply because they have so few options available and because the tax laws have taken the necessary precautions to minimize the tax consequences associated with those few remaining choices. Self-employed people, and especially people with substantial amounts of property, have more options, and because of the magnitude of those options, such people have many important opportunities for tax saving. Our primary concern will be with those opportunities.

## THE MORALITY OF IT ALL

No socially sensitive reader can escape subtle doubts about the morality of finding more and better ways to reduce his or her own tax liability when taxes are supposedly collected and then expended for the greatest common good. These doubts, however, might be resolved on at least two grounds. First, tax avoidance has been found by the courts to be wholly legal. Perhaps the most celebrated statement on this point was delivered in 1947 in the case of *Commissioner* v. *Newman*. In a dissenting opinion, Justice Learned Hand wrote:

> Over and over again courts have said that there is nothing sinister in so arranging one's affairs as to keep taxes as low as possible. Everybody does so, rich or poor, and all do right, for nobody owes any public duty to pay more than the law demands: taxes are enforced exactions, not voluntary contributions. To demand more in the name of morals is mere cant.[1]

Even though Justice Hand's words are from a dissenting opinion, and therefore of no legal significance, they have been widely quoted as authoritative. Other legal opinions have reached the same conclusion, but have stated it in less colorful language.

Granting the legality of tax avoidance does not necessarily lead to the conclusion that it is in the country's best interest that knowledge of tax opportunities be more widely disseminated. However, there is even less to be said for restricting the knowledge of tax opportunities to any select few. All validated observations support the conclusion that the rich have been substantially more successful than the poor in tax avoidance. Nothing in this book is going to change that result because, as noted earlier, the mere own-

---

[1] *Commissioner v. Newman*, 159 F.2d 848 (CA–2, 1947).

ership of property gives the wealthy taxpayer a greater number of alternatives that make tax savings possible. To the extent that this book facilitates greater utilization of existing tax opportunities, it will serve to diffuse the benefits of tax avoidance among a larger number of less wealthy people. If the results of these tax opportunities are finally deemed to be socially unacceptable by the masses, the widest possible dispersion of knowledge about them can only hasten the adoption of corrective political mechanisms. In the interim, reduced taxes should lead to increased consumer spending and savings—both of which are generally deemed to be socially and politically desirable goals.

## BASIC TERMINOLOGY

Taxation, like every other discipline, relies upon some basic terminology to convey fundamental ideas. In tax planning, understanding a few common terms is essential. Among the most critical words and phrases are the following: *exclusion, deduction, tax base, tax rate,* and *tax credit*. Virtually every successful plan to save taxes is based on the manipulation of one or more of these variables. Because the concepts behind these words and phrases are so critical to tax-saving opportunities, it seems advisable to clarify their meaning before we turn our attention to more specific details.

### Exclusions

In tax parlance the word *exclusion* is used to refer to any item that, in ordinary English usage, would be considered part of a more general class of items or events that has been made the basis for a tax but has been specifically removed from the tax base by law. For example, the sales tax imposed by most states is generally imposed on all retail sales. At the same time, virtually all of the state legislatures have decided to exclude from the sales tax base all sales of foodstuffs for off-premise consumption. Thus, the retail sales of food items in a grocery store frequently constitute an exclusion from the general retail sales tax base.

In tax planning, one of the simplest and most effective methods of tax minimization involves the maximization of exclusions. As you might suspect, the list of exclusions is typically very brief, and therefore the amount of tax-planning potential in this area is limited. Our federal income tax does provide one very major exclusion. It does not tax the interest earned by taxpayers who invest their capital in a state or local government's bonds. Consequently, investors can reduce their federal income tax liability on investment income to zero simply by switching their portfolios from corporate stocks and securities to state and local government bonds. The major economic cost that attaches to this simple tax-saving plan is the reduced earnings that usually result because of the tax-exempt feature. That is, state and local government bonds typically pay lower rates of interest than do bonds of equivalent risk precisely because high-tax-bracket investors are willing to accept lower rates of interest that produce a higher aftertax return on their investment. To illustrate, the taxpayer in a 28 percent marginal tax bracket is better off investing in 7 percent state bonds than in 9 percent commercial paper because the aftertax return remains at 7 percent in the former instance but is reduced to 6.48 percent in the latter case. A taxpayer in the 15 percent marginal tax bracket would not, of course, reach the same conclusion.

## Deductions

In tax literature, the word *deduction* is used to refer to any item that the law authorizes as a reduction of a gross quantity to a net quantity designated as a tax base. Because both exclusions and deductions serve to reduce the net tax base, it is very easy to confuse the two concepts. For purposes of interpreting and applying certain tax rules, however, it is important that a clear distinction be maintained. As a simple illustration of this difference, consider the need of two taxpayers to file a federal income tax return. Taxpayer A earns $50,000 in interest on State of California bonds but incurs no authorized expenses in connection with that income. Taxpayer B earns $50,000 in rents from an apartment house and incurs $50,000 in deductions for depreciation, property taxes, interest, maintenance costs, and so forth. The law provides that a single taxpayer whose gross income exceeds some *de minimis* amount (generally $4,950 in 1988) must generally file an income tax return. Application of this filing requirement provision means that taxpayer A need *not* file a return, but that taxpayer B must. A has a gross income of zero because all of his or her income can be excluded from the gross tax base by definition. B has a gross income of $50,000 because his or her expenses are deductions, not exclusions from the gross tax base. Neither A nor B, of course, will pay any income tax if this is their only income, since both will have a net tax base of zero.

Obviously, taxes can be minimized to the extent that deductions can be maximized. The first step in maximizing deductions consists of learning which items are deductible simply to avoid overlooking one or more authorized deductions. Sometimes maximizing deductions may also require the rearrangement of one's business affairs and the creation of a particular form of business organization. The tax-saving value of a deduction is also directly related to the marginal tax bracket of the taxpayer incurring it. Thus a taxpayer in the 28 percent marginal tax bracket will save $2,800 in income taxes for every additional $10,000 in deductions claimed; a taxpayer in the 15 percent marginal tax bracket would save only $1,500 in taxes from the same deduction. It is therefore important that the taxpayer ensure, to the extent possible, that all authorized deductions are incurred at the most advantageous time (for example, in an unusually high income year) or by the most advantageous taxpayer (for example, by a corporation rather than an individual under certain circumstances).

### Tax Base

The term *tax base* simply refers to the net quantity on which any particular tax is levied. For purposes of income taxation that net quantity is called *taxable income*; for estate taxation, *taxable estate*; and for gift taxation, *taxable gifts*. The key word in each instance is the adjective *taxable*. What it connotes, of course, is that the residual quantity is the dollar value that remains after the taxpayer has given adequate consideration to all pertinent definitional problems, exclusions, and deductions. Careful attention to these three items makes possible the minimization of any tax base.

A taxpayer may be able to further minimize a tax liability by making certain that the tax base is divided among the maximum number of taxable entities. Because the tax rates utilized in income, estate, and gift taxation are progressive rates—that is, the marginal tax rates get higher as the tax base increases in amount—it is generally to the taxpayer's benefit to split a tax base among a number of taxable entities. Each reporting unit may therefore begin by applying the rates at the lowest possible level rather than have a single entity report the entire tax base and thus be forced to apply higher and higher marginal tax rates to the same aggregate amount of tax base.

### Tax Rate

A *tax rate* is a specified percentage, or series of percentages in the case of a progressive tax, which the law stipulates as the appropriate multiplier in the determination of a gross tax liability. Stated another way, any tax liability is calculated by multiplying the tax base by the statutory tax rate(s). For example, a state legislature may stipulate that it will utilize a 5 percent tax rate in determining the retail sales tax liability in a particular year. In that event anyone who purchases a $100 item that is subject to the retail sales tax will pay a sales tax of $5 on that purchase ($100 × 5 percent).

In income taxation, Congress has specified four different rate schedules for individual taxpayers (one each for single persons, heads of households, married persons filing jointly, and married persons filing separately), another totally different rate structure for corporate taxpayers, and yet another rate schedule for fiduciaries (i.e., for estates and trusts). Obviously, then, the tax liability of a taxpayer with a given amount of income will change automatically any time the taxpayer's affairs are rearranged so that a different rate schedule will be applied to that amount of income. Perhaps the most obvious rearrangement is marriage: a single individual earning a taxable income of $60,000 can currently reduce his or her 1988 tax liability by $2,935.50, from $15,322 to $12,386.50, simply by getting married *to a person who has no taxable income to report*. This illustration also demonstrates clearly the importance and complexity of the nontax considerations that must often be weighed before rushing headlong into perfectly legal tax-planning ideas. In addition, this illustration emphasizes the importance of details to tax conclusions because, for example, the marriage of two single persons, each earning a $30,000 taxable income, will actually increase their combined tax liability by $773.50, from $12,159 to $12,932.50 in 1988.

Taxpayers (and students of taxation) should learn to distinguish the difference between a marginal tax rate and an average tax rate. The former is by far the more important to tax planning. It is the tax rate which will apply to any *incremental amount* of gross income or deduction. The average tax rate is simply a number determined by dividing the total amount of tax paid by the total tax base for a given time period. Although the average rate may be informative from historical perspective, it cannot be used to make business decisions about the future; for that purpose you must utilize the taxpayer's marginal tax rate.

### Tax Credit

A *tax credit* is any specially authorized reduction in a gross tax liability. Note that tax credits are fundamentally different from deductions and exclusions even though all three items are subtracted at one point or another in the tax calculation procedure. A $500 tax credit reduces a gross tax liability by the full $500; a $500 deduction will reduce a tax liability by some smaller amount, the specific reduction being determined by the marginal tax rate of the taxpayer authorized to claim the deduction. Once again the list of tax credits is typically short.

To summarize the basic terminology introduced in this chapter, we might construct the following simple computational guide to illustrate the various steps followed in the tax determination process.

A gross measure of any general class of items or events declared a tax base by legislative action minus *exclusions* equals the gross tax base.

The gross tax base minus *deductions* equals the *net* tax base.

The *net tax base* multiplied by the *specified tax rate(s)* equals the gross tax liability.

The gross tax liability minus *tax credits* equals the net tax payable to the government.

As you consider the various tax-saving propositions detailed in the remaining chapters, you should attempt to categorize each one in the context of this computational guide. In other words, you should ask yourself exactly why that particular tax saving is made possible. You will very often discover that the answer depends upon the combined effect of two or more variables; for example, by a timely maximization of deductions, the taxpayer may be able to modify the effective tax rate in a most favorable manner. The reason for attempting to place each idea in this perspective is simply that, by the act of analyzing each illustration carefully, you will become attuned to the often simple differences that constitute a common thread among all tax-saving opportunities. The sooner you can identify these common threads, the sooner you will be able to apply the same basic idea to your own particular situation.

## THE MORE IMPORTANT TAXES

The U.S. tax structure differs significantly from those in many other countries because it depends so heavily on the income tax. Excluding social insurance contributions—more commonly known as Social Security or FICA taxes—*approximately* 60 percent of all tax revenues collected in the United States come from an income tax, 20 percent from sales tax, 10 percent from property taxes, and the remaining 10 percent from all other taxes combined. In most other countries, the indirect taxes—that is, the sales, property, and excise taxes—play a more dominant role; the income tax a lesser role. Because the federal income tax is so dominant in the United States, and because it is so readily subject to managerial manipulation, our primary attention in this book will be given to that one tax, which, incidentally, provides over $1 billion in federal revenue every day of the year! Most other taxes—such as state and city income taxes, sales taxes, property taxes, real estate transfer taxes, customs duties, and excise taxes—will be wholly dismissed from consideration. The only nonincome tax discussed here is the federal donative transfers tax, which, until 1976, was two separate taxes: the federal estate tax and the federal gift tax. Although the federal donative transfers tax plays a modest role in our total tax structure, it can be of significance to those few people who either inherit or accumulate substantial amounts of wealth. Furthermore, it too is generally amenable to successful tax-planning techniques. We will, therefore, consider the fundamentals of tax planning for the federal donative transfers tax in Chapter 14. With that one major exception, however, all other chapters of this book are primarily concerned with tax planning for the U.S. federal income tax.

## THE ELEMENTS OF TAX PLANNING

An *element* may be defined as the fundamental unit that, singly or in combination with other elements, constitutes all matter. Using that definition, the world of tax planning might be divided into three elements:

1. The law.
2. The facts.
3. An administrative and (sometimes) judicial process.

Singly, or in combination, these three elements constitute the essential ingredients of every tax plan.

## The Law

The current statutory law of federal income taxation is technically known as the Internal Revenue Code of 1986 (as amended to date). Unfortunately, that legal document is approximately 2,000 pages long. To make matters worse, some portions of the code are nearly unintelligible, even for those whose native tongue is English. As one example, consider the first two sentences of Section 274(n), which read as follows:

(1) In general—the amount allowable as a deduction under this chapter for—
    (A)  any expense for food or beverages, and
    (B)  any item with respect to an activity which is of a type generally considered to constitute entertainment, amusement, or recreation, or with respect to a facility used in connection with such activity,
shall not exceed 80 percent of the amount of such expense or item which would (but for this paragraph) be allowable as a deduction under this chapter.
(2) Exceptions—Paragraph (1) shall not apply to any expense if—
    (A)  subsection (a) does not apply to such expense by reason of paragraph (2), (3), (4), (7), (8), or (9) of subsection (e),
    (B)  in the case of an expense for food or beverages, such expense is excludable from the gross income of the recipient under section 132 by reason of subsection (e) thereof (relating to de minimis fringes),
    (C)  such expense is covered by a package involving a ticket described in subsection (l)(1)(B), or
    (D)  in the case of an expense for food or beverages before January 1, 1989, such expense is an integral part of a qualified meeting.

Because the code is filled with such obscure language, and because the primary objective of this book is restricted to the recognition of major income tax opportunities, we fortunately will devote minimal attention to the exact words of the statute. Nevertheless, in following this approach, you should always remember two things. First, even the best paraphrased general rules are not the words of the code, and they may be misleading in some circumstances. Second, the law itself is constantly being revised by Congress. The latter observation is important for two reasons. First, it means that one or more of the tax-planning ideas discussed here could be made obsolete at any time. It also implies one legal, albeit unusual, method of tax planning: In rare circumstances, a few persons may actually get Congress to change the extant law so that it will be more favorable to their specific situation.

Federal tax laws originate in the House of Representatives. They are referred to the Committee on Ways and Means for study and debate before being considered on the floor of the House. This procedure gives the chairman of the Ways and Means Committee considerable political power, since tax bills can effectively be killed by failure of the committee chairman to proceed. Before major tax legislation is considered by the entire House, the Ways and Means Committee will ordinarily hold public hearings on the proposed legislation and will prepare a formal report that explains both the changes being initiated and the reasons for them. If the proposed legislation is approved by the committee and, later, by the entire House, it goes to the Senate where it is referred to the Senate Finance Committee and the same procedure is repeated. This also makes the chairman of the Senate Finance Committee a major player in the tax legislative process.

Typically when a tax bill leaves the Senate, it has been significantly modified from the earlier House version; therefore, a Conference Committee—consisting of both House and Senate members—will be appointed by the two committee chairmen to reconcile the two bills and prepare a final draft for acceptance or rejection by the Congress and (eventually) the president. At this stage in the legislative process, it is not unusual for the conferees to insert into the bill new amendments that are called "transition rules." The reason for these transition rules is typically the need to get the support of a few key Senators and Congressmen for the proposed tax change. These rules typically provide temporary or transitional relief for an important political constituent who would be adversely affected by the bill and who resides in the key politician's district. The transition rules are, of course, the legal but unusual method of tax planning noted above. Fortunately facts, an alternative variable in tax planning, are much more readily modified by the average taxpayer.

### The Facts

Most successful tax planning involves nothing more sophisticated than a rearrangement of some intended events. Taxpayers who enter into unfamiliar business transactions without the aid of a competent tax adviser frequently reach an unfavorable tax result. Tax liabilities ordinarily depend upon what taxpayers actually do, not on what they might have done. Because competent tax advisers understand the importance of facts to tax results, they are often able to recommend a method of achieving a tax-preferred result by a sometimes simple rearrangement of facts *before* they transpire. For example, the distribution of $1 million in corporate assets by a financially successful corporation to its owners might be subject to an individual income tax of anything from zero (i.e., no tax) to $330,000. If the distribution is a repayment of a corporate security—created through foresight when the business was first incorporated—there would be no income tax to the recipient because the $1 million would represent a return of capital. On the other hand, if the original incorporators failed to include adequate debt in the original capital structure of the corporation, the subsequent distribution of $1 million would very likely be treated as an ordinary dividend and be subject to an individual income tax of up to 33 percent. As this one illustration suggests, the importance of facts to tax planning can never be overestimated.

### An Administrative and/or Judicial Process

No system of taxation will function smoothly without independent administrative and judicial authorities. By definition, a tax necessarily transfers control over a certain amount of wealth from the private to the public sector. Because taxpayers nearly always desire to minimize their own tax liability, and thereby maximize their personal wealth, someone must enforce the laws that accomplish this transfer. Furthermore, because the code is so complex, someone must officially interpret and translate that document for public consumption. These basic tasks of law enforcement and interpretation have been assigned to the Internal Revenue Service, which is part of the Treasury Department.

The administrative interpretations that ordinarily carry the greatest authority are known as Treasury regulations. They represent the government's interpretation of the Internal Revenue Code, stated in general terms that are intended to have broad application to many taxpayers. The government will also respond to an inquiry from a specific taxpayer asking for an interpretation of the law in very detailed circumstances. These latter interpretations take the form of either private letter rulings or "public" revenue rulings. In the last few years, all private rulings have been made available to the general public, but only the published revenue rulings are generally distributed by the Government Printing Office. Although everyone can rely on Treasury regulations as authoritative, only the taxpayer who made the request for a private ruling can firmly rely on that interpretation, and, even in that instance, the private ruling will be deemed authoritative (i.e., controlling) only if the taxpayer revealed all facts openly and in complete detail.

Taxpayers frequently disagree with the IRS interpretation of the code; if carried to extremes, such disagreements can only lead to litigation. As explained in Chapter 15, tax litigation can be initiated in any one of three courts: the Tax Court, a federal district court, or the Claims Court. The decisions of the first two courts can be further appealed to a circuit court of appeals; the decisions of the Claims Court to the U.S. Court of Appeals for the Federal Circuit; and all appellate court decisions may be finally appealed to the U.S. Supreme Court. Thus a diverse array of interpretative authority exists on tax matters, and all of this is properly considered a part of the tax law. The initial interpretation, however, remains within the province of the IRS.

The IRS is not, however, given carte blanche in matters of taxation. It does represent the government's interest, but its interpretations and administrative actions are also subject to judicial review whenever challenged by a taxpayer. Even though the administrative and judicial processes are not ordinarily subject to manipulation in the same manner as the law and the facts, every taxpayer should carefully consider the very human nature of the administrative and judicial processes in tax planning. This warning may translate simply as "too much is still too much." In other words, even if a tax plan seems otherwise to be entirely within the law, if it is abhorrent to human sensitivities, it just *may* fail when put to the human test implicit in every administrative and judicial hearing. This element in tax planning will be examined in greater detail in Chapter 15. In all the other chapters, we will limit our attention to matters of fact and law, the two more malleable elements.

## TAX AVOIDANCE VERSUS TAX EVASION

Finally, every reader should understand that the contents of this book are restricted to wholly legal methods of tax minimization. Legitimate means of reducing taxes are known as tax avoidance; illegal means to the same end are called tax evasion. Thus, for example, this book does not recommend that a taxpayer simply fail to report an income-producing cash transaction, even though the low probability of an IRS audit that might uncover such a transaction is noted in the final chapter. Tax evasion is characterized by fraud and deceit; tax avoidance, by open and full disclosure. That difference does not imply, however, that legal tax planning is always a cut-and-dried affair. Many tax avoidance plans involve major questions of judgment; the conclusions of the IRS agents and those of the taxpayer may very well differ. Those who engage in tax planning must assume the potential risk of litigation if they are to be successful in some circumstances. The areas of tax avoidance in which disagreements are common will be discussed in this book so that a taxpayer might better assess the wisdom of proceeding with a questionable course of action.

This concludes our introduction to tax planning. Chapters 2 and 3 lay the statutory groundwork for most of the tax-planning ideas developed in Chapter 4. Chapters 5 through 8 explain some accounting rules that are unique to federal income taxation. Many of these rules can be viewed as a tax trap for the unwary. In the remaining chapters, the tax law and the planning concepts common to many specific business decisions are developed within the confines of a single chapter. These latter chapters, therefore, can be read independently. The author recommends, however, that every reader read the next seven chapters before pursuing any specific topic developed later.

## PROBLEMS AND ASSIGNMENTS

1. Convert the general "computation guide," suggested for any tax on page 6, to a simple arithmetic formula specifically for the federal income tax.

2. Smith paid a net tax of $100,000, had credits of $12,000, deductions of $75,000, and exclusions of $25,000. Smith's average tax rate is 28 percent. Using the computational guide on page 6, find Smith's *gross tax base* and *net tax base*.

3. Based solely on your general knowledge—that is, without doing any research beyond reading Chapter 1—list two examples each of (*a*) gross income, (*b*) exclusions, (*c*) deductions, and (*d*) tax credits for federal income tax purposes. Be prepared to explain why you think that each of these eight items should be classified in that manner.

4. In a very practical sense, a single course directed at the symptom-recognition level of learning may be more socially important than highly technical professional learning, which typically requires many years of

specialized study and experience. Explain this statement briefly. Include as part of your explanation one or more examples from the fields of medicine, law, or business.

5. What is the most likely danger of a symptom-recognition level of learning? Explain briefly.

6. In 1989, Young purchased $100,000 of corporate bonds yielding 12.5 percent; the interest income from these bonds was taxed at a rate of 28 percent. During the same year, Newman purchased $100,000 of municipal bonds yielding 9 percent. The interest from these bonds is tax-exempt. The bonds have similar maturities and risk.
   a. Who benefited from this tax "loophole"? Is Newman "paying taxes" in any sense here?
   b. Is the goal of tax planning to minimize taxes? If not, what is the goal of tax planning?

7. Tax provisions—sometimes called tax *loopholes*—that either deliberately or accidentally allow one taxpayer to pay substantially less tax than another very similarly situated taxpayer are alternately praised and condemned. Explain how a single tax provision can be viewed so differently by two commentators. If possible, illustrate this difference in viewpoint with the provision that exempts the interest paid on state or local bonds from the federal income tax.

8. The text suggests that both the federal income tax and the donative transfers tax are subject to managerial manipulation. Explain as best you can how a manager can legally manipulate any tax liability.

9. The Tax Foundation, Inc., has publicized "Tax Freedom Day" for several years. That day supposedly represents the day of the year on which the average person's aggregate salary is sufficient to pay his or her total tax liabilities for the year, leaving the remainder of the year available to earn an income for personal objectives. In 1988, Tax Freedom Day was determined to be May 5; in 1970, April 30; in 1930, February 13. What does this say about the average tax burden of Americans?

10. Approximately $370 billion was collected by the federal government from the tax on income reported by individuals in 1986. Suppose you were to arrange all of the 1986 individual income tax returns in one stack, starting with the return indicating the least amount of tax due on the bottom (actually, this return would be the one requesting the largest refund), and continuing with each return based on the amount of tax liability owed, until you placed on the very top the one return that indicated the largest tax liability for that year. Now split that stack, mentally, into two parts:
    1. The top 50 percent; then
    2. The top 1 percent.

    Now estimate the approximate percent of the total revenue collected (i.e., the $370-plus billion) from each of those parts of the total stack.

a. I estimate that the top half of the stack produced about ⎽⎽⎽⎽ percent of the $370 billion collected.

b. I estimate that the top 1 percent of the stack produced about ⎽⎽⎽⎽ percent of the $370 billion collected.

11. Various estimates suggest that somewhere between $75 billion and $200 billion of income goes unreported for tax purposes each year. This results in an estimated revenue loss of $13 billion to $17 billion. Are these estimates concerned with tax avoidance or tax evasion? Explain.

# Case  1–1

Dave Mest is the chief financial officer of Three Initial Corporation (TIC). The president of the company has asked him to decide how to use $100,000 in funds that the company has to invest.

One option is to pay off a short-term note payable on which TIC is paying 11 percent interest. Another option is to purchase a municipal bond which is yielding 8.5 percent interest, tax-free. A third option is to invest the $100,000 in an experimental process designed to reduce TIC's production costs. The research department expects that the process will only reduce costs by $84,000; however, the expenditure will generate a tax deduction of $100,000 *and* a tax credit of $20,000.

Which use of the money should Dave choose if TIC pays a tax rate of 15 percent? of 25 percent? of 34 percent?

# Case  1–2

A group of politicians and businesspeople in River City have decided that their city needs a new 1.2 million dollar civic center. The city is willing to give $200,000 to the project. The remaining construction capital will have to come from issuing bonds.

One proposal is to create a new nonprofit corporation to build and operate the center. Bobby Calhoun, a local attorney, has informed the group that if this proposal is adopted the interest income on the bonds will be taxable to the investors. Mr. Calhoun proposes that the River City Development Authority (RCDA) own and operate the civic center. If RCDA issues the bonds, they will be treated as municipal bonds, and the interest received by the investors will be exempt from federal income tax. Mr. Calhoun would be glad to have his law firm do the necessary legal work with RCDA; he estimates that this would increase legal costs by $50,000.

What would be the difference in the cost of the civic center between the two proposals? Assume that investors demand a 10 percent aftertax rate of return on their investment and that the average tax rate of the investors is 30 percent. The bonds will mature at the rate of $200,000 per year for five years. Interest will be paid at the end of each year on the outstanding balance. Do *not* consider the time value of money.

# CHAPTER 2

# The Income Concept: General Rules and Common Misconceptions

Perhaps the most accurate but least useful definition of taxable income is that attributed to unnamed skeptics who have suggested that taxable income is what the Internal Revenue Code says it is and nothing more pretentious. In lieu of such useless accuracy, this chapter will attempt to simplify and restate some of the more important general rules used to measure income for tax purposes. These general rules tend to be harsh in their application. The reader should not, however, give up hope too early. Most of the remaining chapters explain how taxpayers may be able to mitigate the generally harsh criteria established in this chapter.

Virtually all readers of this book have had some exposure to the income concept. If nothing else, most of them will have filed their own tax returns at one time or another. Some readers will have examined or even prepared an income statement for a business enterprise. Notwithstanding those experiences, this chapter will review some basic elements of the income concept as it is applied in federal income tax matters. Primary attention will be given to the basic concepts that are most frequently misunderstood or misapplied in particular circumstances. The chapter is divided into two major sections. The first section deals with gross income, the positive element in income determination. The second section deals with tax deductions, the negative element in income determination. Taxable income is, of course, the arithmetic difference between the aggregate number used to represent gross income and the aggregate number used to represent deductions.

## GROSS INCOME

Before we even attempt to define *gross income,* the reader should get accustomed to the first basic rule of federal income taxation. That is, *all income is taxable income unless the taxpayer can find good authority for excluding it.* To help the reader interpret this basic rule as it applies to gross income, the next several pages will examine some of the more important corollary rules used to implement the basic rule in specific circumstances. These corollary rules explain the importance of the realization criterion, the insignificance of the form of payment, the unimportance of the direct or indirect status of a benefit received, and the relative significance of accounting methods, statutory exclusions, and assignment-of-income principles.

### The Realization Criterion

Stated in its simplest form, the realization criterion says that mere appreciation in value will not be considered taxable income. Alternatively, it says that income will not be recognized for tax purposes until it has been realized. The reader must be careful to avoid misinterpretation of the alternative definition; the realization criterion does *not* say that an increase in cash, or even an increase in current assets, is a precondition to income. Income is generally associated with an increase in net wealth, and most increases in wealth, unless attributable to mere appreciation in value, do constitute taxable income. However, an increase in wealth in the current year is not essential to the presence of taxable income. To illustrate this conclusion, assume that a taxpayer purchased common stocks 15 years ago and that these stocks steadily increased in value for the first 9 years and then remained constant in value for the next 6 years. In the first nine years of ownership, the taxpayer would not report any taxable income even though the stocks might have appreciated from their cost of $10,000 to a value of $100,000. In the next six years, the taxpayer would not perceive that he or she had any income, excluding the possibility of dividends, because the stock value failed to increase further. If, however, at the end of the 15th year, the taxpayer exchanged those stocks for a plot of land, for other stocks or bonds, or for almost any other property, the taxpayer would be deemed to have realized the $90,000 income that had previously gone unrecognized. Even though this taxpayer had realized no increase in net wealth during the six years prior to the exchange, and even though the property taken in exchange for the stock was relatively unmarketable, the taxpayer would have to recognize the entire $90,000 taxable income in the one year in which the exchange was made. That conclusion is the essence of the realization concept.

Virtually any change in the form or the substance of a property or property right is sufficient to constitute realization for income tax purposes. To the frequent surprise of taxpayers, income may be realized when others forgive their outstanding debts, when they win a prize in a contest, when they embezzle funds, when they incorporate an extant business, when they take separate title to part of a former joint property, or when they find a buried treasure on their property. Because realization is such a pervasive concept, and because an income tax generally must be paid in the year that income has been realized, a taxpayer should consult an adviser on the potential tax consequences that may attach to any action that will modify either the form or the substance of the taxpayer's property rights *before* that action is actually undertaken.

## Accounting Methods

The subject of accounting methods will be considered in greater depth in Chapter 5. At this juncture we need only note that the code technically provides that taxable income shall be computed on the same basis of accounting as taxpayers use in maintaining their regular set of books. This provision, unfortunately, is often as misleading as it is helpful when applied to the notion of gross income. Most noncorporate taxpayers operate on a cash basis of accounting, and this sometimes causes them to conclude that they need not report any taxable income unless and until they receive cash. This conclusion is not justified in many circumstances. A taxpayer on a cash basis of accounting will utilize a cash-receipts test only to determine the proper year of reporting such routine items of income as wages, salary, interest, dividends, and rents. The same cash-receipts test will ordinarily not apply to such nonrecurring transactions as the sale of an investment or the sale of a home. In all nonroutine transactions other than cash-deferred installment sales, the authorities will apply a *cash-equivalence* rule and proceed to tax the individual just as if cash were received in an amount equal to the fair market value of the noncash property received on the disposition. Return momentarily to the earlier illustration in which a taxpayer exchanged stocks purchased 15 years ago for $10,000, but which stocks were currently worth $100,000 for, say, a plot of speculative desert land; even if that taxpayer were ordinarily a cash-basis taxpayer, the authorities would insist that the land received must also have been worth $100,000 and would tax the $90,000 gain accordingly. Tax administrators generally assume that a taxpayer will not enter into an exchange unless an equivalent value is received. Hence, they tend to value the most easily valued property and assume the value equivalence for the other item exchanged. Special rules are applied to transactions between related taxpayers where there is reason to suspect that an exchange was not made at arm's length.

The cash-equivalence rule is generally *not* applicable to casual sales of property on an installment basis. In other words, if a taxpayer sells a property for the buyer's promise to pay cash at a later date, the tax law ordinarily does *not* require that the seller immediately estimate a value for the buyer's promise to pay and tax the seller's gain before that cash is received. Rather, in the case of many cash-deferred installment sales, the tax law provides that the seller must report the gain and pay the income tax as the money is received. This rule is applied to most installment sales unless the seller is a "dealer" in the property sold or a special depreciation-recapture rule applies.

## Constructive Receipt

A taxpayer on the cash method of accounting will occasionally attempt to postpone the recognition of even routine taxable income by refusing to exercise domination over funds received. A taxpayer might, for example, defer picking up a paycheck until January 2, refuse to open an envelope known to contain a dividend check until the first day of a new year, or fail to withdraw or record interest that had accumulated on a savings account in the current year. In each of these situations, the tax rules would find that the income in question was taxable in the current year because it had been constructively received. Whenever a taxpayer has the authority to exercise control over the income, he or she has constructively received it, regardless of when the actual exercise of power or domination is completed.

The tax authorities occasionally stretch the concept of constructive receipt well beyond the boundaries of common sense. For example, employees of many state agencies are required by law to participate in a state retirement program. Frequently this participation requires a contribution from the employee which can be regained and enjoyed only upon (1) quitting the job, (2) retiring, or (3) dying. A reasonable person might well argue that the withheld portion of the salary is not constructively received until the employee quits, retires, or dies. The tax authorities disagree and the courts sustain their contention that the full salary, including any amount withheld, is fully taxable when earned. Their conclusion apparently rests upon the belief that the taxpayer does receive an indirect benefit immediately (the security of retirement program coverage) and that the value of the benefit is equal to the amount withheld from the salary. Alternatively, the true rationale may be that the taxing authorities and the courts realize that any other interpretation would be *very* costly to the government. Since it may be unduly costly to correct an error of long standing, bad decisions sometimes become permanent decisions in matters of taxation.

## Form of Payment

As previously observed, the asset form in which a taxpayer receives income is wholly immaterial to the tax consequence. A wage is equally taxable whether it is paid in the form of a case of good scotch, a book, or cash. Noncash payments necessitate the determination of a fair market value. This may create administrative problems in obtaining agreement between the taxpayer and the Internal Revenue Service (IRS) agent. Typically the taxpayer will undervalue the asset received and the IRS agent will overvalue it. Both parties realize that a reasonable estimate can usually be agreed upon during the administrative or judicial proceedings that accompany a tax dispute.

The author has known numerous instances in which taxpayers erroneously believed that they had cleverly avoided the income tax by taking their rewards in noncash forms. Three illustrations may be helpful. In one instance, a university professor took pride in the fact that he always elected to receive the honorarium for speeches in the form of personally selected books, which he added to his library. In the second instance, a dentist exchanged services with his laundryman neighbor. That is, the dentist kept the teeth of the laundryman and his family in good repair in exchange for free laundry and dry-cleaning services for the dentist and his family. The third instance involved a new corporate venture in which the young entrepreneurs took their compensation in the form of corporate stocks. Legally the professor, the dentist, and the entrepreneurs all realized taxable income in an amount equal to the fair market value of the goods or services that they received. In each instance the taxpayer erroneously failed to report the income received, and in each instance the error went undetected by the IRS. The chances of the IRS uncovering such an error are admittedly small. Nevertheless, the reader should understand clearly that each of these intended tax-saving plans could be considered fraudulent and that each of the taxpayers could end up in a federal penitentiary for tax evasion. Any tax adviser who condones or recommends such tax planning is grossly incompetent, as well as a party to fraud, and should be dismissed immediately.

### Indirect Benefits

The relative insignificance of the form of payment in tax matters also extends to the direct or indirect status of any benefit received. A taxpayer must recognize as part of his or her own taxable income any amounts earned even though they are paid directly to another person. Suppose, for example, that a physician were to direct a patient to make a payment directly to the physician's grandchild. Even though the physician never received any cash for the service rendered, he or she would be taxed on the amount paid to the grandchild by the patient. The tax authorities would determine the tax liability just as if the physician had first received the fee and then made a gift of it to the grandchild.

The indirect-benefit concept is sometimes more difficult to apply than the previous illustration would suggest. Corporations often expend large sums of money for the benefit of their employees. The corporation may purchase, for example, life, health, and accident insurance policies, recreational facilities, pension plans, and other perquisites. Whether or not the indirect benefits from these corporate purchases will be taxed to the employee depends upon a host of special rules. In general it is safest to assume that all benefits received, directly or indirectly, do constitute gross income. In Chapter 9, we will learn why and how employee benefits in particular may be one of the most promising ways for many taxpayers to achieve substantial tax savings in a wholly legal fashion.

## Illegal Gains

Profits obtained from illegal activities are just as taxable as those earned from legitimate activities. As a matter of fact, income tax evasion has been made the basis for legal prosecution in instances where the government seemed unable to obtain a conviction on other grounds. In recognition of this fact, some underworld characters take unusual precautions to maintain an excellent set of financial records. In the absence of good records, the IRS is authorized to use relatively crude methods of estimating a taxpayer's income, and these estimates are often on the high side. To illustrate, the income of a house of prostitution has been estimated on the basis of a commercial laundry's records, apparently after an IRS special agent determined the modus operandi of the house. In any legal dispute over a tax liability, the burden of proving the IRS estimates wrong usually rests with the taxpayer. Without records, the taxpayer is hard pressed to defeat the commissioner's estimates of gross income.

Although well beyond the scope of this book, and beyond the expertise of the author, the concurrent legal problems created by the need to report illegal gains for income tax purposes appear to be substantial. To what extent the Justice Department should be given access to tax files for purposes other than tax litigation is an interesting question. The danger of self-incrimination is obvious. Any taxpayer receiving illegal gains—whether from the sale of narcotics, gambling, extortion, embezzlement, or air piracy—badly needs a good tax *attorney* as well as a good criminal lawyer.

The word *attorney* was italicized in the prior sentence for good reason. In Chapter 1 the need for a good tax *adviser* was emphasized. Most qualified tax advisers are either lawyers or certified public accountants. To date, the concept of privileged communication has not been extended under federal law to the CPA. It is extremely important, therefore, that income tax records from *criminal* activities be handled initially by an attorney. The attorney can engage a CPA on behalf of a client if appropriate and thereby extend the attorney's privileged communication to the accountant's workpapers.

## Source of Payment

Even well-educated taxpayers occasionally get the notion that certain receipts will not be taxed if they are paid by a particular kind of taxpayer. A prominent university professor, for example, believed that he was correct in not reporting his summer compensation for income tax purposes because it had been paid to him by a tax-exempt research organization. As a matter of fact, the taxable status of the organization making a payment is seldom of significance in determining the tax consequences of the payment to the recipient. In the case of this professor, a portion of the money received could be excluded under some very special rules for fellowship grants, but not simply because they were paid by a tax-exempt organization.

Other taxpayers have been amazed to learn that income paid by a foreign entity and received in a foreign country may be subject to the U.S. income tax. We have what is known as a global income tax. This means that U.S. citizens and resident aliens, as well as all domestic corporations, are generally subject to the U.S. income tax regardless of where their income is earned, paid, or received. Nonresident aliens—that is, citizens of another country who are not physically in the United States and who may never have been here—may also be subject to the U.S. income tax, but only on their income from U.S. sources. Needless to say, the rules applicable to the taxation of multinational transactions are doubly complex. Often a single income stream is subject to taxation by more than one country. This necessitates a series of tax treaties and other tax credit provisions to avoid double taxation. The code does provide limited relief for income earned abroad by individual taxpayers under prescribed conditions. A few of the more important aspects of multinational transactions will be discussed later in this book. Suffice it to observe here that the source of an income payment is generally not pertinent to the determination of tax consequences to the recipient.

One exception to the general rule just stated applies to the first $70,000 of personal service income earned each year by a U.S. citizen working overseas. A citizen who remains outside the United States for 330 days or longer in any consecutive 12-month period may elect to exclude from gross income any compensation for services rendered up to the $70,000 maximum. This provision encourages citizens to accept overseas assignments. The importance of the exclusion varies, however, depending upon the income tax laws of the host country. It is of most benefit in those countries with low individual income tax rates and/or those which exempt foreign labor from local tax law.

### Assignment of Income

Sometimes the most difficult tax problem is not determining whether a particular receipt constitutes gross income but identifying whose income it is. Because the detailed discussion of taxable entities is deferred to Chapter 3, this discussion of assignment-of-income problems will be very brief. Income ordinarily derives from one or more of three events: (1) the rendering of a service, (2) the disposition of a property, or (3) the payment by one person for the use of another's property. For some analytic purposes, we combine the last two notions into a single class and say that income is derived either from services or from property (or capital).

Initially it seems clear that income derived from the rendering of a service must be reported by the person rendering that service and that income derived from property must be reported by the person who owns (or holds legal title to) that property. One need not venture far into the world of business to discover how limited these concepts are for determining tax consequences.

Applied literally, they would say that all employees should report the gross value of their services, notwithstanding the fact that they personally may receive only some fractional share of that value. A study of taxation would further prove that our general notions of property and services are amazingly ill defined. Much of the intrigue of tax planning comes from the sometimes deliberate confusion of those ill-defined notions.

To illustrate this tax confusion, consider the income earned by entertainers or athletes. If they conduct their business simply and solely as individuals, there is not much doubt that any fees received for services rendered will be attributed and taxed to the individual personally. If this same individual incorporates his or her talent, and then the corporation negotiates for all appearance contracts, is the income received by the corporation, for the service performed by its employee, taxable to the corporation or to the person as an individual?

Or take another example. If an individual spends time writing music or tinkering with mechanical devices and subsequently obtains a copyright for a musical score or a patent for a gadget, is the income received attributable to a service (writing music or tinkering with mechanical devices) or to a property (a copyright or a patent)?

Finally, consider the father who clipped a series of interest coupons from some bonds and made a gift of those coupons, but not of the bonds, to his son. Is the interest paid to the son, at the maturity date of the interest coupons, taxable to the son as the owner of the coupons or to the father as the owner of the bonds from which the coupons were clipped?

These three brief illustrations suggest both the breadth of opportunity for tax planning and the need for expert assistance. The answers to the questions are not always clear-cut. As you will discover later in this book, the corporate veil is sometimes, but not always, pierced, so that the income earned by a corporation may or may not be attributed and taxed to the individual owner. Gains from the sale of patents are generally treated as gains from the disposition of a capital asset, whereas gains from the sale of a copyright are taxed in the same way as income earned directly by an individual. Income from property may not be transferred in most circumstances to another taxpayer without transferring the basic property. All of these problems are discussed later in more depth.

### Exclusions

Our final consideration pertinent to the gross income concept will consist of a brief review of the items of economic income that are not deemed to constitute gross income for tax purposes. The vast majority of these exclusions are statutory in origin. Before we turn our attention to the statutory exclusions, however, we might note in passing the few exclusions that exist by judicial or administrative interpretation. As a class, virtually no items of imputed income are deemed to constitute gross income. Economists in particular like to point out the reality of such items of imputed income as owner-occupied homes, home-produced and home-consumed foods, and the services of the housewife. Even though the value of these items could be imputed, and even though not taxing them may create an inequity between homeowners and renters, between farmer-gardeners and city dwellers, and between house-wives and career wives, the U.S. income tax has never been extended to items of imputed income on the ground that such an extension would be admin-istratively difficult to implement.

Prior to 1984, most social security and other public-assistance type pay-ments were also excluded from our income tax base by administrative fiat. Tax administrators originally believed that it would be unwise to tax away any part of the payments made by welfare agencies designed to help people deemed to be in particular need. Over the years it became apparent, however, that not every recipient of social security and unemployment insurance was necessarily in great financial need. Therefore the tax law was amended to provide that part or all of these payments may now be subject to the federal income tax. For example, up to one half of an individual's social security payment may now be included with gross income; the other one half (or more) may be excluded, depending on the total (economic) income of the recipients for that year.

Most statutory exclusions are contained in Sections 101 through 133. Even a cursory reading of the section titles will suggest how narrow in application some of the exclusions really are. Because this book is intended as a layper-son's introduction to tax planning, rather than as a complete treatise on tax rules, many of these items will not be discussed. Consideration of the exclu-sions of more general interest to tax planning is deferred to subsequent chap-ters for pedagogic reasons. For example, the discussion of all exclusions requiring that the recipient be an employee is deferred to Chapter 9, where these exclusions can be treated as part of the larger problem of compensation considerations. Before we begin a discussion of the remaining items of general interest, it may be desirable for the reader to review the titles of the sections that create the statutory exclusions. These titles are:

Sec. 101. Certain death payments.

Sec. 102. Gifts and inheritances.

Sec. 103. Interest on state and local bonds.

Sec. 104. Compensation for injuries or sickness.

Sec. 105. Amounts received under accident and health plans.

Sec. 106. Contributions by employer to accident and health plans.

Sec. 107. Rental value of parsonages.

Sec. 108. Income from discharge of indebtedness.

Sec. 109. Improvements by lessee on lessor's property.

Sec. 110. Income taxes paid by lessee corporation.

Sec. 111. Recovery of tax benefit items.

Sec. 112. Certain combat pay of members of the Armed Forces.

Sec. 113. Mustering-out payments for members of the Armed Forces.

Sec. 114. Sports programs conducted for the American National Red Cross.

Sec. 115. Income of States, municipalities, etc.

Sec. 117. Qualified scholarships.

Sec. 118. Contributions to the capital of a corporation.

Sec. 119. Meals or lodging furnished for the convenience of the employer.

Sec. 120. Amounts received under qualified group legal service plans.

Sec. 121. One-time exclusion of gain from sale of principal residence by individual who has attained age 55.

Sec. 122. Certain reduced uniformed services retirement pay.

Sec. 123. Amounts received under insurance contracts for certain living expenses.

Sec. 125. Cafeteria plans.

Sec. 126. Certain cost-sharing payments.

Sec. 127. Educational assistance programs.

Sec. 128. Interest on certain savings certificates.

Sec. 129. Dependent care assistance programs.

Sec. 130. Certain personal injury liability assignments.

Sec. 131. Certain foster care payments.

Sec. 132. Certain fringe benefits.

Sec. 133. Interest on certain loans used to acquire employer securities.

Sec. 134. Certain military benefits.

Sec. 135. Cross references to other Acts.

Other statutory exclusions are scattered throughout the code in such diverse sections as:

Sec. 22.    Retirement income. (Technically this provision is worded as a tax credit for the elderly and the permanently and totally disabled, rather than as an exclusion, but it has the same effect as an exclusion.)

Sec. 74(c). Employee achievement awards.

Sec. 79(a). Group-term life insurance purchased for employees.

Sec. 621.   Payments to encourage exploration, development, and mining for defense purposes.

Sec. 872(b).   Gross income. (Subsection (b) deals with special exclusions for nonresident aliens.)

Sec. 892.   Income of foreign governments and of international organizations.

Sec. 893.   Compensation of employees of foreign governments or international organizations.

Sec. 911.   Citizens or residents of the United States living abroad.

Sec. 912.   Exemptions for certain allowances. (This section contains special rules for foreign service officers and Peace Corps volunteers.)

Sec. 933.   Income from sources within Puerto Rico.

Simply reading this list should help to sensitize the reader to any personal situation for which an unusual exclusion may apply. It should also emphasize the relatively restricted scope of most exclusion provisions. The most common exclusions will be discussed in greater detail in later chapters. In this chapter, we will consider briefly the exclusions for gifts and bequests, state and local bond interest, scholarship and fellowship grants, and the rental value of parsonages.

**Gifts and Inheritances.**   Section 102 provides that "gross income does not include the value of property acquired by gift, bequest, devise, or inheritance." The major problem involved in the interpretation of this brief section is the difficulty of distinguishing on any operational basis between transfers that are truly gratuitous and those made for other reasons. Gifts are frequently defined as transfers based on detached generosity, out of affection, respect, admiration, charity, or similar impulses. This definition is often difficult to apply. To illustrate this, consider the following situation. Paul Hornung was given an automobile by a publishing company because of his prowess on the football field. Could the value of this automobile be excluded by Hornung under the authority of Section 102? In Hornung's case, the court believed that the transfer was not gratuitous, but that it was made with the hope that it either had provided or would provide better sports stories, and, therefore, greater magazine sales.

In general, if the recipient has rendered (or will render) any service to the apparent donor, Section 102(c) provides that the transfer is not gratuitous and, therefore, that any amount received constitutes gross income. Similarly, ordinary tips given to waiters and waitresses, bellhops, and other service personnel are includable in gross income. So are traditional gifts to members of the clergy following weddings and other religious ceremonies. A more delicate problem of statutory interpretation was presented to the courts in the cases of *Greta Starks* and *Everett Brizendine*. To state the essential fact of those two cases succinctly, each involved a "kept" woman. The delicate tax question involved the need to distinguish between a gift and compensation for services rendered. After "all of the facts and circumstances" were examined, the amount received was classified as ordinary income in one case and as a tax-free gift in the other.

Relative to inheritances, the reader should be cautioned to observe the difference between a basic bequest and income that may accrue on that bequest. Generally only the former can be excluded from gross income. For example, a taxpayer can generally exclude from taxable income any amount received as the beneficiary of a life insurance policy purchased by another individual. The income derived from the inheritance, however, is as taxable to the heir as is income derived from property that he or she has personally accumulated.

**State and Local Bond Interest.**  As noted in Chapter 1, the interest derived from bonds issued by a state or local government is generally excluded from gross income for federal income tax purposes. Upper-bracket taxpayers consequently may find it financially advantageous to invest in state and local government bonds. The governments issuing these bonds are able to float them at lower rates of interest because of the tax shelter they provide the purchaser. Tax reformers have contended for many years that this exclusion should be ended because the results are highly inequitable in that they benefit most the wealthiest segment of our society. The tax reformers usually cite estimates to support the contention that the federal government could increase its *net* tax revenues even if it were to grant direct subsidies to the state and local governments in an amount sufficient to compensate them for any increase in interest costs. Whether or not the estimates are realistic, Congress thus far has refused to terminate this statutory exclusion both because of genuine concern for the greater bureaucracy that would attend a direct subsidy and because of pressures brought by governors, mayors, and investment bankers.

**Scholarship Grants.**  Section 117 excludes from gross income amounts received by an individual degree candidate as a scholarship or fellowship grant. The amount that can be excluded is limited, however, to the amount expended for tuition, fees, books, supplies, and equipment required by the school. (Special rules apply to scholarships awarded before 1987.)

Implementation of this exclusion is made difficult by the definitional imprecision common to such terms as fees, supplies, and equipment "required for" enrollment or attendance. If an instructor or course requires the student to utilize a personal computer, is that an item of required equipment if such computers can be rented? In any instance where a specific service is required of the grantee, Section 117(c) provides that the grant is compensation for services rendered and, therefore, included in gross income. Hence stipends paid to medical residents and interns, teaching and research assistants, and other graduate students who render a service to their educational institution constitute taxable income, not scholarships, even though the work experience is an important and integral part of the student's education.

**Rental Value of Parsonages.**    Section 107 excludes from gross income the fair market value of a home furnished to a "minister of the gospel" as part of his or her compensation (or the rental allowance paid in lieu of a parsonage, to the extent used to rent or purchase a home). This section would not be worthy of specific comment in a book on general tax planning were it not for the fact that some of the more radical elements in our society have seized upon this and related sections as their intended legal basis for paying no income tax to the federal government. In a nutshell, this radical element typically recommends that every reluctant taxpayer create a "church" and proclaim himself or herself to be a "minister of the gospel." For the more reluctant, the radical group will sell, at a bargain price, appropriate degrees and clerical titles in their own organizations. The advertisements and "news" reports that extol these tax plans typically fail to report the ease with which the IRS and the courts have seen through the deceit implicit in most of these schemes. The courts have consistently held that these "churches" have no status as religious organizations; furthermore, the individuals "creating" them are *not* deemed to be "ministers of the gospel."

The recent activity in this area does serve, however, to emphasize an important aspect of all legitimate tax planning—namely, the importance of statutory interpretation. It is extremely difficult to define with any precision many words and phrases in the code. For example, precisely who should qualify as a minister of the gospel? Should it include the minister of music or minister of youth in a large congregation? Should it include only ordained persons; and, if so, what minimal requirements should exist for ordination? Should it include ordained ministers temporarily serving in a purely administrative capacity? These questions related to Section 107 are typical of those found in virtually every other section of the code. The tax expert must know how to locate and interpret authority to answer these and similar questions if he or she does not already know the answers.

Exclusions and deductions both reduce the size of the income tax base and therefore the tax liability. The list of possible income tax deductions is considerably longer than the list of statutory exclusions. Deduction rules are additionally confused by frequent limitations and options. The remainder of this chapter is devoted to an elaboration of the general rules governing the deductions authorized in the computation of taxable income.

## DEDUCTIONS

Deductions may be defined only as those items that collectively constitute the difference between the quantity called gross income and the quantity called taxable income. The basic rule applicable to deductions is just the opposite of that stated earlier for gross income—that is, *nothing is deductible unless the taxpayer can find good authority for deducting it.* Even momentary reflection on the general proposition just stated should cause the reader some concern, because income is generally thought to be a net concept. In accounting, *income* is usually defined as the difference between properly matched revenues and expenses. A tax on income, therefore, seems to provide implicitly for an automatic deduction of all properly matched expenses. Technically this is not true for income tax purposes. The code does include a provision (Section 162) that authorizes the deduction of all ordinary and necessary expenses paid or incurred in carrying on any trade or business. Nevertheless, some items that are deductible in computing financial accounting income are not deductible in computing taxable income, and a few items that are not deductible in computing financial accounting income are deductible in computing taxable income. Especially as used in the income taxation of an individual, the word *deduction* is a much broader, more legalistic word than the word *expense.*

In addition to the provision authorizing the deduction of all ordinary and necessary business expenses, the code authorizes many other more restrictive deductions. These include a personal and dependent exemption deduction; deductions for certain interest and taxes, losses, bad debts, depreciation, charitable contributions, research and experimental expenditures, and soil and water conservation expenditures; and a dividend-received deduction for corporate taxpayers only. In addition, there are many other special deductions. For example, some deductions are restricted to certain industries, such as railroads, the extractive industries, exempt organizations, banks, and insurance companies. As noted earlier, the details of all tax provisions cannot be examined in this book. Only the more important deductions for tax-planning purposes will be considered here. The important thing for the reader to remember at this point is that unless an expenditure fits the definition of an ordinary and necessary expense incurred in a trade or business, it generally cannot be deducted without very specific authorization in the code.

The rules applicable to tax deductions are complicated by the need to distinguish carefully among (1) expenditures incurred in a trade, business, or profession; (2) expenditures incurred in an income-producing venture that cannot be deemed to constitute a trade or business, either because of its special nature or because of its limited size; and (3) expenditures of a purely personal nature. The first of these three classes of expenditures is usually deductible without limit; the second is probably deductible, but sometimes only in an amount that does not exceed the income produced; and the last is not deductible at all unless a very specific provision authorizes its deduction, notwithstanding its purely personal character.

The difficulty of distinguishing between a trade or business and an income-producing venture is well demonstrated by many hobbies. The breeding of animals, the racing of horses and automobiles, the restoration of antiques, and even farming may be a primary source of recreation for a harried taxpayer.

The same activities often produce some gross income. Because the rule applicable to gross income says that all receipts must be included in gross income, it seems only fair that the related expenses should be tax deductible. On the other hand, since most purely personal expenditures are not deductible, it seems equally unfair to authorize the deduction of expenses related to certain hobbies and not to others just because some occasionally produce income. Thus the tax authorities are frequently faced with the need to determine whether or not a particular activity constitutes a full-fledged trade or business or something else. To assist in making this decision, the code was amended to include a statutory presumption, subject to rebuttal by the taxpayer, that any activity that does not produce a profit in any three of five consecutive years will be deemed to constitute a hobby. Expenses related to a hobby may be deductible, but in general only to the extent that gross income is reported.

Finally it should be noted that a return of capital does not constitute gross income. In other words, in measuring gross income derived from property transactions, the tax law automatically permits a taxpayer to subtract any unrecovered capital investment from the value received. To illustrate, consider a taxpayer who today sells a few shares of stock for $100 that he purchased for $80 just six months ago. Today's sale will *not* create gross income of $100. Rather it will produce gross income of only $20—namely the $100 received less the $80 of capital previously invested. The statutory rule which underlies the return of capital concept can be found in Sec. 1001 of the Code. It suggests that income (gain or loss) from the sale or exchange of property is equal to the arithmetic difference between (a) the *amount realized* and (b) the *adjusted basis* of the property surrendered. Unfortunately both of these technical terms— amount realized and adjusted basis—are far more complicated than is implied by the simple example of a sale of stock for $100. "Adjusted basis" is the technical term that is used in income tax parlance to represent the unrecovered capital concept. It is a term from the tax lexicon that represents an idea often directly comparable to the concept of "book value" in financial accounting.

For example, a taxpayer could purchase a business building for $1 million and claim depreciation deductions for tax purposes totaling $600,000 during the next several years before selling the building for $550,000. The taxpayer's adjusted basis in the building at the time of sale would be $400,000. Hence a sale of the building for $550,000 would produce a gross income (or gain) of only $150,000—that is, $550,000 amount realized less $400,000 adjusted basis.

Additional complexities concerning the basis concept are scattered throughout the text. Chapter 7, for example, includes the basis rules for property acquired as a gift, as well as those for property acquired by inheritance. Chapter 11 includes a discussion of the basis rules that must be followed when property is acquired in a wholly or partially tax-free transaction. Although many of these and other basis rules are difficult to understand, it is important for anyone who wants to be involved in tax planning to comprehend the significance of the basis concept and to anticipate the kinds of events which will cause a taxpayer's basis to change and generally modify the amount of gross income that must be recognized by that taxpayer. The automatic right of a taxpayer to subtract basis in the calculation of gross income derived from property stands in direct contrast to the rules concerning the right of a taxpayer to subtract deductions in the calculation of taxable income.

## Deductions and Expenses Compared

The basic criteria that must be considered before assuming that an expenditure directly related to a trade or business can be deducted can be separated into three positive and three negative tests. That is, an expenditure incurred in a trade, business, or profession will generally be deductible if:

1. It is "ordinary," which has been interpreted to mean that it is common to other taxpayers who find themselves in similar circumstances.
2. It is "necessary," which has been interpreted to mean that it is helpful to the conduct of the taxpayer's trade or business.
3. It is "reasonable in amount," which has been interpreted to mean that any other taxpayer would pay an equivalent sum for an equivalent good or service.
4. It is *not* a personal expense.
5. It is *not* a capital expenditure.
6. It does *not* relate to tax-exempt income.

Unlike taxation, accounting has no explicit rule that says that an expense must be reasonable in amount. This difference occasionally accounts for reported differences between financial accounting income and taxable income, especially in closely held corporations. Owners of these corporations often overstate their own salaries, as well as the salaries paid to other members of their immediate family, for tax reasons that will become clearer in the next two chapters. Whenever this happens, the authorities may find that what purported to be a salary must be treated as if it were a dividend, a gift, or some other distribution, and taxed accordingly. The reasonableness criterion has been applied in the opposite direction as well. A salary paid to Victor Borge by his own corporation was found to be unreasonably small, with the unpleasant consequence that the corporation ended up being treated as one engaged in a hobby rather than a *bona fide* business. Mr. Borge, the famous pianist-comic, probably did not find it funny that this meant paying a personal income tax on the extra compensation attributed to him, in addition to finding that the expenses incurred by his Rock Cornish hen (farm) corporation were nondeductible.

The rule that precludes the deduction of expenses related to the production of tax-exempt income may also explain some differences between the income reported by financial accounting and by taxation. Businesses often insure the lives of the owners to guarantee the availability of a sufficient amount of cash to purchase any deceased owner's share of the business from his or her estate. As noted earlier, the insurance proceeds received following the death of an owner would be excluded from gross income by Section 102. Consequently the premiums paid to obtain the insurance are not deductible by businesses for tax purposes in the years preceding the owner's death. Accounting, on the other hand, generally reports some or all of the insurance premium as an expense of doing business. Accounting may also report some portions of the insurance proceeds as income.

Some deductions are subject to limitations for tax purposes. For example, charitable contributions made by corporation's are limited to 10 percent of the corporation's adjusted taxable income; percentage depletion (when allowed at all) is limited to 50 percent of the net income from the depletable property; deductions for business meals and business entertainment are limited to 80 percent of the amount expended; and corporate capital losses are deductible only to the extent of capital gains in any one year. Because there is no financial accounting convention that similarly limits any of these items, the amounts deducted for financial accounting purposes in any given year may vary substantially from those deducted for income tax purposes. The major differences between these two figures, however, are attributable to tax provisions which have been written into the code for economic, national defense, or social reasons.

**Economic Policy Considerations.**   During the past two decades, Congress has enacted several major tax provisions relating to deductions with the apparent intention of promoting economic growth, maintaining reasonable price stability, and/or reducing unemployment. Still other tax measures have been justified on the ground that they are essential to the maintenance of a strong national defense. When these policy considerations are deemed sufficiently important, the implications of the tax provisions for the traditional conventions used to measure income are not given much weight. Thus it is not unusual to discover that in instances where economic or defense considerations are primary, tax rules differ substantially from accounting rules for essentially identical expense items.

**Social Policy Considerations.**   The primary objective of other tax provisions that seem peculiar in light of accounting conventions may also be related in some way to a social goal. Such sociological factors as family size, blindness, old age, marital status, or condition of health have little or nothing to do with problems of income measurement for financial accounting purposes. Income is simply the difference between revenues and the properly matched expenses incurred to produce those revenues. Special problems peculiar to a person earning an income may influence his or her disposition of that income but these problems in no way influence the size of the income measure. For tax purposes, however, sociological factors are often important to the procedure used to measure the size of the income stream. Congress tries, sometimes in an obscure manner, to recognize that equal financial accounting incomes need not represent equal taxpaying abilities. To achieve a degree of social equity, the code recognizes some of the differences in the ability to pay taxes by allowing special deductions for large families, for blind taxpayers, for persons 65 or older, for persons who incur large medical expenses, and for a host of other persons in special circumstances. In a few instances, these provisions intended to achieve a higher degree of interpersonal tax equity can be used to benefit taxpayers whom they were not intended to benefit.

### Accounting Methods

We observed earlier in this chapter that the code provides that taxable income shall be computed on the same method of accounting as the taxpayer uses in maintaining his or her regular books. The cash-basis method of accounting for expenses produces relatively few problems pertinent to tax deductions since both financial and tax accounting require that no deduction be made until cash is actually paid. The accrual method of accounting, however, presents more serious problems in application. That method of accounting is based on the notion that expenses should be deducted in the same year that the revenue which they produce is reported. Accountants refer to this notion as the matching concept. Application of that concept often necessitates the estimation of expenses in advance of the time that they are actually known with certainty. The expense associated with a guarantee or warranty, for example, is typically not known with precision until several years after the sale of the guaranteed product. Good financial accounting requires that such expenses be estimated in advance and that they be deducted in the same year in which the gross revenue from the sale is reported. The code generally forbids the deduction of any expense for tax purposes until the amount of that expense is fixed by more objective evidence than statistical estimates based on historical records. In summary, therefore, there really is no "matching concept" for federal income tax purposes.

### Losses

The proper tax treatment of losses is often confusing. In this introductory chapter we will only get acquainted with some of the more important general distinctions in the tax treatment of losses. Additional details of some of these distinctions will be discussed later, whereas other details will have to remain outside the confines of this work. To begin with, we might distinguish between (1) the loss attributable to a specific transaction and a specific property and (2) the loss more generally associated with the nonprofitable conduct of a trade or business, considering all of the many transactions common to that business.

The correct tax treatment of a loss derived from a specific transaction and a specific property is determined primarily by the purpose for which the property was held. If it was held for the production of income in an ordinary trade or business, any loss associated with the disposition of the property will generally be fully deductible for tax purposes. If the property was held solely as an investment, any loss associated with the investment will generally be deductible, but will be subject to special limitations applicable only to passive activity losses and/or to capital losses. If the property was held solely for personal purposes, any loss associated with the disposition of the property will generally not be deductible unless the disposition is attributable to a casualty or a theft. According to these diverse rules, the loss on the sale of a machine used in a business would be fully deductible; the loss associated with the sale of a common stock would be deductible only as a capital loss; and the loss associated with the sale of a personal residence would not be deductible (even though a gain on the sale of that same residence would be taxable). But note that part of the loss associated with the destruction of a personal residence by fire might be deductible as a casualty.

The general loss associated with the nonprofitable conduct of a business, considering the effect of all transactions common to that business, is called a *net operating loss* (NOL). If the authorized deductions exceed the gross income, the negative difference between the two sums effectively eliminates any tax for the current year. The question remains, however: What, if anything, can be done with that excess to offset taxable income in other years? The answer is that, after making several possible adjustments to the amount of this difference, the taxpayer may carry the net operating loss back three years and treat it as a newly discovered deduction to be subtracted from the gross income reported in that year. If the taxpayer reported a taxable income in that year and paid a tax, the new NOL deduction will create a refund of some or all of the tax paid three years ago. This refund even includes interest for the interim years. If the NOL deduction is larger than the taxable income of the third prior year, the taxpayer treats any remaining loss as a deduction in the second prior year. If that is still insufficient to absorb the loss, the taxpayer proceeds to offset it against the income of the immediately preceding year. Finally, if that is still insufficient to absorb the total net operating loss, the taxpayer is allowed to carry the remaining NOL forward and to offset it against any gross income earned in the next 15 years.

In lieu of the tax treatment described in the prior paragraph, the code gives every taxpayer another option. Instead of carrying the NOL back and offsetting it against the taxable income of the 3 prior years, a taxpayer may elect to forgo the *carry-back* and opt only for a 15-year carry-forward. Whether or not this new election is advantageous depends largely on the marginal tax rates applicable in the various years involved.

Special problems are created when one taxable entity tries to utilize another taxable entity's net operating loss. Thus if corporation A acquires all of the stock or assets of corporation B, and if corporation B had an unused net operating loss carry-forward, special rules must be applied to determine whether or not the surviving corporation is entitled to any part or all of the losses originally incurred by corporation B. Before these special rules were enacted, there was a brisk business in our country for worthless corporate shells because they provided valuable tax deductions for the acquiring tax-payer. The catch-22 tax effect was to make the most socially worthless corporation the most valuable one! For the same reason, unlucky persons with accumulated net operating losses might make an excellent marriage prospect, financially speaking, for the more fortunate taxpayer who has need of some big tax deductions.

Still other special tax problems are created when an individual taxpayer attempts to utilize losses derived from certain passive investments to offset income from such active sources as salaries, business profits, and professional fees. Prior to 1987 there were relatively few limits on a taxpayer's right to make such offsets. As a consequence, an entire tax-shelter industry had evolved in a 20-year period. This industry was, unfortunately, tainted by a substantial number of fraudulent deals. In all too many instances the only person to really benefit from the deal was the tax-shelter salesperson. Investors frequently lost big money at the same time that they decreased their federal income tax liability in a big way. Policing the tax deductions derived from these investments required an ever-increasing amount of time for IRS agents, Treasury personnel, and judicial authorities. Although the initial corrective efforts were largely directed at minimizing the opportunities for gross abuse, the 1986 Tax Reform Act finally slammed the door on most tax-sheltered investments by severely limiting the amount of loss from a passive investment that a taxpayer can deduct from gross income derived from more active sources. A discussion of the details of these new rules must be deferred to Chapter 8.

In summary for now, the reader should remember two very important rules of income taxation. First, remember that all income is deemed to constitute taxable income unless you (or your tax adviser) can find good authority for excluding it. Second, remember that nothing is deductible in the computation of taxable income unless you (or that same adviser) can find good authority for deducting it. In the remaining chapters we will discover how the harshness of these two rules can be mitigated.

## PROBLEMS AND ASSIGNMENTS

1. The income concept is among the most difficult of those concepts common to matters of economics, accounting, business, and taxation. Test your understanding of the income concept as it applies to federal income taxation by stating whether or not (in each of the following situations) taxpayer A has realized any gross income. Observe that this instruction is really asking you to do two things: (1) state whether or not taxpayer A has any income and (2) if income is present, state whether or not taxpayer A has realized that income for federal income tax purposes. If gross income has been realized, state the amount of income that taxpayer A must recognize. (Incidentally, if you dislike the small numbers used in

this exercise, add as many zeros as your imagination demands; the principle will not change.)

a. Taxpayer A washes B's windows and is paid $10 (cash).

b. Taxpayer A washes B's windows and is given, in return, a bottle of Beefeater Gin that retails for $10 and wholesales for $8. (Assume that B operates a liquor store.)

c. Taxpayer A washes B's windows in return for B's promise to play tennis with A once a week.

d. Taxpayer A sells B four "joints" (of marijuana) for $5 (cash); A had purchased the marijuana for $3 one week earlier.

e. Taxpayer A sells B a watch for $10; A had paid $10 for the watch one week earlier.

f. Taxpayer A sells B a watch for $10; A had paid $15 for the watch one week earlier.

g. Taxpayer A borrows $10 from B on a 90-day, 10 percent note.

h. Taxpayer A embezzles $10 from his employer, B.

i. Taxpayer A finds buried Spanish coins, valued at $10, on his land.

j. Taxpayer A finds natural gas deposits, valued at $10, on his land.

k. Taxpayer A purchases one share of XYZ common stock for $10. At the end of A's year, XYZ common is selling for $17 per share.

l. Taxpayers A and B jointly purchased a plot of land for $10 five years ago. Since then the value of this land has increased from $10 to $50. This year a dispute developed between A and B because A wanted to sell the land while B wanted to continue to hold it undeveloped for still more appreciation in value. To settle the dispute A and B divided up the property and each took separate title to one half of the total plot of land.

2. In January 1989, Jim Korp purchased stocks for $10,000 and a tax-free municipal bond for $20,000. During 1989, Korp received $1,000 of dividends from the stocks and $1,500 of interest from the bond. On December 31, 1989, the stocks were worth $13,000 and the bond was worth $19,600.

   On January 4, 1990, Korp sold the stocks for $13,200 and the bond for $19,700.

   Compute Korp's economic income, accounting income, and taxable income for 1989 and 1990 from these transactions.

3. In 1989, Acme Truck Rental, Inc. made the following expenditures:

   a. Purchased a truck for $20,000.

   b. Paid the president's wife $40,000 for secretarial services worth $5,000.

   c. Paid speeding fines of $1,500.

   d. Made political contributions of $10,000.

   None of the above expenditures is fully deductible. Using the criteria for a deduction found on page 29, briefly explain why each expenditure is not deductible.

4. Your text suggests that virtually any change in the form or substance of a property or property right is likely to trigger realization for income tax

purposes. There will be no income tax consequence, however, unless a second taxpayer is involved in the transaction.

a. Review each of the 12 situations considered in Problem 1, and see how well (or poorly) this general rule works.

b. Explain one significant difference between a sole proprietorship and a corporation when it comes to applying this general rule. (To illustrate, suppose taxpayer A were to transfer land purchased several years ago for $10 to a business. Assume further that the land had a fair market value of $17 on the day it was transferred. What difference, if any, would it make to taxpayer A if the business were a sole proprietorship or a corporation?)

c. There are at least three exceptions to this general rule. (If you think of any others, please notify the author. Seriously.) The three exceptions are (1) dying, (2) making gifts, and (3) mortgaging property. Explain the significance of each of these exceptions for income tax purposes. In other words, of what significance is it that death (or making a gift of property) is not deemed to be tantamount to realization for income tax purposes? [Again, to illustrate, assume that taxpayer A purchased land for $10 and that he or she died (or gave it away) when the land had a fair market value of $17.]

5. Explain in general what each of the following methods of accounting mean.

a. Cash method:
   (1) For revenue (gross income) recognition.
   (2) For expense (deduction) purposes.

b. Accrual method:
   (1) For revenue (gross income) recognition.
   (2) For expense (deduction) purposes.

6. Explain the correct federal income tax treatment of each of the following taxpayers.

a. Taxpayer A purchased her home for $60,000. Three years later, A sold the same home for $75,000.

b. Taxpayer B purchased her home for $60,000. Three years later, B sold the same home for $50,000.

c. Taxpayer C purchased her home for $60,000. Three years later, when it was valued at $50,000, C's home was destroyed by fire.

7. Explain the one common income tax problem implicit in the three following scenarios.

a. Taxpayer A bought a single-family home for $100,000 and immediately rented the home to B for $1,000 per month.

b. Taxpayer C bought a fourplex for $100,000 and immediately rented each of the four units for $250 per month.

c. Taxpayer D bought a beachfront condominium for $100,000. Whenever D was not using the property—particularly during the "off season"—D would rent it to others.

8. Explain the correct income tax treatment of each of the following taxpayers.
   a. Corporation A insures its commercial dock facility against flood damage. The insurance premium amounts to $100,000 per year.
   b. Corporation B self-insures its property. B assumes that it will, over the long haul, sustain property damage due to floods in the amount of $500,000 once every five years.

9. Under what circumstances would a taxpayer make an intelligent election to forgo the right to carry *back* a net operating loss and opt, instead, only to carry that loss into future years?

10. Assume that corporations A and B are both trying desperately to acquire Loss Corporation—a corporation with a substantial net operating loss that can (under the circumstances of either proposed acquisition) be utilized by corporation A or B. If corporation A is in a 34 percent marginal tax bracket and corporation B is in a 25 percent marginal tax bracket, who is apt to make the acquisition—corporation A or corporation B? Explain briefly.

11. The statutory definition of gross income is found in Section 61, which reads as follows:

    > Sec. 61. Gross Income Defined.
    > (*a*). General Definition.—Except as otherwise provided in this subtitle, gross income means all income from whatever source derived, including (but not limited to) the following items:
    > > (1) Compensation for services, including fees, commissions, and similar items;
    > > (2) Gross income derived from business;
    > > (3) Gains derived from dealings in property;
    > > (4) Interest;
    > > (5) Rents;
    > > (6) Royalties;
    > > (7) Dividends;
    > > (8) Alimony and separate maintenance payments;
    > > (9) Annuities;
    > > (10) Income from life insurance and endowment contracts;
    > > (11) Pensions;
    > > (12) Income from discharge of indebtedness;
    > > (13) Distributive share of partnership gross income;
    > > (14) Income in respect of a decedent; and
    > > (15) Income from an interest in an estate or trust.

    a. What three phrases in this statutory definition collectively support the general rule suggested in your text that "all income is taxable income unless the taxpayer can find good authority for excluding it?"
    b. In an academic sense, is this a "good" or "poor" definition of income? Explain briefly.

# Case 2–1

Rayco Hardware is planning to build a new store. Rayco owns two sites on which it can build; Rayco plans to build the store on one site and sell the other to help finance construction. Each site can be sold for $500,000.

Site #1 was purchased many years ago; it has a book and tax basis of $100,000. Site #2 was purchased last year; it has a book and tax basis of $500,000.

Jim Musumeci, president of Rayco, must decide which site to build on and which site to sell. If Jim is the sole owner of Rayco, which alternative should he choose? If Jim is not an owner and is evaluated by the board of directors based on Rayco's accounting income, which alternative should he choose? Assume Rayco's tax rate is 34 percent.

# Case 2–2

Mark Maggio bought a condominium in Prosperity City for $100,000 and took out a $95,000 30-year mortgage from Joe Morrow, his uncle. Joe Morrow believed Mark was a good credit risk and expected to be repaid. Mark lived in the condominium for four years until he got a better job 300 miles away in another state. The market value of the condo had fallen to $50,000, and the outstanding balance on the mortgage was $94,000. Unable to find a tenant to rent his condo, Mark packed his furniture and left Prosperity City in the middle of the night. Three months later Uncle Joe foreclosed and sold the property (for $50,000) and decided to forgive Mark's debt. Are there any tax consequences for Mark related to these events?

# CHAPTER 3

# Taxable Entities

The Internal Revenue Code technically imposes an income tax on only three entities. They are the individual, the corporation, and the fiduciary. All taxable income recognized in a single year must, therefore, be attributed to and reported by some individual, corporation, or fiduciary. This means, of course, that the taxable income originally realized by other entities—for example, that realized by a sole proprietorship, a partnership, or a joint venture—must be allocated to one of the three entities that are acknowledged for tax purposes. In some cases the code may require other entities to file a return, but these returns are for information purposes only.

## THE INDIVIDUAL TAXPAYER

Theoretically, every living person is a separate and distinct taxable entity. Age is of no significance: A two-year-old child who models baby clothes or acts in a television production is legally responsible for the payment of taxes and is as much a taxable entity as is each of the child's parents. In the case of the incapacitated or of very young children, the law provides, of course, that the parent or guardian may be equally liable for the filing of the return and the payment of the tax liability. The important point is that the individual, rather than the family unit, is the taxable entity. As a practical matter, however, the technical point just stated is, at best, a half-truth.

### The Married Couple

The code has provided since 1948 for something known as the joint return of married persons. The effect of the joint return provision is to decrease the effective tax rate for literally millions of married persons. The reason for initiation of the joint return was to establish some reasonable degree of federal income tax equity between taxpayers who lived in community property states and taxpayers who lived in common-law states. The inequity of the situation that existed prior to 1948 can be demonstrated by the use of a simple graph. If there were only one progressive income tax rate schedule (as there was prior to 1948), and if the entire income of a married couple were earned by one spouse in a community property state, that income could be treated for federal tax purposes as if half of it had been earned by each of the two partners to the marriage (which was and is the general result of those state laws). Consequently the tax would be equal to two times the tax on an income of an amount equal to distance *ab* in Figure 3–1, not on one amount equal to distance *ac*. The tax saving available to a married couple residing in a community property state, as compared to a married couple in identical circumstances, but residing in a common-law state, can be represented by the crosshatched area in Figure 3–1. To reduce this inequality and to stop a movement by all of the states to adopt community property laws, Congress enacted a provision in 1948 for the joint return of married persons. The important effect of this change was to do for everyone exactly what the community property laws had done earlier for a few. That is, it effectively assumed that one half of the income earned by any married persons was earned by each spouse and then permitted the federal income tax computation to be made accordingly. In order to simplify the administration of the law— by avoiding the assumed division of each spouse's income and subsequently by the addition of the two independently determined income taxes—the IRS created a second tax rate schedule, which could be applied to the combined incomes of the married couple. To achieve the congressional objective, this new rate schedule was necessarily designed so that the marginal tax brackets were exactly twice as wide as those applied to income earned by single persons. In other words, if the first $500 of taxable income of a single person were to be taxed at the marginal rate of 14 percent, then the first $1,000 (2 × $500) of taxable income of the married couple had to be taxed at 14 percent.

## The Head of Household

As a consequence of the introduction of the joint return, the basic entity for individual income tax purposes after 1948 remained the individual-only

**FIGURE 3–1**

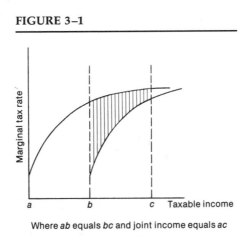

Where *ab* equals *bc* and joint income equals *ac*

for single persons; most married persons filed as a husband-wife team. In the mid-1950s, Congress decided to add a third category of individual taxpayers by creating a head-of-household status. The thought behind the creation of this third subcase of the individual was that for tax purposes some persons were really more like married persons than they were like single persons and that, under these circumstances, they ought to be entitled to some of the tax advantages that attached to matrimony. The basic idea was that if a single person—in most instances, a person who was once married, but was no longer in that status—retained the responsibility of supporting one or more dependent relatives, that taxpayer should be entitled to some tax relief. The relief decided upon took the form of a new rate schedule whose brackets and marginal tax rates were arranged in such a manner as to give this person approximately one half of the tax advantage of being married.

### Single Persons

Although the joint return and the head-of-household rates reduced the tax inequities that had existed between married persons living in different states and, to a lesser degree, between married persons and heads of households, these same tax innovations magnified the tax inequity between single and married individuals. In 1970, the tax on a $32,000 taxable income earned by a married couple was $8,660, whereas the tax on the same income earned by a single person was $12,210, a difference of $3,550 (or an increase of 41 percent) per year. Sufficient pressures were again brought on Congress, and in 1971 a fourth tax rate schedule was introduced for single individuals only. This new schedule was deliberately constructed in such a manner that the tax paid by a single person on any amount of taxable income would never be more than 120 percent of the tax paid by a married couple on the same amount of taxable income. At the same time, the rates applicable to heads of households were also adjusted downward so that they remained approximately midway between the single and the joint return rates. In order to avoid a return to the community property problem that had existed 22 years earlier, Congress required married persons filing separate returns to use a rate schedule that was not the same as that applicable to single persons. The rates were generally higher for married persons filing separately than for single persons earning the same taxable income.

The most interesting consequence of this revision was to introduce a tax inequity for married persons who *independently* earn a substantial and approximately equal taxable income. This result has been dubbed a tax on marriage. The real inequity that results can be simply illustrated. Using the 1989 tax rate schedules, and assuming the taxpayers claim a standard deduction, we can determine that the tax paid by a single person on a $25,000 taxable income is approximately $4,680. If two persons each earning a $25,000 taxable income were to marry, their joint liability would increase to approximately $10,413, which is $1,053 more annually than they were paying separately before saying "I do."

## Definitional Problems

The precise definitions necessary to determine whether or not a particular taxpayer is eligible to use any given rate schedule are not as straightforward as the common words used to describe them would seem to imply. For example, a taxpayer may be eligible to use the rate schedule for married persons filing jointly even though his or her spouse died a year or two earlier. This opportunity exists whenever the taxpayer can qualify for status as a *surviving spouse*, another technical income tax term requiring more than simply outliving the person to whom you were once married. Similarly, status as head of household is determined by some very specific, and sometimes apparently inequitable, criteria. In keeping with the objectives of this book, no details of the pertinent definitions will be examined here. The taxpayer having a personal interest in such definitional problems should consult a current tax return instructional booklet, a reliable tax reference work, or a competent tax adviser to make a correct determination in actual cases.

## Tax Rates for Individual Taxpayers

The tax rates for individual taxpayers were dramatically changed in the 1986 Tax Reform Act. For 1988 and thereafter, there appear to be only two marginal tax rates; that is, one rate of 15 percent that applies to "lower" amounts of taxable income and a second rate of 28 percent that applies to "higher" amounts of taxable income. The maximum amount of taxable income subject to the 15 percent rate varies by filing status. Those amounts for 1988 were as follows:

| Filing Status | Maximum Amount of Taxable Income Subject to 15 Percent Tax |
|---|---|
| Single persons | $17,850 |
| Married persons filing jointly | 29,750 |
| Heads of households | 23,900 |
| Married persons filing separately | 14,875 |

Based on the amounts stated above, the 1988 *apparent* tax rates for single persons can be easily diagramed as in Figure 3–2. The diagram for all other

**FIGURE 3–2**   Apparent 1988 Tax Rates for Single Persons

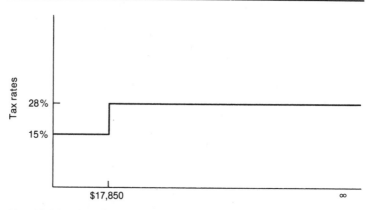

*Note:* The $17,850 will be adjusted for changes in the consumer price index (CPI) by December 15, 1988, in establishing tax rates for 1989. It will be readjusted by December 15, 1989, in establishing the tax rates for 1990.

individuals would, of course, be identical except for the taxable income dollar amounts at which the marginal tax rate increases from 15 to 28 percent. For married persons filing jointly for 1988 that point in Figure 3–2 would increase from $17,850 to $29,750; for heads of households it would increase to $23,900; and for married persons filing separately it would decrease to $14,875. These dollar amounts are to be adjusted in every year after 1988 to reflect any cost-of-living increases. Thus, by no later than December 15, 1988, the above amounts will be adjusted for 1989 to reflect any increase in the consumer price index for 1988 and they will again be readjusted by December 15, 1989, for the year 1990. Because the 1988 CPI adjustments were not available at the time we went to press, we were unable to illustrate the real rate brackets for 1989. The concept, however, will not have changed from that described here for 1988.

A closer examination of the Code will reveal that there is, for all practical purposes, a hidden or third marginal tax-rate bracket for "upper-income" taxpayers. This third bracket was initially created because Congress decided to phase out the benefit of the 15 percent bracket for individuals earning an above-average income. The phase-out is achieved by imposing an additional 5 percent surtax on all individuals reporting a taxable income in excess of a stipulated dollar amount. The specific dollar amounts to which this 5 percent surtax applies, and the taxable income point at which it begins, once again vary by filing status and by year. The amounts and starting points for 1988 were as follows:

| Filing Status | Taxable Income Subject to the 5 Percent Surtax |
|---|---|
| Single persons | from $43,150 to $89,560 |
| Married persons filing jointly | from $71,900 to $149,250 |
| Heads of households | from $61,650 to $123,790 |
| Married persons filing separately | from $35,950 to $113,300 |

The arithmetic of these numbers is (with the one exception noted below) entirely logical, given the intent of Congress. The maximum tax saving associated with the 15 percent bracket for single persons in 1988 was $2,320.50; i.e., $(28\% - 15\%) \times \$17,850$. Hence the 5 percent surtax should logically increase the single person's tax by no more than $2,320.50. Thus we note that $5\% (\$89,560 - \$43,150)$ also equals $2,320.50. The arithmetic for married persons filing jointly is equally logical; i.e.,

$$(28\% - 15\%) \times \$29,750 = \$3,867.50 \text{ and}$$
$$(\$149,250 - \$71,900) \times 5\% = \$3,867.50.$$

The freak case is the married individual filing a separate return. For reasons never explained, Congress decided to penalize these hapless persons via the 5 percent surtax. The $1,933.75 unexplained maximum penalty can be calculated as follows:

$$(28\% - 15\%) \times \$14,875 = \$1,933.75; \text{ but}$$
$$(\$113,300 - \$35,950) \times 5\% = \$3,867.50; \text{ and}$$
$$\$3,867.50 \text{ less } \$1,933.75 = \$1,933.75.$$

It should be noted that the effect of this 5 percent surtax is, at least initially, to impose a flat 28 percent tax on all persons earning income in excess of the maximum amounts indicated above. For reasons to be explained momentarily, however, that is not a totally accurate conclusion.

Because the true marginal tax rate is the only tax rate that is critical to all tax planning, it is important to understand that, in spite of the apparently simple, two-step rates explained earlier, there really is a third marginal tax rate of 33 percent. Based only on the information presented thus far, it would be prudent to modify the concept first introduced in Figure 3–2, above, to reflect this 5 percent surtax, as shown in Figure 3–3 below. The reason for entering a question mark, rather than a taxable income of exactly $89,560, to indicate the point at which the 33 percent marginal rate ended in 1988, is due to another new tax provision not yet explained. That provision states that a taxpayer must also "recapture" the value of any personal exemption deduction(s) claimed at the same 5 percent rate. The amount of the personal ex-

**FIGURE 3–3**   Real 1988 Tax Rate: for Single Persons

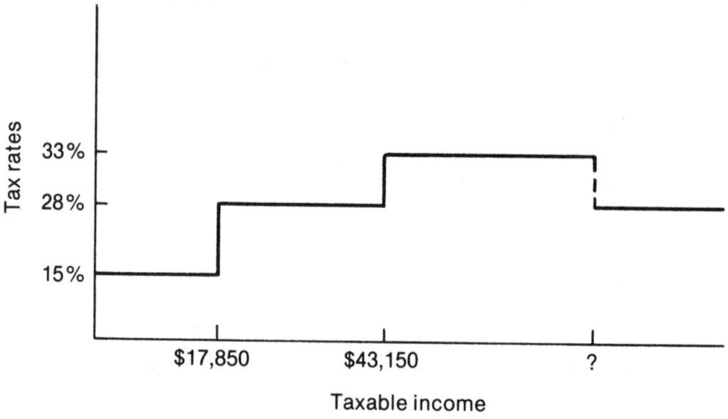

Note: Both the $17,850 and $43,150 numbers will be adjusted, for changes in the CPI, by December 15, 1988, in establishing tax rates for 1989.

emption in 1988 is $2,000; for all years after 1989, the $2,000 amount is to be adjusted to reflect inflation. The maximum tax-saving value of a $2,000 deduction is equal to $560; i.e., 28% × $2,000. Hence the law provides that the 33 percent marginal tax rate will continue to apply to varying amounts of taxable income above the end-points indicated earlier (on page 44). Exactly how far the 33 percent rate will extend depends, of course, on the number of personal exemption deductions that the taxpayer claims. Note that you must add taxable income of $11,200 to "recapture" $560 in additional taxes at a 5 percent rate; i.e., $560 divided by .05 = $11,200. In 1988 the amount of the personal exemption deduction was $1,950; hence in that year there was an addition of $10,920 for each exemption deduction (i.e., 28% × $1,950 = $546; and $546 ÷ .05 = $10,920). For a single individual claiming only one personal exemption deduction, the 33 percent marginal rate for 1988 ended at a taxable income of $100,480; i.e., $89,560 + $10,920. For a single person claiming two personal exemptions, it ended at $111,400; i.e., $89,560 + 2($10,920). For a married couple filing a joint return and claiming a total of four personal exemption deductions (which they would ordinarily do if they had two children living at home) the 33 percent marginal tax rate bracket for 1988 ended at $192,930; i.e., $149,250 + 4($10,920).

Although this is a cumbersome way to proceed, all readers should be prepared to calculate their own personal "real" or "true" tax-rate bracket for 1989 and 1990, as soon as the CPI adjustments have been announced. To double-check their understanding of this tax-law legerdemain, readers may want to see if they can reconstruct the following tax rate schedules for 1988:

Real 1988 Tax Rate Schedule for Married Persons Filing Jointly and Claiming Four, Three, and Two Exemption Deductions

| If Taxable Income Is: | | Then the Gross Tax Payable Is: | | |
|---|---|---|---|---|
| Over | But Not Over | Dollar Amount | Plus (percent) | Of the Amount Over |
| (Schedule for Couple Claiming Four Exemptions) | | | | |
| $  –0– | $ 29,750 | $   –0– | 15 | $  –0– |
| 29,750 | 71,900 | 4,462.50 | 28 | 29,750 |
| 71,900 | 192,930 | 16,264.50 | 33 | 71,900 |
| 192,930 | | 56,204.40 | 28 | 192,930 |
| (Same Schedule for Couple Claiming Three Exemptions) | | | | |
| $  –0– | $ 29,750 | $   –0– | 15 | $  –0– |
| 29,750 | 71,900 | 4,462.50 | 28 | 29,750 |
| 71,900 | 182,010 | 16,264.50 | 33 | 71,900 |
| 182,010 | | 52,600.80 | 28 | 182,010 |
| (Same Schedule for Couple Claiming Two Exemptions) | | | | |
| $  –0– | $ 29,750 | $   –0– | 15 | $  –0– |
| 29,750 | 71,900 | 4,462.50 | 28 | 29,750 |
| 71,900 | 171,090 | 16,264.50 | 33 | 71,900 |
| 171,090 | | 48,997.20 | 28 | 171,090 |

Note: Once the CPI adjustments are announced, similar schedules can be prepared for 1989 and 1990.

Even a cursory examination of these three 1988 tax rate schedules reveals one very interesting anomaly in the new law. That is, for the first time ever in the history of the United States, we now tax upper-upper incomes at a *lower* marginal tax rate than we tax upper-middle incomes.

## THE CORPORATE TAXPAYER

The corporation, like the individual, has for many years been recognized as a taxable entity for income tax purposes. This fact creates about as many tax opportunities as it does tax traps. Most of the traps revolve around the obvious fact that a corporation is nothing but a legal fiction that is responsible ultimately to the people who own the shares of stock that represent the corporate entity; when a small group of people, or even a single individual, owns all of the shares, it becomes exceedingly difficult to distinguish between personal and corporate interests.

## Legal Entities

The propriety of taxing a legal entity seems, at first blush, to be questionable. Legal entities, after all, cannot consume the incomes they earn because consumption is a purely human opportunity. Corporations and other legal entities can reinvest the incomes they earn, and they can transform resources into (one hopes) more valuable forms, but they cannot destroy or consume these resources if they want to survive. Why, then, should these entities be taxed? Many people delight in pointing out that the taxation of income earned by any nonhuman entity necessarily means that a single income stream faces double income taxation. In the case of the corporation, that income stream must first be taxed as part of the corporation's taxable income and later as part of the stockholders' taxable incomes when whatever is left after paying the corporate income tax is distributed as a dividend. This double tax observation is generally applicable to the large, publicly held corporation, but the smaller, closely held corporation finds it quite easy to circumvent much of the double tax.

Among the alternatives to the double tax inherent in the present system is the option of ignoring the corporate entity and allocating all corporate income immediately and directly to the stockholders, whether or not the corporation distributes any of its earnings. This alternative would be administratively cumbersome for large, publicly held corporations since ownership of these corporations changes on a daily basis and income simply cannot be measured that frequently. In addition, this alternative could create major hardships were the corporation to earn a large income and distribute none of it; under those conditions, a stockholder could have a large tax liability with very limited funds to pay the income tax. As a consequence, if this alternative were enacted, corporate boards would be under tremendous pressure from stockholders to distribute most or all of the corporation's income as a dividend. For this reason alone, corporate boards are not likely to give much support to an early demise of the corporate income tax. Another extreme alternative would permit the corporation's income to remain untaxed until distributed to the owners. If applied to a corporation, this would result in vast hoarding of corporate earnings and in widespread tax evasion. After all, anyone can create a corporation for $200 or less, and even persons of very modest means would find that cost immaterial if there were no tax on corporate income until that income was distributed. Although other intermediate positions can be designed to overcome many of the objections to each of these alternatives, none of them have ever gained the support of a majority of Congress. Options currently available to the small, closely held corporation are explained later in this chapter.

To note that the corporation, like the individual, is recognized as a separate taxable entity is to tell only half the story. The tax rate structure applicable to most corporations' taxable income is significantly different from that applied to an individual's income. In the absence of any complications, in 1988 a corporate entity will pay an income tax of 15 percent of its first $50,000 in taxable income; 25 percent of its next $25,000; and 34 percent of any remaining taxable income (plus a 5 percent surtax on taxable income between $100,000 and $335,000). For most practical purposes, therefore, we can generally assume that a large corporation—that is, a corporation with a large taxable income—will pay about 34 percent of its taxable income in federal income taxes, whereas a small corporation will generally pay something less. In summary, the corporate tax has three major steps or brackets, plus a limited 5 percent tax that effectively negates the first two brackets for corporations earning more than $335,000 in taxable income. Figure 3–4 illustrates the essential features of the 1988 corporate tax rate structure. Unlike most other corporations, personal service corporations are taxed at a flat rate of 34 percent. These PSCs include corporations engaged in such professions as law, medicine and accounting.

## THE FIDUCIARY TAXPAYER

The estate and the trust are the two common forms of the fiduciary taxpayer. The estate fills a necessary gap following the death of an individual taxpayer. A person's death marks the end of a final income tax period. On the final return of a decedent, taxable income is reported from the date of the last accounting, usually December 31 of the prior year, to the date of death. Years may pass, however, before the assets of a decedent are distributed to the heirs or devisees. An estate must report and pay tax on any taxable income earned on the decedent's assets in the interim period. Once a deceased taxpayer's assets have all been distributed, the estate ceases to exist, and the

**FIGURE 3–4**   Real 1988 Tax Rates for Most Corporate Taxpayers

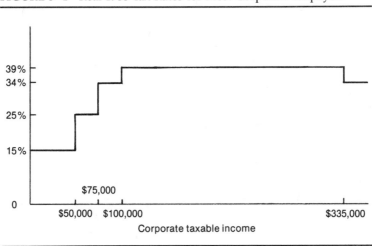

Corporate taxable income

new owners begin to report on their own tax returns the income earned on the property transferred to them.

A *trust* is a legal relationship in which one person, called a *trustee,* holds title to property for the benefit or use of another person, called a beneficiary. The trust may be testamentary (created by a will) or *inter vivos* (created among living persons by a legal document other than a will). *Inter vivos* trusts created after March 1, 1986, may or may not be recognized as a separate taxable entity. Trusts created after that date will be recognized as a separate taxable entity only if the property can not revert to the grantor. Trusts created before March 1, 1986, will be recognized as a separate taxable entity if the term of the trust is for a period of 10 years or longer or for the life of a designated beneficiary. If these or other requirements are not satisfied, the income of the trust will continue to be taxed to the grantor (the person who created the trust through the transfer of property). If all requirements are satisfied, the trust becomes a separate taxable entity, but only to the extent that it does not distribute income to beneficiaries.

The fact that a trustee may be given an option over the distribution of income makes the trust a viable vehicle for tax planning. If conditions are favorable—for example, if the income beneficiary is in a low tax bracket because of his or her age or because of an unusually large tax loss incurred from some other source—the trustee can proceed with an income distribution and avoid or minimize the income tax liability of the trust itself. If conditions are not favorable to a distribution, the trustee may be given the authority to retain the taxable income, in which case the trust pays the income tax. In summary, the trust is, for income tax purposes, a partial entity; it is recognized as a taxable entity only if and to the extent that it does not distribute its taxable income to the beneficiaries.

The 1988 apparent tax rate schedule for fiduciary taxpayers is a simple, two-step affair; that is, a tax of 15 percent on the first $5,000 of taxable income and a tax of 28 percent on any taxable income in excess of $5,000. The tax reduction attributable to the low (15 percent) tax rate on the first $5,000 of taxable income earned by a fiduciary taxpayer is recaptured at a 5 percent rate for taxable income exceeding $13,000. These rates can be diagramed as in Figure 3–5, above. In other words, the *real* fiduciary tax rate structure includes a 33 percent marginal tax bracket that is applicable to taxable incomes of between $13,000 and $26,000. This means, of course, that any fiduciary taxpayer reporting a taxable income of more than $26,000 is subject to a flat tax rate of 28 percent.

## OTHER ENTITIES

For financial accounting purposes, many entities are recognized in addition to the individual, the corporation, and the fiduciary. For example, in financial accounting a sole proprietorship is typically treated as an entity, separate

**FIGURE 3–5**   Real 1988 Tax Rates for Fiduciary Taxpayers

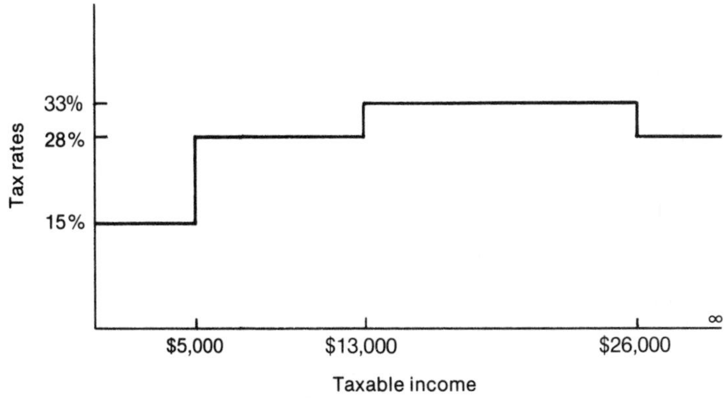

and distinct from its owner. For income tax purposes, however, the income of a sole proprietorship simply becomes one of several schedules that collectively constitute the aggregate income tax return for the owner. Except for the physical separation of financial data on Schedule C, Form 1040, the income of the proprietorship is commingled with the owner's gross income and deductions from other sources, such as interest, rents, dividends, and salary.

### Partnerships

Although a partnership is required to file an annual tax return, Form 1065, this return serves only to indicate to the Internal Revenue Service the amount and kind of income, deductions, and credits that the partners ought to be reporting on their tax returns as their share of the income from the partnership venture. Again, each partner's share of the partnership's income is commingled with income from all other sources on the individual Form 1040 (if the partner is an individual), the Form 1120 (if the corporation is a partner), or the Form 1041 (if the fiduciary is a partner). If the partnership elects to retain all of a sizable taxable income, a partner may owe a large tax liability with only limited resources to pay it. Under the reverse financial circumstances, a partner may discover that sometimes a partnership's losses can be offset against income from other business ventures and therefore be of real tax advantage.

There is one major exception to the general tax treatment of partnerships described in the preceding paragraph. That exception concerns certain master-limited partnerships, or MLPs. Those publicly traded limited partnerships—excluding MLPs in the real estate and the oil and gas business—are to be treated after 1987 as corporations for federal income tax purposes. A grand-father provision in the law allows MLPs that were in existence before December 18, 1987, to defer the effective date of this new provision to years beginning after December 31, 1997.

## Hybrid Organizations

To posit that most partnerships are not recognized as a separate taxable entity whereas a corporation is so recognized begs a very important question: What, exactly, is a corporation? Suffice it to note here that just because a business has been incorporated in compliance with state law does not of itself guarantee the recognition of this entity as a corporation for federal tax purposes. Most corporate entities organized in compliance with state law admittedly are recognized as such for tax purposes, but they need not be so recognized in unusual circumstances. In other situations, businesses that are formally organized as partnerships may discover that for tax purposes they are treated as corporate entities. And, occasionally, what is legally formed as a business trust may be taxed as a corporation. The judicial decisions in this relatively limited area seem to turn upon the presence or absence of such corporate characteristics as continuity of life, centralization of management, transferability of ownership, limited liability, and purpose of organization. The courts have carefully avoided delineation of which, how many, or what combination of corporate characteristics are sufficient to create or to destroy the business association that will be taxed as a corporation. The decisions proceed on an ad hoc basis, and the taxpayer must always be alert to avoid an inadvertent arrangement that could lead to an undesirable classification in a questionable situation.

## Subchapter S Corporations

More important, it is legally possible to organize a business venture as a corporation and then to elect to tax the corporation in a manner similar to that of a partnership, assuming that the conditions for making this election can be satisfied. This provision is contained in Subchapter S of the code; consequently, such corporations are referred to as S corporations. They are alternatively called small business corporations, which is unfortunate for two reasons. First, the qualifying criteria pertinent to this option say nothing about the dollar size of the firm's net worth, sales volume, or number of employees; hence they really may be very large corporations. Second, other special kinds of corporations are also known as small business investment corporations (SBICs) and small business corporations (if their stock is qualified under Section 1244, a special rule to be considered later). The use of very similar terminology for essentially different kinds of organizations only tends to confuse the uninitiated.

At one time, it was legally possible for a business to operate as a sole proprietorship or as a partnership but to elect, under Subchapter R, to be taxed as if it were a corporation. This option was terminated and all prior elections expired several years ago.

Before a corporation can elect Subchapter S treatment it must meet all of the qualifications set out in the code. Among the more important of these qualifications are the following:

1. There can be no more than 35 shareholders, and each must consent to the election.
2. Only individuals, estates, and certain trusts can hold stock in the electing corporation (that is, there can be no corporate or partnership shareholders).
3. There can be only one class of stock (although both voting and nonvoting common stock are permissable).
4. All shareholders must be either U.S. citizens or resident aliens.

Each of these criteria must be satisfied before a corporation can make a valid election; failure to meet any of the four criteria during a year will automatically terminate an otherwise valid election.

There are, of course, a number of other entities that exist for legal and accounting purposes. Because they are of limited significance for tax purposes, they are not discussed here.

## SPLITTING INCOME AMONG TAXABLE ENTITIES

One of the most basic forms of income tax planning involves the splitting of what otherwise would be a single income stream, taxed wholly to one taxable entity, between two or more taxable entities. Income splitting will be beneficial from a tax viewpoint so long as there is some progression in marginal tax rates. And, as we have just observed in the preceding discussion, each of the current U.S. tax rates contains two or more tax brackets. For individuals, corporations, and fiduciaries, the lowest bracket in 1988 is a 15 percent rate.

The fundamental idea behind income splitting is, of course, exactly the same concept as that illustrated earlier in Figure 3–1. Tax minimization will be achieved when an income stream has been subdivided among enough entities and in such a manner that each taxable entity pays tax at the same marginal rate. The creative part of tax planning comes in trying to determine how a person can effectively split what appears to be a single income stream into several apparently separate parts and to have those legal and financial arrangements avoid the many tax rules that have been enacted specifically to derail such exotic schemes. A less interesting but equally important task is determining whether or not the tax savings that still can be achieved in this manner are really worth their cost.

### Income Splitting within Families

To illustrate the potential of income splitting in one very simple example, consider the strange case of a married couple with three children who live entirely on a $100,000 annual taxable income from investments. If the entire $100,000 taxable income is earned by the parents, who file a joint return, their federal income tax liability for 1988 will be $25,537.50. If that same income could be redistributed so that the parents received $55,000 and each of the three children received $15,000, the family tax bill *might* decrease to as little as $18,282.50; a tax savings of $7,255 (about 28 percent of their original tax liability).

Notice that we said the tax liability *might* be reduced to as little as $18,282.50. Whether it would or not depends on (1) exactly how the parents go about diverting $15,000 per year to each of their three children and (2) the ages of their children. The simplest method of redirecting investment income is, obviously, to give away the property that produces the income. Hence, in this example, the parents could give each child sufficient income-producing property to provide the child with a $15,000 annual taxable income. Such a gift would clearly provide the child with the legal claim to the income, but it might not achieve the intended tax objective.

The tax law provides that most of the passive (or "investment") income earned by a child under the age of 14 will be taxed at the *parents'* top marginal rate. This means that, for all practical purposes, the tax will be determined just as if it had been earned by the parents. Therefore, in the above example, the maximum tax saving of $7,255 per year can be achieved only if all three of the children are 14 years of age or older.

Furthermore, many parents would be unwilling to give their child the permanent title to an income-producing property because they believe that they themselves might have a greater need for that same income stream in their own declining years than will their children in their most productive years. Such concerned parents might attempt to temporarily redirect the income stream from themselves to their children for only a limited number of years via some form of trust. At the termination of the trust, clear title to the property would have to be returned to the parents. Although such a temporary income-splitting device often worked before March 1, 1986, similar trusts created after that date are considered to be grantor trusts. For federal income tax purposes that means that the trust income will now be taxed to the parents regardless of how it is distributed for legal purposes.

This somewhat atypical example illustrates both the care with which one must proceed in implementing income-splitting tax plans and the potential nonmonetary costs associated with such plans. A somewhat more typical example could be constructed for the couple earning a $100,000 annual taxable income from an unincorporated trade or business.

### Income Splitting with Corporations

To illustrate the possibility of income splitting through the use of a corporation, suppose that a couple were to incorporate their sole proprietorship mercantile business that had been earning a $100,000 annual taxable income. Their joint tax liability on that income would be $25,537.50 in 1988. If the new corporation were to retain $50,000 of the $100,000 it earned, and distribute the other $50,000 to the couple as a salary, the total tax on that $100,000 income stream would drop to $17,632.50 per year; a saving of $7,905 per year. The tax savings could be increased even more if the parents' salary could be reduced from $50,000 to about $30,000 per year and the other $20,000 could be paid as a salary to their children who also worked for their family corporation. Under those conditions the total bill *might* be reduced to as little as (roughly) $15,000 per year; i.e., 15 percent of $100,000.

Once again note that taxes *might* be reduced via the income splitting plan suggested above. Whether or not it would work depends in part on the reasonableness of (1) any salaries paid to the mythical couple who incorporated their business as well as (2) any salaries paid to their children. In addition, it depends on exactly what kind of business is being carried on in the corporate entity. The tax law has, for many years, authorized a corporation to deduct the wages and salaries paid to its employees only if and to the extent that those salaries are reasonable in amount. Obviously taxpayers and tax collectors have been known to disagree frequently on such subjective opinions as the reasonableness of salaries, especially when those salaries are arranged between individuals and a corporation controlled by the same individuals.

Personal service corporations—that is, corporations engaged in such professional service businesses as accounting, actuarial science, architecture, consulting, dentistry, engineering, law, medicine, or the performing arts—must tax their entire taxable income at one flat rate of 34 percent for all tax years beginning after December 31, 1987. This means, of course, that personal service corporations are for all practical purposes a thing of the past. Since incomes earned in *un*incorporated business forms and in S corrporations will currently not be taxed at a marginal rate in excess of 33 percent, no one should incorporate a professional service business, at least from a tax point of view. Furthermore, professional service corporations created in years before 1988 must now either make the Subchapter S election or liquidate the old corporation to avoid being taxed at the highest possible marginal rate. In summary, income splitting with corporations is still possible, but only under certain favorable conditions.

### Income Splitting with Multiple Corporations

If an individual or a couple can achieve tax savings by splitting the income derived from one single business between the amount retained in a corporation and the amount distributed as a salary, why couldn't even more taxes be saved in somewhat larger businesses by dividing the retained earnings of a single business up among several corporations?

If each corporation is recognized as a separate taxable entity, and if the corporate tax rate structure contains three progressive brackets, it should be possible for the owners of middle-sized firms to split their business ventures in a most tax advantageous way. Suppose, for example, that a taxpayer owned a retail business that provided him with a $200,000 annual taxable income over and above his salary. If this businessman elected to incorporate his venture, should he attempt to form two corporations of approximately equal size or should he put the entire operation into a single corporate shell? Considering only tax factors and ignoring for the moment any possible complications in making this choice, it should be immediately evident that some tax savings would attach to the two-corporation alternative. That is, the corporate income tax on two equal incomes of $100,000 earned by separate legal entities, would appear to be $44,500 [2 × (15% × $50,000) + 2 × (25% × $25,000) + 2 × (34% × $25,000)], whereas the corporate income tax on a single income of $200,000 would appear to be $61,250 [(15% × $50,000) + (25% × $25,000) + (34% × $25,000) + (39% × $100,000)], an increase of $16,750 (or over 37 percent) per year. Ventures retaining more than $200,000 in taxable income should, of course, be able to increase their tax saving even more by creating an appropriately larger number of corporate entities.

Regardless of the details of the corporate tax rate structure, so long as the corporation remains a separate taxable entity, and so long as the corporate tax involves a progressive rate structure, the general tax-planning notion discussed here is certain to remain valid. Only the detailed calculations—and the point at which each idea becomes viable—change. Accordingly, the author urges each reader to concentrate attention on the basic ideas rather than on the arithmetic of a specific example.

### Economic Realities

The simple tax-planning opportunity noted in the preceding paragraph was widely observed and utilized in the United States for decades prior to a critical change introduced in the 1969 Tax Reform Act. That change provided that, after December 31, 1974, controlled groups of corporations must be treated for most tax purposes as if they were a single taxable entity. For a few years prior to 1981, it appeared that economic realities had won out over legal fictions because tax avoidance had reached epidemic proportions. The definition of a controlled group of corporations was expanded in the 1969 Act so that most corporations that were created previously for tax avoidance reasons (as well as some others) were caught in the new definitional web. That definition of controlled corporations encompasses both brother-sister and parent-subsidiary ownership arrangements. The basic differences between these two can be illustrated simply, as shown in Figures 3–6 and 3–7. Figure 3–6 rep-

**FIGURE 3–6**                          **FIGURE 3–7**

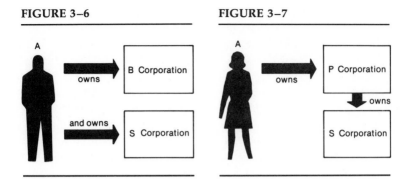

resents a brother-sister ownership arrangement; Figure 3–7, a parent-subsidiary arrangement. If we assume in Figure 3–6 that person A owns all of the stock of both corporations B and S, and if we assume in Figure 3–7 that person A owns all the stock of corporation P and that corporation P owns all the stock of corporation S, then it is very easy to see why it may be more appropriate to tax the corporations on the basis of economic realities rather than legal fictions. To do otherwise permits widespread tax avoidance possibilities.

### Legal Definitions

When Congress tried to close this tax loophole, however, it created some entirely new problems in statutory interpretation. The 1969 definition of the parent-subsidiary form of the controlled group proved to cause little difficulty. It provides that there will be a parent-subsidiary controlled group any time that a parent corporation owns equal to or greater than 80 percent of one or more subsidiary corporation's stock (determined by vote or by value, whichever yields the greater percentage). The parent's ownership interest can be direct or indirect, through third- or fourth-tier corporate structures. For example, corporations A, B, C, and D would constitute a single parent-subsidiary controlled group of corporations if their ownership were distributed as in Figure 3–8.

The interpretation of the new brother-sister controlled group definition proved to be much more difficult. Section 1563(a)(2) provides that two or more

**FIGURE 3–8**

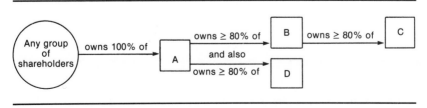

corporations will be considered a brother-sister group if five or fewer persons (individuals, estates, or trusts) own (1) 80 percent or more of the stock of each such corporation *and* (2) more than 50 percent of the stock of each such corporation considering "the stock ownership of each such individual only to the extent such stock ownership is identical with respect to each such corporation." This last phrase, quite obviously, leaves something to be desired in terms of lucidity. Nevertheless, Treasury regulations were promptly issued to help taxpayers understand what Congress supposedly intended. For example, according to the regulations, corporations A and B are considered members of a brother-sister controlled group if their ownership interests are divided between two unrelated shareholders, as indicated in Figure 3–9.

In words, in Figure 3–9 two individuals (X and Y) own (1) 100 percent of corporations A and B and (2) 80 percent of those same corporations considering only their "identical ownership" as that phrase is interpreted by the Treasury regulations, the courts, and the congressional committee reports.

On the other hand, according to these same authorities, corporations C and D would *not* be considered members of a brother-sister controlled group if they were owned by three unrelated individuals, as depicted in Figure 3–10.

**FIGURE 3-9**     In Diagram Format

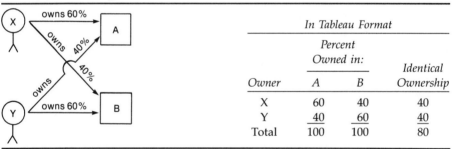

| | *In Tableau Format* | | |
| --- | --- | --- | --- |
| | *Percent Owned in:* | | *Identical* |
| *Owner* | *A* | *B* | *Ownership* |
| X | 60 | 40 | 40 |
| Y | 40 | 60 | 40 |
| Total | 100 | 100 | 80 |

**FIGURE 3-10**     In Diagram Format

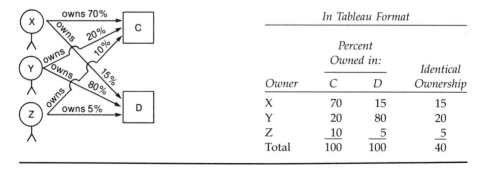

| | *In Tableau Format* | | |
| --- | --- | --- | --- |
| | *Percent Owned in:* | | *Identical* |
| *Owner* | *C* | *D* | *Ownership* |
| X | 70 | 15 | 15 |
| Y | 20 | 80 | 20 |
| Z | 10 | 5 | 5 |
| Total | 100 | 100 | 40 |

In Figure 3–10, three individuals (X, Y, and Z) own 100 percent of corporations C and D; hence, the first (or 80 percent) test *is* satisfied. The second (or 50 percent) test, however, *is not* satisfied. The identical ownership of X, Y, and Z is only 40 percent in this example. The code requires that it be *more than* 50 percent if a brother-sister group is to exist.

The difficulties of statutory interpretation did not end with the identical ownership phrase. Another particularly troublesome issue was determining whether or not every stockholder must own some minimum number of shares in each corporation in order for that corporation to be included in any controlled group. For example, prior to a 1982 Supreme Court decision, the authorities were divided on the issue of whether or not the corporations depicted in Figure 3–11 constituted a brother-sister controlled group.

A majority of the Tax Court contended that corporations E and F could *not* be a controlled group because individual Z owns no part of corporation F. In other words, even though the second (or 50 percent) test is satisfied, the first (or 80 percent) test is not satisfied. Whether the 80 percent test is or is not satisfied depends, of course, on whether or not you include stockholder Z in making the percentage determinations. Treasury regulations, the IRS, and several Circuit Courts of Appeals said that the Tax Court was incorrectly interpreting the code and that corporations E and F (in Figure 3–11) were members of a controlled group. This conflict was resolved by the Supreme Court in *Vogel Fertilizer* when it agreed with the prior opinion of the Tax Court.

Unfortunately for the taxpayer, the definitional complications of controlled groups of corporations do not end with the considerations already discussed. This definition is further complicated by both some overlapping group problems and a maze of constructive ownership rules. Because this book is intended only as a recognition-oriented effort, we will forgo any detailed review of further definitional complications and get directly to the heart of the current tax-planning matter. What is evident today is that the

**FIGURE 3-11**  In Diagram Format

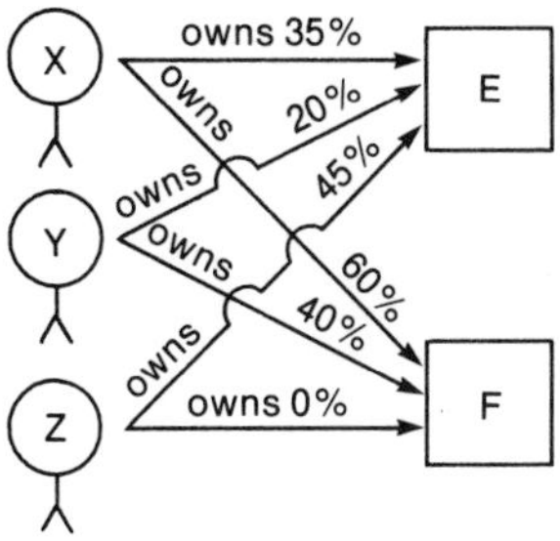

| | In Tableau Format | | |
| | Percent Owned in: | | Identical |
| Owner | E | F | Ownership |
| X | 35 | 60 | 35 |
| Y | 20 | 40 | 20 |
| Z | 45 | 0 | 0 |
| Total | 55 | | |
| | or | | |
| | 100? | 100 | 55 |

1969 tax-law changes are not as harsh as they first appeared to be. Two statutory details are particularly important:

1. The 50 percent identical-ownership test requires that five or fewer persons own *more than* 50 percent of the corporations before the law makes them members of a brother-sister controlled group.

2. There is no attribution between a parent and any *adult* (defined to be persons 21 years of age or older) child so long as neither owns *more than* 50 percent of the jointly owned corporation.

As a consequence of these two details, a family unit consisting of only one parent and two adult children can own 100 percent of six corporations and not have a single controlled group. To achieve that tax magic, the family would have to be willing to divide its ownership interest *exactly* as depicted in Figure 3–12. A deviation of even one percentage point would create entirely different results. In Figure 3–12, there are several potential groups of corporations in which the identical ownership is equal to exactly 50 percent; there is no possible combination in which the identical ownership is *more than* 50 percent.

The Supreme Court decision in *Vogel Fertilizer* also gives renewed vitality to an old multiple-corporate plan. In this scheme one individual typically provides a majority of the capital required by several corporations in exchange for a 79 percent interest in each corporation. Other (unrelated) individuals are then hired to manage each corporation, receiving a 21 percent interest in one corporation in exchange for their services and a possible capital investment. The result of this tax plan would be a group of corporations like that depicted in Figure 3–13. Once again with this carefully arranged ownership distribution there would be no controlled group of corporations for income tax purposes. In other words, the major tax savings described above could be achieved even though one individual owned 79 percent of all six corporations.

In summary, after the Tax Reform Act of 1969 and before 1981, most tax advisers acted as if the golden era of multiple corporations had ended forever. After a few years of living with the new provisions, and after an important Supreme Court decision, however, there was a rebirth of multiple corporations. We again found that what was really a single closely held business was

**FIGURE 3–12**

| Owner | Percent Owned in | | | | | |
|---|---|---|---|---|---|---|
| | A | B | C | D | E | F |
| Parent | 100 | 50 | — | 50 | — | — |
| Adult child 1 | — | 50 | 100 | — | — | 50 |
| Adult child 2 | — | — | — | 50 | 100 | 50 |

**FIGURE 3–13**

| Owner | Percent Owned in | | | | | |
|---|---|---|---|---|---|---|
| | *A* | *B* | *C* | *D* | *E* | *F* |
| Capital contributor | 79 | 79 | 79 | 79 | 79 | 79 |
| Manager 1 | 21 | — | — | — | — | — |
| Manager 2 | — | 21 | — | — | — | — |
| Manager 3 | — | — | 21 | — | — | — |
| Manager 4 | — | — | — | 21 | — | — |
| Manager 5 | — | — | — | — | 21 | — |
| Manager 6 | — | — | — | — | — | 21 |

being divided up among a greater number of corporate entities, largely for tax reasons. To be sure, the owners of these corporations had to take greater care than they did in the pre-1970 era when distributing the stock ownership. It is too early to determine if the 1986 tax law changes will stem this trend. By reducing the top marginal corporate rate from 46 to 34 percent, the relative significance of the idea has been reduced accordingly. Nevertheless, the savings can still be significant. For example, if a single corporation earns approximately $250,000 per year (above the needs of the owner) and that income could be divided equally between five corporations, that business would be worth an additional $2.8 million in 30 years if the tax saving each year were reinvested at a 5 percent aftertax rate of return.

## ENTITIES AND THE TAXABLE INCOME CONCEPT

The calculation of taxable income proceeds on a slightly different basis for corporations than it does for individuals and fiduciaries. The differences in question are sometimes of importance to the achievement of success in tax saving ideas. Consequently, these differences will be examined briefly in the remaining pages of this chapter. To introduce the important differences, let us expand the general formula used to determine the federal income tax liability as it was presented on page 7. The expanded formula can be summarized as illustrated in Figure 3–14.

### Special Corporate Considerations

Relative to the corporate entity, only one additional comment is deemed necessary at this point. Among the special deductions (those available only to the corporate entity) is a dividend-received deduction. A corporation can generally deduct, in the calculation of its taxable income, either 70 or 80 percent of the dividends it receives during a year from other domestic corporate entities. (The deduction is 70 percent if the recipient corporation owns

**FIGURE 3–14**

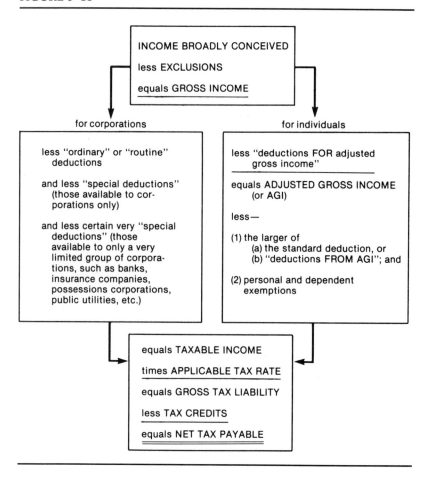

INCOME BROADLY CONCEIVED

less EXCLUSIONS

equals GROSS INCOME

for corporations

less "ordinary" or "routine"
    deductions

and less "special deductions"
    (those available to cor-
    porations only)

and less certain very "special
    deductions" (those
    available to only a very
    limited group of corpora-
    tions, such as banks,
    insurance companies,
    possessions corporations,
    public utilities, etc.)

for individuals

less "deductions FOR adjusted
    gross income"

equals ADJUSTED GROSS INCOME
    (or AGI)

less—

(1) the larger of
    (a) the standard deduction, or
    (b) "deductions FROM AGI"; and

(2) personal and dependent
    exemptions

equals TAXABLE INCOME

times APPLICABLE TAX RATE

equals GROSS TAX LIABILITY

less TAX CREDITS

equals NET TAX PAYABLE

less than 20 percent of the distributing corporation; it is 80 percent if the recipient corporation owns 20 percent or more. In the case of controlled groups of corporations, 100 percent of the dividends received from other corporations in the same controlled group may be deducted.) The reason for this special corporate deduction is obvious if we reconsider a point made earlier in this chapter: Income earned in the first instance by a corporate entity may be subject to a double tax. If one corporation owns another corporation's stock, does that mean that a single income stream will be subject to a triple tax? In the absence of a dividend-received deduction, or of a special exclusion rule available to the corporate entity, that would be the unhappy circumstance. In the absence of such a provision, corporate ownership of another corpo-ration's stock would be of dubious value since the tax consequence would make such relationships prohibitively expensive. To avoid this serious intervention in multicorporate ownership arrangements common to a modern economy, Congress elected to grant the dividend-received deduction to corporate entities.

### Special Considerations for Individual Taxpayers

A few additional comments relevant to the deductions available to individual taxpayers also seem appropriate. First, note that every individual's tax deductions must be divided between deductions *for* adjusted gross income (AGI) and deductions *from* AGI. In the former category, no options are available, and, therefore, the only question is one of definition. Which deductions are properly classified as deductions for AGI?

**Deductions for AGI.**   Deductions for AGI are, generally speaking, the taxpayer's deductions that relate to a trade or business. Unfortunately, like most general rules, this one is replete with exceptions and a satisfactory definition would require a time-consuming investigation of Section 62. In lieu of such an investigation, try to understand the following restatement of the more important limits that apply to deductions *for* adjusted gross income.

1. All deductions that can be classified as
   a. *Nonemployee* trade or business expenses (for example, all routine business expenses associated with the operation of a sole proprietorship).
   b. Expenses associated with the production of rents and royalties, whether or not that activity constitutes a "trade or business."
2. Only very limited expenses incurred as an *employee*, specifically
   a. Any reimbursed business expenses, but only to the extent of the reimbursement; and
   b. Certain expenses associated with activities of performing artists.
3. Certain losses from the sale or exchange of trade, business, investment, or "nonbusiness" assets (not including personal assets).
4. Certain contributions to pension or profit-sharing plans by self-employed individuals.
5. Alimony.
6. Penalties forfeited because of early withdrawals from savings accounts.
7. A few miscellaneous items including certain retirement savings.

Any legitimate income tax deduction not within one of the above classifications is a deduction *from* the adjusted gross income of the individual taxpayer.

**Deductions from AGI.**   An individual taxpayer's deductions from AGI can be subdivided into two major groups: the personal and dependent exemption deductions and all other deductions. As noted earlier, the other or personal deductions should exceed the standard deduction if the taxpayer is to itemize deductions. The personal and dependent exemption deduction was $1,950 in 1988 and will be $2,000 in 1989. (Beginning in 1990, this amount is to be adjusted annually for changes in the consumer price index.) Incidentally, taxpayers who are claimed as dependents on another person's return can not also claim an exemption for themselves on their own returns. The 1988 standard deductions were:

| | |
|---|---|
| Single Persons | $3,000 |
| Married Persons /joint return | 5,000 |
| Heads of Households | 4,400 |
| Married Persons /separate return | 2,500 |

*Note:* These amounts will be adjusted in 1989 for charges in the CPI on or before December 15,1988.

In addition, married taxpayers who are either blind or 65 years of age (or older) will be allowed an *additional* standard deduction of $600. Thus a 65-year-old, blind taxpayer would have an additional standard deduction of $1,200 on a joint return filed with his or her spouse. This additional standard deduction is increased from $600 to $750 for single taxpayers. (All standard deduction amounts will be indexed to reflect inflation beginning in 1989.) If taxpayers' itemized deductions exceed their standard deduction, the former amount should be claimed as a deduction from AGI. No dollar-amount limit is applicable to itemized deductions.

For most individual taxpayers, the important personal or itemized deductions are the charitable contribution deduction, the home mortgage interest expense deduction, and the deduction for certain taxes. To the extent that these items can be manipulated individually in successful tax avoidance, they will be discussed later. However, one very simple tax avoidance idea ought to be noted here since it depends upon aggregate deductions from AGI.

It is not unusual to discover that a salaried individual taxpayer in the lower income bracket finds that his or her legitimate itemized deductions are about equal to the standard deduction. This individual often concludes that not itemizing deductions is advisable because it eliminates record keeping and costs little if anything in additional taxes. Actually this individual may be missing the only available opportunity for tax planning. The cash-basis taxpayer has a great deal of control over the timing of expenditures and can often accelerate or postpone the incurrence of a tax-deductible expense. To minimize the tax liability, a taxpayer may elect to itemize deductions only in alternate years. In the year in which he or she itemizes deductions, the taxpayer can accelerate all charitable contributions, incur and pay larger medical and dental expenses (for example, schedule an annual physical examination late in December to facilitate payment in December or in January, as best suits the tax plan), pay an extra month's mortgage interest, and possibly, to a limited extent, prepay property taxes. In the year in which this taxpayer claims only the standard deduction, he or she should delay (at least in the last two or three months of the year) the payment of any medical or dental bills, the making of any charitable contributions, and the payment of any taxes or interest. These expenditures could be paid early in the following year, which would be another itemizing year. By this simple application of careful timing, the salaried taxpayer may be able to increase aggregate deductions and minimize the net tax liability over several years.

We should also note that to whatever extent a taxpayer can legally classify deductions as deductions for AGI, it may pay to do so. This is especially true if the standard deduction exceeds itemized deductions. That is, a taxpayer who could legally arrange to incur all deductible expenses as deductions for AGI would gain to the extent of the standard deduction. Obviously, the reclassification of deductions is not at the option of the taxpayer and the definitional problems are substantial. Suffice it to note here that the self-employed taxpayer engaged in a trade or business is frequently at an advantage in this regard, as compared to an employee. This is particularly true today because any miscellaneous itemized deductions incurred by an employee are deductible only to the extent they exceed 2 percent of the taxpayer's AGI. Self-employed taxpayers, however, are not subject to this 2 percent floor because they can deduct most of these same expenses as deductions for AGI. The list of miscellaneous deductions that may be involved includes, among others, any unreimbursed travel and transportation expenses; outside salesman expenses; union dues; professional dues and subscriptions; uniforms; tax-return preparation fees; and job-related education expenses.

## PROBLEMS AND ASSIGNMENTS

1. Three families—the Andersons, the Baxters, and the Carters—live in apartments A, B, and C (respectively) at 1040 Tax Hollow, Central City, U.S.A. Each of the three families consists of a father, mother, and two children. Each family household earns a gross income of $60,000 per year; however, the source of each family income differs significantly. Mr. Anderson earns the entire $60,000 as a salary. Next door, at the Baxters, both Mr. and Mrs. Baxter are employed at a salary of $30,000 each. The Carters derive their income as follows: Mr. Carter is an unemployed househusband; Mrs. Carter earns a $40,000 salary, and each of the two Carter children receives $10,000 per year from a trust fund created by their grandparents. One of the Carter children is 10 years of age; the other is 14.

   a. Determine the 1988 federal income tax liability of each family assuming that no family has either any deductions *for* AGI or any itemized deductions. Furthermore, assume that both the Andersons and the Carters file joint returns; the Baxters use the rate schedule for married persons filing separately, each parent claiming one child as a dependent. To solve this problem, you should know that—according to the Internal Revenue Code—the Carter children can claim a standard deduction of only $500 because their income comes solely from passive sources; in addition, they cannot claim a personal exemption deduction for themselves because they are being claimed as dependents by their parents. In other words, each of the Carter children must report a taxable income of $9,500 (i.e., $10,000 − $500 standard deduction). Finally, for the child under 14 only $500 of taxable income can be taxed at the 15 percent rate; $9,000 must be taxed as if it had been earned by the parents. In every instance, use the 1988 tax rate schedules to determine the family tax liability.

b. If the Andersons were to obtain a divorce and he paid her a $30,000 annual alimony, would their tax bill increase or decrease? Explain as best you can; calculate the Andersons' tax assuming each parent claimed one dependent.

Note: Once the CPI adjustments to the 1988 tax rate schedules are announced, your instructors may prefer that you solve this problem using 1989 (or 1990) rates. Please check with them for specific instructions.

2. Mr. and Mrs. Adams own and operate four different businesses—W, X, Y, and Z. The major details of each business for the year can be summarized as follows:

| Business | Legal Form | Taxable Income before Salary Distribution to Owners | Salary Paid to Owners | Taxable Income after Salary Distribution to Owners |
|---|---|---|---|---|
| W | Sole proprietorship | $30,000 | $10,000 | $20,000 |
| X | Partnership | 50,000* | 10,000* | 40,000* |
| Y | Corporation | 40,000 | 10,000 | 30,000 |
| Z | Subchapter S corporation | (20,000)* | 10,000* | (30,000)* |

*The Adams's share only.

a. As detailed above, the Adamses drew salaries totaling $40,000 during the year. What amount of gross income must the Adamses report for federal income tax purposes?

b. Which of the four businesses added more to the Adams's taxable income than to their checking account (cash) balance? Explain briefly.

c. Which of the four businesses added more to the Adams's checking (cash) account than to their taxable income? Explain briefly.

3. Three unrelated individuals—X, Y, and Z—own 100 percent of corporations A, B, and C in the percentages shown below:

| Owner | Percent Owned | | |
|---|---|---|---|
| | A | B | C |
| tX | 60 | 40 | 10 |
| Y | 30 | 20 | 30 |
| Z | 10 | 40 | 60 |

a. Is there a controlled group of corporations in this problem? If so, which corporations are a member of the controlled group?
b. Without doing any research, how do you suppose the problem of overlapping groups is resolved for federal income tax purposes—(1) Theoretically? (2) Practically? (If possible, answer with respect to the situation illustrated in this problem.)

4. Three single taxpayers each had gross income of $20,000 and deductions for federal tax purposes that totaled $4,000 per year, excluding their personal exemption deductions. The type of deductions that each taxpayer could claim, however, differed significantly. These differences can be summarized as follows:

| Taxpayer | Deductions for AGI | Deductions from AGI |
|---|---|---|
| Erica | $4,000 | $   0 |
| Fran | 0 | 4,000 |
| Gail | 2,000 | 2,000 |

a. Which of the three taxpayers would pay the least federal income tax? Explain briefly.
b. Which of the three taxpayers would pay the greatest federal income tax? Explain briefly.

5. You have been hired by the chairman of the Senate Finance Committee to revise the tax rate schedule for married taxpayers. The chairman wants the first $40,000 of taxable income to be taxed at a 15 percent rate, and any income over $40,000 to be taxed at a 30 percent rate. Furthermore,

the benefit of the 15 percent rate and the $2,000 personal exemption should be phased out by imposing a 10 percent surtax on incomes over $100,000. Create the appropriate schedule assuming that the taxpayer has four personal exemptions.

6. Edward Shiflet is a registered architect engaged in private practice. In addition to his professional practice, Ed makes small investments in various stocks and bonds. At present, Ed agrees that this investment activity is too small to constitute a trade or business for tax purposes, but it definitely is an activity that he engages in for profit. Ed subscribes to various publications throughout the year, including the *Architectural Digest, The Wall Street Journal,* and *Playboy.* In all probability how should the cost of each of these three subscriptions be handled for federal income tax purposes by Ed? Explain briefly.

7. Assume that four corporations—A, B, C, and D—each earn a taxable income of $50,000 per year. What is the *aggregate* tax liability of the four corporations if
   a. They constitute a single controlled group of corporations?
   b. None of the four is a member of any controlled group of corporations?

8. Suppose that X, a very wealthy friend, named you as the trustee of a sizable trust fund prior to her death four years ago. As trustee, you are to distribute (or retain) the trust's income as follows:
   a. Minimize the income taxes paid on the trust's income.
   b. As much trust income should be distributed as possible without violating condition a.

   The potential income beneficiaries of this trust include any of X's children (A and B) and grandchildren (C and D). Finally, suppose that you were able to determine the age, filing status, and approximate taxable income of each potential income beneficiary, as follows:

| Person | Age | Relationship to X | Married-Joint | Approximate Taxable Income |
|--------|-----|-------------------|---------------|----------------------------|
| A | 48 | Child | Married-Joint | $ 120,000 |
| B | 35 | Child | Married-Joint | $(100,000) (net operating loss) |
| C | 25 | Grandchild | Married-Joint | $      0 |
| D | 15 | Grandchild | Single | $ 350,000 |

   How should you distribute the trust income of $900,000?

9. Who must report the taxable income earned by the following entities?
   a. A sole proprietorship.
   b. A partnership.
   c. A corporation.

d. A corporation electing to be taxed under Subchapter S.

e. A trust.

f. An individual.

10. Jones and Limberg are both single taxpayers. Jones has a taxable income of $120,000 and Limberg has a taxable income of $60,000. Which taxpayer has a higher marginal tax rate? Which taxpayer has a higher average tax rate? If an "equitable" tax system requires that a higher income taxpayer pay a greater percentage of his or her income in taxes, is the current tax rate schedule equitable?

11. Tom and Dee LeGrand are very comfortable. Together they report a taxable income of approximately $100,000 each year. In addition, Tom and Dee own 100 percent of the outstanding stock of the LeG Corporation, which reports a taxable income of another $25,000 each year.

a. Suppose that this married couple suddenly inherited a block of stock in a domestic (U.S.) corporation and that this block of stock paid the LeGrands another $50,000 per year in dividends. By what amount would the LeGrands' aftertax income increase because of the $50,000 income on this inheritance?

b. Suppose that the LeGrands immediately transferred the block of recently inherited stock to their family-owned LeG Corporation, rather than holding the stocks as individuals. By what amount would LeG Corporation's aftertax income increase because of the $50,000 dividend income on the inherited stocks?

# Case  3–1

Abel, Baker, and Cain own corporations X, Y, and Z in the following proportions:

| Corporation | Abel | Baker | Cain | Taxable Income |
|---|---|---|---|---|
| X | 85% | 0% | 15% | $50,000 |
| Y | 15 | 0 | 85 | 75,000 |
| Z | 15 | 70 | 15 | 25,000 |

Baker has grown tired of Abel's and Cain's constant bickering, and wants to sell his holdings in Z Corporation. What are the tax consequences of Baker selling all of his Z stock to Abel? What are the tax consequences of Baker selling all of his stock to Cain? What are the tax consequences of Baker selling half of his Z stock to Abel and half to Cain? Assume that each corporation expects to earn the same amount of taxable income indefinitely.

# CHAPTER 4

# Tax Aspects of Selecting a Business Form

Successful tax planning is dependent upon a timely selection of the most advantageous alternative. The tax problem is not unlike the problem of transporting oneself or some other object from, say, New York City to Chicago. There are an almost infinite number of alternatives for both problems. Considering the transportation problem, we could begin with such obvious alternatives as flying, driving, taking a bus, riding a bicycle, walking, or even going by ship (up the Atlantic and down the St. Lawrence Seaway). Upon further investigation each of those alternatives yields many further choices. For example, if we elect to fly, will it be by commercial or private plane? By jet, propjet, or propeller-driven aircraft? First class, day coach, economy, or night coach? On United, American, TWA, or some other airline? A morning, afternoon, or evening flight? Do we want to go directly or stop over? If we stop over, should we go via Boston, Philadelphia, Miami, Dallas, Los Angeles, San Francisco, or Seattle?

Planning a trip, fortunately, is typically not all that complicated because we have some general constraints that grossly simplify our decision. For example, we may want to go the fastest, most direct, and cheapest way that will get us to our destination by 10 A.M. and allow us to leave from a specified airport. Alternatively, we may want to drive and take the most scenic route, allowing a maximum of eight days en route. In some tax problems, as in transportation problems, the constraints often dictate a specific answer. In other tax problems, they allow us greater though limited leeway. Fortunately, the number of overriding tax constraints is sufficiently small for us to deal with them adequately in this book. The myriad of possible tax details can be left to the volumes written for professional tax advisers.

## THE BASIC TAX CONSTRAINTS

Most business-oriented people are at one time or another introduced to the nontax advantages and disadvantages of the various forms of business organizations. They learn, for example, that the corporate form of organization provides numerous opportunities for raising large sums of capital, limits the financial liability of the owner to the amount invested in the corporate stock (unless the bank or other lender demands the personal guarantee of the shareholder for all of the corporation's debt, as is common with small corporations), provides for unrestricted transferability of the ownership interest, and makes possible an unlimited life of the business entity. They also know that the sole proprietorship and the partnership are easier to create than the corporation, but that these business forms also provide for the unlimited liability of the owners; that they may be terminated in numerous ways, sometimes at a most disadvantageous time; and that the transferability of their ownership may be restricted. And they may or may not know that corporate officers and shareholders may be personally liable for violations of social and professional duties.

In many situations these nontax considerations are of paramount importance in the selection of a business form for a particular enterprise. However, in an equally large number of small to medium-sized business ventures this is not the case, particularly in ventures owned by a small number of individuals. Here tax considerations commonly play a dominant role in the process of selecting the business form. Unfortunately, some owners form and operate businesses without giving adequate thought to the pertinent tax considerations. This chapter is concerned with precisely those considerations. It will introduce some basic tax-planning ideas; concomitant details will be considered in subsequent chapters. Consequently, it might be advisable to read this chapter twice; once now, and again on completion of the book. It is hoped that, on the second reading, the significance of many items that may seem remote after the first reading will have become obvious.

## Maximum Reinvestment of Income

Many businesses, especially new ventures, want to maximize the capital available for reinvestment in the business. The amount of income that is available for reinvestment is closely related to the taxation of the earnings stream. Obviously, a person can reinvest only aftertax profits. As a consequence, it is particularly important to consider the marginal tax rate that will be applied to a given income stream if the aftertax income and the reinvestment potential are to be maximized. As noted in Chapter 3, the marginal tax rates applied to an individual's taxable income range from a low of 15 percent to a high of 33 percent. The marginal tax rates applied to corporate taxable incomes range from a low of 15 percent to a high of 39 percent. It is apparent, therefore, that one of the prime criteria in the selection of a business form is the aggregate income of the owner of the business. If he or she earns an income subject to a marginal tax bracket that exceeds 15 percent, that taxpayer may very well elect to arrange some portion of his or her business affairs in such a way that a corporate entity may be used to shield that income from higher personal tax rates. Observe also, however, that the top marginal rate on corporate income is greater than that on an individual's income. This means, of course, that at some point a corporation may create a tax trap rather than a tax advantage. The 34 percent marginal corporate tax bracket generally becomes effective when taxable income exceeds only $75,000. Therefore, the owner of a closely held corporation will generally want to avoid the earning and retention of any amount of taxable income in excess of $75,000 per year within a single corporation. In addition, the rate of 34 percent is applicable to any income earned by a personal service corporation. In every year before enactment of the 1986 tax act, the top marginal rate on corporate income was always below that for the top marginal rate on individual income. Hence the idea that the corporation can actually be a tax trap, rather than a tax shelter for high-income individuals, is an entirely new one. Under all prior laws tax advisers were often concerned about justifying the retention of earnings within the closely held corporation; now they will be equally concerned about the details of getting money out of that same corporation with only a single income tax being applicable to the amounts withdrawn. In summary, it is possible to maximize the income available for reinvestment by splitting an income between a corporation and an individual at relatively modest incomes. However, the diversion of too much income into a single corporate entity would be counterproductive. This conclusion is apparent in the bar graphs of Illustration 4–1.

Getting money out of a corporation with a single tax can be tricky business. The owner of a closely held business can avoid any double tax on much of the corporation's income by the use of any of several simple expedients. For example, the owner may pay himself or herself a salary for the service performed in the corporate employ. This salary, so long as it is reasonable in amount, is deductible by the corporation in the calculation of taxable income. Consequently, the salary is taxed only once to the individual owner, as personal compensation. Small corporations may reduce their taxable income to zero, virtually at the owner's discretion, by a simple adjustment of the owner-employee's salary. If the salary reaches the unreasonable range, and the corporation desires to reduce its taxable income still more, it may rent property from the owner and pay a reasonable rent, pay interest on money borrowed, or pay a royalty for the corporation's use of the owner's patent or copyright. Any reasonable amounts paid for these items become a corporate tax deduction at the same time that they create additional gross income for the owner. As illustrated, the closely held corporation may be able to distribute a substantial portion of its income to the owner without incurring a double tax. The only time a double tax is inevitably incurred is when the corporation accumulates the income and subsequently distributes corporate assets to the owner *as a dividend.* Dividends paid are *not* deductible by the corporation in the determination of corporate taxable income even though dividends received by the individual stockholder are generally taxable as ordinary income.

To summarize, we might think of every person as having direct or indirect command over an annual stream of income, which can be represented by the

**FIGURE 4–1**

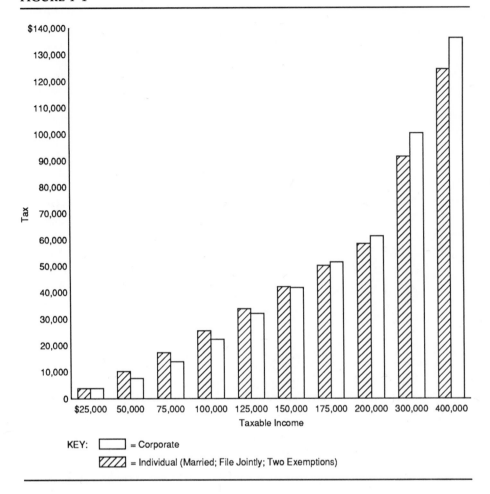

KEY:  ☐ = Corporate
      ▨ = Individual (Married; File Jointly; Two Exemptions)

size of an arrow. If that income is derived from anything other than a salary paid by a corporation not controlled by the owner-operator, then the taxpayer typically has a great deal of discretion over how the income stream should be diffused among business organizations and how, therefore, it will be taxed. The problem can be depicted as shown in Figure 4–2. The person shown in the figure would probably be in a 28 percent marginal income tax bracket because of the size of the annual income stream. This person, who wants to maximize the reinvestment potential, might consider the distribution shown in Figure 4–3 as desirable. If this owner had selected any form of business organization other than a corporation, the $75,000 would have been treated as compensation received directly by the owner, and the owner would have

**FIGURE 4–2**

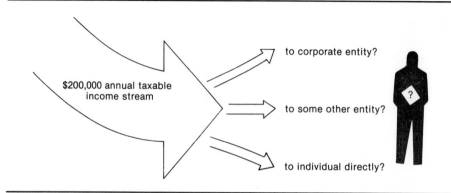

**FIGURE 4–3**

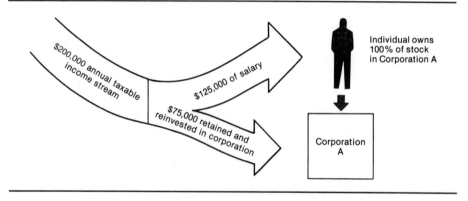

paid an individual income tax of approximately $56,000. This alternative leaves the owner with about $144,000 for consumption spending plus reinvestment in a business. Given the arrangement suggested in the second diagram, the corporation would pay an income tax of $13,750 and the owner would pay an income tax of approximately $35,000. By this rearrangement of business affairs, this taxpayer has reduced the total income tax liability by about $7,250 per year and thereby increased the annual opportunity to reinvest in a business by that same amount. To quantify the importance of this difference we need but observe that an annual tax saving of this size, reinvested at a 5 percent aftertax rate of return, accumulates to something like $875,000 over a 40-year period. The question is this: Is the $7,250 annual tax saving worth the cost and trouble for the owner? Keeping a separate set of corporate records, filing an extra tax return, and making certain that no more than $75,000 per year is retained in the corporation may not be worth the effort.

Also, observe the tax disaster that would be created by running a $200,000 annual taxable income from a professional service business through a corporate entity. If, as in Figure 4–3, the professional who owned and operated corporation A were to allow $75,000 of his or her $200,000 annual professional income to be retained and reinvested in the A corporation, this taxpayer would actually increase the total annual income tax bill by $4,500; from about $56,000 to about $60,500 per year. Clearly in these circumstances a professional service corporation should be avoided unless it can make the Subchapter S election.

## Retention of Special Income Characteristics

A second important tax factor pertinent to selecting a business form concerns the desirability of retaining certain tax characteristics that are attributed to select kinds of income. The notion of exclusions was introduced in Chapter 1 and explained further in Chapter 2. What was not noted, however, was that the designation of certain income as exempt income may be lost when this income is commingled with other income in a corporate entity. That is, if a corporation earns interest on state or local government bonds, the corporation, like the individual, need not report this interest as part of its taxable income for the year. Suppose, however, that, after the corporation earned this interest, the corporate board voted to distribute this same income as a dividend to the stockholders. Would the cash distributed retain its tax-exempt characteristic? No. So long as the distributing corporation had either current earnings and profits or earnings and profits accumulated after March 1, 1913, the distribution would be taxed as ordinary dividend income. Even if the corporation had no such earnings, any distribution of that same income as a salary would be subject to tax by the employee receiving it. There is nothing that the corporate board could do by way of isolating or separating this income from other corporate income to make it retain its tax-free characteristics.

Based on even this limited discussion, it is apparent that whenever a business venture earns a significant amount of tax-favored income it is generally desirable to have that venture organized in such a form that the tax laws will treat it as a conduit rather than as a separate entity. This result is generally possible if the venture is organized as a sole proprietorship, a partnership, or a Subchapter S corporation. It is not possible when the business venture is incorporated unless the Subchapter S option can be exercised, and even then special limits become applicable in some instances. For example, the revocation of an S election ordinarily bars a corporation from electing that status again for the next five years. Otherwise, corporations could move in and out of Subchapter S status simply to preserve the special tax-favored status of income recognized in certain years.

## Utilization of Net Operating Losses

Net operating losses may present a tax situation exactly the opposite of that mentioned in the preceding paragraph. That is, combining a business venture that incurs a loss with a highly profitable venture within a single taxable entity may be desirable. This is true because the corporation can generally use the operating loss from one venture to offset taxable income from another venture on one tax return.

Business entities that frequently or continually incur tax losses overall were usually organized as sole proprietorships, partnerships, or Subchapter S corporations so that the owners could deduct the tax loss on their personal tax returns. The 1986 Tax Reform Act has, however, limited this possibility by denying the individual taxpayer the right to offset certain losses (from activities in which he did not materially participate) from income the taxpayer may earn in other ways. In other words, losses from "passive activities" cannot be offset by the individual taxpayer against either "active income" or "portfolio income." Those losses can only be offset against income from other "passive activities."

The conclusion that loss operations are best located in a corporate form presumes, of course, that the corporation would be in a higher marginal tax bracket than the owner. If this presumption is not valid, an opposite conclusion is correct. In other words, if a net operating loss can be carried back to prior years by a corporation and offset against its own taxable income that was taxed at 34 or 39 percent, this alternative is preferable any time the owner would have to utilize that same net operating loss in offsetting his or her own taxable income that was taxed at a marginal rate of 28 or even 33 percent. A second aspect of net operating losses is also pertinent to the business-form question. The owner of corporate stock generally gets no personal tax advantage from a corporation's losses until some or all of the corporation's stock is sold. At that time, the shares presumably will be worth less because of the losses incurred by the corporation. If the stockholder does sell the shares at a loss, that is a capital loss and, as such, is restricted in the amount deductible in a particular year. As a general rule, an individual taxpayer cannot deduct more than $3,000 per year in capital losses from ordinary income. Admittedly, a taxpayer may use capital losses to offset capital gains without limit, but some taxpayers may not have realized sufficient capital gains in a particular year to make such an immediate offset. As explained above, the owner of a sole proprietorship or partnership interest is not faced with the necessity of disposing of a business interest before reaping the tax benefit of the loss incurred by the business unless (1) that loss is derived from an individual's investment in a "passive activity," and (2) the individual does not have a sufficiently large income from other similar investments in the interim period. These rules will be explained in greater detail later in this book.

If a C corporation makes a Subchapter S election while it has a net operating loss carryforward, that NOL can *not* be carried over to the S corporation or be utilized by the S corporation's shareholders. In fact, if a C corporation with an NOL converts to S status and sometime later reverts again to C status, any prior NOL may be permanently "lost." That is, the NOL can not be claimed by the C corporation in the later years if the time limits on the NOL have expired in the interim.

## Employee Status

The owner of a sole proprietorship or a partnership interest is generally not considered an employee of his or her own firm for tax purposes. The owner of a corporate entity may, however, be an employee of his or her own corporation. This difference constitutes another consideration in selecting from among alternative business forms. There are a few tax advantages available to an employee that are not available to a self-employed individual. In those cases, therefore, it is to a particular taxpayer's advantage to achieve employee status. Among the tax advantages granted to an employee but denied to the self-employed person are tax-free group life and wage continuation insurance plans, certain death benefits, and the chance to receive meals, lodging, and recreational facilities without increasing taxable income.

In a closely held corporation, employee benefits may provide the best of all possible tax worlds. This happy result occurs whenever the corporate entity is permitted a tax deduction for an item that need not be reported as gross income by the owner-employee recipient. In effect, the owner's left pocket (the corporation) has obtained a tax deduction for an item that the right pocket (the individual owner) may treat as an exclusion. A next-best alternative is to get the corporation an immediate tax deduction for an item of gross income that the individual owner need not report for a number of years.

The major tax disadvantage that may attach to classification as an employee stems from the deduction problem discussed in Chapter 3. An employee is more restricted than the self-employed person in deducting items *for* adjusted gross income. Many trade or business expenses incurred by an employee must be categorized as deductions *from* adjusted gross income. Those itemized deductions are generally of no tax value except to the extent that they exceed 2 percent of the employee's adjusted gross income. Even then they will have value only if the employee itemizes deductions rather than claiming the standard deductions.

## Gaining a Special Tax Deduction

For most purposes, the individual taxpayer and the corporation are entitled to claim essentially the same deductions, at least so far as business-related expenses are concerned. A major exception to that general rule exists relative to the dividend-received deduction. As explained earlier, a corporation is granted a deduction equal to 70 or 80 percent of the dividends it receives from most other domestic corporations. An individual taxpayer gets no similar deduction.

Because of this important difference in the tax treatment of individuals and corporate entities, a major opportunity for tax avoidance exists. Any individual earning a substantial *dividend* income must consider the possibility of transferring some dividend-paying investments into a corporate entity. By doing this, the taxpayer may significantly lower the effective tax rate on the dividends received. Ignoring complications that will be discussed later, suppose for a moment that a married individual receives $100,000 in taxable income from a salary plus $50,000 in dividends annually. This taxpayer would incur a 1988 tax liability of approximately $16,500 on the dividends received. If this same individual were free to transfer the stocks that paid the dividends into a corporation (created simply to receive them), the annual tax liability on the same income could be reduced to as little as $1,500 were it not for some special restrictions. This low tax liability would be the direct result of the corporate dividend-received deduction, which might operate as follows:

| | |
|---|---|
| Dividends received by new corporation | $50,000 |
| Less 80 percent of $50,000 dividends received* | 40,000 |
| Corporate taxable income | $10,000 |
| Times applicable corporate tax rate | ×    15% |
| Equals gross tax liability | $ 1,500 |

*This illustration assumes that the corporation receiving the dividend owns at least 20 percent of the corporation paying the dividend.

Recognizing this tremendous opportunity that a corporation creates for sheltering the dividend income of wealthy persons, Congress enacted a personal holding company tax. The critical effect of this tax is to take away the tax shelter provided for dividends received by the corporation, but the special tax is applicable only in the more obvious and extreme cases. It becomes effective only when the *passive* income of a corporate entity is *relatively* more important than income earned in more *active* business endeavors. That is, if a corporation is created to do little more than collect dividends, clip interest coupons, and/or cash rent checks, the personal holding company tax will probably prevail. On the other hand, the dividend-rich taxpayer who is careful to blend into a single corporate shell both some active business ventures and some passive business investments may be able to reduce the effective tax rate paid on the dividend income to between 3 and 4.5 percent (that is, 15 percent of 20 or 30 percent of the dividends received). This kind of tax planning reduces consumption options, but it obviously permits a maximization of reinvestment by gaining a tax deduction that would not be available in the absence of the corporate entity.

A second example that illustrates how a taxpayer might benefit from obtaining a special deduction does not actually require the existence of a corporate entity, but its existence may facilitate the objective. This second illustration turns on the fact that every individual is generally entitled to claim a personal exemption deduction and a standard deduction. For many years, wealthy families were able to take advantage of the standard deduction, which was originally intended for low-income people, by making certain that every member of the family received a minimum income. Children and grandchildren were given sufficient property—sometimes nonvoting, high-dividend preferred stocks in a closely held corporation—to ensure their receiving an income equal to the sum of the personal exemption deduction and the standard deduction. The tax result was significantly restricted after 1986 because Congress passed a rule that disallows personal exemption to any individual claimed as a dependent by another taxpayer and limits the standard deduction to the lesser of (1) $500 or (2) the taxpayer's *earned* income. Thus, it is now necessary to ensure that every child *"earns"* at least $3,000 of his or her income—perhaps as a salary paid by the family business—if the maximum tax saving is to be achieved. Although the dollar amounts are relatively small, the tax savings can still be meaningful. In an extreme situation this simple device can remove $3,000 of taxable income from the corporation's highest bracket and thereby save $1,170 in taxes each year per child, since the new recipient would typically pay no tax on that income.

### Disposition of a Business

The form in which a business is organized can also be important when a taxpayer dissolves or otherwise disposes of that business. Upon disposition of a sole proprietorship, an owner is generally assumed to have disposed of the individual assets that constitute the business venture for tax purposes. The proceeds of the sale are allocated among all of the assets, based on their relative fair market values. As a consequence of this presumption, some of the profit realized upon disposition will result in ordinary income, since the sale of those same assets individually would have produced ordinary income. By contrast, the owner of a corporate entity usually has an option: The owner can either allow the corporation to sell specific assets or dispose of the business by selling the corporation's stock. In most instances the owner will report any gain realized from the sale of the corporation's stock as a capital gain.

A corporation also provides a good vehicle for partial dispositions. It is relatively cumbersome to sell a partial interest in either a sole proprietorship or a partnership. A partial interest in a corporate entity is often more marketable. Disposition of a partial business interest through the sale of some part of a larger block of stock will ordinarily be reported as a capital gain. The relative ease of making stock dispositions makes the corporate form of business organization of special importance to tax planning for wealthy taxpayers.

### Fluctuating Income

Business ventures that are characterized by wide variations in annual income may find it advantageous to incorporate for two reasons. First, the adjustments that are required in converting a negative taxable income into a net operating loss carry-back involve a greater chance for the loss of a tax deduction in the case of an individual taxpayer than they do in the case of a corporate taxpayer. Second, a corporation is generally presumed to be engaged in a trade or business; activities conducted directly by an individual carry no such presumption. Consequently, business ventures that could be considered hobbies (which are often characterized by widely fluctuating incomes) may be better able to withstand an IRS challenge if they are incorporated.

Although the preceding discussion is by no means exhaustive, it should give the reader some appreciation of the basic tax consequences that attach to the selection of any one of the various possible forms of business organization. What may not yet be apparent is that selecting the most advantageous organizational form is often dependent upon a diverse array of unknowns, including the amount of a taxpayer's future income or loss from all sources, the dispersion of that income or loss over several annual periods, the ultimate size of the taxpayer's family, the length of the taxpayer's life, the possibility that either the accumulated earnings tax or the personal holding company tax may be imposed, and subsequent changes in the tax laws. Recognizing the imprecision implicit in these variables, many knowledgeable taxpayers will concentrate their attention on one or two variables deemed to be of primary importance in the hope that other tax consequences can be reasonably accommodated as the business proceeds. In some circumstances, however, nontax considerations may be sufficiently dominant to override what might otherwise be preferable from a tax standpoint. Any reader contemplating a new business venture should seek competent tax advice before selecting the business form within which he or she is going to conduct that venture. Special consideration must be given to business activities that involve more than one country.

## SPECIAL CONSIDERATIONS FOR
## MULTINATIONAL BUSINESSES

The tax rules applicable to multinational business operations are inordinately complex. What appears here is only a capsule summary of a very few of the more critical tax aspects of doing business abroad. This brief discussion has been divided into unincorporated and incorporated business activities. The more substantial tax-planning opportunities involve the utilization of a corporation.

### Unincorporated Businesses

The U.S. income tax is, as previously noted, a global tax; it reaches the taxable income of all citizens and resident aliens, regardless of where that income is earned. As was also noted, the U.S. income tax in general does not recognize unincorporated businesses as separate taxable entities, but prefers instead to attribute any taxable income from an unincorporated business directly and immediately to the owners of the business. As a consequence of these two rules, any U.S. citizen must generally pay a U.S. income tax each year on any income earned through business operations conducted outside the United States, even though none of that income is immediately repatriated. Special rules are applicable, however, if a foreign government has blocked repatriation by currency restrictions.

Income earned in a foreign country by U.S. citizens is often taxed by the foreign government as well as by the U.S. government. To eliminate a double tax on the single income stream, the United States usually allows the taxpayer to claim a credit against the U.S. gross tax liability for any foreign income tax paid. The net effect of this arrangement is to tax an unincorporated business venture, operated by a U.S. citizen or resident alien, at the highest effective rate that is operative in the countries involved. For example, if a U.S. citizen receives income from a Canadian source and pays $250 of income tax to Canada, yet the U.S. tax on that same income is only $150, the U.S. taxpayer could claim a foreign tax credit of $150. Alternatively if the effective U.S. tax is $300, the taxpayer could claim a $250 foreign tax credit on the U.S. tax return. In the latter example, $250 would be paid to Canada and $50 to the U.S. for a total of $300.

### Corporate Businesses

U.S. corporations doing business abroad must reconsider the business-form question with specific reference to foreign operations. The corporation with a domestic (U.S.) charter can conduct its foreign operations as a branch of the domestic corporation, as a separate but domestic subsidiary of the U.S. parent, or as a foreign subsidiary corporation. In some instances a business can also achieve its objectives through a licensing arrangement with a foreign corporation that is not a subsidiary. The tax consequences of each alternative are different and sometimes substantial.

**Branch Operations.**    Domestic corporations engaged in foreign business through branch operations are in essentially the same position as individual taxpayers conducting an unincorporated business abroad. That is, the domestic corporation must pay the U.S. income tax on all operations of a foreign branch immediately, regardless of the disposition of the taxable income earned by the branch. A tax credit may be claimed for any foreign income taxes paid by the branch. Branch losses may also be offset against other income generated by domestic (U.S.) operations. They are, however, subject to "recapture" if the branch subsequently becomes profitable.

**Subsidiary Corporations.**    A domestic corporation can, of course, create a subsidiary corporation to handle its foreign operations. This subsidiary can be either a second domestic corporation or a corporation created under the laws of a foreign country. Subject to a few major exceptions, which are discussed below, the domestic subsidiary doing business abroad will be treated with regard to taxes like most other domestic corporations. However, the creation of a foreign subsidiary gives birth to a host of new problems and opportunities.

Recall the general rules which provide (*a*) that a stockholder is generally not taxed on the taxable income earned by a corporation until the corporation distributes its previously accumulated taxable income, and (*b*) that nonresident aliens are subject to the U.S. income tax only to the extent that they have income from U.S. sources. If applied literally, as they were until about 1962, these rules provided tremendous tax-planning opportunities for foreign subsidiary corporations. A U.S. taxpayer could create a foreign corporation (thus creating something comparable to a nonresident alien) and retain all earnings of that corporation, until the most propitious moment, without incurring a U.S. income tax. In addition, by a careful selection of the country in which the subsidiary was incorporated, the tax on the corporation's income could be minimized or even obliterated. No fewer than 25 countries, most of them tiny nations, clamored for years for such corporate shells by creating the most favorable possible corporate tax laws. These became known as "tax haven countries," and the corporate shells created in such countries became known as "base country corporations."

In their heyday, these foreign operations were further blessed by price gerrymandering of grand proportions. To glimpse briefly the glorious tax opportunities of the past, consider the corporate superstructure shown in Figure 4–4. Although goods were shipped directly from Corporation P to Corporation S2 for sale in Country E by Corporation S2, the legal title to those goods passed momentarily through island empire Z (a tax haven country)

**FIGURE 4–4**

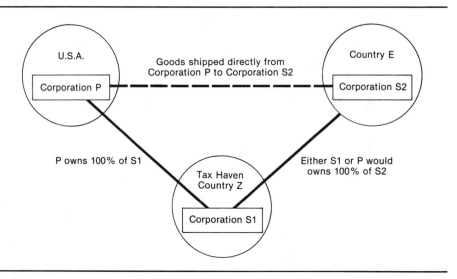

and Corporation S1. Corporation P would price its sales to Corporation S1 at something close to its cost, thereby reducing to a minimum or even to zero the reportable taxable income on foreign sales of Corporation P. Corporation S1 would resell the same goods to Corporation S2 at a price comparable to the ultimate sales price of the goods by Corporation S2 in Country E (which imposed a corporate income tax), thereby reducing Corporation S2's taxable income to zero. Needless to say, Corporation S1, in Country Z, was a fantastic financial success! The owners of Corporation S1 were twice blessed by the coincidence that neither the United States nor Country Z would tax those profits until Corporation S1 paid Corporation P a dividend or until Corporation P sold its Corporation S1 stock.

So much for history. Specific statutory changes in the Internal Revenue Code, as well as more vigorous attempts by the IRS to force related taxpayers to deal with each other at something like arm's-length prices, have changed the foreign scene considerably. In the process, the IRS has also created some of the most complex tax provisions ever known to humankind. The important results of the new rules are (*a*) that under prescribed conditions a U.S. stockholder of a foreign corporation *may be* required to report the taxable income earned by the foreign corporation immediately (as the taxable income is earned) and without regard for any actual repatriation of income from the foreign corporation to the U.S. stockholder; and (*b*) that related parties must be careful in all dealings with each other if they want to avoid a reallocation of their reported gross income and deductions by the IRS. The exact rules charting these dangerous waters can be understood and interpreted only by an expert. International business ventures simply must have such an expert on board. A few special tax-saving opportunities related to foreign operations that, by design, remain in our tax code, should be examined briefly.

**The FSC and DISC.**    In 1971, Congress created a set of special tax provisions intended to reduce the perennial balance of payments problem. These provisions originally established a special kind of corporation called the Domestic International Sales Corporation, or DISC. Various foreign nations protested our DISC provisions as constituting an illegal export subsidy under GATT, the General Agreement on Tariffs and Trade. Therefore, in 1984, Congress enacted a revised set of provisions intended to achieve the same general objective through what is now called the Foreign Sales Corporation, or FSC. A modified version of the prior rules was retained for small exporters (i.e., $10 million or less in qualified export receipts) in what is now known as an "interest charge DISC" or the "small FSC." To qualify as an FSC a corporation, among other things, must:

1. Be created in a qualified foreign country or a U.S. possession other than Puerto Rico.
2. Have 25 or fewer shareholders.
3. Issue only common stock.

4. Maintain a foreign office (with a permanent set of books and a bank account).

5. Have one or more non-U.S. resident on its board of directors.

6. Have a foreign economic substance and perform specified activities outside the U.S.

Corporations that qualify as an FSC can exclude a portion of their foreign trade income from the U.S. income tax. The exact portion that may be excluded depends on both (1) who owns the FSC and (2) the way in which the foreign income is determined (which can be through either the use of an arm's length pricing method or special administrative pricing rules). In general terms, the exclusion may vary from 30 percent to $15/23$ of the "foreign trade income."

**The Possessions Corporation.**    A subsidiary corporation that does most of its business in a possession of the United States may be eligible for other tax benefits. Specifically, a subsidiary corporation that earns 80 percent or more of its income from a possession and that earns 70 percent or more of its gross income from an active trade or business is eligible for a possession tax credit (also known as a Section 936 credit), whether or not it actually pays an income tax to the possession. Some U.S. possessions, such as Puerto Rico, have deliberately excused new business ventures from any local income tax for a period of from 10 to 15 years, just to attract new business. Consequently a U.S. parent corporation that owns a subsidiary doing business in Puerto Rico might well be excused from paying any Puerto Rican income tax because of Puerto Rican law and, at the same time, be excused from paying any U.S. income tax on the income of its subsidiary because of the possession tax credit. The U.S. tax credit is a phantom credit determined as if the subsidiary had paid a tax to the possession at the tax rate that would have prevailed had that corporation earned the same taxable income in the United States. Furthermore, because of the corporate dividend-received deduction, the subsidiary can repatriate all of its current earnings to its U.S. parent with minimal tax. Such a dividend distribution may, however, be subject to a "tollgate" tax in Puerto Rico of from 10 to 15 percent. In addition, income generated from intangibles (such as patents or trademarks) is subject to special limitations.

The special tax considerations for multinational business operations could be expanded to include other exotic special provisions. Because most readers could not take advantage of the tax-saving opportunities of those provisions, they are dismissed without discussion. It is hoped that this brief and limited introduction to foreign operations will trigger ideas in some readers. Imagination often pays large dividends in tax matters, and this kind of imagination sometimes involves the careful selection of both a business form and a country of incorporation. Perhaps a classic example of creative imagination came to light in the case of *U.S. Gypsum*, 304 F. Supp. 627. There the court found that a corporation created to own gypsum rock for the split second it took for the rock to fall from a related corporation's conveyor belt to the hold of a ship, which was owned by another related corporation, was not a valid Western Hemisphere Trade Corporation (WHTC) because it was not actively involved

**FIGURE 4–5**

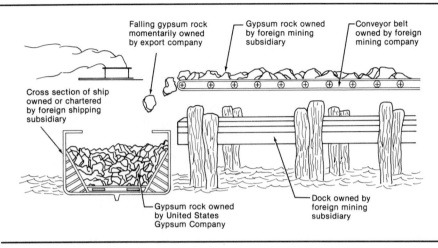

in the conduct of a trade or business. The court report's diagram of the critical facts, which is reproduced in Figure 4–5, is most informative. Although the WHTC tax advantages were phased out, the case should stand as a monument to creativity for years to come.

## PROBLEMS AND ASSIGNMENTS

1. a. Carol Gabriel operates a small manufacturing business and wants to estimate her income tax liability under various alternative amounts of operating income as either a proprietorship or a regular corporation. Assume that all of the operating income would be included in gross income on her tax return and that she and her family have no other income and no other itemized deductions. She is married and has three children under the age of 15. Complete the table below.

| Operating Income | Income Tax Liability | |
| --- | --- | --- |
| | *Proprietorship* | *Corporation* |
| $     30,000 | | |
| $     50,000 | | |
| $   100,000 | | |
| $   175,000 | | |
| $   300,000 | | |
| $   500,000 | | |
| $1,000,000 | | |

b. The message implicit in the above tabulation seems to be that any business earning more than $100,000 should not be incorporated. Why is that conclusion *not* necessarily valid? (Explain briefly.)

c. Would your answer change if Carol's business was a consulting firm and she performed many of the key services herself?

2. a. Suppose that a married businessperson receives a sufficiently large income from interest on investments in municipal bonds so that he or she has no desire whatsoever for any additional personal income. If this fortunate person owns 100 percent of an incorporated manufacturing business that produces an annual taxable income equal to the amount indicated in the left-hand column below, indicate—by filling in the blanks in the next two columns—how that "extra" income should be distributed between the corporate entity that earns it and the owner, assuming that the current year's federal income tax is to be minimized. Assume the taxpayer claims six exemption deductions. Assume also that the businessperson has no sources of income or deductions other than the municipal bonds and the business.

| | Distribute as Follows: | |
|---|---|---|
| "Extra" Income | To Owners | Hold in Corporation |
| $  16,700 | _____ | _____ |
| 96,450 | _____ | _____ |
| 121,450 | _____ | _____ |
| above $121,450 | _____ | _____ |

b. What general principle did you apply in making the determinations of how to distribute the taxable income in the above tabulation? (Be as precise as possible in stating the general principle.)

3. Suppose the situation described in Problem 2 really did exist; what other tax factors would you have to consider before you could actually conclude that the suggested distribution of the extra income was the best solution?

4. After a taxpayer has observed the potential tax benefits of splitting what is essentially a single income stream between two entities—that is, between the owner and the corporation—the next tax question investigated for some closely held businesses may concern multiple corporations. In other words, if one corporation is good, wouldn't two corporations be even better? In general, Sections 1561 and 1563 limit the tax benefits that might accrue to multiple corporations. For the moment, ignore those statutory limitations and determine, by completing the tabulation below, the potential federal income tax benefit that could otherwise be derived

in 1989 by creating multiple corporations and retaining the four different amounts of taxable income indicated below:

| Number of Multiple Corporations (as opposed to one only) | Annual Federal Income Tax Savings if Multiple Corporations Collectively Retain Income in the Amount of | | | |
| --- | --- | --- | --- | --- |
| | $50,000* | $100,000* | $150,000* | $250,000* |
| 2 | $_____ | $_____ | $_____ | $_____ |
| 3 | _____ | _____ | _____ | _____ |
| 4 | _____ | _____ | _____ | _____ |
| 5 | _____ | _____ | _____ | _____ |

*Assume that any retained taxable income is divided equally between/among the multiple corporations.

5. Closely held businesses are not always profitable. What form of business organization is ordinarily recommended if such a business is experiencing recurring tax losses? Answer this question by answering the two questions below. Assume that XYZ experienced the following taxable income (losses) during its first five years of business.

| | 19×1 | 19×2 | 19×3 | 19×4 | 19×5 |
| --- | --- | --- | --- | --- | --- |
| Net operating income (loss) | ($100,000) | ($50,000) | ($25,000) | $50,000 | $225,000 |

    a. If XYZ is an ordinary corporation, what is the economic value (ignoring the present-value-of-money concept) of the NOLs incurred in years 19x1 through 19x3?

    b. If XYZ is a sole proprietorship, partnership, or Sub S corporation, what is the economic value of those same NOLs? Explain briefly.

6. The S corporation is often a viable alternative to the sole proprietorship or partnership form of business organization where losses are concerned. There are, however, some special factors to consider whenever dealing with an S corporation. Use additional references available in your school library to research and answer the following questions.

    a. What are the major requirements that must be satisfied before an incorporated business can elect to be taxed under Subchapter S?

    b. An existing corporation has *not* been operating as an S corporation for the past several years, but, because of anticipated tax losses in the current year, its stockholders desire to make a Subchapter S election for the current year.

  (1) When must the election be made if it is to be effective for the current year?

  (2) Who will report the corporate loss for the year (assuming that a timely election has been made)?

  (3) What general limits are placed on the deduction of tax losses that are realized by a Subchapter S corporation but are recognized by (or passed through to) a stockholder?

  c. An existing S corporation *made* a valid election several years ago, but its stockholders desire to terminate the election for the current year. How can that termination be effected?

7. From a tax point of view a domestic corporation is comparable to a U.S. citizen; a foreign corporation is like a nonresident alien. Explain briefly.

8. If each of the three corporations below earned a taxable income of $200,000, which would most likely pay the most federal income tax? Which would most likely pay the least federal income tax? Explain briefly.

  Corporation R: a regular, domestic corporation.

  Corporation F: a Foreign Sales Corporation.

  Corporation P: a new domestic corporation doing business exclusively with Puerto Rico.

9. Loftus Co. was founded 20 years ago with a $20,000 cash investment, and all of its assets have been acquired from internally generated funds and bank loans. The Loftus Co. is about to be sold. This business has only three significant assets, namely:

| Asset | Basis | Value |
|---|---|---|
| Inventory | $100,000 | $300,000 |
| Equipment | 200,000 | 300,000 |
| Land | 300,000 | 300,000 |

  a. How will Cleo and Mona Loftus, who have always been the sole owners of Loftus Co., report their taxable gain on the sale of this business for $900,000 if—

  (1) Loftus Co. is a partnership?

  (2) Loftus Co. is a corporation and the buyer purchases all of their Loftus stock?

  b. Why might a potential buyer be willing to pay $900,000 for the assets but only some lesser amount for all of the Loftus Co. stock?

10. Richard has been hired by a professor to write homework problems for his textbook. Richard incurred $700 in expenses during this project. Rich-

ard's "adjusted gross income" before considering these expenses is $10,000. Richard's only other deductions are $5,500 of home mortgage interest and real estate taxes. He has no dependents.

a. What is the aftertax cost of these expenses if Richard is considered to be self-employed?

b. What is the aftertax cost of these expenses if Richard is an employee?

# Case 4–1

Doug Fox is planning to open a record store. In order to protect his personal assets from the liabilities of this venture, he wants to operate the business as a corporation. Doug, who is single, earns about $150,000 in taxable income a year from his other investments.

Doug has come to you for tax advice. In which year should he elect to have his record store be taxed as an S corporation or as a regular corporation, assuming a projected $50,000 loss in year one and

a. $125,000 income in year two, $200,000 income in all future years.

b. $200,000 income in year two, $50,000 income in all future years.

c. $50,000 income in all future years.

(The time value of money can be ignored in this analysis.)

# Case 4–2

Clarence Yuppie is an eager young entrepreneur fresh from business school. Clarence, a smooth-talking salesman with several years of experience as a real estate sales agent, wants to get into the real estate development business. His meager savings has been depleted by his years of schooling, and he does not have any wealthy relatives to invest in his deals.

Bob Bigbucks has been investing in land and buildings in Beanville for many years. Bob has a substantial income from his law practice. Bob thinks Beanville is about to boom and wants to organize an active real estate development company. Bob has no children or young relatives that he wants to bring into the business.

Bob and Clarence have met and they have similar views toward the real estate prospects for Beanville, so they would like to go into business together. Bob proposes to contribute land and serve as an officer. Clarence will be responsible for most of the day-to-day selling and management activity. Since Bob is very familiar with business law, he proposes that they organize their business as a corporation.

Bob and Clarence have come to you for tax advice on how they should organize their business. What do you recommend that they do?

# CHAPTER 5

# Accounting Method Options

Code Section 446 provides the general accounting method requirements that must be satisfied by every taxpayer. This code section is subdivided into five subsections. Subsection *(a)* states that a taxpayer must compute taxable income on the same method of accounting as is used in keeping the regular books. Subsection *(b)* gives the Secretary of the Treasury authority to designate a particular accounting method if either the taxpayer has no regular method or the method used does not clearly reflect income. Subsection *(c)* lists several methods that may be used, including a cash method, an accrual method, and a modified cash method prescribed by Treasury regulations. Subsection *(d)* allows a taxpayer to use more than one method of accounting if he or she is engaged in more than one trade or business. And Subsection *(e)* requires the prior consent of the commissioner if a taxpayer desires to change the method of accounting. Collectively, these requirements are sufficiently flexible to permit most taxpayers a maximum opportunity to select the most favorable method of accounting. Except for an occasional refusal to authorize a change in accounting methods, the statutory requirements have been interpreted rather liberally. Thus, it is doubly important for every taxpayer to make the initial selection wisely.

In addition to selecting one general method of accounting for each trade or business, a taxpayer must select many specific accounting procedures and conventions to be utilized in implementing a single method of accounting. The number of alternative accounting procedures and conventions is substantially larger than the number of generally accepted accounting methods. Each election can have a significant impact on the tax liability ultimately reported for any taxpayer. In this chapter, we shall consider some of the more important planning aspects of the various accounting methods and conventions. The first portion of the chapter will be concerned with general methods of accounting; the second portion, with more specific accounting procedures and conventions. The code contains over 50 elections that must be made within the first tax year of any taxable entity and several hundred additional elections that can be made in any year in which they are applicable to a taxpayer. We shall consider a few of the more important elections.

## GENERAL METHODS OF ACCOUNTING

The most commonly known methods of accounting are the cash receipts and disbursements method, usually called the *cash method*, the accrual method, and the completed contract method. For tax purposes, a fourth method of accounting, called the *installment method,* has been accepted for reporting specific transactions. The income reported by a taxpayer in any single year will differ importantly under each of these accounting methods. Although the aggregate net differences tend to be reduced over a long period of time, they are still important for tax purposes because of the time-preference value of money. The longer a taxpayer can defer a tax liability, other things being equal, the smaller the real economic cost of the tax.

### The Cash Method

The vast majority of individual taxpayers report their taxable income on a cash method of accounting. This means, of course, that they report their items of gross income in the year in which they receive cash or other property and that they report deductions in the year in which they pay a deductible expense. The only financial records typically maintained by such taxpayers are a checkbook and an odd collection of canceled checks, "paid" vouchers, sales receipts, and some miscellaneous notes and diary type records. These documents, along with the Form W–2 (the "Wage and Tax Statement," prepared by the taxpayer's employer) and the Forms 1099 (the "U.S. Information Returns" prepared by banks, savings and loan associations, dividend-paying corporations, and other payers of miscellaneous earnings), are somehow combined to provide the necessary information required to complete an individual tax return (Form 1040, 1040A, or 1040EZ) by April 15 each year.

Most service-oriented businesses, including the professions of medicine, dentistry, law, and accountancy, also report their taxable income on a cash method. In these instances, however, it is common to find a more complete and accurate set of financial records. Farms, restaurants, gasoline stations, and other businesses that combine a service orientation with sometimes large capital investments typically report on a modified cash basis of accounting. Most of their modifications are attributable to capital investments in fixed assets the costs of which must be capitalized and recovered over some arbitrary time period.

**Specific Limitations.**    The only general restrictions historically placed on the cash method of accounting were those for capital improvements and for businesses in which the sale of merchandise is a material income-producing factor. The prescribed treatment of capital investments will be explained in Chapter 10. In businesses in which merchandise is important, the law usually requires an adjustment to the cash method of accounting for changes in year-end inventories. If this adjustment were not mandatory a taxpayer could very easily reduce reported net income by increasing the stock of inventory and could increase reported net income by depleting the normal inventory. The effect of the required adjustment is to change only the computation of the income from gross sales and the tax deduction for the cost of merchandise sold from a strict cash basis to an accrual basis of accounting. The deduction for the cost of merchandise sold must be made as follows:

$$
\begin{array}{l}
\phantom{+}\text{Cost of merchandise on hand at first of year} \\
\underline{+\text{Cost of merchandise purchased during the year}} \\
=\text{Cost of merchandise available for sale} \\
\underline{-\text{Cost of merchandise on hand at end of year}} \\
=\text{The tax-deductible cost of merchandise sold}
\end{array}
$$

In other words, a cash-basis taxpayer can deduct only the amount shown on the last line of the above formula, not the amount shown on the second line of that formula, as the cost of goods sold. Except for the "sales" and "cost of goods sold" figures, the other components of of taxable income can generally be reported on a cash receipts and disbursements basis. This is what the Treasury regulations refer to as a *modified cash basis of accounting*.

Congress recently prohibited the use of the cash method of accounting by regular corporations (called C corporations), partnerships which have one or more corporate partners, and tax-shelter businesses. In general, however, this prohibition does not apply to entities, other than tax shelters, with gross receipts of $5 million or less. Because corporations and partnerships of that size are apt to have their own source of good tax advice, the new limitations will not be detailed further here.

In addition to the new restrictions for C corporations as well as the long-standing limitations for capital expenditures and for the cost of goods sold, a number of special restrictions on the cash method of accounting have been imposed by the IRS and the courts in particular instances. For example, we noted in Chapter 2 that a constructive receipt rule may often modify a strictly cash-basis result.

For obvious reasons, the IRS and the courts generally require that a cash-basis taxpayer report extraordinary transactions on a cash-equivalent basis rather than on a literal cash basis. If they had not made this interpretation, all barter-type transactions would remain tax-free for all cash-basis taxpayers. Quite obviously, that temptation would be too great to resist. Given our present tax rates, the nation could be turned into a semibarter economy overnight by any contrary interpretation of a cash basis of accounting. This means that even if a taxpayer reports recurring salary, dividends, interest, professional fees, rents, royalties, and other items of routine income on a cash basis, the sale of an investment or "capital-type" asset cannot be reported on that basis *unless it involves an installment sale*. In all barter transactions, the authorities will require that the taxpayer determine the fair market value of any assets received and that taxable income be reported on a cash-equivalent basis. If a cash-basis taxpayer desires to defer the recognition of income from an extraordinary transaction until actually receiving cash, it is necessary either to arrange an installment sale or to fall within the nontaxable exchange provisions, some of which are discussed in Chapter 11. The installment sale provisions are discussed later in this chapter.

**The Advantage of the Cash Method.**    Except for the specific limitations just observed, a taxpayer reporting taxable income on a cash receipts and disbursements basis has some ability to control the timing of many tax-critical events. The importance of proper timing will be noted throughout this book. In Chapter 10, for example, we will note how the proper timing of asset acquisitions can change the depreciation expense deduction allowed in the first year. In Chapter 3, we noted how a taxpayer might maximize use of the standard deduction by the careful timing of personal or "other itemized" deductions.

There are literally hundreds of other ways a cash-basis taxpayer can change a tax liability by changing the date on which certain things are done. A taxpayer who has earned an unusually large income in a particular year might be able to reduce the marginal tax rate that would be applied to that income by either deferring additional income or (to the limited extent allowed) by accelerating the payment of tax-deductible items. A professional person may, for example, defer the mailing of all bills to clients during the last month of a high-income year and thereby discourage many clients from paying until early in the next accounting period. Alternatively or concurrently, a taxpayer might purchase an unusually large stock of expendable supplies in a high-income year and deduct them by making a timely payment. A farmer, for example, could purchase extra feed, fertilizer, or seed near the year-end. Another taxpayer might pay property taxes early, or make early charitable contributions, if more tax deductions are needed in the current year. (Incidentally, except for a limited number of "points" paid on the original purchase of a home, taxpayers generally cannot deduct any amount of interest expense they prepay.) If an extraordinary sale is made at a large profit near the year-end, the sale might be arranged as an installment sale and the first payment deferred until the next year. These general ideas apply to any taxpayer who has some basis for predicting a substantially smaller taxable income in a subsequent accounting period as well as to years in which the taxpayer knows that the tax rates are going to be reduced. Just the opposite kind of action would be recommended for any taxpayer anticipating a substantial increase in taxable income or in any year the tax rates are going to increase.

In a limited number of circumstances, the IRS and the courts may disallow an otherwise authorized tax deduction claimed by a cash-basis taxpayer on the ground that the item distorts the reported income of the taxpayer. In the case of "investment interest," the Treasury Department persuaded Congress to pass restrictive legislation. The effect of this statutory provision is to disallow a deduction for interest expense incurred on a loan made to finance investments that do not produce taxable income. This statutory disallowance of investment interest will generally not apply until the interest expense exceeds the net income produced by the investments. Taxpayers should always remember that the IRS *may* be able to deny any otherwise legitimate cash-basis tax deduction if that deduction distorts taxable income in a given year. The potential hazard of disallowance notwithstanding, the taxpayer reporting income on a cash method of accounting retains some opportunity for successful tax planning.

Most taxpayers will find that it is preferable to keep their routine books on a cash basis if they desire to report income for tax purposes on a cash basis. If cash-basis books are adequately maintained, it is relatively easy for an accountant to convert a cash-basis income determination to an accrual basis income determination anytime the need arises. If, for example, a bank or other credit institution demands an accrual basis income statement from a cash-basis taxpayer, a certified public accountant can usually prepare such a statement at a minimum cost so long as a good set of cash-basis records has been maintained.

## The Accrual Method

The accrual method of accounting is utilized by virtually all large corporate businesses. Most professional accountants would insist that only an accrual method of accounting can determine a meaningful income figure, at least for purposes of financial reporting. The essence of the accrual method of accounting is the notion that revenues (or gross income) should be recognized when *earned,* regardless of when cash is received, and that expenses should be matched against the revenues they produce and thereby be deducted in the year the correspondent revenue is recognized, not in the year the expenses happen to be paid. Professional accountants admittedly have problems in deciding exactly when some revenues have been earned and in determining the causal relationship between certain expenditures and the corresponding revenues. They have other problems in measurement relative to both revenues and expenses. Nevertheless, most practicing accountants agree on the general procedures utilized in measuring income on an accrual basis. In recent years, the Financial Accounting Standards Board has attempted to reduce the number of acceptable alternative procedures that can be applied in common situations. Although accrual accounting for tax purposes is frequently similar to accrual accounting for financial purposes, there is a growing difference between the two concepts each year.

Two frequent differences involve items received as prepaid income and items received under a claim of right. Generally speaking, for federal income tax purposes both of these income items must be recognized when they are received; for financial accounting purposes they typically are deferred. Special tax rules may, however, apply in limited circumstances.

Differences also exist for many expenses that have to be estimated for financial accounting purposes. In a number of instances the tax law denies a taxpayer the right to claim any deduction that has to be estimated. For example, even though estimates are required by the rules of generally accepted accounting principles, most taxpayers cannot claim a tax deduction for either *estimated* warranty expenses or bad debts. In these two instances the taxpayer cannot claim the tax deduction until the actual loss is experienced. This means, of course, that a number of routine expenses are recognized for tax purposes in a later year than they are for financial accounting purposes.

**Special Limitations.**    Even if a taxpayer both maintains regular books and files a tax return on an accrual method of accounting, typically there will be a number of differences between specific items as reported on the financial statements and the tax return. Most of the significant differences can be traced to code provisions that were enacted to achieve particular economic or social objectives. The ACRS (or cost recovery) and percentage depletion provisions are just two examples of such differences. Other differences can be attributed to administrative considerations peculiar to taxation. For example, the denial of a taxpayer's right to deduct estimated expenses is, at least in part, attributable to the desire for administrative simplicity. Even though the traditional explanation for this difference is made in terms of the large revenue losses for the government, another explanation is the fear that acceptance of such estimated amounts as an authorized tax deduction would lead to widespread disagreement between the taxpayer and the tax collector. To the maximum extent possible, the trend over the past several years has been to reduce the areas of potential disagreement. In other situations, the differences between accrual method accounting figures for tax and financial accounting purposes can be explained on a wherewithal-to-pay concept. The nontaxable exchanges, explained in Chapter 11, have no counterpart in financial accounting. The apparent difference is in no small measure related to the fact that, even if there is a substantial realized gain, a taxpayer has no dollars with which to pay a tax when a nontaxable transaction has been completed. In select situations, Congress has found this sufficient reason to permit the deferral of the tax liability. In financial accounting there is no comparable reason for deferring the recognition of income, and therefore financial accounting typically recognizes all gains and losses as soon as they have been realized.

In addition to these general differences between the use of the accrual method of accounting for financial purposes and for tax purposes, the code provides some very special limitations in unusual situations. A subsection of Section 267, for example, disallows any tax deduction for the loss realized on a sale or exchange of property between certain related taxpayers. The disallowance is applicable for tax purposes, no matter how real the transaction might be in legal or economic terms, if the stipulated code conditions are satisfied. Another subsection of Section 267 disallows the deduction of certain expenses *accrued* by one taxpayer for the benefit of another closely-related cash-basis taxpayer until the accrued liability is paid.

The reason for this second provision is most easily understood in the context of a closely held corporation that reports its taxable income on an accrual method of accounting. If the statutory prohibition did not exist, the owner of the corporation could declare a salary payable to himself or herself and thus obtain an immediate tax deduction for the accrual basis corporation. As a cash-basis taxpayer, the owner would not have to report any taxable income from such a salary until the corporation made a payment on the accrued salary. The owner-operator could obviously defer any recognition of taxable income until a most convenient year and still have the benefit of the immediate tax deduction in the corporate entity.

Section 267 defines related parties rather broadly. The proscribed relationships include, among others:

1. Members of the same family.
2. Individuals and a corporation in which they own 50 percent or more of the outstanding stock.
3. Two corporations which are both members of the same controlled group.
4. Numerous other closely related parties, such as the fiduciary and beneficiary of a trust.

In summary, because of Sec. 267, transactions between closely related parties may be subject to very unusual accounting treatment.

## Long-Term Construction Contract Methods

For financial accounting purposes construction projects that require longer than a single accounting period for completion can usually be reported under one of two alternative methods of accounting, namely, the percentage-of-completion method or the completed-contract method. These same two accounting methods were also available for tax purposes prior to 1987. In 1986 Congress generally repealed the right of many taxpayers to use the completed contract method of accounting for federal income tax purposes. The new law carves out an exception, however, for certain real property construction or improvement contracts if: (1) the project will take two years or less to complete; and (2) the taxpayer has had average annual gross receipts of $10 million or less for the past three years. Those few taxpayers may still defer the recognition of both gross income and deductions from these construction projects until all work on the contract is completed. All other taxpayers involved in long-term contracts must now use either (1) the percentage-of-completion method or (2) something new called the percentage-of-completion/capitalized-cost method.

Under the former method of accounting a taxpayer must recognize a portion of the gross income each year. The percent recognized is determined by comparing the costs incurred during the year to the total estimated contract costs. The latter method requires a taxpayer to use the percentage-of-completion method for 70 percent of the contract; the remainder may be reported using the taxpayer's "regular" method of accounting (which may be the completed contract method). Special, complex rules determine how the various costs are to be assigned to a contract. At the end of the long-term contract, the taxpayer must look back and recompute the annual tax liability for prior years utilizing the actual contract costs incurred in the project. Underpayments in prior years will result in an interest charge; overpayments will generate an interest refund.

The reason for this latest aberration in tax accounting rules can evidently be attributed to the fact that several large defense contractors were able to pay little or no federal income taxes in years prior to 1987 because they had utilized the completed-contract method of accounting for tax purposes. This embarrassed Congress and the rules were amended in the way just described. Presumably this will accelerate the collection of taxes from persons engaged in the defense and construction industries.

## The Installment Method

The installment method of accounting is no longer accepted as a tax accounting method for dealers in property. Rather, it is a special tax provision that is applicable only to a *profitable* deferred-payment sale made by a person who is otherwise a cash-basis taxpayer and who is *not* a dealer in the property sold. When it is allowed, the fundamental idea is to defer the recognition of taxable income until the receipt of cash. The taxpayer must determine a gross profit ratio for an authorized installment sale and then apply this ratio to each cash collection to determine the amount of gross income that must be recognized. For example, if a taxpayer sold an investment property with an $80,000 adjusted tax basis for $100,000, a $20,000 gross profit would be realized on the sale. Thus, the taxpayer's gross profit ratio would be 20 percent ($20,000 gross profit divided by $100,000 sales price), and the taxpayer would recognize only 20 percent of any collections on this sale as taxable income in each year.

Observe that the rules for installment sales are automatically applicable to most non-dealer sales made at a gain (unless the taxpayer formally elects not to have these rules apply) and that they never apply to sales made at a loss. This ability to defer the recognition of income, until the receipt of cash, through an installment sale does *not* extend to sales of depreciable properties subject to certain "depreciation recapture" rules or to sales of publicly traded property (including stocks and securities). In addition, special rules apply if at the end of a year a taxpayer holds more than $5 million in uncollected installment obligations acquired during the year from the sale of business or rental *real* properties (other than farm properties) with a selling price in excess of $150,000 each. These special rules require the taxpayer to pay interest to the government on any deferred tax attributable to the installment obligations in excess of $5 million. Furthermore, if the taxpayer pledges any installment receivables as security for a loan, the net proceeds from the pledge will be treated as the equivalent of receipts from a sale and thus trigger the realization of any gain that would otherwise have been deferred by the installment sale method of accounting. Finally, other special rules that are not detailed here may apply to installment sales by dealers in timeshares, residential lots, or properties used (or produced) in the farming business.

The major advantage of the installment method of accounting is that it defers the payment of the income tax as long as possible. Also, if a taxpayer anticipates a reduction in the marginal tax rate in the future, perhaps because of a change in the tax law or because of a lesser income in retirement, it is especially important to arrange a deferred-payment sale. In this instance the tax is both deferred as long as possible and taxed at the lowest marginal rate. On the other hand, a taxpayer looking forward to a substantially increased taxable income in the future might want to avoid an installment sale, even if this means an earlier payment of the tax. An increase in the marginal tax rate could offset any time-preference value of a tax deferral.

## ACCOUNTING PROCEDURES AND CONVENTIONS

The number of alternative accounting procedures and conventions is substantially greater than the number of alternative general methods of accounting. We will read in Chapter 10, for example, that the code authorizes a limited number of accounting procedures to determine the cost allocations common to depreciation. The acceptable depreciation procedures include both an accelerated cost recovery system (ACRS) and a straight-line method. Earlier in this chapter, we also observed the need to determine the deduction for the cost of goods sold on an accrual basis, without regard for the taxpayer's usual method of accounting. We did not note there, however, that the cost-of-goods-sold determination can be made under any of several alternative inventory costing conventions, including FIFO (first-in, first-out), LIFO (last-in, first-out), weighted average, moving average, retail sales, and specific identification. Each of these accounting conventions or procedures will yield a different taxable income in anything other than a perfectly static economy.

### Inventory Costing Conventions

Time and space constraints preclude any detailed examination of each of the inventory costing conventions just noted. The reader should be aware, however, that the selection of an inventory costing convention may have a substantial impact on the amount of taxable income that must be recognized. During a period of rising prices, it is generally to the taxpayer's advantage to utilize the LIFO costing technique because, as the name implies, the assumption under that costing convention is that the very last goods to be purchased during a year were the first to be sold! During a period of rising prices, the last goods to be purchased are the most costly. If we assume that the most costly goods were the first to be sold, we are in effect charging the highest priced goods to the tax-deductible cost of goods sold and charging the least expensive goods to the ending inventory, a nondeductible asset. During a period of falling prices, the FIFO costing technique would yield the largest tax deduction and the lowest inventory valuation. The other inventory costing techniques tend to yield an intermediate measure of both the cost of goods sold and the ending inventory. If a taxpayer desires to use the LIFO method of inventory costing for tax purposes, it generally must also be used for financial accounting purposes. And if a taxpayer desires to change from one inventory costing convention to another, the consent of the commissioner must be obtained and an appropriate adjustment made to the reported taxable income in the year of change.

### The Unit of Account

The basic unit of account selected for any single element of a larger accounting system may have a substantial impact on the income reported by that system in a given year. The phrase *unit of account* refers to the lowest common denominator in any accounting classification. Relative to an automobile, for example, the unit of account may be each specific car, some portion of a car (say, the motor), or an entire fleet of cars. Generally, the broader we make the unit of account, the more likely it is that we can treat a particular related expenditure as an immediately deductible expense and the less likely it is that we will need to recognize a gain on the disposition of each small element within the larger unit. The selection of the most tax-advantageous unit of account can only proceed on an item-by-item investigation.

### Interest Expense

Interest payments also create special problems for income tax purposes. These problems derive from the fact that the code contains many special rules that limit the right of a taxpayer to deduct some portion or all of the interest expense that they incur. The limitations generally depend upon how the proceeds of the debt are utilized. Interest incurred on purely personal debts— i.e., debts unrelated to any business or investment purpose—are, since 1986, generally *not* deductible. That general rule, however, is subject to at least three major exceptions:

1. Interest incurred on the debt incurred to acquire, construct, or improve a taxpayer's primary residence as well as one additional home is, fully deductible as "qualified residence interest" so long as the total of this debt does not exceed $1 million;
2. Interest incurred on a "home-equity debt" not in excess of $100,000 is fully deductible, regardless of what the taxpayer does with the proceeds from a home-equity loan; and
3. Interest incurred on other purely personal debts may be partially deducted because of certain transition rules. In general these rules allow a taxpayer to deduct 40 percent of the otherwise disallowed personal interest expense in 1988; 20 percent in 1989; and 10 percent in 1990. Thereafter, of course, this third exception to the general rule will no longer apply. Subtle distinctions between residence-acquisition debt and home-equity debt are

created in the first two exceptions noted above. Taxpayers with large debts on their primary and/or secondary residence(s) should investigate these distinctions elsewhere.

Interest on debts incurred to finance any part of a trade, business, or profession in which the taxpayer materially participates is fully deductible. Interest on debts incurred to finance the acquisition of investments that produce only tax exempt income is wholly disallowed. And interest on debts incurred to acquire other investments may be subject to still other special rules that apply to "investment interest," "passive activity losses," and/or "portfolio income." The rules for investment interest were noted earlier in this chapter; the other rules are discussed briefly in Chapter 8.

The practical problems encountered in applying these tax provisions are substantial. Money is, after all, a fungible commodity. The proceeds of many loans are commingled with funds derived from a wide variety of sources in a general bank account. It is virtually impossible, therefore, to physically trace many specific debt proceeds to their eventual use. Nevertheless, that is what the code now requires. The Treasury Department has issued regulations intended to help taxpayers comply with this new law.

As a practical matter, these regulations (Temp. Regs. 1.163-8T) provide a host of administrative presumptions that the IRS will follow in the classification of interest expense incurred by taxpayers barring valid accounting records that clearly support an alternative conclusion. For example, if a tax payer borrows money and deposits the loan proceeds in an extant checking account, and no checks are written from that account for the next 40 days, the interest expense for the 40-day "inactive" period will automatically be classified as "investment interest." Furthermore, if borrowed funds are comingled in a single account with unborrowed money—for example, savings—the first withdrawals will be presumed to come from the borrowed funds until the total amount withdrawn equals the amount borrowed. And if two or more loans are deposited in a single account, the proceeds of the various loans will be presumed to be withdrawn on a FIFO (first-in, first-out) basis. If the proceeds of a single debt are used to pay for multiple activities, a partial repayment of that debt is assumed to first repay any personal use of the debt; next any investment debt; then passive debt; and, finally, trade or business debt. Many additional assumptions, too numerous to explain here, can be found in the Treasury regulation.

To avoid unintended results and sometimes unfavorable presumptions, most tax advisors currently recommend that clients keep separate bank accounts for borrowed funds. They also recommend that taxpayers keep good records of the business use of any assets acquired with borrowed funds; for example, an automobile used for both business and personal purposes. Finally, many tax advisors recommend that individual taxpayers consolidate their consumer debts and pay them off with a home-equity loan of $100,000 or less. The intent in every instance is, of course, to maximize the amount of interest expense that can be deducted by the taxpayer.

To summarize, interest expense deductions are presently subject to various statutory limitations that can be paraphrased as follows:

1.  Personal interest is generally not deductible except for (1) acquisition debt of $1 million or less on a primary and/or secondary residence; (2) home-equity loans of $100,000 or less; and (3) certain transition rules for 1988–1990.

2.  Investment interest is deductible only to the extent of net investment income plus (under the 40-20-10 percent transition rules) an amount not to exceed $4,000 in 1988; $2,000 in 1989; and $1,000 in 1990. Any excess may first be deducted under the personal interest transition rules and any remaining excess will be carried forward and deducted against any excess net investment income in later years.

3.  Passive interest is deductible only when and to the extent that passive income equals passive expenses or on the total disposition of a passive activity. (See Chapter 8 for additional details.)

4.  Interest on debt used to acquire tax-exempt income is not deductible at any time.

5.  Trade or business interest is currently deductible without limit.

Although the regulations do not modify any of the statutory rules, they may help a taxpayer, by way of an assumption, to determine how any given interest expense should be classified for federal income tax purposes.

### Other Convenient Tax Assumptions

A taxpayer may be required to make many other assumptions to further simplify even the best tax accounting system. For example, no taxpayer of any substantial size can calculate depreciation on a daily basis. Fixed assets are bought, sold, and traded throughout the year, and a taxpayer usually could not afford to make separate depreciation determinations for each of these many transactions. Therefore, in addition to granting the limited right to group certain fixed assets in a single account, the code requires a taxpayer to make certain standard assumptions about the timing of all property acquisitions and dispositions made during a year. For example, current law requires that a taxpayer assume that all acquisitions of personal (or nonreal) properties occurred in the middle of the year unless more than 40 percent of all additions for the year are made during the last quarter. In that event, a mid-quarter convention must be used. Acquisitions of real property, on the other hand, are assumed to be made in the middle of the month in which the real property is acquired. These rules all explained in greater detail in Chapter 10.

## The Fiscal Year

A year is the period commonly used to measure income for tax purposes. Until recently that year could be either a calendar year or a fiscal year for almost all taxpayers. Today, however, there are special restrictions that apply to certain entities. For example, S corporations are *generally* required to use a calendar year. Partnerships and personal-service corporations *generally* must conform their tax years to the same year as that used by their majority owners. Thus a partnership must *ordinarily* report taxable income using the same year as that used by the partners who own a majority interest in the partnership. Partnerships and S corporations, may utilize a pre-1987 fiscal year, however, if they are willing to make a "required payment" that effectively takes away any monetary advantage associated with the tax deferral. This option—known as a Sec. 444 election—is not available to personal service corporations.

If a taxpayer wishes to modify the taxable year of any taxable entity, it is generally necessary to get the consent of the commissioner before making the change. It is sometimes easier to make an initial election wisely than to obtain the commissioner's permission to change. If a taxpayer obtains permission to modify a tax year, a short-period return must generally be filed. In some situations, the adjustment procedure required in preparing a short-period return may result in an unusually large tax liability, which can be corrected only if the taxpayer first pays the tax and then, at the end of the regular accounting period (prior to the change), files a claim for refund based on actual results for the previous 12 months. A failure to file the refund claim on a timely basis may result in the permanent loss of the right to do so.

## Records: Good and Bad

Every taxpayer should remember that, in tax matters, the usual presumption of the court is that the IRS is correct until proved wrong. This presumption for the government argues for a good accounting system. At one time in our history, a taxpayer could rely on the mercy of the court to grant a reasonable allowance for any tax item that could not be proved. That doctrine was known popularly as the "Cohan rule" because of a court case between the IRS and the famous entertainer George M. Cohan over certain entertainment expenses. In the recent past, the courts have exhibited an increasing reluctance to follow the Cohan rule, and taxpayers are well advised to keep the best possible records if they wish to obtain the most favorable tax result.

Small taxpayers in particular may be surprised to discover the reluctance of the IRS to accept what appear to them to be perfectly reasonable validation records. In the case of the charitable contribution deduction, for example, the IRS has sometimes refused to accept a canceled check as sufficient evidence of the fact that a contribution has in fact been made. The reason for its hesitancy in this instance stems from a case in which a taxpayer cashed a check each Sunday with the church treasurer for the alleged purpose of obtaining sufficient change to open an office on Monday morning. The taxpayer in fact used the check as evidence of an apparent charitable contribution. The ruse was discovered, and the canceled check suddenly lost much of its potential value as evidence of a valid tax deduction under suspicious circumstances.

Although it is almost impossible to overestimate the value of a truly good set of accounting records in income tax matters, it is very easy to underestimate the potential value of other records. In some situations, an IRS agent or a court will accept a purely personal (and often sloppily prepared) diary as evidence of certain tax-deductible expenditures. Although such personal records may be worthless in suspicious cases, they tend to corroborate other evidence of good faith, and sometimes spell the difference between getting administrative agreement and going to court. The taxpayer should not destroy charge slips, guest lists, convention programs, and other evidence that may support a questionable tax deduction for travel, entertainment, or other business expenses. Guest logs are necessary to support some tax deductions for club memberships and the use of entertainment facilities. Even a good color photograph may help to sustain a claim for a casualty loss deduction. A taxpayer sensitized to the many tax opportunities and pitfalls should also begin to comprehend the need for validation records, good or bad.

### One-Time Elections

The code contains numerous elections that pertain to newly organized businesses. A few of these provisions are worded in such a way that the taxpayer has a minimal opportunity to correct an initial "bad" decision. Code Section 248, for example, authorizes a corporation to amortize organization expenses over a period of 60 months or longer. If the corporate officers fail to make the election on a timely basis, however, none of the organization expenses can be deducted until the corporation is dissolved.

The details of each election are sufficiently intricate, and the methods of compliance sufficiently peculiar, that further discussion is best left to the books written for those concerned with tax compliance rather than with tax recognition. The good business manager need understand only the importance of obtaining qualified help on a timely basis.

## PROBLEMS AND ASSIGNMENTS

1. Phil N. Pullem, D.D.S., opened his first dental office immediately after graduation from State University in June. During the remainder of the year, he recorded the following:

|  | Amount Earned | Cash Received | Liability Incurred | Cash Paid |
|---|---|---|---|---|
| Services rendered | $48,000 | $37,000 | — | — |
| Assistant employed | — | — | $ 5,500 | $ 5,000 |
| Dental supplies/utilities | — | — | 14,000 | 10,000 |
| Dental equipment | — | — | 80,000 | 8,000 |

Assume that the depreciation on the dental equipment is $12,000 for tax purposes.

a. Based solely on the above information, what amount of taxable income does it appear that Dr. Pullem must report from his dental practice if—
   (1) He uses the cash method of accounting?
   (2) He uses the accrual method of accounting?

b. Which of the items detailed above are readily amenable to modification for tax planning purposes if—
   (1) He elects a cash method of accounting?
   (2) He elects an accrual method of accounting?

c. Assuming that there are some things that Dr. Pullem could do before the end of the year that would legally minimize his federal income tax liability, do you recommend he do them? Explain briefly.

2. Vera Greenleaf is engaged in the retail sale of tropical plants. Vera buys her plants from the Rio Valley Nursery at wholesale prices and resells them at considerably higher prices through her retail store, Vera Green. During her first year of business, Vera recorded the following:

|  | Sales Made | Cash Received | Liability Incurred | Cash Paid |
|---|---|---|---|---|
| Retail sales | $48,000 | $37,000 | — | — |
| Wholesale purchases | — | — | $40,000 | $25,000 |
| Assistant employed | — | — | 5,500 | 5,000 |
| Supplies and utilities | — | — | 14,000 | 10,000 |

The Vera Green has a year-end inventory of $20,000 at wholesale, or $50,000 at retail.

a. Based solely on the above information, what amount of taxable income does it appear that Vera Greenleaf must report from her retail store if—
   (1) She uses the cash method of accounting (or at least as close to that method as she can possibly get)?

(2) She uses the accrual method of accounting?

b. Which of the items detailed above are readily amenable to modification for tax planning purposes if—

(1) She elects a cash method of accounting?

(2) She elects an accrual method of accounting?

3. Jody Cool runs a small retail ice cream store. Jody buys his ice cream from Local Dairy at prices determined on the first day of each month. During the current year, the price per gallon increased exactly one cent each month from January through December. In January, Jody paid $1 per gallon; in December, $1.11 per gallon. Jody sells an average of 500 gallons of ice cream each month.

a. At what price should Jody's year-end inventory of 300 gallons be costed if—

(1) He elects the FIFO inventory method?

(2) He elects the LIFO inventory method?

b. If Jody initially elected the FIFO method, can he independently change to LIFO this year? Explain briefly.

4. Joan Smithe owns 100 percent of the outstanding stock of Smithco. Joan is a calendar-year, cash-basis taxpayer; Smithco is an accrual basis taxpayer whose year ends on January 31. As president of Smithco, Joan receives a salary of $60,000 per year; she also is entitled to a year-end bonus based on a previously arranged contract. On January 31, 19x1, Smithco accrued on its books a year-end bonus payable to Joan in the amount of $32,000.

a. What amount of salary expense for Joan Smithe may Smithco deduct for the fiscal year ended 1/31/x1 if—

(1) It pays the bonus to Joan on January 31, 19x1?

(2) It pays the bonus to Joan on March 1, 19x1?

b. What amount of this bonus must Joan report on her 19x0 federal income tax return that she files on April 15, 19x1? Explain briefly.

5. David Burrow, CPA, sold a 10-acre lot of land on April 1, 19x1, for $100,000. David had purchased this land as an investment five years ago for $60,000. The sale contract calls for a $29,000 down payment plus two equal payments of $35,500 (plus interest) on April 1, 19x2, and April 1, 19x3. The interest due on April 1, 19x2, was $3,550; that due one year later, $1,775.

a. May David report this sale on an installment basis?

b. If an installment method is available, what amount of taxable gain must David report for 19x1?

c. Considering the total sale, what aggregate amount of ordinary income and capital gain must David report as the contract is written?

6. Aaron Plucket lost his billfold on the way to the airport. Unfortunately, Aaron's billfold contained $1,000 in cash at the time he lost it. Sharon Tucket was robbed by an armed bandit of her new $1,000 engagement ring on her way home from the theater.

a. Might either Aaron or Sharon be entitled to a federal income tax deduction because of their unfortunate experience?

b. If Aaron or Sharon is entitled to a deduction, what kind of accounting or other records should be retained to support any deduction claimed?

7. In 1989, Jim Musumeci borrowed $160,000. He used $50,000 to buy stocks, $100,000 to invest in his business, and $10,000 to buy a car. His interest expense for the year was $16,000. His income from investments in 1989 was:

| | |
|---|---|
| Taxable interest income: | $1,500 |
| Tax-free interest income: | 2,000 |
| Gain on sale of stocks: | 1,000 |
| Dividend income: | 2,000 |

What is Jim's interest expense deduction for the year, and is the deduction for AGI or from AGI?

8. In 19x1 Tom and Helen bought themselves a new primary residence for $500,000. They paid $300,000 down and borrowed the balance on a 15-year, 10 percent mortgage note. In 19x3 Tom and Helen decided to borrow $150,000, at 10 percent interest, using a home-equity loan.

a. What maximum amount of interest expense may they deduct on the loan made in 19x3?

b. What might Tom and Helen have done differently that would allow them to deduct a larger amount of interest expense in 19x3?

9. Some drug dealers, gamblers, prostitutes, and other seamy characters keep surprisingly good accounting records.

a. Explain briefly why these people might keep good records.

b. In the absence of records, how do you suppose the IRS might estimate the amount of income earned by a taxpayer? Explain briefly; do no research beyond your book.

---

# Case 5–1

Athena Pappas has just died and left $100,000 to be divided equally between her twin daughters, Prudence and Persephone. Both daughters have exactly $50,000 of principal remaining on their home mortgages to be paid at a 12 percent annual rate over the 60 months remaining on the mortgage. The monthly mortgage payment is $1,112.22 on each mortgage.

Prudence plans to take her $50,000 and pay off the mortgage immediately. She will then take the aftertax cost of the monthly payments and put them into an ordinary savings account with an 8 percent annual interest rate calculated monthly.

Persephone plans to take her $50,000 and put it into an ordinary savings account with an 8 percent annual interest rate calculated monthly. Persephone will continue to make the monthly payments of $1,112.22 on the mortgage for five years.

Both daughters expect to have a marginal tax rate of 28 percent for the indefinite future. Neither daughter plans to sell her house in the next five years.

At the end of five years how much does each daughter have in savings?

If Prudence needs to borrow $20,000 next year to send her son to school, what would you recommend for her?

# CHAPTER 6

# The Alternative Minimum Tax

The alternative minimum tax (AMT) can be conceptually described as a tax on embarrassment! That is, taxpayers who would otherwise embarrass the government by earning a substantial amount of economic income, but paying little or no federal income tax, will very probably be required to pay something called the alternative minimum tax. The name for this second income tax derives from the fact that all taxpayers must, at least theoretically, calculate their federal income tax liability in two rather different ways. If the income tax determined in the regular way is less than the income tax determined in an alternative way, then the alternative tax is the minimum amount of tax that must actually be paid. As a practical matter, the average individual and the very small corporate taxpayer will not even make the alternative computation simply because there are exemption provisions of sufficient size to excuse them from having to pay the alternative minimum tax. For the individual with a higher than average economic income, however, both tax calculations must be made. That same unfortunate conclusion now also applies to all but the smallest corporations, estates, and trusts.

This chapter is little more than a brief overview of a very complex subject. The problem of understanding this material is doubly difficult because many of the rules to be explained here depend upon the reader's understanding of concepts that are introduced much later in the text. Pedagogically this chapter might, therefore, be better postponed and covered just before the final chapter. In the opinion of the author, however, the fundamental notion of an alternative minimum tax is best discussed in the context of accounting methods, business entities, and income concepts; subjects just covered in prior chapters.

This introduction to the alternative minimum tax is divided into three major parts. The first part explains general rules applicable to all taxpayers; the second part, those rules of special importance to corporate taxpayers; and the final part, rules of most importance to individual taxpayers. An appendix has been added at the end of the chapter for those readers who may desire more detail on one of the most common complications of the AMT; i.e., the adjustments required in the depreciation deduction calculations for AMT purposes.

# FACTORS OF IMPORTANCE TO ALL TAXPAYERS

As implied in the introductory remarks, the alternative minimum tax is really a second income tax system, parallel to, but separate from, the regular income tax described in all of the other chapters of this text. The intent of Congress in enacting these unusual Code provisions was clearly to assure that all taxpayers earning any significant amount of economic income will pay their fair share of the federal income tax. The first provisions, enacted in 1969, were largely intended to impact individual taxpayers; the current provisions seem clearly directed at the larger corporate taxpayers. Nevertheless, most of the technical provisions are equally applicable to all taxpayers. At the same time, however, some of the AMT provisions are narrowly directed at only a few very specific taxpayers. For example, one rule applies only to corporations that build merchant and fishing vessels; another applies only to certain Blue Cross, Blue Shield operations. Consistent with the general thrust of this book, we will dismiss from discussion all provisions other than those of the most general interest, and even those provisions will be discussed in the most general terms.

## Computing the Alternative Minimum Tax

The computation of the AMT begins with taxable income computed in the regular way, but before considering any net operating loss (NOL) deduction or adjustment. That amount is then adjusted in various ways, described later, to derive a new tax base called the alternative minimum taxable income (AMTI). AMTI, after one possible additional adjustment, is then multiplied by a flat tax rate to determine the gross AMT liability. Finally, this amount may be reduced by two tax credits to determine the net AMT liability. In skeletal form this computation can be diagrammed as in Figure 6–1.

**Adjustments.**   Observe that the first series of adjustments identified in Figure 6–1 can cause AMTI to be either larger or smaller than taxable income in any year. This set of adjustments includes items that are strictly a matter of timing differences. In other words, even though the Code requires (or permits) one set of calculations for regular income tax purposes, it may require another set for AMT purposes. In that event any difference between these two sets of tax rules will completely balance out over the long run. Examples include special rules for the completed-contract accounting methods and for depreciation calculations.

Timing problems are commonly encountered with alternative accounting procedures. For example, as you will discover in Chapter 10 and/or the appendix to this chapter, fixed assets are generally depreciated using an accelerated cost recovery system (ACRS) for regular income tax purposes. For AMT purposes, however, somewhat different accounting procedures must be followed. In almost every instance the depreciation deduction for AMT purposes

**FIGURE 6–1**   Calculating the AMT

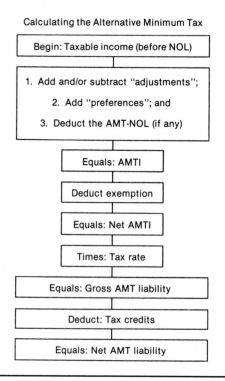

Calculating the Alternative Minimum Tax

| Begin: Taxable income (before NOL) |

1. Add and/or subtract "adjustments";
2. Add "preferences"; and
3. Deduct the AMT-NOL (if any)

| Equals: AMTI |

| Deduct exemption |

| Equals: Net AMTI |

| Times: Tax rate |

| Equals: Gross AMT liability |

| Deduct: Tax credits |

| Equals: Net AMT liability |

will be less in the early years and greater in the later years. Additional details of the adjustment are explained in the appendix to this chapter.

A more complete identification of the items requiring "adjustment" for AMT purposes is as follows:

|  | *Adjustment Applies to—* | |
| --- | --- | --- |
| *Adjust for—* | *Corporation* | *Individual* |
| Depreciation of real property | x | x |
| Depreciation of personal property | x | x |
| Completed-contract method | x | x |
| Book-tax accounting difference | x | |
| Passive activity losses | | x |
| Net farm losses | | x |
| R & D expenditures | x | x |
| Circulation expenditures | x | x |
| Mining exploration and development costs | x | x |

As is apparent in the preceding list, most of the common adjustments are required of both corporate and individual taxpayers. Two important exceptions to that rule are the "book-tax accounting difference" and "passive activity losses." Because these two adjustments are of particular importance to corporate and individual taxpayers, respectively, they will be discussed in greater detail later in this chapter. Further explanation of most of the other required adjustments is better left for further study at another time.

Most of the details required to actually understand and calculate the AMT adjustments are of limited interest to general business managers. The really important thing for them to understand is the fact that they may be required to keep three entirely different sets of books; i.e., one for financial accounting purposes; a second for regular income tax purposes; and a third for alternative minimum tax purposes. Furthermore, almost every taxpayer should understand that the amount of income tax payable in any year is the larger of the regular income tax or the AMT.

**Preferences.**    Tax preferences, unlike the "adjustments" described above, will always be added to taxable income determined in the regular way. In general, tax preferences are income items that are excluded, for one reason or another, from the definition of taxable income. The list of tax preferences is somewhat shorter than the list of adjustments. The more important preferences include the following:

| | Preference Applies to— | |
| --- | --- | --- |
| *Tax Preference* | *Corporation* | *Individual* |
| Certain tax-exempt interest | x | x |
| Percentage depletion in excess of cost basis | x | x |
| Unrealized appreciation in the value of property contributed to charity | x | x |
| Some part of the gain in an incentive stock option | | x |
| Portions of certain intangible drilling and development costs | x | x |

Unlike the adjustments described earlier, tax preferences will ordinarily not balance out over time. In other words, tax preferences have the general effect of making AMTI a larger amount than taxable income determined in the normal way.

For example, tax-exempt interest on most state and local bonds is forever excluded from gross income for regular income tax purposes. Tax-exempt interest attributable to certain state and local bonds—specifically, to "private activity bonds" issued by a state or local government after August 7, 1986—will, however, have to be included in AMTI. This difference will never balance out, even in the long run.

A second example of tax preferences is that attributable to the unrealized appreciation in capital gain properties contributed to a charitable organization. The good reasons that taxpayers have for giving these particular properties to charity is explained in Chapter 14. The amount of the tax preference for AMT purposes is easily explained by a simple example. To illustrate, assume that taxpayer A gave common stock having a fair market value of $100,000 to a local nonprofit hospital. If A had paid $20,000 for this stock several years ago, there would be $80,000 of unrealized appreciation (i.e., $100,000 value less $20,000 cost) in the stock on the date of the gift. Although this $80,000 would forever escape being reported as part of A's taxable income, computed in the regular way, that same $80,000 would have to be included in the determination of A's AMTI.

**NOLs.**   The net operating loss deduction is computed differently for both regular and minimum tax purposes. The details of the many differences required in making these two computations are of limited importance to tax planning generally; hence they are dismissed without discussion here. Perhaps, however, every taxpayer should know that an NOL may not offset more than 90 percent of AMTI. As a consequence, businesses with very large NOLs may still be subject in some cases to a relatively small amount of income tax because of the AMT.

**Exemptions.**   Taxpayers with only relatively small amounts of taxable income and limited adjustment and preference items can generally ignore the AMT because of the basic exemptions allowed. The precise amount of the exemption varies by taxpayer, as follows:

| | |
|---|---|
| Individuals— | |
| Married persons/joint return | $40,000 |
| Married persons/separate returns | 20,000 |
| Single persons | 30,000 |
| Fiduciaries | 20,000 |
| Corporations | 40,000 |

These basic exemptions, however, are phased out for all taxpayers earning a substantial amount of income. The phase-out rules are as follows:

1. For married persons filing jointly, reduce the exemption by 25 percent of the excess of AMTI over $150,000.

2. For married persons filing separate returns and for fiduciaries, reduce the exemption by 25 percent of the excess of AMTI over $75,000.

3. For single persons, reduce the exemption by 25 percent of the excess of AMTI over $112,500.

4. For corporations, reduce the exemption by 25 percent of the excess of AMTI over $150,000.

As a result both corporations and married persons filing jointly will have no basic exemption when their AMTI exceeds $310,000; fiduciaries and married persons filing separately, when their AMTI exceeds $155,000; and single persons, when their AMTI exceeds $232,500.

**Tax Rates.**    The AMT rate is a flat 21 percent for individual and fiduciary taxpayers; a flat 20 percent for corporate taxpayers. Observe that the difference between the AMT tax rate and the top, marginal, regular income tax rate is relatively small. For individual taxpayers it is only 7 percentage points (i.e., 28 percent versus 21 percent); for corporate taxpayers it is 14 percentage points (i.e., 34 percent versus 20 percent).

Because AMTI is generally larger than taxable income, determined in the normal way, and because the AMT and top regular tax rates are now so close together, many taxpayers may be surprised to discover that their AMT is greater than their regular income tax. As explained earlier that means, of course, that they owe the larger amount. If this has caused a taxpayer to make insufficient estimated tax payments on a timely basis, that taxpayer may discover that an additional interest and penalty charge is also payable. In short, today the AMT is a potentially significant trap for the unwary taxpayer.

**Tax Credits.**    The only two tax credits that may be claimed against the AMT are an investment tax credit (ITC) and a foreign tax credit. Because the ITC was generally discontinued for years after 1985, except for transition-rule properties, this means that an ITC will be available only to taxpayers with an ITC carry-forward from earlier years. The details associated with the determination of the exact amount of ITC or foreign tax credit available for AMT purposes are sufficiently complex that they are best omitted from this overview. As a general proposition, however, corporate taxpayers can offset up to 25 percent of the AMT with an ITC carry forward and all taxpayers can offset up to 90 percent of the AMT with a foreign tax credit. Hence the bottom line once again is that a few taxpayers who may completely avoid the regular income tax, by reason of these two credits, may still owe some relatively small amount of federal income tax because of the AMT provisions.

### Miscellaneous Considerations

Incidentally, the way in which both the Code and the tax forms are worded may cause the taxpayer a little confusion in understanding exactly how much AMT they may be paying. Officially a taxpayer computes both the AMT (A) and the regular tax (R); subtracts (R) from (A) (assuming A is greater than R); and pays the difference "as the AMT." This procedural detail can easily mask the real significance of the AMT. To illustrate the point, consider the following two cases as shown on the next page:

|                              | Case A    | Case B    |
|------------------------------|-----------|-----------|
| Net AMT liability            | $800,000  | $800,000  |
| Net regular tax liability    | 900,000   | 600,000   |
| AMT payable per Code/form    | $  –0–    | $200,000  |

Although clearly no amount of AMT is payable in Case A, because the regular tax is greater than the AMT, the true amount of AMT payable in Case B is confusing. Is it only $200,000 (as suggested by the wording of the Code and the IRS forms) or is it $800,000? Because the AMT and regular tax are today the product of two parallel, but effectively separate income tax systems, the author would argue that the true AMT in Case B is $800,000, not $200,000.

Finally, since the AMT may be payable solely because of income timing differences, the Code includes an AMT credit mechanism. This credit avoids a double tax on the same income that is simply reported in different time periods under these two parallel income tax systems. The amount of the AMT credit is equal to the excess of the AMT (A) over the regular tax (R). Thus, in Case B of the example in the preceding paragraphs, the $200,000 excess can be carried forward and credited against (R) in any later year when (R) exceeds (A). No carry-*back* is permitted. This description of the AMT credit is grossly oversimplified; it ignores numerous adjustments that must be made in converting an excess of (A) over (R) into a tax credit. Nevertheless, it does serve to explain conceptually how Congress got around a sticky theoretical problem when it tightened the AMT rules as part of the 1986 Tax Reform Act.

## FACTORS OF SPECIAL IMPORTANCE TO CORPORATIONS

One tax adjustment unique to corporate taxpayers is destined to play a major role in our federal income tax law for years to come. It was identified earlier in this chapter simply as a "book-tax accounting difference."

The book-tax difference is the AMT adjustment that Congress put into the tax law largely in response to research reports revealing that several Fortune 500 companies paid little or no federal income tax, between 1981 and 1985, even though they reported sizable profits to their shareholders during those same years. Hence the adjustment provision requires that corporations include in AMTI one half of the excess of (1) an adjusted *pretax* financial statement or "book" income over (2) an adjusted AMTI. The idea is simple: no corporation will now be able to report substantial profits to shareholders, creditors, government agencies, and/or other interested parties, and, at the same time, report little or no income to the IRS.

The starting point for this adjustment is obviously "book income" as reported on some more or less formal financial statement; but which financial statement is to be used as the ultimate reference point? To answer that question, the Code provides the following priority list:

1. First, any income statement filed with the Securities and Exchange Commission (SEC).
2. Second, any income statement that has been audited and certified, by a CPA, for any substantial nontax purpose.
3. Third, any income statement that must be filed with a federal, state, or local government agency (other than the SEC).
4. Fourth, any income statement prepared for any substantial nontax purpose.

If a corporation has no income statement, or it has *only* a statement described in the fourth category, it may make an irrevocable election to use a tax concept known as earnings and profits (E & P) as its reference point.

For all years after 1989, the Code further provides that all corporations will use something new, called adjusted current earnings (ACE), as the ultimate reference point for making this same book-tax adjustment. The Treasury Department is supposed to issue regulations clarifying the ACE concept before 1990. In the interim years, for the first time in U.S. history, generally accepted accounting principles derived for financial accounting purposes may have a direct impact on the federal income tax liability of a corporation by operation of this AMT provision. Hence the age-old tendency of some corporations to report little or no taxable income, but a substantial amount of financial income for the same year, may come quickly to a halt.

Many knowledgeable observers fear that this intrusion of the federal income tax law into the standard-setting process of financial accounting will do great harm to financial reporting. They fear that the pressure to reduce corporate income taxes may compromise the evolution of standards that could more accurately report income for strictly financial purposes. In fact, the acceptance of ACE in 1990 and thereafter was, in large measure, an attempt by Congress to placate those who champion this position. Their refusal to make that change immediately and directly, however, is a good measure of the embarrassment that many in Congress felt toward our federal income tax system in 1985 and 1986.

The details of the numerous and sometimes extremely complex adjustments required to convert book income to adjusted financial statement income, and AMTI to adjusted AMTI, are once again left for reference works well beyond this introductory chapter. Suffice it to observe here that these required adjustments will sometimes include the elimination of income derived from foreign subsidiary corporations; the coordination of different fiscal years by related taxpayers; the correct treatment of dividends received from related domestic corporations; and other equally exotic and difficult accounting topics. It would be nearly impossible to overestimate the added complexity required by this one new rule alone. Hence many taxpayers and their advisers will continue to wonder if a better way couldn't have been found to deal with the perceived problem.

## FACTORS OF SPECIAL IMPORTANCE TO INDIVIDUALS

Another tax adjustment, this one unique to individual taxpayers, may also play a relatively important role in the AMT for the next few years. It was identified earlier in this chapter simply as an adjustment attributable to "passive activity losses." Chapter 8 explains both the history and the importance of the passive activity loss provisions. Although we will not repeat here much of the information included in that chapter, a few highlights may help the reader understand the role of this adjustment in the general scheme of the AMT.

Prior to 1986 many individuals who earned relatively large amounts of economic income were able to pay little or no federal income tax on that income because they invested in certain tax-sheltered investments. These tax-sheltered investments were deliberately arranged business ventures intended to throw off "paper" or "tax" losses during their first several years of operations. The paper losses from these investments would offset the taxpayer's taxable income from other sources. Once a successful investment began to produce taxable income, rather than paper losses, the taxpayer would invest still more capital in still bigger tax-sheltered investments and thus continue to avoid paying any income tax even though his or her economic income and net assets both continued to increase.

To stop this embarrassing parlay, Congress made many changes in the 1986 Tax Reform Act. Most importantly, perhaps, it enacted new rules to prohibit a taxpayer from offsetting certain losses (i.e., passive activity losses) from most other sources of income. Then, to decrease the retroactive quality of these harsh, new provisions, it turned around and allowed a partial deduction of those same losses against other income during a phase-in period (1987–1990). Finally, however, to be sure that it would not continue to be too embarrassed by the investors who earned large incomes, but somehow still managed to pay little or no taxes, Congress made the passive activity losses allowed by the transition rules a positive adjustment in the determination of AMTI. This is intended, obviously, to assure that these individual investors will also pay their fair share of the federal income tax.

One other adjustment that must be made in the calculation of an individual's AMTI, which has not yet been mentioned, is the add-back of many itemized deductions that a taxpayer can claim for regular income tax purposes. For AMT purposes only the following deductions *from* AGI are allowed: home mortgage interest; charitable contributions; medical expenses; casualty and theft losses; and gambling losses. Among the *disallowed* personal deductions, for AMT purposes, are: the state and local property and income tax deductions; the portion of consumer interest allowed for regular tax purposes under the phase-in rules; investment expenses; tax return preparation fees; the standard deduction; and personal exemptions.

## GENERAL CONCLUSIONS

It is too early to predict with much certainty exactly which or how many taxpayers will be subject to the AMT. From even this brief description of the general rules, however, it seems safe to conclude that many taxpayers will have to determine their federal income tax liability in two similar but separate ways before they can safely file their tax return for any year. Among the most obvious targets for this greatly expanded alternative minimum tax are:

1. Capital intensive businesses—whether or not incorporated—that report little or no regular taxable income, especially in the early years of their existence, because of large ACRS (i.e., depreciation) deductions.

2. Incorporated business ventures that report little or no regular taxable income, but whose ordinary financial statements reflect substantially greater profits.

3. Individual investors who continue to own tax-sheltered investments that produce substantial paper losses, even if the investor is now subject to more than a trivial amount of income tax determined in the regular way.

4. Taxpayers reporting any significant amount of income on the completed-contract method of accounting for regular tax purposes.

Although these may be among the more obvious candidates for the remodeled AMT, there will certainly be many others who are affected. Even those who are not directly subject to the payment of the AMT will be affected by the cost and difficulty of complying with these complex rules. The interaction between the regular tax and the AMT is nearly impossible to predict in many situations. Hence every taxpayer must now do tax planning with attention to both income tax systems concurrently.

Unfortunately, good tax planning becomes doubly complex in those years in which a taxpayer is subject to the AMT. Prior to the institution of the AMT credit, the general planning strategy under these circumstances was relatively straightforward. It usually called for the acceleration of income into, or the deferral of expenses from, an AMT year to a regular tax year because of the lower AMT rate. Today that same strategy may backfire because of the way the minimum tax credit is determined. If the AMT is attributable solely to exclusion preferences, or the marginal regular-tax rate is lower in the AMT year, the old strategy generally remains viable. If the AMT is attributable solely to deferral preferences, however, the old strategy may now serve only to accelerate taxes without decreasing the aggregate tax liability. If the AMT is atributable to both exclusion and deferral item—as it frequently will be— a skilled tax adviser must be engaged to determine if (and to what extent) income acceleration or expense deferal makes good tax sense. To fully understand the technical explanations which support the general conclusions suggested above requires that one understand the details of the minimum tax credit computation. That task is best left for those who must solve tax issues—not for those who only need to reognize them.

## PROBLEMS AND ASSIGNMENTS

1. Manny Hernandez, a married individual who files a joint return, has a net AMT tax liability of $10,750, allowable tax credits of $5,000, $10,000 of preferences, and $15,000 of positive adjustments. What is his taxable income?

2. Identify the following items as (1) an AMT adjustment (2) a preference item or (3) neither for an individual.
   a. ACRS depreciation on personal property.
   b. ACRS depreciation on realty.
   c. Income recognized under the completed-contract method.
   d. Income from private activity municipal bonds issued in 1990.
   e. Income from public activity municipal bonds issued in 1990.
   f. Percentage depletion in excess of cost basis.
   g. Income deferred using the cash method of accounting.

3. Janet Jones, a single individual, is considering contributing common stock with a basis of $2,000 and a value of $10,000 to her church in 1989. Janet's regular taxable income without regard to her contribution is $40,000. She has $36,000 of positive adjustments from depreciation. Assuming Janet itemizes her deductions, what would be the tax savings from the proposed contribution?

4. Ginshu Knives, Inc., had $1 million in taxable income before NOL carryover in 1989. Ginshu has no AMT adjustments or preference items. Ginshu has $2.5 million of NOL's (for either AMT or regular tax purposes) which could be carried to 1989. What is Ginshu's 1989 tax liability?

5. What is a married couple's alternative minimum tax if their AMTI before exemption is
   a. $100,000.
   b. $250,000.
   c. $400,000.

6. Le-Sung Ho's regular tax and AMT for 1991–1993 (before consideration of the AMT credit) are shown below.

| Year | Regular Tax | AMT |
|------|-------------|------|
| 1991 | $20,000 | $45,000 |
| 1992 | 25,000 | 20,000 |
| 1993 | 60,000 | 15,000 |

The differences between the regular tax and AMT is due to his use of the completed-contract method of accounting for regular tax purposes. What is Ho's tax liability in each year? What is the effect of the alternative minimum tax in this situation?

7. Prior to the Tax Reform Act of 1986, the alternative minimum tax for individuals usually came into play only when an individual had substantial capital gains and/or investment tax credits. The 1986 Act repealed both the investment credit and the preferential treatment of capital gains. Nevertheless, the alternative minimum tax will probably affect more taxpayers today than ever before. Why?

8. Alex Grant, a married taxpayer, had the following items of taxable income from his widget business (a proprietorship) and personal activities in 1989:

| | |
|---|---|
| Sales revenue | $1,250,000 |
| Cost of goods sold | 1,000,000 |
| Operating expenses | 150,000 |
| Depreciation | 80,000 (AMT depreciation is $50,000) |
| Dividend income | 50,000 |
| Home mortgage interest | 4,000 |
| State income tax | 2,000 |

Alex also received $20,000 in interest income from newly issued tax-exempt private activity bonds (face value $250,000, yielding 8 percent) and is entitled to two personal exemptions.

a. What is Alex's regular tax liability?

b. What is Alex's AMT liability?

c. What is Alex's aftertax rate of return on his municipal bonds?

9. Amazing Ronco Products, Inc., had the following items of income and expense for regular tax, AMT, and book purposes in 1989:

| | Regular Tax | AMT | Book |
|---|---|---|---|
| Sales revenue | $2,200,000 | $2,200,000 | $2,200,000 |
| Cost of goods sold | 1,700,000 | 1,700,000 | 1,700,000 |
| Operating expenses | 200,000 | 200,000 | 200,000 |
| Depreciation | 200,000 | 140,000 | 160,000 |
| Tax-exempt interest | –0– | –0– | 100,000 |
| Federal income tax provision | –0– | –0– | 40,000 |

The interest income is from a $1,250,000 public activity municipal bond yielding 8 percent.

a. Compute Ronco's regular tax liability.
b. Compute Ronco's AMT liability.
c. What would Ronco's tax liability be if it did not have the interest income?
d. Compute Ronco's aftertax rate of return on the bond for 1989 assuming the bond price is constant.

# Case 6–1

Unisynthesis, Inc. projects the following regular tax, AMT, and book income figures:

|  | Regular Tax | AMT | Book |
|---|---|---|---|
| Sales revenue | $2,800,000 | $2,800,000 | $2,800,000 |
| Cost of goods sold | 2,200,000 | 2,200,000 | 2,200,000 |
| Operating expenses | 300,000 | 300,000 | 300,000 |
| Depreciation | 250,000 | 170,000 | 200,000 |
| Federal tax provision | –0– | –0– | 7,500 |

Unisynthesis is considering three investments: a $1 million corporate bond yielding 11 percent; a newly issued $1 million private use municipal bond yielding 9 percent; and a $1 million public use municipal bond yielding 8 percent. Rank these investments in terms of their aftertax yield.

# Case 6–2

Good and Plenty, Inc. is a very successful food and beverage company owned by Gerry Good, age 50, and Peter Plenty, age 40. The success of the firm has been built largely on the extraordinary marketing ability of Mr. Good. Corporate profits (book and tax) after the bonuses paid to the owners have averaged $50,000 per year.

Both owners are concerned that the firm might be in grave difficulties if Mr. Good were to die in the next few years. They are considering purchasing a keyman life insurance policy on the life of Mr. Good. The corporation would own the policy and pay the premiums. If Mr. Good should die while the policy is in force, the policy would pay a death benefit of $1 million to the corporation.

Their insurance agent has told them that they can buy either a straight term life insurance policy for about $4,000 per year or a universal life insurance policy for about $10,000 per year. The term policy would build up no cash surrender value (CSV). The universal policy would increase in CSV each year and would have a CSV of approximately $40,000 after five years. The firm could borrow against this cash surrender value.

The annual increase in cash surrender value would be in the firm's book income, but not in its taxable income. The premiums paid under either policy would be included as an expense in the financial statements, but would not be deductible on the federal return.

a. Would there be any tax effect if Mr. Good dies after six years under either policy?

b. Would your answer (above) differ if the firm were a partnership?

# *Appendix to Chapter 6*

Among the more important changes in the AMT rules enacted in 1986 are those dealing with depreciation deductions stemming from both real and personal property acquired after 1986. In general, as explained in Chapter 10, the depreciation (or ACRS) deduction for personal property in the regular tax system is computed by applying a declining-balance depreciation method (usually double declining balance) over an estimated useful life that is significantly shorter than the more realistic useful life implied by the asset depreciation range (ADR) midpoint classification. Depreciation deductions for real estate acquired after 1986 are, in general, determined using a straight-line method over an estimated useful life of 27.5 or 31.5 years. For AMT purposes the longer ADR midpoint lives must be used and, in most instances, a less rapid depreciation method must also be applied. Table 6–1 summarizes the major differences between the ACRS deductions computed under the regular income tax provisions and those computed under the AMT rules.

To illustrate he numerical significance of these differences, assume that in 1988 a taxpayer invested $1 million in 7-year personal property and another $1 million in residential rental property. The 1989 ACRS deduction generated by those two investments for regular and AMT purposes would differ dramatically, as summarized below.

| Property | Regular Tax Deduction | AMT Deduction |
|---|---|---|
| 7-year property | $244,900 | $108,727 |
| Residential rental property | 36,400 | 25,000 |

**TABLE 6–1**   ACRS Deductions under Regular and AMT Provisions

| | Regular Tax | | AMT | |
| --- | --- | --- | --- | --- |
| Class of Property | Depreciation Method | Useful Life (years) | Depreciation Method | Average ADR Life (years) |
| Personal Property— | | | | |
| 3-year class | DDB* | 3 | 150% DB* | 4 |
| 5-year class | DDB | 5 | 150% DB | 7 |
| 7-year class | DDB | 7 | 150% DB | 13 |
| 10-year class | DDB | 10 | 150% DB | 18 |
| 15-year class | 150% DB | 15 | 150% DB | 23 |
| 20-year class | 150% DB | 20 | 150% DB | 25 |
| Real Property— Residential | | | | |
| rental | SL* | 27.5 | SL | 40 |
| Nonresidential | SL | 31.5 | SL | 40 |

*Note: DDB means double declining balance method; 150% DB means 150 percent declining balance method; and SL means straight-line method.

The potential impact of these differences for AMT purposes should be obvious. The aggregate ACRS deduction of approximately $280,000 for regular income tax purposes might very easily reduce this taxpayer's regular taxable income to little or nothing. The comparable deduction for AMT purposes, however, would approximate only $133,000. The $147,000 difference could help to trigger a substantial AMT, even though little or no regular income tax was payable.

The amount of gain (or loss) to be reported on the sale or exchange of a fixed asset will also differ substantially for regular and AMT purposes. To illustrate, assume that a $100,000 personal property in the 7-year class was sold for $50,000 sometime during the fourth year following its acquisition. Further assume that, for AMT purposes, this property had a 13-year ADR life. Given these assumptions, the gain (or loss) on the disposition of this property would be determined as follows:

| | Regular Tax | | AMT | |
| --- | --- | --- | --- | --- |
| Sales price | | $50,000 | | $50,000 |
| Original cost | $100,000 | | $100,000 | |
| Less ACRS claimed | 63,555 | | 39,408 | |
| Adjusted basis | | 36,445 | | 60,592 |
| Gain/(loss) | | $13,555 | | ($10,592) |

In this example the taxpayer would report a $13,555 gain on the sale of the property in the fourth year for regular tax purposes and a $10,592 loss on the same property for AMT purposes.

Incidentally, the method used to calculate the tax preference for AMT purposes differs importantly for properties acquired before 1987 compared to those acquired after 1986. The examples included in this appendix illustrate only the rules applicable to properties in the latter category. As a matter of fact, there was no AMT tax preference for *personal* properties, other than leased personal properties, prior to 1987. The difference applicable to leased personal properties and real properties acquired before 1987 are once again omitted from this brief overview.

# CHAPTER 7

# Capital Gains And Losses

Income taxes can be conceptually divided between unitary income tax systems and schedular income tax systems. A unitary income tax, at least in theory, brings together all of the income and deduction elements, recognized by each taxpayer during the year, and taxes the one, final, net amount utilizing a single set of prescribed tax rates. A schedular system of income taxation, by contrast, subdivides each taxpayer's income and deductions among a predetermined set of separate schedules and typically taxes the net balance reported on each separate schedule at different tax rates. For example, in a schedular system the net income from all wages and salaries might be subject to one set of tax rates; the net income from interest and dividends to a second set of rates; the net income from farming to a third set of rates; and net income from all other activities to a fourth set of tax rates.

The U.S. federal income tax is alleged to be a unitary tax system. So far as net gains are concerned, that categorization is essentially correct today. That is, each taxpayer generally combines all of the various positive elements of net income—from whatever sources derived—and taxes the grand total net income utilizing the one set of tax rates, described earlier in this text, applicable to that particular taxpayer. Losses from selected activities are, however, subject to numerous special limitations. To illustrate, let us assume that a U.S. taxpayer is engaged in four separate activities that are intended to be income-producing activities. In this year, however, assume that only two of the four activities produce net gains, while the other two activities produce net losses, in the following amounts:

| | |
|---|---|
| Activity #1 | $60,000 |
| Activity #2 | 50,000 |
| Activity #3 | (10,000) |
| Activity #4 | (30,000) |

If we can combine all four activities, to determine this imaginary taxpayer's net income, the result in a pure unitary system would obviously be a single $70,000 net income. To understand the current U.S. tax system, it is necessary that you understand that some portion or all of the losses generated by activities numbered three and four, in this example, may not be recognized in the current period. Thus, this imaginary taxpayer's income for tax purposes could be anything from as little as $70,000 to as much as $110,000 (if both losses are wholly disallowed). Because of these limitations, the U.S. income tax system really has some attributes more typical of a schedular system.

In this chapter we will examine one of the two most pervasive general loss limitation provisions in the U.S. Code. It applies to what is technically known as a net capital loss. The other important general loss limitation—applicable to passive-activity losses—will be explained in the next chapter.

## CAPITAL GAINS IN HISTORICAL PERSPECTIVE

Most U.S. taxpayers probably think of capital asset transactions as something beneficial or desirable for federal income tax purposes. That common perception is attributable to the fact that from 1922 until 1987 certain net capital gains were given preferential tax treatment. Although the precise details of the preference varied from year to year as well as from taxpayer to taxpayer, the overall effect was clearly beneficial in almost every instance. It will, therefore, be difficult for some persons to grasp the fundamental notion that under the tax laws in effect today, capital asset transactions can never result in good news, and may result in bad news, particularly when net capital losses exceed net capital gains for the year.

### A Word of Caution

When Congress was rewriting our income tax law in 1986, it deliberately elected to leave many of the old capital gain and loss provisions intact. It explained this decision by noting that it would make the reinstitution of capital gains benefits easier if, because of subsequent increases in the marginal tax rates on ordinary income, that option should once again become desirable in future years. This fact is important for at least two reasons. First, it partially explains why the rules that appear in the remaining pages of this chapter are so complex. Second, it should temper the taxpayer's natural instinct to argue now that all losses sustained stem from ordinary assets, rather than capital assets, if the definitional status of the asset is somewhat uncertain.

To illustrate, assume that taxpayer A, a practicing attorney, also sells four different parcels of land in 1990 for a net loss of $100,000. Assume also that the tax status of the land sold is somewhat uncertain: i.e., the taxpayer could defensibly argue that either the four properties were purchased and held (1) only with the intent to resell them as quickly as possible or (2) only as long-term investments. Under the former argument the $100,000 loss might be classified as an ordinary loss and, therefore, immediately deductible in full. Under the latter argument the $100,000 loss might be classified as a capital loss and, therefore, be limited to an immediate deduction of $3,000 (for reasons to be explained later in this chapter). Certainly the attorney would be inclined to make the former argument. To do so, however, might permanently identify the attorney as a dealer in land for all future years. And, if tax rates should rise and capital gain privileges should return, that classification could be detrimental. In summary, all taxpayers must exercise unusual care in reporting capital asset transactions during the next few years. No really intelligent choices can be made with much certainty until we have a better feeling for just how permanent the 1986 tax law revisions are likely to be.

## DEFINING THE BOUNDARIES

Most people believe that capital gains and losses are those gains and losses attributable to transactions involving either stocks and bonds or plant-and-equipment-type assets. This common belief is both incomplete and at least partially incorrect. Fortunately, however, we do not have one set of definitions for one kind of taxpayer and another set for another kind of taxpayer. For individual, fiduciary, and corporate taxpayers alike, a capital gain or loss is simply any gain or loss attributable to the sale or exchange of a capital asset. The real question, then, becomes one of defining a capital asset.

Surprising as it may seem, the code defines capital assets by exception. That is, the code states that *all assets are capital assets unless they are specifically excluded*. The list of excluded assets is initially both limited and surprising. It includes:

1. Inventory items, "or property held by the taxpayer primarily for sale to customers in the ordinary course of his trade or business."
2. Real or depreciable property used in a trade or business.
3. A copyright, a literary, musical, or artistic composition, a letter or memorandum, "or similar property," but only if such an asset is held either by the taxpayer who created it or by one who has assumed the tax basis of that creator—in the case of letters, memorandums, and similar property, the exception also applies to the person for whom it was prepared or produced.
4. Receivables acquired in a trade or business.
5. A few miscellaneous items of limited significance.

### Inventory Assets

The first group of assets excluded from the capital asset category—that is, inventory items—is self-explanatory. If such an exclusion were not made, all routine profits of a merchandising operation would be capital gains by definition. The only practical problem with this first exclusion is the difficulty in applying it to situations in which a taxpayer frequently, perhaps regularly, buys and sells certain assets, but this activity is not deemed to be the primary business activity of the taxpayer. A lawyer, for example, was surprised to discover that the IRS and the courts found that his dealings in real estate constituted a trade or business even though he did not have a broker's license and did not take an active part in the sales activity. The court found that the frequency and the substantial nature of this activity were sufficient to sustain the IRS contention that such purchases and sales did constitute a trade or business, and that the profits were, therefore, ordinary income from the sale of real estate held primarily for sale rather than capital gains from investments. Just why this same criterion should not be applied to nonbroker investors who are heavily engaged in stock market transactions is not at all clear. Suffice it to say that the frequency criterion has not generally been applied when the asset in question was a security, although the literal wording of the code makes no such distinction. The IRS and the courts seem to have implicitly adopted a hands-off attitude in applying the primarily-for-resale test inherent in the capital asset definition to securities for reasons known only to themselves. Only regular securities dealers realize ordinary income from trading transactions. With this notable exception, however, the reader should understand that there is absolutely nothing inherent in any particular kind of property that makes it capital or noncapital. That definitional result is based solely on the relationship between the taxpayer and the property: If an asset is held primarily for resale in the ordinary course of a trade or business, it is not a capital asset for that particular taxpayer. And any one taxpayer can be engaged in multiple trades or businesses at the same time.

## Real or Depreciable Property Used in a Trade or Business

The second group of assets excluded from the capital asset category—that is, real or depreciable property used in a trade or business—is probably the most surprising entry in the list of noncapital assets. If the exclusion were applied without further modification, this would mean that all profits and losses from the sale of plant-and-equipment-type assets would be ordinary income or loss by definition. Stated in another way, it would mean that any profit on the sale of farmland by a farmer or a rancher, or the sale of a factory by a manufacturing corporation, or the sale of a cash register by a retail business, would be categorized as ordinary income. There are several additional sets of rules that modify this conclusion in varying circumstances.

Before we concern ourselves with those modifications, we should observe that *this exclusion applies to either real or depreciable property, but only if such property is used in a trade or business.* When the adjective *real* is used to modify the noun *property,* the expression generally means land and anything permanently attached to land. Thus the term *real property* would include most buildings and building components, a lot of heavy equipment, and fences, tanks, tracks, and other assets permanently attached to the earth, directly or indirectly. The adjective *depreciable* tries to distinguish a wasting asset from a nonwasting asset. Any property, whether realty or nonrealty, that will deteriorate over time can be considered a depreciable property. In this context, however, the code has reference to more than this physical wasting characteristic. The term *depreciable property* as used here demands wasting plus a profit motive. Thus a taxpayer's personal residence would *not* constitute a depreciable property for purposes of this definition because no profit motive is present in the taxpayer's owership of that house. A single dwelling rented by a taxpayer to another person for a reasonable rent, however, generally constitutes a depreciable property, since the code permits that taxpayer to claim a depreciation deduction against the income derived from the property. Note that a property can be depreciable, then, without being part of a trade or business. When we classify an item for tax purposes from a profit motivation standpoint, we utilize a trichotomy, which includes (1) a full-fledged trade or business class, (2) a profit-oriented, but less than trade or business status, and (3) a wholly personal or not-for-profit category. This definitional distinction is diagramed in Figure 7–1. The term *nonbusiness* is often used in tax matters to describe something held for profit, but not classifiable as a full-fledged trade or business. The definitional distinctions are sometimes very hazy, even though the distinction may be critical to the capital asset definition. Returning to our earlier illustration, if a taxpayer rents a single dwelling unit to another party and this rental activity is not deemed to constitute a trade or business, the rented unit remains a capital asset since the statutory exception applies only to real or depreciable properties *used in a trade or business.*

A book devoted to tax-planning ideas is not an appropriate place to review all of the complex rules that modify the ultimate tax treatment of even the most straightforward trade or business-type asset. Given our objective, it seems more appropriate to provide some summary statements that will usually be correct and then to remind the reader that these statements should not be used in actual circumstances without first verifying their applicability in those specific settings. Table 7–1 summarizes, correctly in most circumstances, the present tax treatment of the gain and loss realized on the sale or

**FIGURE 7–1**

exchange of a real or depreciable property used in a trade or business. The reference to Section 1231 gain or loss in Table 7–1 obviously requires an explanation.

**TABLE 7–1**    The Usual Tax Treatment of Gain or Loss Realized on the Sale or Exchange of Real or Depreciable Property Used in a Trade or Business

| Kind of Property | If Result Is Gain | If Result Is Loss |
|---|---|---|
| 1. Depreciable "personalty" (that is, nonrealty) such as a business car and factory or office equipment | Usually ordinary income* | Sec. 1231 loss |
| 2. Land | Sec. 1231 gain | Sec. 1231 loss |
| 3. Depreciable "realty" *other than* an apartment house or other residential rental property if— | | |
| a. Acquired *before* 1981 *and a—* | | |
| (1) Rapid depreciation method was used | Partially or wholly ordinary income† | Sec. 1231 loss |
| (2) Straight-line depreciation method was used | Sec. 1231 gain | Sec. 1231 loss |
| b. Acquired *after* 1980 but before 1987 and— | | |
| (1) ACRS tables were used to determine the depreciation (or capital recovery allowance) | Partially or wholly ordinary income‡ | Sec. 1231 loss |
| (2) Straight-line method was used to determine the capital recovery allowance | Sec. 1231 gain | Sec. 1231 loss |
| c. Acquired *after* 1986 | Sec. 1231 gain | Sec. 1231 loss |
| 4. Depreciable apartment house or other residential rental property (*excluding* low-income housing) if— | | |
| a. Acquired after 1975 but before 1987 and either (1) a rapid depreciation method or (2) the ACRS tables were used to determine the depreciation/capital recovery allowance | Partially or wholly ordinary income† | Sec. 1231 loss |
| b. Acquired on any date and the straight-line method was used to determine the depreciation/capital recovery allowance | Sec. 1231 gain | Sec. 1231 loss |

*Gain to extent of any depreciation previously claimed will be ordinary income; any remainder, Sec. 1231 gain. See Code Sec. 1245.

†Gain to extent of "*excess*" depreciation will be ordinary income; any remainder, Sec. 1231 gain. See Code Sec. 1250. (Special rules apply to corporate taxpayers.)

‡Gain to extent of any capital recovery allowance claimed will be ordinary income; any remainder, Sec. 1231 gain. See Code Sec. 1245. (Special rules apply to corporate taxpayers.)

Section 1231 is a very peculiar part of our income tax law. In effect, it provides that specified items shall be brought together and their ordinary or capital character held in suspense until the end of the year when a net result can be determined. If the net result of all Section 1231 transactions is a loss, each of the items is treated as if it involved a noncapital asset; if the net result of all Section 1231 transactions is a gain, each of the items *may* be treated as if it involved a long-term capital asset, unless "excess" Section 1231 losses— i.e., Section 1231 losses in excess of Section 1231 gains were claimed in the prior five years. From a tax-planning standpoint, ordinary losses are always preferred to equivalent amounts of capital losses.

Combining this terse explanation of Section 1231 with Table 7–1, we should note that a taxpayer may recognize capital gains from the sale or exchange of depreciable real property used in a trade or business. The like- lihood of this result is increased if the gain is attributable to the sale or exchange of land, or if the taxpayer claimed only straight-line depreciation on depreciable real property before it was sold or exchanged. Suffice it to note here that the exclusion of property used in a trade or business from the capital asset definition does not always mean that transactions involving such assets will necessarily produce ordinary income or loss. As suggested in Table 7–1, capital gain is still possible if the gain can be attributed either (1) to land or (2) to certain buildings.

### Copyrights and Similar Properties

The third group of assets excluded from the capital asset category includes copyrights, literary, musical, or artistic compositions, letters, memorandums, and similar property. The rationale for the exclusion of most of these items turned on the belief that under prior law, taxpayers should not have been able to reap the rewards of their individual efforts in the form of a capital gain just because those efforts culminated in the production of a property. The potential inequity between a taxpayer who rendered a personal service without the production of a property (for example, a physician, an accountant, or salesclerk) and a taxpayer whose service produced a property (for example, an author, a composer, or an artist) would have been tremendous under prior law except for this rule. The obvious failure to include patents in this list of noncapital assets is notable. Congress apparently believed that it was pref- erable for our citizens to tinker and to invent machines than to spend time in other creative ways. At least the substantial tax reward of a capital gain was retained solely for such activities for many years.

The exclusion of letters and memorandums is closely related to the tax rules applicable to the charitable contribution deduction. Without explaining these rules here, we might note that the important result of this exclusion is to deny a taxpayer a sizable tax deduction for any gift of property that would produce ordinary income if sold. As specifically applied to letters and mem- orandums, this means that all U.S. presidents taking office after Lyndon

Johnson have been denied a substantial tax deduction for the value of the many papers they typically donate to their presidential libraries.

Note that this third category of exclusions usually applies only to persons who create the property, or to those who receive it as a gift from such persons. If a taxpayer purchases a copyright or a literary, musical, or artistic composition from the creator, that property may be a capital asset for the purchaser. Whether or not it will, depends largely on the reason for acquiring the asset and the way it is used after acquisition. If the property was purchased with the intention of reselling it in the ordinary course of business, or if it becomes a depreciable property used in a trade or business, it will remain a noncapital asset. If, on the other hand, the purchase was made as an investment or for personal enjoyment, it will become a capital asset of the purchaser.

### Other Exceptions

Accounts and notes receivable are generally not considered to be capital assets for the same reasons that inventory assets are excluded from the capital asset definition. If the receivables are derived from the ordinary conduct of a trade or business, any gain or loss on the disposition of the receivables should be treated in the same way that the income produced by those receivables would be treated. The exception of receivables from the capital asset definition effectively accomplishes this result.

In summarizing this portion of Chapter 7, we should remember that the capital or noncapital status of any asset is determined by the relationship between the asset and the taxpayer. There is no inherent characteristic in a property that leads to a correct classification. For example, a car would be a noncapital asset to an automobile dealer because it is part of the inventory; it might also be a noncapital asset to a contractor, who uses it entirely for trade or business; but it would be a capital asset to a taxpayer who uses it solely for purposes of personal enjoyment. Actually a single property may be both a capital and a noncapital asset. If, for example, a physician used a car 80 percent of the time for business purposes and 20 percent of the time for personal purposes, that car would be both capital (20 percent) and noncapital (80 percent). The importance of the definition of a capital asset, and the complications it can create, will be demonstrated after we investigate further the rules associated with the measurement of a capital gain or loss.

## MEASURING A CAPITAL GAIN OR LOSS

The amount of a capital gain or loss is simply the difference between (*a*) the amount realized on the sale or exchange of a capital asset and (*b*) the basis of the capital asset surrendered. The amount realized is, in turn, the sum of (1) any cash received, (2) the fair market value of any noncash property received, and (3) the amount of any liability that the buyer assumes from the seller. To illustrate, assume that in 19x1 a taxpayer purchased, solely for investment purposes, a parcel of land for $50,000, paying $10,000 down and assuming a $40,000 mortgage for the balance. If the taxpayer sold the land in 19x6 for (1) $30,000 cash, (2) a boat worth $25,000, and (3) the purchaser's assumption of the $20,000 mortgage that remained outstanding against the property, the selling taxpayer would realize a long-term capital gain of $25,000. The amount realized would be $75,000 (that is, $30,000 + $25,000 + $20,000), and the adjusted basis of the property surrendered would be $50,000 (the original cost of the land). The difference of $25,000 represents the taxpayer's capital gain.

In the real world, of course, it may not be easy to determine the fair market value of many properties. A determination of that value is, nevertheless, necessary to the measurement of the gain or loss realized, and the IRS and the courts generally insist that taxpayers make such a determination immediately. In some situations the tax authorities will infer the value of the more-difficult-to-value property on the basis of an easier-to-value property, believing that a taxpayer would not engage in an arm's length sale or exchange of the two properties if those values were not equal. To return to the illustration in the prior paragraph, if the value of the boat received in that exchange were difficult to determine, but the value of the land surrendered were easier to determine, the IRS and the courts would not hesitate to infer the $25,000 fair market value for the boat if they could readily determine that the land was worth $75,000 at the date of the exchange.

Another difficult problem in measuring a capital gain or loss involves the determination of the tax basis of the capital asset surrendered. This difficulty is attributable to the fact that the basis rules differ depending upon the way in which a taxpayer acquired the capital asset. One set of basis rules is applicable to purchased property, another set to property acquired by gift, another set to inherited property, and yet another to property acquired in a nontaxable exchange. The first three of these four sets of rules are considered here; the basis rules applicable to property acquired in a nontaxable exchange are deferred to Chapter 11.

### The Tax Basis of Purchased Property

The tax basis of purchased property is generally equal to its cost plus the cost of any subsequent capital improvements, less the amount of depreciation (or other capital cost recovery deduction) claimed for tax purposes. The term *cost* includes both the basic purchase price and all associated costs necessary to acquire the asset and make it operative. Thus, the cost of a security includes the broker's commission; the cost of equipment includes the freight and installation charges that may be incurred before the equipment can be put to its intended use; and the cost of land may include fees paid to real estate agents and lawyers. If a taxpayer purchases more than one asset for a single purchase price, the total cost must be allocated among the assets acquired. This allocation is based on relative fair market values.

After an asset is acquired, and before it is sold or exchanged, a taxpayer typically incurs numerous costs to keep it going. Any costs that do not extend the original estimated life of a depreciable asset are usually treated as current expenses and (if authorized) deducted immediately for tax purposes. Costs that extend a property's original life, or improve it in some material way, are called capital expenditures, which simply means that at the time they are incurred they are properly charged to the asset account rather than to an expense account. Because of the time preference value of money, a taxpayer typically wants to expense everything (and thereby reduce an income tax liability) as soon as possible; the IRS agent seems to think that everything should be capitalized. The distinction between an expense and a capital expenditure is sometimes very hazy; in such instances, tax disputes are commonplace.

The portion, if any, of a fixed asset's cost that may be deducted (or "recovered") in any particular tax year changed significantly in 1981 and again in 1986. Before 1981, the depreciation deduction rules controlled that determination. After 1980, ACRS (accelerated cost recovery system) rules applied. These concepts are sufficiently complex to justify a separate discussion in Chapter 10. For our immediate purposes—the quantification of a capital gain or loss—we will avoid any problems associated with determining which costs must be capitalized and how large a deduction can be claimed, so that we may concentrate on the problems peculiar to the measurement of a capital gain or loss.

To summarize and illustrate the rules applicable to the determination of the tax basis of purchased property, consider the plight of a taxpayer who purchased land and a building in 19x1 and sold that same property in 19x9 if, during the interim period, this taxpayer incurred the following expenditures or charges:

| | |
|---|---:|
| Initial purchase price | $400,000 |
| Legal fee associated with title search made at purchase date | 10,000 |
| Capital improvement to building made three years after purchase | 80,000 |
| Cost of routine repairs, taxes, and so on during ownership | 120,000 |
| Cost recovery deductions claimed on building during ownership | 100,000 |

Before this taxpayer can determine the amount of gain or loss on the sale made in 19x9, it is necessary to determine the tax basis of the assets sold. This begins with a separation of the initial purchase price of $400,000 between land and buildings. Assuming that the taxpayer has good evidence of their relative fair market values, $300,000 might be allocated to the building and $100,000 to the land. Questions then arise concerning the $10,000 legal fee: Must this cost be capitalized, or could the taxpayer deduct that expenditure in 19x1? If the legal fee must be capitalized, should the cost be divided between the land and the building, or is it entirely allocable to the land? The answers to those questions are not obvious, but further investigation would probably substantiate the conclusion that the legal fee would have to be capitalized and that it should be allocated entirely to the land. Capital improvements would be added to the basis of the building; routine costs would be deducted as they were incurred. In summary, then, this taxpayer could determine the tax basis of the assets in 19x9, as follows:

$$\text{Building: } \$300{,}000 + \$80{,}000 - \$100{,}000 = \$280{,}000$$
$$\text{Land: } \$100{,}000 + \$10{,}000 \qquad\qquad = \$110{,}000$$

If the taxpayer sold the land and building for $600,000 and at the time of the sale $200,000 was properly allocated to the land and $400,000 to the building, a gain of $90,000 on the land and $120,000 on the building would have been realized. By reviewing the way the taxpayer utilized this building and by reference to the rules implicit in Table 7–1, the taxpayer could finally determine the correct tax treatment of the $210,000 gain.

## The Tax Basis of Property Acquired by Gift

The tax basis of property acquired by gift is usually either (a) the donor's cost basis or (b) the fair market value of the property on the date acquired. The tax basis of property acquired by gift will be the donor's cost unless the fair market value of the property on the date the gift is made is lower than that cost. In the event that the fair market value is lower than the donor's cost on the date of the gift, the basis of the property cannot be determined until the donee finally disposes of the property. In this latter instance, if the donee eventually sells the property for less than the fair market value on the day the property was received, the basis becomes the value on the day it was received; if the donee eventually sells the property for more than the donor's original cost, the basis becomes the donor's cost; if the donee sells the property for any value between the value on the day it was received and the donor's cost, the basis is equal to the value on the date sold.

These rules may seem unduly complex, and they probably are. However, they become easier to remember and to apply if the reader will only observe that the one thing the tax law will *not* tolerate is passing a paper loss to a donee in a high tax bracket. In other words, if a taxpayer purchased a stock for $100,000 and that stock declined in value to $60,000, the law would not permit the original owner to transfer this $40,000 paper loss to another tax-payer in a higher marginal tax bracket prior to selling it. If the taxpayer gave the stock away and the donee sold the stock immediately after receiving it, the basis would have become $60,000 and thus the donee would not realize any loss on the sale (that is, $60,000 amount realized less $60,000 basis). On the other hand, observe that the law will not penalize the donee who waits and sells the shares at a date when their value has returned to something more than the donor's cost basis of $100,000. In that situation the donee's basis reverts to $100,000 and the gain is calculated from that value. If the donee sells for any price between $60,000 and $100,000, the tax rules essentially tell the taxpayer to forget it—there is neither gain nor loss to report.

Observe again that the critical fact that initially determines the tax basis of property acquired by gift is the relationship between the donor's cost and the fair market value on the date a gift is made. If the fair market value on the date of the gift is equal to or greater than the donor's cost, the donee's basis will under all possible circumstances remain the donor's cost—subject only to a relatively minor modification if the donor pays a gift tax on the transfer. As a practical matter, a taxpayer should only rarely make a gift of property that has decreased in value since it was purchased. To do so risks the possibility that an income tax loss may go forever unrecognized by anyone. Some of the important tax-saving opportunities that remain because of the basis rules will be discussed in later chapters.

### The Tax Basis of Inherited Property

The basis of inherited property to the heir or devisee is determined by one of three rules. Generally, it is equal to the fair market value of the property on the date of the decedent's death. An exception to that general rule applies if the executor or executrix elects to value the decedent's property for estate tax purposes on the alternate valuation date. Stated briefly, the administrator of the estate may have an option to value the deceased's estate either on the date of death or exactly six months after death. If the administrator elects the latter date, then the heir or devisee who eventually receives the property must also take, as his or her basis, the fair market value of the property six months after the decedent's death. In the rare case in which the administrator elects the alternate valuation date but distributes a particular piece of property prior to that date, the property so distributed will take as its basis the fair market value on the date of distribution. To summarize: (1) the basis of any inherited property is generally its fair market value on the date of the decedent's death; (2) an exception exists for any property included in an estate for which the administrator elects the alternate valuation date—in this special case, the basis of any inherited property is the value of the property six months after the decedent's death; and (3) if the administrator elects the alternate value date *and also* distributes a property prior to that date, then for any property so distributed the heir's basis is the fair market value of the property on the date distributed.

For income tax planning purposes the significance of the rule just stated can hardly be overemphasized. Note that no one ever pays the *income tax* on the appreciation in the value of the property that is retained by its owner until death. Any heir can sell inherited property immediately after receiving it and report absolutely no gain or loss! If the deceased taxpayer had sold or exchanged the same property prior to death, any previous appreciation in value between the date of purchase and the date of sale would be subject to the income tax. In addition, the administrator of the decedent's subsequent estate would still have to pay the estate tax on the aftertax proceeds realized on the sale or exchange. Thus the tendency to retain appreciated assets and to allow them to pass through a decedent's estate is very great for persons of substantial means. This strong tendency is commonly referred to as the "locked-in effect." The lock-in has obvious reference to the wealthy, older person who feels that it would be unwise to dispose of an appreciated asset prior to death because of the extra tax that would be imposed on that disposition. People of less means have, of course, more limited opportunities. Very often they must dispose of the few appreciated properties that they have prior to death simply to live decently during their retirement years.

Application of the basis rules for property acquired by gift and for inherited property is important to family tax-planning ideas. The possible tax savings will be explained in Chaper 14, after we have reviewed the rules common to gift and estate taxes. For the moment, it is sufficient to observe that the income tax can be permanently avoided by application of the basis rules for inherited property, but that it cannot be avoided by the basis rules for property transferred by gift. Since a donee can never get a basis higher than a donor's cost (except for minor increases due to the gift tax), a donee will eventually recognize the income implicit in appreciated property that is made part of a gift.

## THE TAX TREATMENT OF NET CAPITAL LOSSES

If a taxpayer realizes in the aggregate more capital losses than capital gains in any particular year, special tax rules come into play. Unfortunately, the rules for individual and fiduciary taxpayers differ from the rules for corporate taxpayers. We will review the rules applicable to individual and fiduciary taxpayers first and then consider the corporate rules.

### Individual and Fiduciary Taxpayers

An individual or fiduciary taxpayer who realizes in the aggregate more capital losses than capital gains in any single year, must offset a maximum of $3,000 of such losses against ordinary income in that year. What happens, however, if the taxpayer's aggregate net capital losses exceed the $3,000 maximum?

In the case of individual and fiduciary taxpayers, any capital losses in excess of the maximum $3,000 that may be offset against ordinary income can only be carried *forward* and offset against the taxable income of future years. There is no dollar limit on the amount of capital losses that can be offset against capital gains in either the current or future years. If, however, a capital loss is carried forward and the taxpayer does not realize sufficient capital gains in the next year to offset such a carry-forward, he or she once again is limited in the next year to a maximum $3,000 offset against ordinary income. All remaining losses are carried to later years until they have finally been utilized or the taxpayer dies.

### Corporate Taxpayers

If a corporation realizes in the aggregate more capital losses than it does capital gains in a single year, it cannot offset any of that capital loss against its ordinary income. However, the corporation can carry that loss *back* and offset it against any capital gain it reported in the third prior tax year. If the capital gains in that year are insufficient to absorb the current year's capital loss, the excess is carried to the second prior year and, if necessary, to the last taxable year. If the total capital loss in the current year exceeds the amount of capital gain reported by the corporation in the three prior years, any balance can be carried forward and offset against capital gains realized in the next five years. If the loss has not been utilized by the end of the fifth subsequent year, it expires without tax benefit. If a corporation has capital-loss carryforwards from more than one year, they will be exhausted on a FIFO (first-in, first-out) basis.

## A WORD OF CAUTION

The actual tax rules applied to the sale of many assets are not as simple as they may seem. Consider the tax consequences attaching to the disposition of an automobile by a taxpayer who had used that automobile 80 percent of the time in business and 20 percent of the time in personal use from the date of acquisition until the date of disposition. If we assume that the taxpayer-owner originally paid $8,000 for the car, subsequently deducted a total of $5,800 of the original cost for tax purposes, and finally sold it for $2,000, we might be tempted to conclude that there was a $200 loss on the sale ($2,000 amount realized − $2,200 adjusted basis) and that $160 of this loss (80 percent × $200) was ordinary loss and $40 (20 percent × $200) was capital loss. Such a conclusion would be incorrect under the circumstances described. Tax rules essentially view this transaction as involving two entirely separate assets, one capital and the other noncapital. The correct calculation of gain and loss is shown in the table on p. 136.

To the dismay of the taxpayer, the correct determination of the tax consequences of this simple transaction would produce a $1,000 ordinary income and a nondeductible $1,200 capital loss! The tax treatment of the $1,000 gain is determined by the basic tax rules implicit in the preparation of Table 7–1. Those rules provide that any gain on the sale of depreciable nonrealty used in a trade or business will probably be ordinary income. The correct tax treatment of the $1,200 loss is derived from the basic rules stated in Chapter 2. It was noted there that all income is taxable income unless the taxpayer can find some authority to exclude it; on the other hand, nothing is deductible unless the taxpayer can find some authority that makes it deductible. Search as he may, except in the case of casualty losses, the taxpayer will find no authority for the deduction of any loss incurred in the sale or exchange of purely personal assets. In other words, if a taxpayer sells a personal residence, car, or clothing at a profit, he or she must pay tax on that profit as a capital gain. However, if the taxpayer sells a personal residence, car, or clothing at a loss, such a loss is properly classified as a capital loss; but more importantly, it constitutes a capital loss for which no tax deduction can be claimed since no code section authorizes the deduction of losses from the sale or exchange of purely personal assets. As explained in Chapter 2, losses arising from the sale of specific properties are deductible if attributable to (1) properties used in a trade or business or (2) nonbusiness properties (that is, income-producing properties that do not constitute a trade or business), but not if attributable to purely personal properties. The only exception for purely personal properties applies to possible casualty and theft loss deductions. In our illustration, no casualty was involved in the sale of the car for $2,000, and therefore the $1,200 loss attributable to the 20 percent of the car used for personal reasons would not be deductible.

| | Noncapital Portion (80 percent business use) | Capital Portion (20 percent personal use) | Total (100 percent) |
|---|---|---|---|
| Original cost | $6,400 | $1,600 | $8,000 |
| Less cost recovered | 5,800 | 0* | 5,800 |
| Adjusted basis on sale | $ 600 | $1,600 | $2,200 |
| Amount realized | $1,600 | $ 400 | $2,000 |
| Less adjusted basis | 600 | 1,600 | 2,200 |
| Gain or (loss) realized | $1,000 | ($1,200) | ($ 200) |

*Personal-use assets are not depreciable for tax purposes because they are not income-producing.

Suppose that the taxpayer had converted the car from 20 percent personal use to 100 percent personal use for one week preceding the disposition at $2,000. Would this change in use for one week magically transform the classification of the transaction to one solely involving a personal property and thereby get rid of the $1,000 ordinary gain that otherwise would attach to the 80 percent of the car that had been used previously for business purposes? Anyone familiar with the tax game would immediately predict that such a simple tax plan would fail, either because of a specific Code section or on some rather nebulous judicial doctrine. On numerous occasions, the courts have not hesitated to look through a "rigged" transaction to find either that the transaction had no "business purpose" or that "form should give way to substance" in tax matters. When a court makes this finding, it usually is trying to find good authority for ignoring the code as it is literally written and to apply it as Congress probably intended it to be applied. The interesting aspect of such nebulous judicial doctrines is that they are not applied consistently and that taxpayers can help to improve their chances for nonapplication of such judicial rules by slightly modifying their own behavior.

Returning to our illustration of the car sold for $2,000 just one week after it had been converted to wholly personal use, we might note that the most questionable aspect of that transaction was the short time period that elapsed between the date of the alleged conversion from 20 percent to 100 percent personal use and the date of disposition. If the taxpayer had allowed one year rather than one week to elapse, several things would have happened. Most important, perhaps, the time lapse would have provided evidence that the conversion in use was "real," or "had substance," beyond its obvious tax-saving result. It is likely that this difference would have been sufficient to convince any court that such judicial doctrines as "substance over form" or "business purpose" were not applicable to this transaction. A favorable tax result would also have been buttressed by the fact that values would have changed sufficiently during the intervening time period to make any allocation of earlier and undetermined amounts difficult if not impossible—an interesting corollary of the realization criterion.

This illustration could easily be dismissed as unimportant because of the small dollar amounts involved. Such a peremptory dismissal would be unwise. The same principle can sometimes be applied in circumstances in which larger sums are involved. Consider, for example, the plight of the taxpayer who purchased a personal residence for $80,000 and found a few years later that the home has decreased in value so that it could be sold only if the taxpayer were willing to realize a nondeductible loss on the sale. Instead, this taxpayer might convert the former home to a rental property and then, some years afterward, proceed to sell it and thereby try to convert a nondeductible personal loss to a deductible loss on rent-producing property. In this instance, the tax rules have specifically attempted to preclude the deduction of such a loss by providing that the tax basis on the date of conversion from a personal residence to a rental property must be the *lower* of (*a*) the owner's cost or (*b*) the fair market value on the date of the conversion in use. The only fact that works to the taxpayer's benefit in this circumstance is that fair market values are exceedingly difficult to determine, especially retroactively, and the taxpayer may be able to achieve the intended objective if he or she (*a*) is sufficiently patient and allows a reasonable time to lapse before realizing any loss, and (*b*) is sufficiently adamant in maintaining a position on assumed fair market values at the earlier date. At least the taxpayer has given the real economic facts a maximum opportunity to become sufficiently confused so that a revenue agent might be persuaded to yield on a debatable point that the agent recognizes as a distinct risk if the controversy proceeds to judicial settlement. Finally, even if the taxpayer cannot convince the revenue agent that the contention is reasonable, a court or jury has been given potential grounds on which to render a decision favorable to the taxpayer.

### Three Additional Rules

Although there are many other rules that we could study in conjunction with this introduction to the world of capital gains and losses, three specific rules appear to be of continuing interest to a large number of investors. We will, therefore, dismiss from our consideration all of the additional rules except those dealing with wash sales, short sales, and Section 1244 stock.

**Wash Sales.** If a taxpayer purchases "substantially identical securities" within 30 days before or after selling a security, that sale will be classified as a wash sale. The tax law disallows any *loss* recognized in a wash sale; it says nothing about gains recognized in wash sales.

To understand the potential consequences of the wash sale rule, consider the plight of a taxpayer who has already recognized $60,000 in capital gains and $20,000 in capital losses during the year. Near the end of the year it would be prudent for the taxpayer to review his or her security portfolio in an attempt to identify additional stocks with paper losses—i.e., stocks whose current fair market value is less than cost—for potental sale before the end of the year. Ideally this taxpayer would find and sell stocks with a total paper loss of $43,000. That action would completely wipe out the $40,000 net capital gain that otherwise would have to be added to ordinary income and, in addition, would provide the taxpayer with an extra $3,000 deduction. This tax planning will work perfectly so long as the taxpayer does not purchase stock substantially identical to that sold within 30 days before or after making the sale. If the taxpayer did make such a purchase, the loss associated with that stock would not be recognized for federal income tax purposes.

To illustrate the potential benefit of a wash sale resulting in a gain, consider the plight of a taxpayer who has realized a capital gain of $20,000 and a capital loss of $60,000 in a given year. If this taxpayer does nothing further before the end of the year, the gain of $20,000 will be offset by the loss of $60,000, leaving a net $40,000 capital loss. Only $3,000 of that loss could be offset against the taxpayer's ordinary income; the remaining $37,000 would have to be carried forward to future years. If this taxpayer has $37,000 in potential or "paper" capital gains that could be realized, this would be an ideal time to do so. He or she could sell the shares with the paper gain and immediately repurchase them if that were deemed desirable. Such a transaction would cost the taxpayer only the broker's fee in exchange for the right to immediately offset the $40,000 of previously realized capital loss against potential capital gain. By doing this the taxpayer would have increased his or her tax basis in the shares repurchased; hence any sale at a later date would be made with much less concern for tax consequences since a good part of the total gain would already have been absorbed.

**Short Sales.**    Taxpayers occasionally will discover that they have already so arranged their affairs that they are in the most desirable tax position, but their prediction of future economic events is such that they would very much like to "freeze" a particular economic gain or loss in the current year. If such a taxpayer proceeds to freeze this gain or loss in the usual manner, this action will upset the already arranged preferable tax position. To illustrate, suppose that a taxpayer had already realized $80,000 in net capital gains and has no "paper losses" available to offset the gain. The taxpayer may be willing to pay the income tax on the $80,000 capital gain, but he or she may also have an additional $60,000 potential gain, which must be realized very soon if it is not to be lost, but the taxpayer is unwilling to pay the tax on the additional $60,000 gain at this time. Furthermore, the taxpayer is aware that if he or she does realize this gain, there are no paper losses immediately available to offset it.

Under the conditions just described, this taxpayer is a prime candidate for a "short sale against the box." A simple *short sale* involves the sale of something a person does not own. In the case of short sales of securities, the broker typically borrows the shares sold short for the seller, and at some future date the seller goes into the market and purchases the shares sold earlier and delivers those shares to the broker to "cover" the prior short position. If the value of the shares decreases in the interim, the seller obviously profits on the transaction, because he or she was able to sell for more than cost. If the value of the shares increases between the two dates, the seller obviously loses, having sold for less than he or she eventually paid.

The tax magic of the short sale is due entirely to noneconomic factors. The pertinent question involves the selection of a date that must control for tax *reporting* purposes. Two dates are potential candidates: the controlling date might be the date of the short sale (that is, the date on which the seller had the broker sell short), or it might be the date on which the short sale was covered (that is, the date on which the seller purchased and delivered to the broker the shares borrowed in the interim period). In a pure short sale, the amount of the gain or loss cannot, of course, be determined until the cover date. Therefore, the tax rules provide that the cover date will control for purposes of determining the correct year of reporting gain or loss.

One final twist must be clarified before we can solve this taxpayer's problem. A short sale against the box is like a pure short sale except that in this instance the seller already owns what is purportedly sold short. However, the seller allows the broker to go out and borrow the stock temporarily, and only after the new year has dawned does the seller deliver the original shares to the broker to cover the short sale. By application of the short-sale rules, this taxpayer has been able to defer the recognition of a $60,000 gain into the next taxable year by withholding delivery of the shares against the earlier short sale. Through this simple device, the taxpayer has maintained a desirable tax position and put the additional short-term gain into a new tax year. This adds an entire year during which the taxpayer can again offset the gain in the most appropriate manner.

**Section 1244 Stock.**    Based on the normal rules already reviewed in this chapter, we know that a taxpayer must generally report a capital loss when he or she sells or exchanges corporate stocks or securities for an amount less than basis. We also know that capital losses are generally not as tax advantageous as ordinary business losses. Section 1244 is worth investigating precisely because it allows a taxpayer to treat a loss from the disposition of certain common stock as an ordinary business loss rather than a capital loss. The conditions specified before this result can be obtained, include the following:

1. The taxpayer claiming the loss must be an individual.
2. The loss must be attributable to stock issued to the taxpayer by the corporation—that is, it cannot be purchased from a prior owner, acquired by gift, and so on.
3. The stock must have been issued for property—that is, shares issued for services are not eligible.
4. The corporation must qualify as a "small business corporation"—this qualification includes specified dollar limitations (generally available only to corporations with equity capital of $1 million or less) and which derive 50 percent or more of their gross receipts from any active trade or business.
5. The amount deducted as ordinary loss under this provision cannot exceed $50,000 per taxpayer per year. (Thus, on a joint return, $100,000 per year is allowable.)

Any taxpayer who invests in a closely held corporation should make certain that a maximum amount of stock is qualified under this special provision. In the initial planning stages, the owner-operator may be so optimistic that the need for anticipating tax differences that become pertinent only if the new venture fails will be overlooked. Historical data support the conclusion, however, that many more small businesses fail than succeed. For those businesses that do fail, the opportunity to obtain a tax refund based on a $50,000 or $100,000 ordinary loss deduction is generally more valuable than the potential use of a capital loss carry-forward.

## PROBLEMS AND ASSIGNMENTS

1. Jim Sejd, a professional engineer who is self-employed, owns the following assets. Determine which are capital assets.
   a. A small computer used solely in Jim's professional work.
   b. The land on which Jim's office building is located.
   c. Land directly across the street from Jim's office, which he purchased as an investment. (This is the third property that Jim has purchased as a speculative investment.)
   d. A sailboat, which Jim sails on Chesapeake Bay when he needs to "get away from it all."

e. An automobile used 70 percent of the time for business purposes and 30 percent of the time for personal purposes.

f. Jim's private residence.

g. An oil painting that Jim received as a gift from an artist friend.

h. Twenty ounces of gold held as a speculative investment. (Jim buys and sells approximately 100 such investments each year. Although he has not earned a lot of income in this way, he thoroughly enjoys the excitement of keeping up with the market on a daily basis.)

i. A 10-year note received from a client for professional services rendered.

j. Twenty shares of GE common stock. (Jim buys and sells approximately 100 such investments each year. Although he has not earned a lot of income in this way, he thoroughly enjoys the excitement of keeping with the market on a daily basis.)

2. Leah Morphy spent $8,000 in creating a golden statue of the Roman goddess, Caissa. To her bitter disappointment, an independent appraisal valued the statue at only $5,000. Leah decided to give the statue to her friend, Howard Staunton. Is the statue a capital asset? What is Howard's basis in the statute?

3. Paul Nelson sold each of the following assets sometime during 19x4. Determine in each sale the amount and the kind of income realized—that is, ordinary income or loss, Section 1231 gain or loss, short-term capital gain or loss, or long-term capital gain or loss.

a. Ten shares of ABC common stock purchased on 2/4/x1 for $500. Paul sold these shares for $5,000 on 4/2/x4.

b. A tractor used in Paul's business. The tractor had cost Paul $10,000 on 1/1/x1. He depreciated the tractor $7,000 prior to its disposition. Paul sold the tractor for $4,000.

c. A vacant lot located next door to Paul's office. Prior to its sale, Paul had used this vacant lot as a parking facility for vehicles used in his business. Paul paid $10,000 for this lot on 4/1/x2; he sold it for $15,000 on 1/4/x4.

d. A desk used in Paul's business office. The desk had cost Paul $500 on 8/10/x3. He depreciated the desk $50 prior to its disposition. Paul sold the desk for $375 on 12/11/x4.

e. A high school class ring that Paul no longer wore. Paul paid $25 for the ring on 3/10x0; he sold it to a "gold vendor" for $30 on 9/5/x4.

f. Ten shares of DEF common stock that Paul received from his deceased mother's estate. Paul's mother had purchased the shares on 2/2/x1 for $1,000. She died on 5/5/x3, when the shares were worth $1,500. The executor of Paul's mother's estate valued all property as of 5/5/x3. The shares were distributed by the executor to Paul on 7/3/x4, when they had a fair market value of $1,700. Paul sold the shares on 10/10/x4 for $1,650.

g. Ten shares of GHI common stock that Paul received as a gift from his father. Paul's father had purchased the shares on 2/2/x1 for $1,700. He gave the shares to Paul on 7/3/x4, when they had a fair market value of $1,500. Paul sold the shares on 10/10/x4 for $1,450.

4. The XYZ Corporation realized the capital gains and losses detailed here.

|  | 19x1 | 19x2 | 19x3 | 19x4 | 19x5 | 19x6 |
|---|---|---|---|---|---|---|
| Net long term | $10,000 | $20,000 | $30,000 | ($40,000) | ($50,000) | $60,000 |
| Net short term | $ 5,000 | ($10,000) | $50,000 | $60,000 | ($10,000) | $20,000 |

*Note:* Amounts in brackets indicate losses.

Assuming that the XYZ Corporation also realized an ordinary income of $200,000 in each of the years 19x1 through 19x6, explain the following.

a. The correct treatment of the $10,000 net short-term capital loss in 19x2 and the $40,000 net long-term capital loss in 19x4.

b. The correct treatment of the $50,000 net long-term capital loss and the $10,000 net short-term capital loss in 19x5. Calculate the value of any tax refund to which XYZ may be entitled.

5. Linda Nelson, a single taxpayer, realized the capital gains and losses detailed below.

|  | 19x1 | 19x2 | 19x3 | 19x4 | 19x5 | 19x6 |
|---|---|---|---|---|---|---|
| Net long term | $1,000 | $2,000 | $3,000 | ($4,000) | ($5,000) | $6,000 |
| Net short term | $5,000 | ($1,000) | $5,000 | $6,000 | ($1,000) | $2,000 |

*Note:* Amounts in brackets indicate losses.

Assuming that Ms. Nelson also realized an ordinary income of $20,000 in each of the years 19x1 through 19x6, explain the following using 1989 rules.

a. The correct treatment of the $1,000 net long-term capital gain and the $5,000 net short-term capital gain in 19x1.

b. The correct treatment of the $2,000 net long-term capital gain and the $1,000 net short-term capital loss in 19x2.

c. The correct treatment of the $4,000 net long-term capital loss and the $6,000 net short-term capital gain in 19x4.

    d. The correct treatment of the $5,000 net long-term capital loss and the $1,000 net short-term capital loss in 19x5.

6. In 1986 the top marginal tax rate for individuals was 50 percent, and 60 percent of a taxpayer's net long-term capital gain was deductible in the computation of taxable income.

    a. Determine the maximum effective marginal tax rate on capital gains for individuals in 1986 and 1988 and beyond.

    b. Determine the maximum effective marginal tax rate on dividend income for individuals in 1986 and 1988 and beyond.

    c. Considering *only* the change noted in your answers to parts **a** and **b** above, what should have happened to the relative price of "growth stocks" versus "high-yield stocks" after 1986?

7. Fifty years ago, each of three brothers—Tom, Dick, and Harry—inherited $100,000 in cash from the estate of a recently deceased aunt. Each brother immediately invested his inheritance in a capital asset. Today the financial circumstances of the three brothers differs significantly. Their general circumstances can be detailed as follows:

Tom: The lucky brother. Tom's investment of the $100,000 that he inherited has appreciated fantastically in value; in fact, that asset is currently worth over $10 million. This is by no means Tom's only stroke of good luck. Because of his many good investments, Tom is today worth over $200 million.

Dick: The ambivalent brother. Some of Dick's investments have been very successful; others, very unsuccessful. Dick's investment of the $100,000 that he inherited is one of his least successful investments. Today that investment is valued at only $1,000. Fortunately he has other assets available to maintain a comfortable standard of living. Thus he has no real financial need to sell this investment prior to his death.

Harry: The unfortunate brother. Harry has recently been the victim of cancer. In order to pay his medical bills, it will be necessary for him to sell the good investment he made 50 years ago. That investment of $100,000 is worth $500,000 today. It is just too bad that Harry needs this money to meet his current medical expenses.

    a. Which of the brothers, if any, is "locked in" to his investment? Explain the meaning of the term *locked in*.

    b. Should Dick sell his 50-year-old investment prior to his own death? Explain briefly.

    c. Comment on the equity of our federal income tax in the three circumstances depicted in this problem.

8. Consider Harry's dilemma in problem **7.** What tax-saving alternative to selling his stock might you recommend?

9. Mary Black and Tom White, two unrelated taxpayers, each sold a duplex owned during the current year. Mary sold her duplex at a $20,000 profit; Tom sold his duplex at a $20,000 loss. Assume that this duplex was the only rental property owned by either taxpayer. Are Mary and Tom likely to report the sale of their duplexes in the same manner? Why or why not? Explain briefly.

10. Rossco, Inc. wants to invest $100,000 in National Motors, Inc. NMI's preferred stock sells for $100 per share and pays a 10 percent dividend. Analysts do not expect the stock to appreciate. Rossco plans to use its dividends to purchase more NMI stock. NMI's common stock also sells for $100 per share; no dividends are planned in the near future, but analysts expect the stock to increase in value by 10 percent per year. Rossco plans to liquidate its investment in three years in order to invest in real estate. If Rossco is in the 34 percent tax bracket, which stock should Rossco purchase?

11. Mary Gomez, M.D., began buying and selling a few pieces of real estate in 1984, the year she graduated from medical school and set up a general practice in McAllen, TX. She bought and sold one to four properties each year from 1984 through 1989. Mary's income for each of these six years can be summarized as follows:

| Year | Income from Medical Practice | Income or (Loss) from Property Sales | No. of Property Transactions |
|------|------------------------------|--------------------------------------|------------------------------|
| 1984 | $ 50,000 | $ 5,000 | 1 |
| 1985 | 75,000 | 10,000 | 2 |
| 1986 | 100,000 | 15,000 | 3 |
| 1987 | 125,000 | 20,000 | 4 |
| 1988 | 150,000 | 10,000 | 3 |
| 1989 | 175,000 | (30,000) | 2 |

Mary spends virtually all of her time on her medical practice. Until the real estate market "fell apart" in 1989, Mary simply thought of these property transactions as good investments. Today she is less sure of that conclusion.

a. If you were Mary's tax adviser, how would you recommend that she report the $30,000 loss on her two property transactions for 1989 federal income tax purposes?

b. What fundamental tax problem is implicit in your answer to part a, above? Briefly explain the most interesting problem.

# Case 7–1

Wendy Hines is a wealthy real estate developer who lives in Houston, Texas. In 1979, she acquired a tract of land for $700,000 with the intention of holding it for appreciation.

The faltering Houston economy has seriously hurt Wendy's financial position. She receives about $600,000 in taxable income annually from her rental properties, but each of her real estate investments are now worth less than they cost. In 1989, she received an offer from a residential home builder to sell the land for $500,000. Her own market analysis indicates that she could install the appropriate utilities at a cost of $200,000, subdivide the property, and sell the lots for about $705,000 over the next three years.

Her chief financial officer has recommended that Wendy sell the property in order to recognize the loss immediately for tax purposes instead of dragging it out over three years, since the time value of money outweighs the extra $5,000 she can make by subdividing the property. Do you agree?

# Case 7–2

Things are not going well for Lake Austin Condominiums. Six years ago units sold for $100,000; today their market value is only $70,000.

Rita and Tom Cedillo have owned and lived in a Lake Austin condo for five years. They stopped making payments on their mortgage when it had an outstanding balance of $90,000. Their mortgage company foreclosed on the unit and sold it for $70,000. Although the Cedillos are still solvent, the mortgage company has accepted $10,000 from the Cedillos as full settlement for the $20,000 deficiency.

Billy Joe Buttrick bought a condominium five years ago as an investment. Billy Joe rented this condo and was allowed $40,000 of depreciation. Billy Joe also stopped making payments on his $90,000 mortgage and the mortgage company foreclosed and sold it for $70,000. Billy Joe is still solvent and the mortgage company will "go after" Billy Joe for the entire $20,000 deficiency.

   a. Discuss the tax effects for the Cedillos.
   b. Would the Cedillos have been better off renting the condo to someone else for a year and then abandoning it?
   c. Discuss the tax effects for Billy Joe.
   d. How would your answer be different if Billy had taken only $20,000 of depreciation?

# CHAPTER 8

# Special Limitation
# on Passive-Activity Losses

Taxpayers reporting certain "passive-activity losses" will often discover that these losses, like net capital losses, cannot be used to reduce taxable income from other sources, at least in the year in which they are first realized. The special limitations on passive-activity losses were put into the Code in 1986. Because these rules are entirely new and unusually complex, it will be many years before anyone fully comprehends all of the tax opportunities and pitfalls buried within these provisions. One thing that is certain is that Congress intended the passive loss limitations to put an end to the tax-sheltered investment industry.

Prior to 1986 many high-income taxpayers were making investments expected to produce tax losses for several years. The losses reported for the first few years after making the investment were used to reduce the taxpayer's income from other sources and thereby served to reduce the amount of income tax payable currently. If the investments were good economic investments, they eventually would begin to produce additional amounts of taxable income for the investor. Instead of paying still larger amounts of income tax at that time, however, these taxpayer-investors were often inclined to make even larger tax-sheltered investments to reduce their increased taxable income and thereby continued to avoid paying any income tax while their investment portfolio and net wealth continued to increase. Although the scenario just described may sound idyllic, so far as both the taxpayer-investor and the salesperson are concerned, not everyone was happy, even when things turned out well. Because some high-income persons made tax-sheltered investments while other equally high-income persons made more traditional investments, a great disparity developed between the income tax liability of the two groups. In short, apparently equally situated taxpayers were no longer treated equally; hence a form of horizontal inequity in the distribution of the federal tax burden soon became apparent. Furthermore, because of the major tax advantages associated with certain investments, a serious misallocation of national resources also became evident. In general this resulted in far too many resources going into buildings and too few into other productive assets. Finally, many of the investments sold were not good economic investments and they often failed to produce any amount of income at any time. Under these circumstances the investor-taxpayer also became unhappy. Although the tax-shelter salespersons, who typically collected their sales fees in advance, remained satisfied with the status quo, almost everyone else was at least somewhat dissatisfied. The latter group included both the income tax authorities and the courts because they eventually inherited the mess of trying to sort out the legitimate tax investment loss deductions from the shams.

Given this chaotic economic and political setting, it is little wonder that Congress enacted the special limitations on passive-activity losses in 1986. What is unfortunate, however, is that the provisions which were enacted primarily to put an end to tax-sheltered investments were (perhaps necessarily) worded so broadly that they may very well affect many taxpayers in unintended ways. There is no doubt that the complexity added by these few new provisions alone will make self-compliance in a tax loss situation a virtual impossibility for anyone engaged in a start-up trade or business as well as anyone making an investment that even temporarily loses money.

In this chapter we will examine the new passive loss limitation rules beginning with an overview and moving to a more detailed consideration of the most important general provisions. The reader should understand, however, that many details critical to a genuine understanding will not be known for several years. Specifically, we must wait until the Treasury Department issues interpretive regulations and the courts arbitrate numerous disputes between taxpayers and the IRS before we really comprehend the import of at least this portion of the new law.

## A GENERAL OVERVIEW

Taxpayers—other than certain "regular" corporations—must effectively separate each of their gross income and deduction items into one of three categories:

1. Passive-activity sources;
2. Portfolio sources; and
3. Active sources.

Net losses from passive activity sources cannot be deducted currently from any income reported from any other source. Net losses from portfolio or active sources can, however, be deducted currently from other sources. To illustrate, assume that an individual recognized the following amounts of net income (and loss) this year:

| | |
|---|---|
| Source #1 | ($20,000) |
| Source #2 | 5,000 |
| Source #3 | 50,000 |
| Total net income | $35,000 |

If source #1 was from passive activity sources, this taxpayer would—ignoring for the moment certain transition rules and other special exceptions—report a net taxable income of $55,000, not $35,000! On the other hand, if source #1 was a net loss from active sources, then this taxpayer would report a net taxable income of only $35,000. Based on even this simple example, it is immediately apparent that the definition of certain new words and phrases used in the 1986 Code are of utmost importance. We will, therefore, subsequently examine those definitions in greater detail. Before doing that, however, let us complete this overview of the special limitations on passive-activity losses.

Even though net losses from passive activities cannot be currently deducted against income from other sources, they can be carried forward and offset against income from those same sources in later years. To illustrate, let us expand on the example introduced earlier by adding assumed information for two more years, as follows:

| | 19X1 | 19X2 | 19X3 | Three-Year Total |
|---|---|---|---|---|
| Passive activities | ($20,000) | ($ 5,000) | $ 30,000 | $ 5,000 |
| Portfolio sources | 5,000 | 7,000 | 10,000 | 22,000 |
| Active sources | 50,000 | 63,000 | 70,000 | 183,000 |
| Net income | $35,000 | $65,000 | $110,000 | $210,000 |
| Taxable income | $55,000 | $70,000 | $ 85,000 | $210,000 |

As illustrated in this example, the special limitation on passive activity losses is generally intended to be only a deferral mechanism, not a denial mechanism.

What happens if before its disposition a passive activity fails to produce a sufficient amount of income to absorb all of the losses carried forward from prior years? In that event the aggregate remaining loss, effectively put into a suspense account in prior years, can be totally recognized—i.e., it can be offset against any net income from other sources—in the year in which the taxpayer completely disposes of the activity in a taxable transaction. Note that the deferred but full recognition of any suspended loss requires (1) a complete disposition (2) of an entire activity (3) in a taxable transaction. The latter term means only that the disposition not be made in a "nontaxable" transaction. It does *not* mean that the transaction must result in a gain or that some minimal amount of tax must be payable because of the disposition event. Incidentally, dispositions made to a related party do not qualify, even if made at an arm's length price. Family members and 50 percent owned corporations are two common examples of related parties. Special rules, to be explained later, apply if the disposition occurs at death or by gift.

# DEFINITIONS

The practical application of the special limitation on passive-activity losses depends on many definitions not yet articulated. At the date of this writing, we know only the broadest outline of the intended but critical definitions of Section 469. Eighteen months have elapsed since these provisions were enacted, and the Treasury Department has issued only one of three promised sets of interpretative regulations and they are subject to challenge.

## Passive Activity

A passive activity is in general a trade or business in which the taxpayer does not materially participate. The term *passive activity* is specifically defined to include rental activities, but those rental activities are also subject to their own special limitations and definitions. (For example, income from renting hotel rooms is not generally considered to be a rental activity.) The statute also clearly carves out an exception for working interests in oil and gas properties; those interests are automatically defined to be from active, rather than passive, sources. Finally, portfolio activities are specifically excluded from passive activities.

The intent of Congress, explained in the introductory paragraphs of this chapter, is reasonably clear. Congress intended that taxpayers be denied the right to offset net losses from most tax-sheltered investments against either active income sources (i.e., against wages, salaries, or active trade or business profits) or portfolio income (i.e., against interest, dividends, and royalty income).

The relationship between each taxpayer and each specific business activity will have to be carefully reviewed to correctly categorize every activity as (1) passive, (2) portfolio, or (3) other (i.e., active). All nonportfolio income and deductions will generally be deemed to stem from passive activities unless the taxpayer *materially participates* in the operations of the activity *on a regular, continuous, and substantial basis.* Although the Code fails to state how often this material participation test is to be applied, it seems reasonable to assume that it must be applied on an annual basis. Both the Conference Committee Report and the first set of temporary regulations make it clear that a deliberate change in a taxpayer's level of participation each year to achieve the most favorable tax result, will not be tolerated.

In most cases, the taxpayer's principal business will yield active income. However, secondary businesses may be classified as a passive activity, even if they are operated as part of a sole proprietorship and are owned by the taxpayer. If, for example, a sole proprietor turns over the day-to-day management functions of a secondary business to an employee or to a management firm, the income and deduction items generated by that business may be categorized as passive. In addition, a single business entity may be engaged in more than one separate activity and, if it is, each activity must be accounted for separately, at least for federal income tax purposes. As a safe haven, the temporary regulations provide that a taxpayer's involvement in an activity for more than 500 hours per year the activity will generally be sufficient to qualify as one characterized by material participation.

## Separate Activities

The practical application of the new passive-activity loss limitation might call for the separation of many previously unitary businesses into active and passive components both (1) to determine the annual loss limitation, if any, and (2) to trigger the release of any previously suspended losses when the entire activity has been completely disposed of in a taxable transaction. Businesses operated under a common name, with common management and financing, need not be treated as a single activity unless they could not be independently operated. The Senate Finance Committee Report (p. 739) that accompanied the 1986 Act attempts to explain this new concept as follows:

> The determination of what constitutes a separate activity is intended to be made in a realistic economic sense. The question to be answered is what undertakings consist of an integrated and interrelated economic unit, conducted in coordination with or reliance upon each other, and constituting an appropriate unit for the measurement of gain or loss.

The separate-activities test is, obviously, a subjective one and, therefore, one likely to inspire a good bit of litigation in the years to come. The Committee reports suggest that most farms and most rental properties are to be treated as separate activities. This may (or may not) imply that geographically separate retail outlets of a single venture should also be treated as separate activities. Alternatively, a professional engineer engaged in a business offering both engineering and construction services could discover that losses suffered in the latter activity might not be offset against income from the former activity if the proprietor-engineer had relatively little day-to-day involvement in the construction supervision work done by his own firm and the IRS and the courts took a narrow view of the critical definition. The second set of temporary regulations—not yet released—promises to give guidance on this question.

## Portfolio Activities

The Committee reports make it clear that the term *portfolio activity* is intended to include the income and expenses from traditional investments such as interest, dividends, and royalties. Observe, however, that these income items are *not automatically* classified as portfolio income. The interest and dividends earned by a securities dealer in the ordinary course of business, for example, would be categorized as active income, not portfolio income.

The 1987 Tax Act included a new provision that automatically classified income from publicly-traded limited partnerships as portfolio income.

Interest income will almost certainly prove difficult to classify in many cases. Interest from assets directly connected to a business—such as interest on installment sales or other deferred payment arrangements—is active income. Interest earned by the same business on temporary investments of excess working capital is portfolio income.

In the vast majority of all cases, the net balance attributed to portfolio activities will be positive rather than negative because investment-related expenses are almost always smaller than the income they help to produce. If those expenses were larger than the income produced over the long run, the investor would almost certainly dispose of the investment. Thus the intent of Congress in separating out portfolio activities is reasonably clear in concept: Congress did not want to permit taxpayers to offset losses from tax-shelter investments against the income earned from traditional investments in stocks and bonds. At the same time, it would have been difficult to classify these items as income from active sources because one who invests in common stocks, commercial bonds, and/or certificates of deposit can hardly be deemed to have material participation in the operations of the interest-paying venture. To solve this dilemma in terminology, Congress created the three-way distinction suggested earlier; that is (1) passive, (2) portfolio, and (3) other (or active) activities. Given this trichotomy, the best way to proceed is possibly to first identify all items of gross income and deduction that derive from portfolio activities and then separate all remaining items between the passive and active categories.

### Active Activities

As explained earlier, the presence or absence of material participation in the operation of an activity by the taxpayer on a regular, continuous, and substantial basis is—in the absence of a statutory presumption to the contrary—the sole factor that determines the correct categorization of an activity as either active or passive. The passive-activity category is apparently a residual class. In other words, items of gross income and deduction that cannot be properly classified as deriving from either portfolio or active activities are subject to the passive-activity loss-limitation rules.

The principal activity in which the taxpayer participates on a full time basis is obviously an active one. In most cases, full-time participation will establish the requisite material participation with regard to all of the separate activities that might be carried on within that line of business unless the business involves either the renting of properties or farming. The taxpayer's involvement in secondary business activities are more difficult to categorize correctly. Factors to be considered include: (1) the frequency of contact; (2) the nature of the work done by the taxpayer; (3) the significance of the taxpayer's effort to the overall operation; and (4) the relationship between the taxpayer and other individuals performing services in the business. The less frequent the contact, the more perfunctory the task, the less critical the contribution, and the more remote the supervisory relationship, the more likely it is that the passive-activity categorization is the correct one. Each situation must be judged separately based on all of the available facts and circumstances.

As noted earlier, the temporary regulations provide quantitative rules that may sometimes help interpret the subjective criteria of the Code. Specifically, those regulations generally define material participation to include activities in which the taxpayer participates for more than 500 hours per year. Curiously, however, those same regulations do *not* require that a taxpayer maintain a contemporaneous time log to substantiate this condition. Apparently annotated calendars, appointment books, or other narrative summaries may suffice.

The temporary regulations go on to suggest that participation of less than 500 hours may also suffice if the taxpayer's participation constitutes "substantially all" of the participation by those participating in an activity. Furthermore, participation by a taxpayer's spouse is ordinarily treated as participation by the taxpayer. And taxpayers who participate for more than 100 hours but less than 500 hours in each of several activities per year may (per the temporary regulations) be subject to certain aggregation rules—that is, the several activities may sometimes be consolidated and treated as one by the IRS (This 100-to-500 hour status is dubbed "significant participation" in the new regulations.) The first impression of these new administrative pronouncements is not entirely favorable because, in some instances, the rules appear to favor the IRS position. For example, in the discussion of potential aggregation in cases involving less than 500 but more than 100 hours per activity per year, the temporary regulations come perilously close to suggesting that aggregation will apply if the overall result is a net income (thus creating active rather than passive income), whereas nonaggregation will apply if an overall net loss is experienced. This "heads-we-win, tails-you-lose" position by the Treasury Department seems untenable. Because of the way the Code provision is written, however, any final regulations *may* have greater than normal status with the courts. Whether they will or not remains to be seen. Taxpayers should note the risks and seek competent advice on a timely basis whenever warranted.

## ENTITIES AFFECTED

The special limitation on passive-activity losses generally applies by statute to all individual and fiduciary taxpayers as well as to closely held and personal-service corporate taxpayers. Thus at first blush it appears that the only taxpayer to escape this new limitation is the C corporation that is not either a personal-service corporation or a closely held one. As will be explained later, however, that conclusion is not entirely justified.

A corporation is deemed to be closely held if, at any time during the last half of the tax year, 50 percent or more of the corporation's stock is held (directly or indirectly) by five or fewer individuals. This ownership test is based on the value of all shares held; not by voting power or number of shares outstanding. Indirect ownership of shares held by other corporations, partnerships, and family members may be attributed to a taxpayer. A corporation is a personal-service corporation if: (1) employee-owners (directly or indirectly) own more than 10 percent of the corporation's stock; (2) the principal activity of the corporation is the performance of a personal service; and (3) these personal services are substantially performed by the employee-owners. Although there are many ill-defined words and phrases in this definition, they would be of limited significance because most personal-service corporations are also closely held and, therefore, it would matter little which definition makes them subject to the passive-activity loss-limitation rules were it not for a special rule explained below.

## Entity Participation

The notion of material participation by an inanimate entity is difficult to comprehend. Therefore, as you probably would surmise, the law transfers the material participation requirement from the taxable entity to one or more persons in all circumstances involving taxpayers other than individuals. Specifically, the test for trusts is determined by the activities of the trustee or fiduciary; for an estate, by the activities of the executor or administrator; and for a closely held (or personal-service) corporation, by the activities of the stockholders who own the requisite stock. Special rules may apply to the closely held C corporation that is involved in more than one activity to allow a reasonable division of labor among the employees.

## Special Rule for Certain Closely Held Corporations

For reasons not at all clear to your author, Congress allowed closely held C corporations (but not personal-service corporations) the right to offset passive-activity losses against any income from an active trade or business (but not against income from portfolio sources). This special exception means, of course, that closely held, profitable corporations, that are not personal-service corporations, can utilize the classical tax-shelter losses with very few restrictions. High-income taxpayers who continue to hold tax-sheltered investments that produce losses, and who also own a profitable, nonservice business that is incorporated, should consider transferring their tax-sheltered investments into their corporate enterprise. Others, who own no such incorporated business at present, should consider acquiring one. Finally, those individuals who have decided to dispose of their tax-shelter investments should look at profitable corporations as potential buyers because the tax-loss benefit inherent in those investments is still of genuine economic value to the right corporate buyer.

The reason for excluding personal-service corporations from this special rule is obvious. To do otherwise would have invited many professionals—such as doctors, lawyers, accountants, and engineers—to continue the precise pre-1986 behavior Congress was trying to discourage. That is, if the law were worded otherwise, these professionals would continue to play the tax-shelter investment game inside their professional-service corporations.

What is strange is the fact that Congress allowed one obvious loophole to remain. Those few tax-shelter salespersons still selling will very likely acquire a new clientele. The new buyer will probably be a corporate executive directly engaged in a closely-held mercantile or manufacturing business rather than a learned profession. Because of other changes in the law—particularly in the areas of depreciation, investment credit, capital gains, and the at-risk rules—most of the real impetus behind the typical tax-sheltered investment has been removed so there are very few real tax-sheltered investments remaining to be sold. Therefore the remaining loophole is more of a selective, but fortuitous, escape from a retroactive law than it is a planning opportunity for the future.

### Passthrough Entities

The active, passive, or portfolio status of any items of gross income or deduction originally recognized by a partnership or S corporation are determined by the relationship between the item and the individual partner or shareholder in the passthrough entity. Therefore, even if a partnership or S corporation is engaged in only one active business, the net income or loss incurred in that business is not automatically deemed to be from active sources. That determination would be uniquely made for each partner or shareholder. All of the gross income and deduction items—other than portfolio items—initially recognized by a partnership will be considered to be from a passive activity unless the individual partner (or shareholder in the S corporation) materially participates in the operations of the partnership (or the S corporation). Items attributed to a limited partner are *generally* deemed to be passine unless the limited partnership is publicly traded; in that event they are portfolio items. To illustrate, let us assume that three individual partners each own a one-third interest in the ABC partnership which recognizes a $30,000 net loss after paying partner A a salary of $25,000 and partner B a deductible professional fee of $6,000. Let us further assume that: partner A is a general partner, who is active on a full-time basis with ABC's only business; partner B is also a general partner, but does not materially participate in ABC's business; and partner C is a limited partner. The correct categorization of ABC's loss would be made as follows:

|  | Active | Passive |
|---|---|---|
| Partner A: |  |  |
| Salary | $25,000 |  |
| Net loss | (10,000) |  |
| Partner B: |  |  |
| Professional fee | $ 4,000 | $ 2,000 |
| Net loss |  | (10,000) |
| Partner C |  | (10,000) |

The allocation of B's $6,000 professional fee between $4,000 active and $2,000 passive sources is equitable, if not obvious. Recall that B does *not* materially participate in ABC's business; hence his allocation of ABC's $30,000 net loss will be treated as derived from a passive activity. Yet B's share of the loss effectively includes a deduction for one third of the professional fee ABC paid to him. Because B must record the full $6,000 he received as income, a special rule will allow him to reallocate $2,000 of his own income to passive sources to mitigate the otherwise unreasonable disallowance of the full $10,000 loss from ABC. The same economic result could, of course, be realized by allowing partner B to reallocate $2,000 of his $10,000 passive activity loss from ABC to active sources. The Conference Committee Report provides that Treasury regulations are to be issued to insure this end result, one way or another. Those regulations have not yet been issued.

The example in the Committee Report deals with interest, a portfolio item. It assumes that a partnership pays $100 in interest to a 40 percent partner who does not materially participate in the partnership's operations. The $100 interest received by the partner would ordinarily be treated as portfolio interest because it derives from a nonbusiness loan. Because this partner must pick up the partnership's $100 interest expense deduction as one derived from a passive activity, and because that includes $40 of interest expense paid to the partner, the Committee Report suggests that only $60 of the partner's interest income be reported as portfolio income and that $40 of it be treated as income from a passive activity.

Limited partners present many special classification problems. As noted in a prior paragraph, limited partners are generally not treated as material participants in an activity. Under some circumstances, however, they may be. For example, participation in excess of 500 hours per year may qualify a limited partner as a material participant, as may their material participation in any five of the preceding 10 years. And, in personal service partnerships, a limited partner may be deemed a material participant in any year if he or she was a material participant for any three previous years. Also, recall from Chapter Three that publicly-traded limited partnerships created after late-1987 will be treated like corporations (as will older MLPs after 1997). This means, of course, that limited partners in those partnerships are not subject to the general flow-through treatment accorded other partners. Income from those MLPs will generally be treated as portfolio income. Furthermore, losses from those MLPs will generally be treated as portfolio income. Furthermore, losses from those MLPs are treated separately—that is, the loss from one MLP can not be offset from the income of another MLP. Those losses can only be carried forward and offset against future income from the same partnership.

### Transition Rules

The potentially devastating and retroactive economic consequences of the passive-activity loss-limitation rules on many taxpayers, who had purchased tax-sheltered investments in good faith before 1987, was apparent to Congress during its deliberation of the 1986 Act. To mitigate an unduly harsh result, Congress eventually agreed upon certain transition rules to reduce the effect of the new rules between 1987 and 1991, the year the rules just described become fully operative. These transition rules generally allow a taxpayer to deduct 65 percent of the otherwise disallowed passive activity loss in 1987; 40 percent in 1988; 20 percent in 1989; and 10 percent in 1990. To qualify, however, that loss must derive from a preenactment activity; i.e., an investment made by the taxpayer before the new law was enacted on October 22, 1986.

The portion of any preenactment-activity loss that is disallowed—for example, the 80 percent disallowed in 1989—can be carried forward and deducted against passive activity income realized in a subsequent year. It cannot, however, be treated as an amount eligible for the preenactment percentage allowance in any subsequent year. New passive activities—those acquired after enactment—can reduce, but cannot increase the amount eligible for deduction under this transition rule. To illustrate these rules, assume the lowing facts for 1989:

|  | Case A | Case B |
|---|---|---|
| Gain or (loss) from— | | |
| Preenactment activity | ($1,100) | ($1,100) |
| Postenactment activity | (100) | 100 |
| Total passive activity loss | ($1,200)* | ($1,000)* |

*The deduction allowed in case A is 20% × $1,100; not 20% × $1,200. In case B the deduction is 20% × $1,000; not 20% × $1,100.

The $880 disallowed deduction in case A (and the $800 in case B) can be carried forward to 1990 and offset against any passive activity income recognized in that year. Those same amounts, however, are *not* eligible for the 10 percent transition rule deduction in 1990.

## *DE MINIMIS* RULE FOR REAL ESTATE

Rental real estate activities are, as noted earlier, automatically deemed to be passive activities. Were it not for another special rule, therefore, many relatively low-income taxpayers (who often own one or two rental properties) could be subject to the new loss limitation on passive activities. To avoid this result, Congress created another special rule intended to minimize the impact of the new law on certain taxpayers. That special rule provides that individuals may deduct up to $25,000 in losses from real estate each year if they satisfy the following criteria:

1. The individual must "actively participate" in the rental business. This active participation test is significantly less demanding than the material participation test otherwise applied to test passive activities. It has only two requirements: the taxpayer must (*a*) have a 10 percent or greater interest in the real estate and (*b*) have a "significant and bona fide" involvement in the rental activity. The Finance Committee Report suggests that the latter requirement can be satisfied by approving tenants, setting terms, approving repairs, or even by selecting a management service to care for the property. The property can not, however, be subject to a net lease.

2. The taxpayer's adjusted gross income (computed without regard to net passive losses, taxable social security benefits, or individual retirement account contributions) cannot exceed $100,000 for the year. If it does exceed that amount, the $25,000 maximum real estate loss deduction otherwise allowed must be reduced by 50 cents on the dollar. Thus no deduction under this special *de minimis* rule is possible for an individual with an adjusted AGI of $150,000 or more in a year.

3. The amount deducted under this special rule cannot exceed the net passive activity loss for the year. Thus, if a taxpayer has a $20,000 net loss from a qualifying real estate business and a $15,000 net passive-activity gain from other sources, the maximum deduction is the $5,000 overall net passive-activity loss; not the $20,000 loss attributable to the real estate alone.

4. Finally, no amount can be deducted under this special provision that would be limited by another provision in the Code. Such limits apply, for example, to the business use of a taxpayer's residence and to the rental of a vacation home. (See Section 280A.)

In summary, this special provision is clearly intended for the individual with relatively small direct investments in real estate rather than the big-time, real-estate syndication investor.

## OTHER DETAILS

Although this chapter can only cover the surface of a very complex subject, a few additional details are deemed necessary to round out the prior discussion. Individuals interested in the specifics of an actual situation will have to research their problem in a current tax service or consult a qualified tax advisor. The following details might, however, be helpful in limited circumstances.

### Loss Allocation

Suppose that a taxpayer is engaged in three passive activities with the following gains and losses for the current year:

| Passive Activity | Gain or Loss |
|---|---|
| #1 | $15,000 |
| #2 | (6,000) |
| #3 | (12,000) |
| Net passive-activity loss | ($ 3,000) |

If neither activity #2 nor #3 qualify for the special deduction available for real estate rentals, we know that overall a $3,000 loss deduction will be disallowed (ignoring the transition rule) but can be carried forward in a suspense account. The question is, to which activity does the disallowed amount apply? The answer is to both of the losing activities. The $3,000 carryforward is to be allocated between activities 2 and 3 on a relative loss basis, as follows:

Activity #2: $6,000/$18,000 × $3,000 = $1,000
Activity #3: $12,000/$18,000 × $3,000 = $2,000

If the year in question were 1989 and the transition rule allowed this taxpayer to deduct 20 percent of the $3,000 net passive activity loss, then only $800 would be carried forward on activity #2 (i.e., $1,000 − $200) and $1,600 on activity #3 (i.e., $2,000 − $400).

### Dispositions on Death

It was noted earlier in this chapter that the complete disposition of a passive activity in a fully taxable transaction will ordinarily permit a taxpayer to deduct the losses accumulated in a suspense account for this activity in prior years plus the loss realized on the disposition, if any. But what happens if a taxpayer dies before disposing of such an activity? In that event only the amount (if any) of previously disallowed loss that would have been deductible had the passive activity been sold becomes deductible. The reason for the partial or total disallowance of the accumulated loss previously disallowed is that the decedent's estate (or heirs) take as their tax basis in the property the fair market value of the property on the date of the decedent's death. (This rule was explained in Chapter 7.) The net effect of this rule is equivalent to the result that would have been reached if the passive-activity property had been sold at a gain before the taxpayer died.

To illustrate, assume that a taxpayer has accumulated a total of $50,000 in previously disallowed losses from a single passive activity. Assume further that this taxpayer's basis in that activity was $10,000 and that the fair market value of the activity was $25,000. In that event, if the taxpayer were to completely dispose of his or her interest in the passive activity by sale, the $15,000 gain realized (i.e., $25,000 amount realized less the $10,000 adjusted basis) would go first to offset the $50,000 in previously disallowed losses, leaving the taxpayer free to deduct the remaining $35,000 disallowed loss (i.e., $50,000 suspended loss less $15,000 gain on disposition). If the taxpayer were to die before selling the passive activity described above, the executor would claim the same $35,000 net loss on the final income tax return of the deceased taxpayer, assuming all facts as stipulated above. If the fair market value of this passive activity had been $60,000 or more (instead of the $25,000 assumed above) then, of course, there would be no amount remaining for the executor to deduct because unrealized gain would be equal to or greater than the previously disallowed losses.

### Dispositions by Gift

If a taxpayer disposes of a passive activity by gift, any previously disallowed losses are added to the basis of the property in the hands of the donee. Under those circumstances, the donor is obviously not entitled to any deduction for the previously accumulated losses.

### Other Miscellaneous Matters

Dispositions of passive activities in nontaxable transactions, other than by death or gift, create unusual problems. In general the disallowed loss remains with the transferor even though all of the assets associated with the passive activity have passed to another taxpayer. Partial dispositions also create unusual problems and are fraught with tax difficulties. In general, therefore, they should be avoided.

The categorization of a passive activity can also be affected by a change in the taxpayer's activities. If a taxpayer begins to materially participate in a previously passive activity, the status of the property also changes but any accumulated losses are *not* triggered for immediate realization. Instead they remain in suspense unless active income is generated in the interim by those same properties; in that event any suspended loss can be offset against the income as it is earned. Any remaining loss will, of course, be deductible at disposition.

Finally, there is some coordination between the rules applicable to passive-activity losses and those for capital gains and losses discussed in the preceding chapter. For example, if an individual taxpayer disposes of a passive activity and that disposition event creates a capital loss of more than $3,000 for the year, any excess capital loss will have to be carried forward if there are no capital gains currently available to offset it. The $3,000 annual net capital loss limit does not, however, apply to the accumulated losses from the passive activity in prior years.

Alternatively, if an individual taxpayer realizes a gain on the disposition of his or her entire interest in a passive activity, and some portion or all of that gain is a capital gain, the entire gain must be offset against any passive-activity losses before it can be used to offset other capital losses.

### Tax Planning Considerations

The passive-activity loss rules obviously present an interesting challenge in tax planning for certain taxpayers; namely, those taxpayers who experience net passive losses in any tax year. The general strategy in these circumstances is to reduce the amount of the current nondeductible loss, assuming that there is no anticipated increase in future marginal tax rates that would more than offset the present-value cost associated with a deferred tax deduction. In many instances, this means that these taxpayers will acquire passive income generators, aptly identified as PIGs by the financial press. The first idea generated following enactment of the 1986 Code was that publicly-traded multiple limited partnerships, involving active securities fund management, could be created to generate passive income for needy investors because of the original presumption that all limited partners would be deemed recipients of passive income or loss via their partnership interests. As noted earlier in this chapter, that idea was short-lined because Congress quickly stepped into the breach and enacted new rules that changed much of that kind of income to portfolio income or effectively taxed the MLP as a corporation.

The second wave of tax planning typically involved the creation of passive income by carefully contrived rental arrangements, since rents are generally presumed to constitute passive income. These early efforts were directly challenged by the first set of temporary regulations governing passive-activity losses. The regulations attacked these tax plans in two ways. First, rental activities were narrowly defined and, second, certain rental income was simply recharacterized as active income.

The temporary regulations excluded from the definition of a rental property both (1) those properties rented for an average of seven days or less and (2) those rented for 30 days or less *if* significant personal services were concurrently provided to the leasee. The former excluded rental of most house-

# Sources of Gross Income and Deductions

| | Active | Portfolio | Passive |
|---|---|---|---|
| Rule: | Net losses can be deducted from other sources. | Net losses can be deducted from other sources. | Net losses cannot be deducted from other sources. However, they can be carried forward to offset income from passive sources in later years. Any aggregate remaining loss may be used to offset income from other sources in the year of a complete disposition. |
| General Definition: | Taxpayer materially participates in the operations of the activity on a regular, continuous, and substantial basis. Each activity of a multi-activitied business must be accounted for separately. | Income and expenses from traditional investments such as interest, dividends, and royalties. May also include income from certain master limited partnerships. | A trade or business in which the taxpayer does not personally participate on a material basis. |
| Examples: | Sole proprietorship run by the proprietor. | Interest from temporary investments of excess working capital. | Secondary activities in which the day-to-day efforts are managed by an employee or a management firm. |
| | Income and loss from investment by a partner or S corporation shareholder who materially participates in the active trade or business of the partnership or S corporation. | | Income and loss from investment by partner of S corporation shareholder who does not materially participate in the active trade or business of the partnership of S corporation. |
| | Rent from hotel rooms and other properties rented for less than one week (or even 30 days if personal services are provided) as well as rent income from properties rented to a related party. | | Rental income or loss (subject to a diminimus rule) but only if rented to an unrelated party. |
| | Working interests in oil and gas ventures. | | Royalties from oil and gas ventures. |
| | Interest expense on loans used to acquire assets directly connected with an active business. | | Income and loss from limited partnership interests that are not publicly traded. |

hold items, motel rooms, and many automobiles; the latter excluded many condo-hotels and other vacation properties. In addition, the regulations provided that rental activities would not include the use of property that was merely incidental to the receipt of a service; for example, hospital or boarding school room as well as properties generally available during defined business hours (e.g., a golf course clubhouse).

The recharacterization of rental income as active income also occurred because: (1) the rented property was used in an active trade or business in which the taxpayer was a material participant; (2) the rented property included little or no *depreciable* property; or (3) the rental income occurred in the year in which the property was sold and the rental income was only incidental to development activity.

The proposed regulations go on to anticipate and shortcut other planning opportunities that involve shared costs; single properties used in more than one activity; and sales of substantially appreciated properties. Although the general thrust of the regulations is clearly intended to interdict any plans which would circumvent the intent of Congress in enacting the PAL (passive-activity loss) provisions, many viable opportunities still exist. These include both careful portfolio management and substantive behavioral changes. For example, taxpayers may elect to use funds previously invested in income-producing assets to pay off liabilities in passive activities and thereby reduce both passive activity losses and portfolio income. Alternatively, they may actually spend more of their time on some activities, and less on others, and thereby increase passive income and decrease active income. Whatever a taxpayer does to mitigate the PAL rules should be checked with a tax adviser before implementation because this area of the law, more than others, is in a state of evolution. Ideas that seem good today may be worthless tomorrow. A summary of the basic rules is contained on page 161.

## PROBLEMS AND ASSIGNMENTS

1.  Tom Heaton makes an investment that will generate a $50,000 loss in 19x1 and 19x2, and $130,000 of income in 19x3. Tom is in the 28 percent tax bracket. Assume that $100 of tax savings in 19x1 is worth $100 today; $100 of tax savings in 19x2 is worth $90 today; and $100 of tax savings in 19x3 is worth $81 today. (Ignore the transition rules applicable to 1987–1990 and the special rule for rental real estate.)
    a.  What is the tax cost of this investment if it is an active business?
    b.  What is the tax cost of this investment if it is a passive investment?

2.  Bob and Mary Tidwell own and operate a grocery store. Their income (loss) from the grocery store and other activities is:
    a.  Grocery store                                           $40,000
    b.  Dividends from stocks                                     2,900
    c.  Loss from condominium that he rents to students          (1,500)

d. Loss from investment in syndicated real estate partnership    (4,500)
e. Income from investment in cattle breeding partnership    3,000
f. Loss from investment in oil drilling partnership (working
   interest)    (3,500)
g. Royalties from oil well and gas interests    2,500
h. Mary's loss from selling cosmetics    (1,000)

Assuming Bob and Mary claim a standard deduction of $5,000 and two personal exemptions of $2,000 each, what is their taxable income? Ignore the transition rules.

3. In 19x1, Susanne Doell recognized a $60,000 income from her business, $2,000 in portfolio income, and a $10,000 loss from a passive investment. Ignore the transition rules and the special rules for rental real estate.
   a. What is Susanne's adjusted gross income?
   b. If the above amounts had been earned by Doellco, Inc., what would its taxable income be?

4. Diversified Investments, Inc., an S corporation owned 100 percent by Kent Leediker, makes and sells widgets, invests in real estate syndicates, and owns stocks. Its 19x1 income and assets are:

| Category | Assets (basis) | Assets (value) | Gross Income | COGS | Expenses |
|---|---|---|---|---|---|
| Widgets | $300,000 | $300,000 | $900,000 | $800,000 | $150,000 |
| Real estate | 250,000 | 400,000 | 350,000 | –0– | 250,000 |
| Stocks | 100,000 | 400,000 | 50,000 | –0– | –0– |

Diversified Investments also incurred $100,000 of interest expense and $30,000 of administrative expenses. Discuss a major problem in trying to determine Diversified Investments' active income, passive income, and portfolio income for 19x1.

5. D owns 25 percent of the ABCD partnership. In 1989, D was paid $8,000 for professional services that he performed for ABCD; D's share of the partnership loss (which is a passive activity for D) is $12,000. If D has no other passive activities, how much of the partnership loss can he deduct if his professional fees were for:
   a. Tax return preparation (deductible by ABCD).
   b. Legal advice relating to partnership organization (assume ABCD amortized $1,600 in 1989).
   c. Title search expenditures (capitalized as part of the land cost by ABCD).

6. In 1989 Brian Buck, a single individual, had regular taxable income of $80,000 and alternative minimum taxable income before the AMT exemption of $85,000, computed without regard to two activities. Activity #1, a

passive investment, increased Brian's regular taxable income by $60,000 and his AMTI by $75,000. Activity #2 created a regular loss of $100,000 and an AMTI loss of $80,000.

a. What is Brian's 1989 tax if activity #2 is a passive investment?

b. What is Brian's 1989 tax if activity #2 is an active business?

7. Lisa Futile purchased a limited partnership interest for $40,000, which generated suspended losses of $30,000. What are the tax consequences if Lisa—

a. Sells her interest to an unrelated party for $25,000?

b. Contributes her interest to a corporation in a Section 351 transaction (see Chapter 11) in which she recognizes $10,000 of gain?

c. Contributes her interest to a partnership in which no gain is recognized?

8. Lawrence Taylor owns a limited partnership interest that cost $50,000 and generated suspended losses of $32,000. Taylor sells his investment for a note receivable of $40,000, which he will collect in four annual $10,000 payments over four years.

a. How much gain (loss) in the first year will Taylor recognize if he treats the sale as an installment sale?

b. How much gain (loss) in the first year will Taylor recognize if he elects not to treat this as an installment sale?

9. Guy Bond, a single taxpayer, earns a taxable income of $200,000 every year. He is also the sole shareholder of a regular corporation that earns a taxable income of $80,000 per year. Guy is considering making a passive investment that will generate a $5,000 loss in 1989 and 1990, and will generate $15,000 in income in 1991. Neither Guy nor his corporation are involved in any other passive activities.

a. Ignoring the time value of money, should Guy make this investment individually or through his corporation?

b. Now assume that $100 of tax savings in 1989 is worth $100 today; $100 of tax savings in 1990 is worth $90 today; and $100 of tax savings in 1991 is worth $81 today. (In other words, Guy has a discount rate of about 11 percent.) Should Guy make this investment individually or through his corporation?

---

# Case 8–1

John C. Calhoun is an attorney in Hooterville; his law firm owns the four-story Calhoun Building on Main Street. Two floors of the building are occupied by the law office and two floors are rented out to a group of doctors. John is so busy with his law practice that he is not involved in negotiating the leases with the tenants. The partners of the law firm selected a real estate agent to find tenants, negotiate leases, and manage the building.

John is one of elven equal partners in the law firm. In 1989 his share of the partnership's income and expense is:

| | |
|---|---|
| *Income* | |
| Legal services fee revenue | $250,000 |
| Rental income | 65,000 |
| *Expenses* | |
| Rental agent's commissions | $ 10,000 per year |
| Depreciation | 100,000 per year |
| Maintenance | 2,000 per month |
| Legal staff (payroll to nonpartners) | 150,000 per year |

The depreciation and maintenance amounts above are John's share of the total for the building. He has no other sources of income or expense and no carryover items from other years. He is not married and has no dependents.

a. What is John's taxable income in 1989?

b. What suggestions do you have for John?

# Case 8–2

Zonker Harris is considering three investments of $10,000. An investment in an active business will generate $700 of income and cash distributions in years one through three. An investment in an oil drilling partnership (working interest) will generate a $5,000 loss in years one and two, and $11,900 of income and $1,900 of cash distributions in year three. An investment in a cattle breeding partnership (passive activity) will generate a $2,500 loss in years one and two, and $7,300 of income and $2,300 of cash distributions in year three. Each investment will be worth $10,000 after three years.

a. If Zonker is in a 15 percent marginal tax bracket and has no passive activities, which investment should he choose?

b. If Zonker is in a 28 percent marginal tax bracket and has $20,000 of income from passive activities, which investment should he choose?

c. If the investment is being made by Zonkco, a corporation in a 39 percent marginal tax bracket, which investment should it make?

For each case, assume that $100 of tax savings in year one is worth $100; $100 of tax savings in year two is worth $90; and $100 of tax savings in year three is worth $81.

# CHAPTER 9

# Compensation Considerations

Employee compensation transactions have been more significantly affected by tax considerations than virtually any other common business occurrence. Some of the tax-saving techniques available in this area demand that the employer be a corporate entity because the law makes the particular privilege available only to employees. Self-employed people—the proprietors of sole proprietorships and the partners of partnerships—are not considered to be employees of their own firms and, therefore, any tax shelter restricted to employee benefits is unavailable to them.

Largely because of the distinction between employees and self-employed people, and the dollar significance of the differences that used to exist between the tax treatment of pensions for employees and those for self-employed people, such professions as medicine, law, accountancy, dentistry, and engineering about 20 years ago brought pressure to bear upon the state governments to pass legislation authorizing professionals to incorporate in professional service corporations. Virtually all of the states responded affirmatively to this pressure. Although the Treasury Department for some time fought the recognition of the new professional corporations, the courts were generally unsympathetic to the IRS view. The dispute was partially resolved when Congress passed legislation providing major improvements in the tax benefits available to self-employed people and, at the same time, put lower limits on the benefits available to corporate employees. Hence today the two limits are generally comparable. Perhaps the final volley in this tax war was fired in late 1987 when Congress amended the tax rates and began taxing most personal-service corporations at a flat 34 percent rate.

The remaining tax shields available in the compensation area can be classified in several different ways. One of the most meaningful ways to classify them seems to be in terms of their differential tax effect on the employer corporation and on the employee. Although equally applicable to the large corporation, the importance of the alternatives comes into particularly clear focus when we think about the small to medium-sized, owner-managed business venture. In terms of priority-ranked preferences, few owner-managers would disagree with the following preferences:

| Preference Ranking | Tax Effect to Employer Corporation | Tax Effect to Employee Recipient |
|---|---|---|
| 1 | Immediately deductible | Never taxable |
| 2 | Immediately deductible | Tax deferred and, if possible, realized in a preferential form |
| 3 | Immediately deductible | Immediately taxed |
| 4 | Deferred deduction | Deferred tax |
| 5 | Never deductible | Taxed immediately or at a later date |

As a matter of fact, each of these five preferences is a viable possibility, and the specific techniques commonly used in compensation arrangements have been classified under these preferences in the remaining pages of this chapter.

## TECHNIQUES PROVIDING AN IMMEDIATE CORPORATE DEDUCTION AND A BENEFIT THAT IS NEVER TAXED TO THE EMPLOYEE

In Chapter 2, we observed that, generally speaking, individuals are taxed on any economic benefits they receive for services rendered, no matter how indirect the benefits may be. In that same chapter, however, we also observed that the Internal Revenue Code does provide a limited number of exceptions to this rule in the form of specific statutory exclusions. We further noted there that a taxpayer is entitled to deduct all ordinary and necessary business expenses incurred in a trade or business, including any reasonable compensation paid to an employee. By carefully combining the exclusion provisions with the deduction authorizations, it is possible in a limited number of circumstances to provide an employee with a real economic benefit which is never taxed, and, at the same time, provide the employer corporation with an immediate deduction.

### Group Term Life Insurance

Code Section 79(a) provides that an employee need not report as gross income the value of group term life insurance premiums paid by his or her employer so long as the insurance coverage provided under this group-term policy does not exceed $50,000. Observe that, before this special exclusion can apply, the insurance in question must be *group, term, life* insurance. In addition the plan generally cannot discriminate in favor of corporate owners or key employees if it is to be recognized as a qualified plan. If the coverage exceeds $50,000, the employee is taxed only on the cost of the premium for the excess; this cost is based on tables provided in the pertinent regulations. Suffice it to note that the tax cost of coverage in excess of $50,000 is relatively inexpensive. An obvious economic advantage attaches to tax-free life insurance in comparison with insurance purchased from aftertax salary dollars.

In the case of life insurance, a double exclusion is actually possible. Note that the employee need not report the premiums paid by his or her employer for this insurance. Furthermore, if the employee dies and the beneficiaries collect insurance under the policy, they need not report as gross income any amount that they received by reason of the insured person's death.

## Health and Accident Plans

Code Section 106 provides for a similar tax treatment of health and accident insurance plans purchased by an employer for the employee. In the case of health and accident insurance, however, it is necessary to distinguish between the tax treatment of the premium payments and the tax treatment of the amounts actually received under such coverage. The cost of the premiums can be excluded by the employee under Section 106. Other sections of the code determine the tax consequence of compensation paid for injuries and medical expenses. The employee can generally exclude amounts received as payment for loss of a body member or body function. Amounts received to reimburse the taxpayer for medical expenses incurred are also excludable in most circumstances. The details of the many rules are best left for other books.

It is again pertinent to note that, relative to health and accident insurance, an employer corporation can provide a very real economic benefit to an employee without tax cost. If the employee were to purchase his or her own equivalent insurance coverage from aftertax salary, the employee would pay more for the same coverage; the exact amount of the increased cost depends upon the employee's marginal tax bracket. Alternatively, of course, the employee might be forced to purchase less desirable coverage for the same dollar cost. Incidentally, this tax-saving opportunity can include the increasing cost of an annual physical examination for any employee; it can also cover the medical expenses of the employee's spouse and dependents.

Self-employed taxpayers may deduct 25 percent of the cost of health insurance for themselves, their spouses, and their dependents. To be eligible for this deduction, however, the health insurance plan must also apply in a nondiscriminatory way to all of the self-employed taxpayer's employees. Finally, no deduction for such a plan is allowed if the self-employed taxpayer is eligible to participate in an accident and health plan maintained by an employer of either the self-employed taxpayer or his or her spouse.

## Meals and Lodging

Code Section 119 permits an employee to exclude from gross income the value of meals and lodging furnished on the employer's premises for the convenience of the employer. The potential benefit of this section seems to have gone largely unrecognized in the past, and it should be carefully examined by many more taxpayers. Section 119 does not include an explicit nondiscrimination requirement; hence posh executive dining rooms and palatial homes for presidents, governors, and chancellors have traditionally been excluded from income. Under Section 132(e), however, the executive dining room is in jeopardy because that section includes a nondiscrimination test for tax-free, subsidized, employee eating facilities. Another critical nexus in succeeding with regard to taxes lies in the employer's ability to establish a valid corporate reason for insisting that an employee eat while at work or live in a particular home. In regard to company homes, the success of beer magnates Adolph and Joseph Coors is encouraging. (See *Adolph Coors Co.*, T. C. Memo, 1968–256.) The undeveloped but potential use of this section by ranchers, farmers, operators of small businesses, and professionals seems to be substantial, since many should find it possible to explain why their constant presence is required by their own employer corporation. The economic impact of this alternative can be significant since it effectively provides the taxpayer, through a closely held corporation, the right to deduct depreciation on a home, the cost of utilities and insurance, and many other costs not otherwise deductible. Note that, under the proper circumstances, even the cost of the food eaten by the employee becomes deductible by the employer corporation. For these plans to succeed, however, it is essential that the corporation pay the bills in the first instance. Corporate reimbursements will generally fail. Furthermore, there must be a valid business reason for the corporation requiring the employee to live and work on the corporate premises.

### Death Benefits

Code Section 101 allows a taxpayer the right to receive up to $5,000 in tax-free death benefits paid by a deceased employee's corporate employer. The employer can also deduct the amounts paid under such a death benefit plan. Although the dollar significance of this opportunity is obviously rather limited, any taxpayer who takes the trouble to incorporate a business in order to obtain other employee tax benefits should also take the necessary action to insure the right to this small additional benefit.

### Other Employee Benefits

Prior to the 1984 Tax Reform Act the correct tax treatment of numerous other employee fringe benefits was in doubt. That tax act, however, attempted to resolve many questionable fringe-benefit issues with the addition of Section 132 to the Code. That section specifically excludes from gross income those fringe benefits that can qualify as a—

1. No-additional-cost service;
2. Qualified employee discount;

3. Working condition fringe; or

4. De minimis fringe.

To qualify as a no-additional-cost service, a fringe benefit must not add any substantial cost to a service already offered to the public in the ordinary course of the employer's business and must be offered to all employees on a nondiscriminatory basis. Although reciprocal agreements between unrelated employers are allowed, the tax-free service generally must be in the same line of business as that conducted by the recipient employee. Thus, for example, airline employees will be able to travel tax-free on their employer airline (and, possibly, on a reciprocating airline) so long as they fly on a space-available basis. Similarly, employees of a hotel corporation may occupy otherwise vacant rooms in their employer's hotel with little or no cost and still avoid the recognition of any imputed gross income for the value received. Employers engaged in more than one line of business on January 1, 1984, may continue to offer multiline fringe benefits tax-free to all employees. Otherwise this statutory exclusion extends only to a single line of business. In other words, if a corporation engaged solely in the airline business were to add a hotel business to its commercial activities in 1989, the employees of that corporation would in general be restricted to one benefit or the other (i.e., free airline passes or free hotel rooms), depending on their primary employee duties. A few top-level administrative personnel, however, would still seem to qualify for both tax-free fringe benefits under the new rules.

Fringe benefits potentially excluded under the working-condition rules include such items as company cars and airplanes (discussed further below); professional dues and publications; and employee parking. In general, non-discrimination rules do not apply to this class of benefits. To be excluded, however, the fringe benefit provided must be one the cost of which the employee could otherwise have deducted had the same item been purchased from personal funds. For example, a professional employee of an accounting firm could exclude from his or her income the dues of a national or state accounting organization, the cost of auditing or tax journals, and parking charges paid by the employer firm to the extent they would otherwise have been deductible.

Fringe benefits excluded under the new de minimis rules apply to such items as cocktail parties and supper money. These and other similar items are excluded solely because the value of the property or service given to the employee is so small that accounting for it more precisely is simply unreasonable or administratively impracticable.

Some employers provide their employees with the personal right to select from a specified group, which perquisites they would like to receive, subject to some maximum dollar amount. These programs are widely known as *cafeteria plans,* for obvious reasons. Section 125 of the code makes it clear that no otherwise tax-free benefit will become taxable merely because it is part of a cafeteria plan, or because some employees elect to receive cash or other taxable compensation. There is, however, an exception for plans that discriminate in favor of highly compensated employees; these cafeteria plans do not qualify for any tax-free status. Furthermore, to qualify for exclusion, the employee must make his selection at the start of each year; not as he wishes on a daily basis.

### Travel and Entertainment

The detailed rules that regulate the correct tax treatment of travel and entertainment expenses are so lengthy that they cannot be examined here. However, it would be equally inappropriate to gloss over the obvious benefits available in this area. Country club memberships, theater tickets, admissions to athletic events, elegant dining, premium-brand alcohol, and other perquisites too numerous to mention may all be partially or wholly deducted under the proper circumstances. Travel that combines business with pleasure is frequently rewarding from a tax standpoint.

Prior to 1987 the entire cost of any qualifying travel and entertainment (T & E) expenses was generally deductible. Today, in many circumstances, only 80 percent of many of those same expenses is deductible. The disallowed 20 percent of the expense is supposed to represent a crude measure of the personal benefit implicit in the expenditure. In general the 80 percent rule applies only to the cost of meals (including tax and tip) and entertainment expenses. It does not apply to transportation, housing, and other travel costs often associated with T & E expenses.

If a taxpayer makes a full accounting of any T & E expenses incurred and is thereafter totally reimbursed for those expenses, regardless of any personal benefits associated with the event, this taxpayer reports no amount of either gross income or deduction. The taxpayer who reimburses the T & E expense will be the party who cannot deduct the cost of 20 percent of the meal and entertainment expenses incurred. This means that the employer, rather than the employee, will eventually suffer the consequences of the decreased tax deduction allowed. Self-employed taxpayers and employees who are not reimbursed will, however, also be subject to the 20 percent disallowance. This new requirement will obviously require more detailed records of all T & E expenses incurred.

Employees who are not reimbursed for all of their T & E expenses may continue to deduct the excess, subject to two important limits. First, the employee must claim itemized deductions, rather than a standard deduction, because these expenses are now categorized as deductions from AGI. Second, because they are also categorized as miscellaneous employee business deductions, they may be included with other itemized deductions only to the extent that, in the aggregate, miscellaneous deductions exceed two percent of the taxpayer's AGI.

In a practical sense, what these rules should say to the members of the entrepreneurial class is that they ought to give adequate consideration to the tax aspects of alternative ways of doing business combined with pleasure. When the conditions are favorable, it is still not terribly difficult to convert a great number of expenditures for personal pleasure into tax deductions. Relative to domestic travel, for example, once the taxpayer can establish that the primary purpose of a trip is business, the entire cost of the transportation and most of the related expenses during business days become tax deductible. Relative to foreign travel, entirely different rules are applied. The interesting little rules required to get a deduction for foreign travel sometimes make the entire scene look like part of a comic opera, and the substantiation requirements appear to be a chapter directly from George Orwell's *1984*. In a nutshell, under the current rules, the deduction for travel to a foreign convention is limited to the lowest economy air fare; and even that deduction depends on the taxpayer spending more days devoted to business than to pleasure. Moreover, in order to deduct other travel costs, the taxpayer must be able to prove that he or she engaged in at least four out of six hours of scheduled business on any one business day. In this area more than any other, an ounce of prevention is worth a pound of cure, so see your tax adviser and go well prepared. The way can be both rewarding and enjoyable for those who know the rules. For the poorly advised, it is filled with pitfalls.

### Automobiles (and Airplanes?)

The company car has become as much a part of the American scene as the winter convention in Arizona or Florida. For the fortunate employee, the company car is the one that produces no taxable income, but whose entire cost is deductible by the employer corporation. The models may vary from four-cylinder compacts to the chauffeur-driven limousines parked two deep around Wall Street and Rockefeller Center at 3:00 P.M. The tax results are the same. Use the car for purely personal purposes, and you suddenly have realized gross income. Use it solely for business purposes, and you just might escape tax-free. Use it for both personal and business purposes, and anticipate an argument with an IRS agent. Business purpose? Personal use? Definitions and tax requirements are a dime a dozen.

Why stop with automobiles? For the jet set, a plane is vastly more effective. After all, if the company plane is scheduled to fly to Acapulco to pick up a business client, why shouldn't the corporate executive (or a member of the family) who happens to have the day off fly along just for the fun of it. Or if Air Force One happens to be flying the president or a member of his cabinet to Hawaii, why shouldn't wives, families, and friends accompany the government official tax-free? And a senator or congressman on a military jet bound for a fact-finding mission in the Orient just may find enough time to stop for Christmas shopping in Hong Kong.

The opportunities for tax abuse are obviously as real as other social inequities. Unfortunately, there are no easy answers. Expenses for business travel and business entertainment are as legitimate as expenditures for heat, light, water, and rent in a place of business. The unique problem created by travel and entertainment, however, is that it is extremely difficult to measure on any reasonable basis the legitimate business expense portion and the truly personal portion. In an attempt to deal with this problem, Congress and the Treasury Department have brought forth a host of new Code provisions and regulations in the past few years. As with the foreign travel provisions, many of the automobile and private airplane regulations would be amusing in their complexity, were it not for the fact that taxpayers, tax advisers, and tax administrators must now attempt to comply with those rules in a serious fashion. Occasionally the tax authorities overstep the boundary of reasonableness— as they did a few years ago when they required that a daily mileage log be maintained for every automobile used in business—and the taxpayers revolt with sufficient fervor to cause Congress to intervene in the endless struggle for tax equity. The final result is typically a very crude provision (not unlike the 20 percent business meal disallowance) which is intended to measure the personal portion of these otherwise legitimate business expenses.

Taxpayers who own and operate a small business must be particularly careful in their use of automobiles for combined business and personal use. Section 280F severely limits the depreciation or lease-rent deduction that can be claimed on "luxury automobiles" and other "listed property" used in this dual manner. Detailed records are once again a necessary evil for taxpayers in these common circumstances.

### Employee Discounts

If an employee is given the opportunity of purchasing the employer's ordinary inventory at a discount, and if this discount is extended to all employees, the employee generally need not report the bargain price element as gross income. On the other hand, if the price discount becomes too great, or if it is not made generally available to all employees, the IRS will be quick to find that the employee must report as taxable income the difference between the fair market value and the lower price actually paid to acquire the employer's property. In general, excluded employee discounts are limited to the employer's gross profit percent in the particular line of business in which the employee works; service discounts are limited to 20 percent of the price charged ordinary customers. Furthermore, this exclusion does not apply to real property or to personal property that is held for investment purposes.

### Interest-Free Loans

Prior to the 1984 Tax Reform Act, some employers also provided select employees with interest-free loans. The idea behind the interest-free loan was conceptually similar to the idea behind employee discounts. That is, neither benefit literally created a tax deduction for the employer. What both of these fringe benefits did, however, was to indirectly reduce the employer's gross income and, therefore, its taxable income, by the amount of the income foregone via (1) reduced sales revenues (in the case of employee discounts) or

(2) investment income (in the case of interest-free loans). The right of the employee to exclude the economic benefits received in these ways was based on somewhat tenuous authority prior to 1984.

The 1984 act specifically authorized the continued exclusion of the employee discount under the conditions described above. At the same time, however, it explicitly made taxable the similar benefit in low-interest and interest-free loans to employees. The latter result is attributable to new rules which now require:

1. The employee to report as additional compensation the value of an imputed interest (equal to the difference between the interest rate charged, if any, and the applicable "federal rate") on the loan; and

2. The employer to report an interest income of an equal amount.

Although the original impact of the change made by the 1984 Act was more or less a wash—that is, the employee reported an equal increase in both compensation (gross income) and interest expense (a deduction) and the employer reported an equal increase in both wage expense (a deduction) and interest income—that is not true today because the executive can no longer deduct the imputed interest expense. Consequently very few persons are expected to continue interest-free loan arrangements.

Special exceptions to the above rules apply to certain loans of $10,000 or less if the loan is compensation-related or is a corporation-shareholder loan. Still other exceptions apply to "gift loans" between individuals of $100,000 or less. The details of these exceptions will not be explained here.

Before we proceed to the second-ranked form of compensation, a word of caution seems to be in order. Obviously, the IRS and the courts are not ignorant of what is taking place in the area of disguised compensation. They examine the records of closely held corporations with particular care just because the opportunity for owner-managers to divert corporate funds for purely personal purposes is substantial. In the large publicly owned corporation, even the very top executives may eventually have to answer to a higher authority at the next stockholders' meeting. The most obvious abuses in this area frequently lead to the courtroom and an eventual judicial settlement. The owner-manager must be particularly careful to establish sound business purposes for whatever he or she does. Extra caution in maintaining proper records, to give any transaction the bona fide look, is essential. This is not a job for an amateur.

## TECHNIQUES PROVIDING AN IMMEDIATE CORPORATE DEDUCTION AND A TAX-DEFERRED BENEFIT TO THE EMPLOYEE

A second class of compensation techniques is characterized by the ability to produce an immediate deduction to the corporate employer and only a deferred (and sometimes preferential form of) gross income to the employee. In terms of the absolute dollar amount of tax-sheltered compensation, there can be little doubt that this class of tax-saving techniques dominates in the aggregate. The most common forms of this second-ranked class are the qualified pension and profit-sharing plans. In the same class of benefits, but of much less common occurrence, is the qualified stock bonus plan. All *qualified* pension, profit-sharing, and stock bonus plans share several common characteristics. On the other hand, two fully qualified plans may differ significantly from each other. In the discussion that follows, we will first examine the common characteristics, then look at some of the more important differences among qualified plans, and finally consider briefly a few of the considerations that should be given careful thought before undertaking the implementation of any of these plans. The technical rules that govern this complex area of taxation were first introduced in the Employee Retirement Income Security Act of 1974, popularly known by the acronym ERISA. Even though those and many subsequent modifications have become part of the Code, most people still refer to these rules as the ERISA requirements.

### Common Characteristics of All Qualified Pension, Profit-Sharing, and Stock Bonus Plans

All qualified pension, profit-sharing, and stock bonus plans attain their preferred tax position because of certain unique tax provisions that are applicable to them. They must all meet certain requirements before they can be considered to be qualified plans. And they all trigger tax consequences for the employee under similar circumstances. Before we consider the many requirements applicable to qualified plans, let us look briefly at the available benefits.

**The Tax Opportunities Available.**    The tax benefits available in most qualified pension, profit-sharing, and stock bonus plans can be separated into six distinct considerations.

1. Subject to varying maximum limits, the corporate employer will get an immediate tax deduction for its contribution to the employee trust fund created to administer these assets.
2. The employee trust fund will be treated as a tax-exempt entity, which allows it to accumulate earnings tax free and thus to grow at a faster rate than would otherwise be possible.
3. The employee will not be taxed on either the employer's current contributions or on the growth from prior contributions until he or she either withdraws the funds or until the funds are otherwise made available to the employee.
4. Employees who designated before 12/31/84 that, in the event of death, their interest in an employee trust fund be paid as an annuity to someone other than the executor of the estate, effectively removed from the value of the

estate (for estate tax purposes) up to $100,000 of their interest in the trust fund that was attributable to the employer's contributions, deductible employee contributions, or IRA benefits.

5. If in one year an employee withdraws all of his or her rights from a qualified employee trust in a lump-sum settlement, certain options exist. The details of those options depend, among other things, upon the age of the taxpayer on January 1, 1986. Individuals who were 50 years of age (or older) on that day have more options than do younger persons. For the latter group the choice is generally between taxing the entire amount as ordinary income or electing something called five-year forward averaging. In many instances the five-year averaging alternative is beneficial; hence a taxpayer can elect it only once in a lifetime (after reaching age 59½). For persons who were 50 years of age or older on January 1, 1986, it will be important to consider other options with the help of a knowledgeable adviser.

6. An employee may sometimes be able to contribute additional funds to a pension trust out of his or her own pocket and thereby put those funds to work in a tax-free environment. In some circumstances, the additional contributions made by an employee may be taken from the employee's salary by the employer on a before-tax basis. In other words, the employee may be able to contribute pretax dollars to the fund if they can be treated as a salary *reduction* rather than as a salary *deduction*. In other cases the employee's personal contributions must come from aftertax dollars, but to the extent that this is true, the employee will be able to recover those same amounts free of any further income tax on separation from service, retirement, or death.

This list of tax benefits available through a qualified pension or profit-sharing plan is truly impressive, and the dollar significance of this opportunity to any employee can hardly be overrated. The magnitude of the tax savings is, of course, directly related to the marginal tax bracket of the employee. For upper-income-bracket individuals, it would require a significant increase in cash salaries to purchase an equivalent retirement annuity in a taxable commercial enterprise. The compounding effect of tax-free contributions and tax-free growth is almost phenomenal over the working life of an individual. To grasp better the significance of the difference, consider two taxpayers in the top marginal tax bracket (i.e., 33 percent) who each divert $15,000 per year to a retirement plan and earn an annual 6 percent return on their retirement investment for a period of 40 years. The only difference between the two taxpayers is that taxpayer A prepares for retirement in a non–tax sheltered way, whereas taxpayer B prepares for retirement through a qualified pension program. At the end of the 40 years, taxpayer B's retirement fund will amount to over $2.3 million, whereas taxpayer A's fund will have grown to less than $1 million. Obviously, these two amounts are not appropriate as a final comparison, since taxpayer B still has to pay an income tax on all retirement income, whereas most of taxpayer A's retirement income will be free of further income tax (that is, all but the additional earnings produced by the remaining assets during the retirement years). Nevertheless, the dollar difference in their retirement pensions will be substantial. Perhaps in no small measure it is because these benefits are so impressive that requirements for qualifications are so demanding.

**Qualification of a Plan.**    A pension, profit-sharing, or stock bonus plan will not qualify for the tax shelters listed previously unless it satisfies the numerous code requirements of Section 401. Among the conditions required for qualification are the following:

1. That the plan be created for the exclusive benefit of the employees and/or their beneficiaries.
2. That the sole purpose of the plan be either to give the employees or their beneficiaries a share of the employer's profits or to provide them with a retirement income.
3. That the plan be a written, permanent plan and that it be communicated to the employees.
4. That the plan *not* discriminate in favor of corporate officers, stockholder-employees, or supervisory or highly paid employees.
5. That the plan provide for a vesting of full benefits after no more than 7 years of service to the employer.
6. That the plan be "funded"—that is, the employer must make annual cash contributions to the fund, often in significant amounts.

Each of these requirements is stipulated with considerable detail in the code and the related regulations. For anything other than the smallest corporate enterprise—that is, for all but the "one-man" corporation—the two most important requirements are perhaps the one that precludes discrimination among employees and the one that insists on funding. Most owner-operators would be delighted to provide themselves with a tax-sheltered pension or profit-sharing plan, but they are reluctant to do so when this also requires that all other employees share the pot. On the other hand, some employers who might be willing to cover all employees may not have sufficient capital to fund a qualified plan. Although a qualified plan cannot discriminate, because contributions to the plan may be made a percentage of the employee's salary, the real benefits obtained are not equal for every employee by any means.

Taxpayers owning more than one corporation might be tempted to be selective in determining which corporation would institute a generous qualified pension or profit-sharing plan. The corporation with the highest ratio of owner-employees to total employees is the obvious candidate. The effort to discriminate through the careful selection of one of several related corporate entities generally will not succeed. In most instances, multiple businesses under common control must be treated as a single business.

Assuming that a pension or profit-sharing plan meets all code requirements for qualification, the accumulated assets of the employee trust fund must sooner or later be distributed to the employees. When this happens, the employee must recognize taxable income. As noted earlier, that income may be subject to special treatment if taken in a lump sum.

**Taxation of Employee Benefits.**   An employee covered by a qualified pension or profit-sharing plan need not report as taxable income any benefits under that plan until they are paid or otherwise made available. Usually, benefits are not distributed by employee trust funds until an employee terminates employment, retires, or dies. Very often a qualified plan will allow the employee to select from several options when deciding how to receive any accumulated benefits. He or she may, for example, be given a choice between (1) a lump-sum settlement, (2) a lifetime annuity for one life, or (3) a smaller lifetime annuity for as long as either the employee or the employee's spouse shall live. Another common option is a refund feature, which guarantees the employee or the heirs the right to receive a minimum payment, regardless of how long the employee may live. The option selected by the employee significantly determines the tax consequence of any distribution. Once again, the specific rules that determine the exact tax results are too numerous and too complex to justify their inclusion in a book aimed at tax recognition rather than tax solution. Suffice it to observe here that no employee should make any election until he or she has fully investigated the tax results of every option. Generally that will require the assistance of a qualified tax adviser.

If all details are properly arranged in advance, an employee may rarely be able to obtain an earlier benefit from an economic interest in a qualified plan without termination of employment and without triggering the usual tax consequences for all accumulated benefits. For example, a few qualified profit-sharing plans provide that employees can borrow against vested rights if they can show need (such as unusual medical costs, college expenses, or acquisition of a new residence). In general, these loans cannot exceed the *lesser* of (a) $50,000 or (b) one-half the present value of the nonforfeitable accrued benefit under the plan (but not less than $10,000). Furthermore, the maximum new loan in any year is decreased by the highest loan balance outstanding in the prior 12 months. And, finally, except in the case of home-construction loans, all loans must be repaid in five years or less. So long as the employee does not have an absolute right to make such loans, but only has the right to request them in appropriate and specified circumstances, the tax deferral privilege may be maintained.

### Some Important Differences in Qualified Plans

Although all qualified pension, profit-sharing, and stock bonus plans have many things in common, such plans also differ in many important ways. Some of the important differences have more to do with everyday economics than with taxation. Some of the differences are of primary importance to the employer corporation; others are of greater importance to the employee. Perhaps the most important differences relate to funding and to the tax deduction limitation.

**Pension Plans.**    A pension plan has as its primary purpose the provision of a retirement fund for covered employees. Once instituted, a pension plan generally becomes a fixed obligation of the employer corporation. This means, of course, that the employer must make the contractual contribution without regard for the presence or absence of corporate profits. Because of the substantial cash requirement implicit in a pension plan covering any sizable group of employees, new and riskier ventures are typically reluctant to institute such a plan. Employees, especially middle-aged and older employees, on the other hand, strongly prefer the relative security of a fixed contractual arrangement. Because pension plans are intended to provide for retirement income, they seldom make provision for any acceleration of benefits, even in cases of demonstrated need. Vesting rights were, for many years, a controversial aspect of qualified pension plans. Today an employee's rights to any employer contributions must vest under one of two different schedules. In every case, an employee's rights must either be 100 percent vested after five years of service or vested at the rate of 20 percent per year in the third through seventh year of employment. This means, of course, that an employee with at least seven years of service with a single employer is now guaranteed certain rights under a qualified pension program, whether or not he or she continues employment with the same employer until retirement. Obviously, an employee who leaves the employ of a corporation after a few years will receive a smaller retirement pension than will an employee with many years of service. By the accumulation of two or three small pensions with different employers, however, the more transitory employee can now look forward to a reasonable retirement income, even if not all of it is paid by a single trust fund.

The maximum tax deduction that an employer corporation may claim in any tax year for its contribution to a qualified pension plan depends in part upon the funding method it elects. The actuarially determined cost of the plan, along with a liability-to-asset ratio, fixes the maximum deduction under any fixed-benefit plan. Pension costs are based upon assumptions about the future, including estimated employee earnings, mortality, turnover, retirement, and vesting rights. Because qualified pension plans include credit for prior service (that is, for services rendered to the employer prior to the institution of a pension plan) as well as for future service, the current year's tax deduction may well exceed the cost that relates only to current employee services rendered to the employer. However, a defined benefit plan cannot provide for a retirement income in excess of *approximately* $95,000 per year; it will be less than that if retirement begins before age 65. (The exact maximum varies from year to year. It was $90,000 in 1987—an amount that is adjusted annually for changes in the consumer price index—and $94,023 in 1988.)

Maximum contributions under a defined-contribution plan are easier to determine because no contractual minimum return is guaranteed. No contribution can be made for any employees' income in excess of *approximately* $210,000 per year under a defined-contribution plan. (Again this is an amount that is adjusted each year for changes in the CPI; it was $200,000 in 1987 and $208,940 in 1988.)

**Profit-Sharing Plans.**   Rights under a profit-sharing plan depend, as the name implies, upon the presence of employer profits. If the corporate employer earns no income in a particular year, it has no obligation to make a contribution to a qualified profit-sharing plan that year. Corporations with highly volatile income find this feature especially appealing. Young, new employees, who look forward to a number of prosperous years, may also find profit sharing a desirable alternative, whereas older employees, with fewer years remaining prior to retirement, generally prefer some other plan.

The maximum deduction for amounts contributed by the employer to a profit-sharing plan is generally equal to 15 percent of the compensation paid to participating employees. In no instance can the deduction in a single year exceed 25 percent of current employee compensation. Amounts contributed in excess of the current year's maximum deduction can generally be carried over and deducted in succeeding years to whatever extent the succeeding years' contributions are less than the maximum deduction, but they are subject to a 10 percent excise tax in the interim period.

**Stock Bonus Plans.**   The tax rules for qualified stock bonus plans generally parallel those applicable to profit-sharing plans. The major difference between the two is the fact that stock bonus plans are payable in the stock of the employer corporations rather than in cash. This means, of course, that the employees' rights under the plan depend not only upon the presence of profits but also upon the value of the employer's stock. New corporations, many of which are critically short on cash, may be especially attracted to stock bonus plans because they minimize cash requirements. Young employees may find that the possible increase in benefits is worth the additional risk associated with the future value of their employer's stock. Older employees and majority stockholders may find stock bonus plans less acceptable because of the extra risk and the dilution of equity, respectively.

As noted earlier, it is easy to underestimate the significance of the benefits available through qualified pension, profit-sharing, and stock bonus plans. Implementing the plans and selecting the most desirable options within those plans are much more difficult tasks. Some of the more important considerations will be reviewed very briefly.

### Related Considerations

Any taxpayer considering the possibility of implementing a qualified pension, profit-sharing, or stock bonus plan should consult with a team of experts to assist in making a wise decision. Normally the team will consist of representatives of the employer and the employees, as well as an accountant, attorney, and actuary (or life underwriter). The team should carefully estimate the cost of implementing any plan, as well as the benefits expected from it. The costs and benefits are doubly difficult to predict, not only because they are based on many estimates of the future, but also because they may significantly influence that future through changes in employee morale, and thus changes in the corporate performance generally. A good plan is one that helps develop and retain a strong and permanent complement of employees who are anxious to do their part to make the corporation more profitable.

Qualified pension plans may provide the retired employee with either a *fixed* or a *variable* annuity. A defined benefit plan stipulates in advance a determinable number of dollars that the employee may claim at some future date under any given option. A defined contribution plan provides benefits of varying amount, depending upon the relative success or failure of the trustee's investment of fund assets during the interim years. Many authors describing fixed annuities suggest that they are less risky than variable annuities because the dollar benefits paid to the employee are not subject to the vagaries of the securities markets. However, that statement is at least as misleading as it is accurate. Although it is true that the employee may be able to determine how many dollars he or she will receive under a fixed annuity, that fact provides no knowledge about what any number of dollars may buy at some future date. The more rapid the inflation prior to retirement, the greater the risk in a fixed annuity. Unfortunately, the risk in a variable annuity may also be sizable because of wide fluctuations in the price of stocks. Few if any employees contemplating retirement in the period from 1960 to 1970 would have accurately estimated the absolute dollar cost of a minimal retirement living in the 1980s. Given the importance of the unknowns, it is often very difficult to select wisely between fixed and variable annuities.

Contributions made by an employer to an employee trust fund obviously do not lie idle pending the employee's retirement. These assets might be directly invested by the fund trustee; they might be turned over to some other professional or to a mutual fund for investment; they might be put into government bonds; or they might be lodged directly with an insurance company, which could provide an annuity contract for each covered employee. The eventual financial success of any employee trust fund is directly determined by the investment decisions.

Prior to the passage of ERISA in 1974, a number of employee trust funds seemed to be manipulated more for the benefit of the corporate employer than for the employees. For example, the assets of some trust funds were loaned back to the contributing employer at low rates of interest. Other funds purchased assets from employers and/or the employer's stockholders at apparently inflated values. Still others hired the employer's stockholders at high salaries. All of these and many other questionable practices were made the subject of severe penalty provisions in the 1974 legislation. As a consequence, most self-serving transactions have been ended. In fact, the new rules may be too restrictive. Some trustees are now being overly conservative; they are thereby reducing the earnings of the employees' trust funds and thus the benefits that will eventually be received, at least under variable annuity plans.

Life, health, and accident insurance are sometimes made a part of the qualified pension, profit-sharing, or stock bonus package. Generally, the presence of any of these benefits makes some part of the employee's rights immediately taxable. Other plans combine pension and profit-sharing plans into a single combined plan. Such plans may maximize the number of dollars that can be tax sheltered. Still other plans facilitate the transfer of employees between related employers by providing a single qualified plan for a group of related employers. Affiliated corporate groups can create plans that allow profitable member corporations to make contributions for the benefit of an unprofitable member corporation's employees. Deciding whether or not to include these or many other benefits within the context of a qualified plan complicates the basic decision. Even with the multiple complexities, however, few tax-saving plans create more impressive benefits than do qualified pension, profit-sharing, and stock bonus plans.

The next class of compensation arrangements to be discussed is the class that includes the most common form of employee compensation—that is, the routine wage or salary. The tax planner should always remember that the aggregate compensation paid to an employee must be *reasonable* in *amount* before it can be deducted by the employer corporation. This reasonableness test encompasses all forms of compensation considered together.

## TECHNIQUES PROVIDING AN IMMEDIATE CORPORATE DEDUCTION AND AN IMMEDIATE TAX TO THE EMPLOYEE

In addition to cash wages and salaries, this third class of techniques includes almost all nonqualified compensation arrangements. For example, if a corporate employee is given the right to make a bargain purchase of a corporate asset, the amount of that bargain generally will be included as part of his or her compensation. If a corporation purchases an entertainment facility—say, a resort condominium or a hunting lodge—and makes it available only to corporate executives, the value of their use of such a facility could very easily be treated as additional compensation. If an employee's spouse and family are provided with a free trip at company expense in connection with a convention or other business trip, the employee can anticipate having to report the amount expended by the employer for the spouse and the family as additional gross income. In summary, assuming that the aggregate value of all of the items paid by the employer primarily for the employee's benefit is a *reasonable* compensation, it will be immediately deductible by the employer and immediately taxed to the employee, unless it can be fitted into one of the special exceptions discussed earlier in this chapter.

## Cash Salary

The regular cash wage or salary is still the most common form of employee compensation. It may be surprising that it qualifies only as a third-ranked class of compensation techniques—that is, as one that produces an immediate deduction for the employer and an immediate gross income for the employee. The reason for its overwhelming popularity is, naturally, the need and desire of every employee to obtain cash and the personal flexibility in spending that goes with it. Even if an expert were able to create a tax-sheltered world in which every employee was adequately provided with a company home, company food, a company car, company entertainment, a company medical plan, and a company pension, the need and desire for additional cash salary would remain. In fact, in such a protected world, the implicit or psychic cost associated with any further tax shelter would almost certainly be greater than the benefit of the additional tax saving under even the most onerous income tax that the human mind could devise.

Because the top marginal rate on a corporation's taxable income now is, for the first time in U.S. history, higher than the top marginal rate on an individual's taxable income, many closely held corporations will be sorely tempted to increase their owner-employee's salary near the end of every profitable year in order to keep the aggregate tax liability of the two taxpayers at the lowest possible level. This tendency promises to lead to a great deal of litigation in years to come. The standard of reasonableness is, obviously, a subjective standard. Decisions can only be made in these cases on a facts-and-circumstances basis. Taxpayers who are successful in their defense of large salary increases will, in most cases, be those who made the changes with sufficient forethought and planning. Large bonuses, declared late in a tax year, and distributed to owner-employees in the same ratio as their capital balances, will be particularly suspect. Here, as elsewhere in tax matters, an ounce of prevention is worth a pound of cure.

## Nonqualified Stock Options

Stock options have had a long and checkered history in the tax annals of the United States. Because of the demise of the special tax treatment for capital gains in 1986, stock options are of much less interest today than they were in prior years. Nevertheless, they are still of some limited interest. To understand the economics involved in a stock option, we must review some basic concepts.

A stock option is nothing more than a right to purchase a corporation's stock for a given period at a given price. If the price is set equal to the market price on the date the option is granted, the option itself has real economic value only if the period of the option is of some reasonable length. To illustrate, if someone were to offer you the guaranteed right to purchase General Motors common stock at today's market price, wouldn't you be willing to pay something for that option if it ran for, say, a period of 5 years? Wouldn't you be willing to pay even more if it ran for 10 or 20 years? Under these conditions, the opportunity to make a substantial profit with a minimum investment is very real. An option holder would simply hold the rights unexercised as long as the value of the stock remained constant or decreased. If the market price decreased and remained depressed for the term of the option, the option would finally expire and prove to be worthless. On the other hand, if the value of the stock increased, the option would become as valuable as the spread between the later market price and the option price multiplied by the number of shares authorized in the option.

At one time, the tax laws were interpreted so that an employee was required to report as ordinary income only the initial spread between an option price and the fair market value of the stock on the date the option was granted. Any subsequent increase was capital gain. Today, the rules that control the tax consequence of a stock option are considerably more complex. At this juncture we will consider the tax rules applicable to *nonqualified* options; the rules applicable to incentive stock options appear later in this chapter. The tax treatment of a nonqualified stock option depends upon whether or not the fair market value of the *option* is readily ascertainable when the option is granted. If it is, the employee must immediately report that value, less anything he or she might have to pay to acquire the option, as ordinary income; the same amount is immediately deductible by the employer corporation. In this situation, any further increment in value will be reportable as a capital gain when sold. If the fair market value of the option is not readily ascertainable when the option is granted, the employee will not realize any taxable income until he or she exercises the option and acquires the property. At that time, the employee reports the entire fair market value of the property received, again less any payment made to acquire the property, as ordinary income; the corporate employer then receives a corresponding deduction at that time. The appropriate rules, although difficult to state in words, can be illustrated simply, as shown in Figure 9–1.

The distance $OA$ represents the amount of capital that the employee must contribute to the corporation to acquire the stock when exercising the option. Distance $AB$ represents the spread between the option price and the fair market value of the stock on the date the option was granted. If distance $AB$ is known on date $t_1$, it is immediately taxed to the employee and deducted by the employer. If the distance $AB$ is not known on date $t_1$, then distance $AC$ is taxed to the employee and deducted by the employer on date $t_2$. In the latter case, the only element of capital gain remaining in the employee stock option is the distance $CD$, the increment in value after the exercise date and before the sale date. If the time lapse between $t_2$ and $t_3$ is more than six months, the distance $CD$ will be capital gain. Stock subject to a restriction—for example, stock that can only be sold to the employer corporation at a fixed

**FIGURE 9–1**

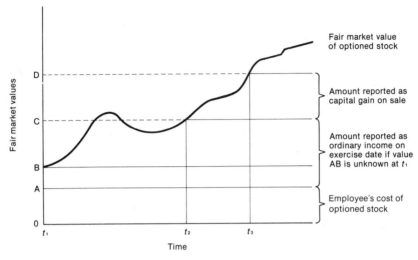

Where

*OA* equals the option price.
*OB* equals the fair market value of the stock on the date the stock option was granted.
*OC* equals the fair market value of the stock on the date the stock option was exercised.
*OD* equals the fair market value of the stock on the date the stock was sold.
$t_1$ represents the date the option was granted.
$t_2$ represents the date the option was exercised.
$t_3$ represents the date the stock was sold.

price if the employee resigns within a prescribed time period—is subject to special rules.

Given the fact that most of any increment in value in a nonqualified employee stock option is taxed as ordinary income, the reader may wonder why that option has any potential compensation value. The answer has to lie in nontax considerations. First, note that the option price (*OA*) can be set low enough to allow even a nonpropertied junior executive a "piece of the action" with a minimum investment. Second, note that the value of any option eventually depends upon the value of the stock. If the stock becomes very valuable, so does the option. For the third and final advantage, note that a stock option may provide a real economic benefit to an employee with no cash cost to the corporation. In fact, if an option is exercised, the corporation may actually receive an additional cash contribution to its own capital. This cash-free cost assumes that the corporation can issue either (1) previously authorized but unissued shares or (2) treasury stock already owned by the employer. The real economic cost is shifted to the stockholders by dilution of their equity interests. In large corporations, where no one person owns anything but a small fraction of the total stock, this dilution of equity is minimized if an executive can increase the stock dollar value of shareholder's stock, notwithstanding a small dilution of each shareholder's relative interest. In summary, under the appropriate circumstances, a nonqualified stock option is still a viable form of compensation even though it presents no tax-saving opportunities.

The possible variations on a basic stock option theme are amazing. Some options involve additional restrictions on the property acquired by the employee, which may affect the date and the measurement of taxable income. Other plans involve phantom stock rather than actual shares. Phantom plans are useful whenever the stockholders want to avoid any dilution of their ownership interests, but still wish to base an employee's compensation on stock values. Under a phantom plan, the employee acquires an "equivalent unit," based on stock prices and on a stock plan agreement. These units even pay "dividend equivalents," which are accumulated and held on the employee's behalf. On separation from service, the employee claims all vested rights and withdraws all accumulated benefits over an agreed time period. Details of these and other plans could be described at length, but those details would add little of significance. Thus it seems preferable to move to other techniques utilized in compensation arrangements and to return later to a discussion of the incentive stock option, which provides no tax deduction for the employer-corporation at any time.

## TECHNIQUES PROVIDING A DEFERRED CORPORATE DEDUCTION AND A DEFERRED TAX TO THE EMPLOYEE

In relatively rare instances, an employee may be provided with an unfunded equivalent of a pension plan. These arrangements, commonly known as *deferred compensation plans*, involve an employer's promise to make continued payments to a particular employee following retirement from service. The payments supposedly represent additional compensation for services already rendered by the employee. If the deferred compensation plan is a nonqualified one, no corporate assets are actually set aside to cover the contractual agreement; the employee's rights are forfeitable; the employee will not report any gross income until he or she actually receives payments under the agreement; and the corporate employer will not claim a tax deduction until that same year. If the plan is funded and the employee's rights become vested, the tax consequences may be accelerated for both parties. Typically, the tax benefit of a deferred compensation plan must derive from the deferral of income to a date at which an executive is in a lower marginal tax bracket. Given the present tax rates, that seems an unlikely possibility. Hence deferred compensation arrangements are of very limited interest today. Economically speaking, these arrangements place the retired employee in the position of a general creditor of a former employer. If all goes well with the corporation financially, a deferred pay contract is valuable and a comfortable retirement is assured. If the employer gets into financial difficulty, however, the deferred compensation arrangement may be essentially worthless to a former employee.

## TECHNIQUES PROVIDING NO CORPORATE DEDUCTION BUT A TAX TO THE EMPLOYEE

A reader might question whether any technique that provides no deduction to a corporate employer can really constitute an employee compensation device. It can be argued that, definitionally, such an item cannot exist. Although that conclusion may be justified on definitional grounds, as a practical matter it will pay to examine two situations in which apparent employee compensation is associated with a nondeductible result to an employer corporation. One of those (the disguised dividend) is a tax trap; the other (the incentive stock option) is largely an anachronism.

### Disguised Dividends

If a court sustains an IRS contention that payments made to an employee are unreasonable in amount, the court is also likely to find that such payments are in effect a disguised dividend if the recipient is also a stockholder of the employer corporation. If a payment is found to constitute a dividend, we know that the corporation will not be entitled to any deduction, even though the recipient shareholder will be required to report the entire amount received as ordinary income. The likelihood of this disastrous tax conclusion is significantly increased in the closely held corporation in which the corporate executives are also the major stockholders and dividend payments are kept to a minimum. Taxpayers in this situation may be able to provide some protection against the initial conclusion if they have an advance, written contractual agreement with their corporate employer that provides that they must return to the corporation any amount finally determined to constitute unreasonable compensation. If successful, such an agreement will remove the initial problem of ordinary income with no deduction, but it may create further problems in the area of the accumulated earnings tax. The need for expert assistance in such a sensitive area is obvious.

The reader should also understand that in making the reasonableness determination, the IRS will look to the entire compensation package, not just to cash salaries. To the extent that fringe benefits increase aggregate compensation, they also increase the likelihood of the reasonableness issue. The successful defense against an unreasonable compensation charge may turn upon such facts as the special skill and ability of the employee, the scope of his or her services, the dividend history of the employer, the relative ownership interests of the employees whose salaries are being questioned, the adequacy of compensation in prior years, and general comparisons with other taxpayers in the same industry. Each case stands on its own facts, and generalization of results is hazardous.

## Incentive Stock Options

As noted earlier in this chapter, recent changes in the tax law have reduced the role of the stock option to minimal significance because capital gains are now taxed like ordinary income. Nevertheless, because of nontax factors, they still are of limited interest.

The proponents of employee stock options have always argued that the value of any corporate executive is totally dependent on what he or she can "do with the company." If an executive can make the firm highly profitable—and thereby substantially increase the market value of the corporation's stock—the executive is a very valuable person to the stockholders and should be compensated accordingly. On the other hand, if the executive cannot increase the value of the stock, the executive should not receive any special compensation. That basic theory is clearly the rationale behind the stock option provisions.

To qualify as an incentive stock option, each of the following seven conditions must be satisfied:

1. The option must be part of a plan (approved by the stockholders within 12 months before or after the plan is adopted) that states both (*a*) the maximum number of shares to be issued and (*b*) the employees or class of employees to be granted an option.

2. The option must be granted to the employee within 10 years from the earlier of the date the plan was (*a*) adopted or (*b*) approved by the shareholders.

3. The maximum option period generally cannot exceed 10 years from the date it is granted. (This period is reduced to 5 years for any shareholder owning more than 10 percent of the employer's stock.)

4. The option holder must be an employee of (*a*) the corporation granting the option, (*b*) a parent or subsidiary corporation, or (*c*) a corporation that has assumed the option as a result of a reorganization or liquidation, for the entire period from the date the option is granted until three months before it is exercised.

5. The option cannot be transferable except at death. (The executor of a deceased employee's estate has a maximum of three months following the decedent's death to exercise an outstanding option.)

6. The option price must be equal to (or greater than) the fair market value of the stock on the date the option is granted. (If the recipient owns more than 10 percent of the corporation granting the option, the option price

must be at least 110 percent of the stock's fair market value on the date granted.)

7. A maximum of $100,000 in stock (valued on the date granted) can be exercised in any one calendar year by any one employee. However, amounts not exercised in one year may be carried forward and exercised in another year and thereby increase the maximum limits in later years.

Any employee stock option that satisfies all of the above requirements will create capital gain, rather than ordinary income, for the recipient shareholder/employee if the stock is finally sold at a gain and (1) the employee has held the stock for more than six months and (2) the date of the disposition is more than two years after the stock option was granted. If the employee does not satisfy both of these last two time requirements, he or she will recognize ordinary income equal to the excess of the lesser of the stock's fair market value on the date of (*a*) exercise or (*b*) sale over the option price. Any remaining gain is capital gain. Incidentally, if the employee does report some amount of ordinary income, then the employer corporation is also entitled to claim an equivalent compensation deduction. Except in the unusual circumstance just described, however, the employee will report no income either when the incentive stock option is granted or when it is exercised; and the employer will receive no deduction at any time.

A careful reading of requirements 2 and 3, on page 188, reveals that an incentive stock option in a publicly held corporation might not be exercised until nearly 20 years after a plan was adopted or approved. That is, if a plan were not granted until 10 years after it was authorized, and if an employee did not exercise an option for 10 years after it was granted, nearly 20 years could have passed between the adoption of a plan and the acquisition of a stock. Under these extreme circumstances it would be very doubtful to assume that the value of the executive was correctly measured by the difference between the option price and the value of the stock on the date the option was exercised. In other words, the theory behind the incentive stock option may sometimes be wholly inappropriate. Because capital gains are of so little interest today, new incentive stock options are also of little interest to most taxpayers. A number of taxpayers will still have available to them, however, options that were granted before the tax law changes made new options largely obsolete.

## SPECIAL TAX CONSIDERATIONS FOR SELF-EMPLOYED TAXPAYERS

Some tax-sheltered compensation techniques are simply not available to the self-employed taxpayer. Those not available to such a person include group-term life insurance and meal and lodging opportunities. Health and accident plans are available, but only on the limited basis noted earlier in this chapter. The major exception to the rule is the pension plan. Since 1962, a self-employed proprietor or partner can claim a deduction on his or her own tax return for amounts contributed to a nonemployee retirement plan. As usual, a number of restrictive conditions and related factors must be considered before anyone can determine whether or not this tax shelter is desirable for a particular taxpayer.

Pension plans for a self-employed proprietor or partner are commonly known as *Keogh plans* or as *H.R. 10 plans,* because Congressman Keogh introduced House Report 10, which first authorized this particular deduction. The most demanding condition for H.R. 10 qualification is that the plan must also include pension coverage for all full-time employees who have worked for the self-employed person or the partnership for three years or longer. Thus, the tax value of the additional deduction for a self-employed taxpayer may be more than lost to the extra cost of covering other employees. The most restrictive condition of a qualified Keogh plan is that the self-employed individual can never deduct more than the lesser of 15 percent of earned income or $30,000. (The current *maximum* corporate contribution to a defined contribution plan for any employee is also $30,000. The maximum deductions noted above were those for 1988; they are adjusted annually for changes in the CPI. In addition, before such a plan will be qualified, the taxpayer must have sufficient income from an unincorporated personal service business; income from passive investments does not qualify.

If a self-employed taxpayer succeeds in creating a qualified pension plan, the tax shelter available is much like that available to the corporate employee in a qualified pension plan. In other words, the important tax results arise (1) because the contributions to the plan (to the maximum amounts) come from before-tax income and (2) because the accumulated amounts can grow tax-free in a retirement fund. Most self-employed people utilize an extant mutual fund, bank trust fund, or insurance plan to administer the assets during the years of accumulation. The self-employed individual, with a sizable income and a small number of permanent employees, is the most likely prospect for a Keogh plan.

### Individual Retirement Accounts

The Individual Retirement Account (IRA) was first introduced by ERISA. It provides some individuals (employees as well as the self-employed) with an additional opportunity to obtain some of the tax advantages associated with a qualified retirement plan. The annual deduction for an IRA contribution cannot exceed the *lesser* of 100 percent of the taxpayer's earned income or $2,000 ($2,250 if a joint account for a qualified taxpayer and spouse is created). Generally the opportunity for tax-free growth of IRA funds is very similar to that of other qualified pension plans. The two major limitations of an IRA are: (1) the low annual contribution ceiling; and (2) the fact that tax-deductible contributions are denied if the taxpayer or spouse is already an active participant in an employer-sponsored plan *and* the taxpayer earns over $50,000 if married (and files jointly) or $35,000 if single. (Couples earning over $40,000, and singles earning over $25,000 get a partial deduction.) Persons otherwise disqualified can make nondeductible contributions to an IRA and achieve tax deferral on the amounts earned on those contributions (up to the usual limits). Nevertheless, this extension of tax benefits for retirement funds is an important alternative, especially for the smaller businessperson. It provides a method for setting aside limited funds for retirement under tax-favored circumstances, without the more onerous requirements common to other pension plans. Incidentally, no five-year forward averaging is available, even in a lump-sum settlement, from an IRA.

Because of the very substantial reporting and funding requirements applicable to all other qualified plans after ERISA, many employers terminated their previous pension plans. The significant reduction in the number of employees covered by a sound pension plan was, of course, exactly the opposite result to that which Congress had hoped to achieve when it passed ERISA in 1974. Consequently, Congress extended the IRA idea to nearly all employers, in what is technically called a *simplified employee pension plan*, or (more commonly) a SEP-IRA. To implement such a plan the employer must include all employees who (1) are 25 years of age or older, and (2) have worked for the employer during any part of the current year and any three of the prior five years. Qualified SEP-IRA plans are eligible for the same contribution deduction limits as H.R. 10 plans. The limits are, of course, considerably more favorable than those applicable to regular IRA accounts. In every instance, a SEP-IRA must have 100 percent, immediate vesting.

## SUMMARY

Compensation arrangements more than almost any other common business transaction provide a host of opportunities for major tax savings. The entrepreneur and the corporate business manager would do well to review their own compensation arrangements in light of the broad outlines described in this chapter. If suggested improvements appear possible, the reader should discuss his or her particular situation in detail with a competent tax adviser.

Before leaving this topic, a final word of caution seems appropriate. Although the ideas in this chapter have been developed along a continuum beginning with the "best" alternative, in reality, the "best" alternative is the one most likely to be challenged by the IRS and recharacterized as the "worst" alternative. It is not unusual for the IRS to contend that a company car, a family vacation, and all other executive perquisites are really disguised dividends, especially if they are identified in a closely held corporation. Thus the person who seeks too much tax advantage is likely to lose under the "pig theory." That theory suggests that one can make money being a bull, or make money being a bear, but will only lose if the IRS perceives his or her actions to be those of a pig. Too much is still too much. Both the IRS and the courts have a special way of dealing with those who are especially greedy in matters of taxation. Careful compliance with all statutory and regulatory requirements is a minimal condition for success. The reader must therefore temper any enthusiasm for the ideas suggested here with a clear appreciation of the need for a tax expert in this important area of federal taxes and management decisions.

## PROBLEMS AND ASSIGNMENTS

1. Without doing any research beyond your text, define as best you can each of the following words or phrases as they are used in tax-sheltered retirement programs.
   a. Annuity.
   b. Term annuity.
   c. Life annuity.
   d. Joint and survivor annuity.
   e. Refund annuity.
   f. Vesting.
   g. Funding.
   h. Nondiscrimination.
   i. Employee trust fund.
   j. Defined benefit plan.
   k. Defined contribution plan.
   l. Contributory plan.
   m. Noncontributory plan.

2. Explain the basic similarities and differences between a qualified pension plan and a qualified profit-sharing plan.

3. Vicki Horikawa, a CPA in Seattle, Washington, would like to visit friends in New York City for a couple of days. The cost of the trip will be $2,000 excluding meals.
   a. Assuming that Vicki is self-employed and in the 33 percent marginal tax bracket, explain an entirely legal plan that will allow her to deduct the cost of her trip. What is the aftertax cost of her trip?
   b. Assume that Vicki is an employee who itemizes deductions, has an adjusted gross income of $25,000, and has no other employee business expenses or miscellaneous itemized deductions. What is the aftertax cost of her trip if her employer reimburses half the cost of the trip?
   c. Assume the same facts as in b, except that Vicki does not itemize deductions.

4. Some individuals retire with taxable incomes as large as or larger than those they experienced during their working years. If such an individual has been a participant in a qualified pension or profit-sharing plan during his or her working years, what tax-related options (or elections) are of special interest? Explain briefly.

5. Jonestown Manufacturing Company recently established a pension plan for its employees. The plan was largely designed by Mr. Jones, who owns 98 percent of the company's common stock and who is, surprisingly, its president and chairman of the board. Every employee with 10 or more years service will be covered by the plan. Funds will be contributed annually to the Jonestown Employee Trust Fund, which will be managed by the trust department of the bank at which both Mr. Jones and the Jonestown Manufacturing Company keep their accounts. The amount to be contributed will be determined as follows: 4 percent of the first $10,000 in wages or salaries earned during the year; 6 percent of the next $10,000; 8 percent of the third $10,000; and 10 percent of any wage or salary earned in excess of $40,000. Do you think this plan will be a qualified plan for federal income tax purposes? Explain briefly.

6. Generous Corporation allows every full-time employee with more than 10 years' service an extra $100 per month to be used, at the employee's discretion, to purchase any one or more of the following fringe benefits:

   1. Ordinary life insurance.
   2. Group term life insurance.
   3. Medical insurance.
   4. Bus tokens (to be used on city buses).
   5. Meals in the employee cafeteria.
   6. Group legal insurance.
   7. Prepaid vacation package tours.
   8. Tennis club membership.
   9. Tickets to local football, baseball, and hockey games.
   10. Cash (i.e., employee can take an additional $100 salary).

   a. Which of the above benefits could the employee elect to receive tax-free? (Assume in answering this question that the cafeteria plan suggested here is nondiscriminatory.)

   b. Would your answer to part *a* differ if this plan were held to be discriminatory? Explain briefly.

7. Jim and Susan McMahon are a married couple. What maximum IRA contribution can they deduct, assuming—

   a. Jim earns $55,000, is covered by a nonvested, but qualified plan and Susan does not work.

   b. Same facts as in *a*, but Jim is not covered by a qualified plan.

    c. Jim earns $35,000 and is covered by a qualified plan; Susan earns $25,000 and is not covered.

    d. Jim earns $16,000; Susan earns $30,000; both are covered by qualified plans.

    e. Jim earns $55,000; Susan earns $75,000; neither is covered by a qualified plan.

    f. Is a nondeductible IRA contribution void of any tax advantage?

8. Gerald Fenig is an employee of Mesa Land Development Corporation. Like all Mesa employees, Gerald is entitled to a 5 percent discount on any Mesa property that he elects to purchase. Because Gerald has been especially helpful in landing a couple of really big contracts lately, the board of directors agree to sell Gerald a particular building lot for $25,000. Ordinarily the same lot would sell for $45,000. The board made the proposition conditional on the fact that Gerald would build his personal residence on this lot and remain there for at least five years. What taxable income, if any, must Gerald report if he accepts this proposition?

9. Joe McVey is the CEO (chief executive officer) of one of the *Fortune* 500 companies. Ed McSpade is the CEO of MC Space Industries, a family-owned corporation. Both Joe and Ed draw a salary of $650,000 per year. In addition, they benefit from a qualified pension plan and receive other executive perquisites common to many business executives.

    a. Is it likely that an IRS agent, on audit of their personal tax returns, will claim that either Joe or Ed is receiving an unreasonably large salary? Explain briefly.

    b. What factors will be considered in any dispute between the IRS and Joe or Ed over unreasonable salaries? Explain in as much detail as possible.

10. Amy Dunbar, a self-employed tax attorney, travelled out of town to attend a three-day seminar. Her flight cost $600; taxicab costs to hotel, $40; hotel room, $80; meals, $50; and seminar fees, $200. How much of a deduction does Amy get for these seminar costs?

# *Case 9–1*

Charley Huff and Walt Bratic are junior executives for two plumbing companies. Charley earns a $48,000 salary, but receives no fringe benefits; Walt earns a $40,000 salary and the following fringe benefits:

| Benefit | Value |
|---|---|
| Group-term life insurance | |
| ($40,000 face value) | $  200 |
| Medical insurance coverage | 1,200 |
| Employee travel expense | |
| reimbursements | 1,000 |
| Discount on plumbing services (15%) | 120 |
| Contribution to profit-sharing plan | 3,000 |
| Total benefits received | $5,520 |

Both Charley and Walt are in the 28 percent marginal tax bracket; neither itemizes deductions. Assume that the profit-sharing contribution will compound at a rate of 8 percent for 35 years, when it will be taxed at a rate of 28 percent. Neither man will make an IRA contribution or invest in a savings account. Which person is getting a better deal?

# Case 9–2

Palm Valley Development Company of Los Angeles plans to hire real estate sales agents for a 200-unit residential subdivision that it is building in New Jersey. These agents would be hired only for this project. The following two alternative compensation plans have been proposed.

One plan would have the company hire real estate agents as independent contractors. The agents would be paid $3,338 for each home they sell. The company has a legal opinion that indicates the agents would be treated as independent contractors and would *not* be reclassified as employees for payroll tax purposes under this plan. These independent contractors would pay for a $200 training seminar and $150 of health insurance for themselves each month.

The other plan is to hire experienced real estate agents as employees and pay them a base salary of $1,500 per month plus $2,000 of incentive compensation for each home sold. The company would have to pay payroll taxes of 15 percent on the salary and incentive compensation. The company would provide each employee with a $200 training seminar and $150 of health insurance benefits each month. These employees would be participants in the company's defined benefit retirement plan that has a three-year vesting provision. The actuary estimates that the cost of benefits average $1,200 per year for each participant.

Under either plan the company estimates that the sales people will sell two homes per month.

Assume the company is in a 34 percent marginal tax bracket and that the individuals are in a 28 percent bracket. Disregard any payroll taxes that would be paid by the independent contractors or withheld from the employees' pay.

a. What is the aftertax cost per home to the company of each plan?

b. What is the aftertax benefit per month to each agent under each plan?

c. Which plan do you think will be adopted? Why?

# CHAPTER 10

# Tax Factors in the Acquisition, Use, and Disposition of Fixed Assets

The term *fixed asset* is used to refer to any asset that will benefit more than a single accounting period. Thus, this term usually encompasses such mobile assets as cars, trucks, and airplanes, as well as more "fixed" assets, such as buildings, land, and utility poles. The term also covers both tangible and intangible properties. For tax and financial accounting purposes, income is generally measured in intervals of one year. Because fixed assets benefit more than one year, they present some unique problems in income measurement. One basic problem involves the proper method of allocating the total cost of a fixed asset over its estimated useful life.

The tax rules governing the acquisition, use, and disposition of fixed assets had become increasingly volatile in recent years because Congress apparently was convinced that changes in those rules had a greater-than-normal impact on the way our economy performed. In years when economic stimulation was deemed necessary, we found that Congress tended to increase the portion of the cost of any fixed asset that could be deducted and, in some years, to allow an investment tax credit based upon the cost of certain fixed assets purchased during the year. In years when an economic depressant was deemed necessary, we came to expect the opposite changes; that is, the amount of the cost recovery deduction was typically reduced and the investment tax credit was reduced or rescinded. In 1986 Congress either gave up these old beliefs or chose to ignore them. Because change has been so frequent, and because the rules are so diverse, we will concentrate our attention in this chapter on the general planning opportunities associated with additional investments in fixed assets and give much briefer coverage to some of the older rules that may apply to fixed assets, acquired in prior years, that are still in use.

Before we look at more specific details, we might pause to observe the range of alternative treatments available for fixed assets in general. At one extreme, it is possible for the law to authorize as an immediate deduction the entire cost of a fixed asset, notwithstanding the fact that the expenditure will benefit one or more future accounting periods. The consequence of this alternative is, of course, to understate income in the year of purchase and to overstate it in subsequent years. In a limited number of circumstances, the Internal Revenue Code actually authorizes such an immediate deduction. At the other extreme, it is possible for the law to deny a taxpayer the right to claim any deduction for any portion of the cost of a fixed asset until disposition. Generally, this is the tax treatment prescribed for all nonwasting assets, such as investments in stocks and land, which are deemed to be indestructible. The third and intermediate alternative requires the taxpayer to capitalize the cost of a fixed asset initially, but then allows a recovery of this cost over some arbitrary period and using some predetermined cost allocation technique. This last alternative is the most widely used one and the cost allocation technique authorized was (until 1980) commonly known as a depreciation method. Since 1980 the old depreciation deduction has been replaced by an ACRS (accelerated cost recovery system) deduction.

This chapter is divided into four major sections. The first section explains the fundamental relationships between tax rules, present value concepts, and profit opportunities. The second, third, and fourth sections deal with tax factors related to the acquisition, use, and disposition of fixed assets, respectively. Although this organizational arrangement has certain pedagogic advantages, the reader should understand that he or she may have to examine several sections of this chapter for the "whole story" on one specific form of investment. For example, a reader who really wants to understand the tax factors associated with ownership of an apartment house or an oil well must sequentially evaluate the tax factors pertinent to the acquisition, use, and disposition of that particular form of fixed asset.

## FUNDAMENTAL RELATIONSHIPS BETWEEN TAX LAWS, THE PRESENT VALUE CONCEPT, AND SIMPLE ECONOMICS

The reader should observe that acquisition of a fixed asset may provide a tax deduction without an immediate cash disbursement. Suppose, for example, that a taxpayer acquired in one day two identical fixed assets to be used for the same purpose by paying $10,000 cash for asset 1 and signing a $10,000 promissory note, due in five years, for asset 2. In each case the taxpayer's basis in the asset is $10,000. Furthermore, the taxpayer would be entitled to exactly the same tax deductions (and credits, if any are authorized) on each asset. This ability to acquire a tax deduction, and possibly a tax credit, with a minimal cash disbursement is a basic reason why high-marginal-bracket taxpayers have a continuing interest in certain fixed assets.

To illustrate the critical interaction between tax rules and fundamental economics, let us begin with a grossly oversimplified illustration. If on January 1, 19x1, taxpayer A acquires a $200,000 fixed asset with a four-year life by signing a $200,000, 10 percent simple-interest note, which will be payable on January 1, 19x5, and if we know with 100 percent certainty that this fixed asset will provide its owner with new assets that can be sold on January 1,

19x5, for exactly $280,000, and that the initial fixed asset will vanish into dust on exactly that same date, the reader might conclude that the taxpayer should not proceed with the investment. If we assume that there is no income tax, the result can be detailed as follows:

| Year | Item | Cash Inflow | Cash Outflow |
|------|------|-------------|--------------|
| 19x1 | No cash transactions | — | — |
| 19x5 | Sale of new assets | $280,000 | — |
| 19x5 | Payment of note | — | $200,000 |
| 19x5 | Payment of interest | — | 80,000 |

Obviously, this investor would have to utilize the entire sales proceeds to pay off the note and would have no profit for the effort expended.

If we want to illustrate the critical interface between tax rules and simple economics, we will have to begin to modify our stated assumptions. This time let us assume that taxpayer A lives in a country that imposes a flat-rate 50 percent tax on all income, that authorizes the amortization of fixed asset costs equally over the life of an asset, that authorizes the deduction of interest expense, and that collects the income tax on January 1 of each year for income earned in the previous year. (Note: none of the assumptions made in this extended illustration are intended to reflect the law currently applicable in the United States; rather, imaginary rules have been assumed simply to illustrate some basic tax consequences.) These extreme assumptions might still lead a reader to conclude that taxpayer A should not proceed with this investment since the inevitable result will be cash-receipt equivalents equal in value to cash disbursements. The revised calculations would be as follows:

| Year | Item | Cash Inflow or Equivalent | Cash Outflow |
|------|------|---------------------------|--------------|
| 19x1 | Tax saving due to new $50,000 depreciation deduction allowed taxpayer | $ 25,000 | |
| 19x2 | Same as 19x1 | 25,000 | |
| 19x3 | Same as 19x1 | 25,000 | |
| 19x4 | Same as 19x1 | 25,000 | |
| 19x5 | Payment of note—face amount | | $200,000 |
| 19x5 | Payment of interest (the deduction for interest provides new tax savings) | 40,000 | 80,000 |
| 19x5 | Sale of new assets | 280,000 | |
| 19x5 | Income tax on sale of new assets | | 140,000 |
| | Total over life of investment | $420,000 | $420,000 |

Interestingly, the effect of introducing a 50 percent income tax into our earlier illustration is simply to increase the cash-receipt equivalents and the cash disbursements by 50 percent—that is, from $280,000 to $420,000. The desirability of the investment does not seem to be changed by this fact alone.

The next step in understanding the interface between tax rules and simple economics involves appreciation of the present value concept. Stated in its most elementary terms, this concept suggests that money has a time-preference value. A dollar today is worth more than a dollar that you cannot have until one year from now, and a dollar that you cannot have until one year from now is worth more than a dollar that you cannot have until five years from now. The exact difference in the present value between these dollars depends upon the investor's discount rate. Stated crudely, the discount rate is the rate of return that an investor can earn on capital during an interim period. If we assume that a taxpayer has a discount rate of 5 percent, a dollar deferred for one year is now worth about $0.95238095. In other words, if the taxpayer puts that latter amount to work at 5 percent (after taxes), it will be worth exactly $1 one year later. A dollar that a taxpayer could not have for five years, discounted at 5 percent, would be worth approximately $0.78352617 right now.

Returning to our previous calculations, we can now determine the discounted present value of the investment opportunity, based upon an assumed 5 percent (aftertax) rate of return, as shown below. In other words, the effect of the tax law is to give this investor dollar-receipt equivalents (in the form of tax savings), which can be invested at 5 percent (after taxes). Assuming that the taxpayer actually makes these investments at this rate of return, the investment opportunity will actually provide a $10,297 profit (i.e., $339,378 less $329,081) *solely because of the combined effect of tax laws and the time-preference value of money.*

| Year | Item | Present Value of Inflows | Present Value of Outflows |
|------|------|--------------------------|---------------------------|
| 19x1 | $25,000 tax saving discounted for one period ($25,000 × 0.95238095) | $ 23,810 | |
| 19x2 | Same tax saving discounted two periods | 22,676 | |
| 19x3 | Same tax saving discounted three periods | 21,596 | |
| 19x4 | Same tax saving discounted four periods | 20,568 | |
| 19x5 | $280,000 sale discounted five periods | 219,387 | |
| 19x5 | $200,000 note discounted five periods | | $156,705 |
| 19x5 | $80,000 interest discounted five periods | 31,341 | 62,682 |
| 19x5 | $140,000 tax liability discounted five periods | | 109,694 |
| | Total present value of investment | $339,378 | $329,081 |

If we were to make a systematic study of this example to discover the magic of the $10,297 profit and what it has to say about pragmatic investments in fixed assets, we would not have to tarry long to observe that the sooner the tax deduction (and thus the cash-inflow equivalent) can be realized, and the longer the taxable income can be deferred, the greater the opportunity to profit. The tax magic of many fixed assets can be explained this simply: They provide immediate tax deductions with deferred income recognition possibilities. Obviously, it is possible to create illustrations in which the nondiscounted cash outflows actually exceed the cash-inflow equivalents but which still yield an actual profit on a discounted basis. In the daily financial press, such losses are often termed *tax losses* to distinguish them from real economic losses. The longer the time period between the tax deduction and the income realization, and the higher the discount rate, the greater the opportunity to reap a tax loss and a real economic gain.

Additional study would demonstrate that the real economic success of an investment in any fixed asset is critically affected by several variables, including: (1) the timing of the tax deduction; (2) the timing of the income recognized; (3) the marginal tax rate applicable to the tax deduction and to the income recognized; and (4) the discount rate assumed by the taxpayer. Generally speaking, real economic profits will be increased if the time between the tax deduction and the income recognition is lengthened and the discount rate is increased. These differences can influence investors' decisions relative to the acquisition, use, and disposition of various fixed assets.

## TAX FACTORS PERTINENT TO THE ACQUISITION OF FIXED ASSETS

When a taxpayer first considers the prospect of acquiring a fixed asset, he or she should give adequate consideration to the form of that acquisition, since each form may produce significantly different tax and financial results. The most obvious and common form of acquiring a fixed asset is, naturally, by direct purchase. Even in this simple case, however, we have observed how the tax result may vary depending upon whether the taxpayer pays cash for the asset or borrows the funds required to make the purchase. As an alternative to the direct purchase of an asset, a taxpayer sometimes has the opportunity to acquire a controlling interest in the stock of a corporation that owns the desired asset. In this way a taxpayer can acquire the effective use of a desired asset, even though ownership of the asset is indirect, through the corporate entity. This alternative may create tax problems or opportunities for the unsuspecting investor. As an alternative to either a direct or an indirect purchase, the taxpayer should also consider the possibility of leasing an asset. In this way, he or she acquires the use of an asset without acquiring legal title to the asset. That taxpayer will probably be entitled to a deduction for the lease rents paid. Finally, in some circumstances a taxpayer may be able to construct or develop a desired asset. This method of acquisition may present several new and interesting tax consequences.

### Direct Purchases

The most common form of acquiring a fixed asset is the outright purchase of the finished product from an unrelated party. Tax factors in this sort of acquisition are reduced to such fundamental problems as determining the correct amount to capitalize in the fixed-asset account (for example, the cost of freight charges and installation expenses are properly added to the asset account in addition to the initial purchase price), determining the correct ACRS classification of the property, and, at least in some circumstances, selecting the most appropriate depreciation method. Each of these tax factors will be discussed in remaining portions of this chapter.

### Indirect Acquisitions through Stock Ownership

If taxpayer A desires to acquire a certain collection of assets which are owned by XYZ Corporation, essentially two alternatives exist. Taxpayer A can try to negotiate for the direct purchase of these assets with the executives of the XYZ Corporation, or A can negotiate for the purchase of a controlling interest in the stock of XYZ with its stockholders. Significant tax differences attach to each alternative from the standpoint of both the buyer and the seller.

To understand the important differences between direct and indirect acquisitions of assets from the standpoint of a buyer, consider the two alternatives which appear in Figure 10–1. In this illustration, taxpayer B owns 100 percent of the stock of XYZ Corporation, and XYZ owns assets 1, 2, and 3.

**FIGURE 10–1**

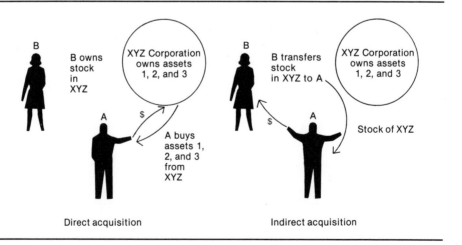

Let us assume that all parties agree that the fair market values of assets 1, 2, and 3 are $10,000, $20,000, and $30,000, respectively. If the only assets owned by XYZ are assets 1, 2, and 3, and if XYZ owes no liabilities, one might conclude that the stock of XYZ ought to be worth $60,000 since the ownership of this stock gives the stockholder the indirect ownership of the same assets. If we assume, however, that XYZ has, for income tax purposes, recovered most of the original cost of these assets (and the remaining tax basis in them is only $1,000, $2,000, and $3,000, respectively) a special problem in valuation is presented. If A acquires the assets *directly* for $60,000, A's tax basis in these assets will be $10,000, $20,000, and $30,000, respectively. This means, of course, that A can recover his cost in the assets and thereby reduce his future taxable income by that same amount.

If A had made an *indirect* acquisition for $60,000, A's tax basis would be *in the stock of XYZ, not in assets 1, 2, and 3*. The assets would still have their low tax basis ($1,000, $2,000, and $3,000), and the taxable income of XYZ would be substantial in the future because it would have only very limited amounts of cost left to deduct.

If, in Figure 10–1, a corporation (rather than individual A) were to have purchased 80 percent or more of XYZ's stock within a 12-month period that acquiring corporation would have a statutory right to elect to treat the purchase of the stock as if it had been a direct purchase of assets 1, 2, and 3. To do this, however, the acquiring corporation must either literally or figuratively liquidate the acquired corporation (here, XYZ). Hence XYZ Corporation will have to recognize as taxable income the "paper gain" on assets 1, 2, and 3 in the year of liquidation. This means, of course, that XYZ may have to pay a corporate income tax on a $54,000 taxable income in its final year, and, therefore individual B, who is selling XYZ, may ask for more than $60,000.

To summarize, if the management of XYZ understands the tax factors associated with A's indirect acquisition of assets 1, 2, and 3, they might not, under the circumstances described here, be willing to sell 100 percent of the stock of XYZ for $60,000, even though the assets were individually "worth" that amount. The appropriate price increase for an indirect acquisition would depend upon the amount of income that would have to be recognized on the liquidation of XYZ. Observe also that under the reverse conditions—that is, when the fair market value of assets is less than their tax basis—an indirect acquisition may provide an economic benefit to the purchaser because he or she may be willing to pay more than the apparent fair market value of the assets to acquire the tax advantage that goes along with an indirect acquisition.

### Leasing Fixed Assets

A lease obviously provides a taxpayer with an opportunity to acquire the use of a fixed asset without acquiring other risks or benefits of ownership. In many instances the utilization of a lease in preference to other methods of acquisition is predicated upon financial considerations alone. A new company with limited capital, for example, may find the lease to be the only effective way to acquire certain assets. A leasing arrangement may prove to be more expensive than direct ownership because it must include a profit for the lessor. Thus, under some circumstances, the lease is less attractive to an established firm with large amounts of capital and adequate credit. However, even under these conditions, the tax consequence of a lease may make it more profitable than ownership.

Perhaps the easiest situation in which to demonstrate the potential tax value of a lease arrangement is in connection with land. If a taxpayer purchases land (for cash or on credit), there will be no tax deduction for that investment until the taxpayer disposes of the land, since land is a nonwasting asset. This means, of course, that a taxpayer may make a substantial real economic investment with no immediate tax benefit. We observed earlier that the chances of obtaining a real economic profit usually increase if we can accelerate the timing of a tax deduction. Thus, for tax reasons, a taxpayer may be inclined to lease land rather than purchase it. The cost of a few hundred feet of ocean frontage in Honolulu, Miami Beach, Southern California, or New England might be prohibitive for any taxpayer but the largest hotel corporation. A lease arrangement, with attendant tax deductions for (land) rents paid, might change this financial requirement substantially.

Taxpayers with little or no taxable income may also benefit from a lease arrangement because a profitable lessor with a substantial tax liability may be able to acquire the property desired by the lessee at a lower real (aftertax) economic cost. In other words, if the tax savings associated with the cost-recovery deductions are sufficiently great, a profitable corporation in the top marginal tax bracket may be willing to acquire the technical or legal title to an asset and immediately lease it to a less profitable firm at a lower price than the latter could acquire that same property directly, even after allowing a reasonable profit to the lessor firm. To the extent authorized by law, this effectively allows taxpayers to pass the tax advantages associated with the acquisition of certain fixed assets to those entities most capable of utilizing them.

### Constructing or Otherwise Creating Fixed Assets

A taxpayer will sometimes construct or otherwise create a fixed asset simply because the desired asset is not already in existence and because the taxpayer knows no one else willing to make it. In other cases, a taxpayer will construct or create an asset because that option is less costly. In many more situations, however, taxpayers' reasons for constructing or otherwise creating fixed assets are that that is their primary business.

**Constructing Assets.**   Taxpayers who construct fixed assets are generally required to capitalize all direct costs plus an allocable portion of most indirect costs "that benefit the asset," following uniform capitalization rules. These rules, found in Section 263A, were added to the Code in 1986. The Treasury Department issued temporary regulations to help implement the new rules but business has been slow in responding. Without waiting for final regulations, however, the committee reports make it clear that allocable indirect costs are to include general and administrative overhead, pension costs and other pension benefit expenses, and any excess of tax depreciation deductions over book depreciation. In most instances, therefore, a taxpayer must now capitalize more costs for tax purposes than may be capitalized for financial accounting purposes following GAAP (generally accepted accounting principles).

Under prior law, different capitalization rules had developed for manufacturers, wholesalers, retailers, and taxpayers who constructed assets for their own use. Although increased uniformity may be desirable as a general goal, the cost of compliance with the new rules will be substantial and the overall gain to society from these changes is questionable. What is certain is that both tax revenues and accounting costs will increase because of this change.

As always, the new law provides a list of special exceptions or exclusions. For example, the statute provides that certain costs are not to be allocated and capitalized, including: research and development costs; minerals; and most selling, marketing, and distribution costs. In the case of interest costs, taxpayers must now capitalize any construction-period interest associated with the construction of most (1) real estate; (2) other properties with a class life of 20 years or longer; (3) properties requiring 2 years or longer for construction; and (4) properties requiring 1 year or longer to construct if they cost more than $1 million. These rules apply to both properties constructed for resale and to those used in a taxpayer's trade or business. If the actual production expenditures exceed the amount specifically borrowed to finance the construction of a property, an additional amount of imputed interest (based on the average actual rate paid by the taxpayer on all indebtedness) must be added to the actual construction-period interest incurred.

**Locating and Developing Oil and Gas Wells.**    The tax law provides that all *intangible* drilling and development costs associated with locating and developing an oil or gas well can be deducted immediately. These costs often represent as much as 80 percent of the cost of a producing well. The obvious benefit of the right to deduct 80 percent of an investment in a fixed asset is one reason these investments are more attractive than many others to certain taxpayers. Incidentally, large oil companies (called integrated producers in the Code) cannot expense more than 70 percent of their IDC. The remaining 30 percent must be amortized ratably over five years. The cost of all dry holes can, however, be expensed.

It should be obvious, however, that the right to an immediate tax deduction is *not* tantamount to the promise of an economic profit. The odds of drilling a dry hole are something like 8.5 to 1. And a dry hole is essentially worthless to everyone. The tax law authorizes the deduction of any remaining costs associated with an attempt to locate and develop an oil or gas well when the drilling venture proves to be worthless. The right to immediately deduct the entire cost of a worthless venture, as well as a majority of the costs of a successful oil or gas venture, helps to make them attractive to high-marginal-bracket taxpayers. If things go badly, the government stands ready to share up to 33 percent of the losses (through tax savings to the investors). Special limits apply to the IDC expenses incurred by integrated oil companies.

Risks are high in the oil and gas business. The wealthy taxpayer, however, might find those high risks to be preferable to low-risk investments because of the liberal tax treatment of the initial investment and the income produced from a successful investment.

**Land Development and Agricultural Growth.**    In a series of special provisions, the code has tried to encourage investments in agriculture. Again, the exact limitations of the separate rules are too detailed to justify our investigating them. However, we should note in passing that, under prescribed conditions, the tax rules do authorize the immediate deduction of (*a*) soil and water conservation expenditures, including "leveling, grading and terracing, contour furrowing, . . . drainage ditches, earthen dams, watercourses, outlets, . . . and the planting of windbreaks"; (*b*) expenditures for fertilizer and "other materials to enrich, neutralize, or condition land used in farming"; and (*c*) certain land-clearing costs.

## The Investment Credit

An investment tax credit was first introduced into the federal income tax in 1962. It was revised in 1964, suspended in 1966, reinstated in 1967, repealed in 1969, reenacted in 1971, liberalized in 1975, expanded in 1978 and 1981, reduced in 1982, and once again repealed in 1986. Given this checkered history, one is tempted to totally ignore the investment credit and to proceed with more stable aspects of our tax system. Because some taxpayers are still able to claim an investment tax credit carried forward from prior years; because others may have to recapture a credit claimed in a prior year, should they make an "early" disposition of an asset today; and because a small part of the credit, known as the rehabilitation credit, remains available, a few additional words concerning the investment credit are deemed necessary.

Under prior law, investment tax credits (ITC) could generally be used to offset up to $25,000 plus 85 percent of any tax in excess of $25,000. Taxpayers with insufficient taxable incomes and, therefore, too little tax liability to utilize immediately the full ITC they had generated through the purchase of qualifying assets, may still claim those credits under carry-forward provisions. In general, however, they must reduce ITC carry-forward amounts by 35 percent to reflect the general decrease in tax rates. Furthermore, in determining the amount that can be claimed in the current year (and the amount that must be carried forward to future years) the maximum current ITC was decreased to $25,000 plus 75 percent (down from 85 percent) of the current year's tax liability in excess of $25,000.

The amount of ITC that a taxpayer claimed in prior years depended, among other factors, on the class life of the asset placed in service. Three-year properties generally qualified for a 6 percent credit, longer lived assets, and a 10 percent credit, if the taxpayer would reduce the depreciable basis of the property by 50 percent of the investment credit claimed. Alternatively, the taxpayer could claim a 4 percent credit on three-year properties and an 8 percent credit on longer lived assets. The former option was known as the basis-reduction method; the latter as the credit-reduction method. If a taxpayer disposes of an asset before that predetermined period has expired, some portion of the ITC previously claimed must be recaptured in the year the asset is disposed of. This recapture remains possible even though the ITC was in general repealed after 1985. When it does apply, a minor adjustment can be made to the tax basis of the property sold or exchanged if the basis-reduction method of calculating the ITC had been used. The effect is to decrease any reported gain or increase any reported loss by some amount deemed too small to justify discussion here.

Taxpayers who purchase and remodel old buildings may still claim a "rehabilitation credit." In general this credit is equal to 20 percent of qualifying expenditures for certain historic structures and 10 percent for (nonhistoric) buildings that were originally placed in service before 1936. The former credit applies to both residential and nonresidential buildings; the latter, to non-residential buildings only. To qualify for this substantial rehabilitation credit, a prescribed portion of the external walls and the building's internal structural framework must be retained. This credit reduces the basis of the property for purposes of determining the ACRS deduction by the amount of any credit claimed. In addition, an expenditure must exceed the *larger of (a)* the property's adjusted basis or *(b)* $5,000 before it can be considered a substantial rehabilitation.

## TAX FACTORS PERTINENT TO THE USE OF FIXED ASSETS

After a taxpayer acquires a fixed asset, another series of tax considerations is typically encountered. Traditionally, the first three questions of major importance involved were: (1) determining the probable useful life of the asset; (2) estimating salvage value at the end of that life; and (3) selecting the most desirable cost recovery (or depreciation) method. Since 1981, however, those questions are no longer of much significance. Although the old "useful-life" rules will continue to be utilized by most taxpayers for many years—i.e., until all property put into service before 1981 has been sold or exchanged—those rules will not be described in detail in this text because they generally have little or nothing to do with today's managerial decisions.

Since 1981 an accelerated cost recovery system (ACRS) has more or less replaced the traditional useful-life depreciation deduction. Unfortunately, however, the ACRS system has already been modified more than once in the past five years and, therefore, fixed assets acquired and placed in service in years prior to 1987 will continue to be subject to some "old" ACRS rules, not to the "new" modified ACRS rules described later in this chapter. Because these cost-recovery techniques have been so frequently modified, taxpayers must now keep multiple records for nearly identical fixed assets that were purchased within a few years of each other. As deplorable as this result may be, it seems intuitively less offensive than having Congress retroactively change the rules—especially when the trend is generally antitaxpayer in most instances.

## Classification of Personal Property

Today's tax law requires that all tangible personal property of a character subject to depreciation (which includes both property used in a trade or business and property held for the production of income) be classified in one of six categories, namely:

1. 3-year property;
2. 5-year property;
3. 7-year property;
4. 10-year property;
5. 15-year property; or
6. 20-year property.

Properties are assigned to each of the six classes based on the useful lives estimated for them by the Treasury Department in the asset depreciation range (ADR) system. (The ADR system is described in Treas. Reg. Sec. 1.167(a)–11.) Some examples are as follows:

| New ACRS Class | Properties Assigned an ADR Midpoint Life of— |
|---|---|
| 3-year | Less than 4 years. (Note: in the original ACRS system cars and light trucks were assigned to the 3-year class; in the modified ACRS system they have been shifted to the 5-year class). The present 3-year class includes, for example, small tools used in manufacturing, some race horses and breeding hogs, and special handling devices used in food manufacturing. |
| 5-year | 4 or more, but less than 10 years. It includes, for example, cars, light trucks, computers, typewriters, and cargo containers. |
| 7- year | 10 or more, but less than 16 years. It includes, for example, office furniture, railroad track, and single-purpose agricultural and horticultural structures. (It also includes property with no specified ADR midpoint life.) |

| New ACRS Class | Properties Assigned an ADR Midpoint Life of— |
|---|---|
| 10- year | 16 or more, but less than 20 years; e.g., assets used in petroleum refining and vessels and barges. |
| 15-year | 20 or more, but less than 25 years; e.g., land improvements, telephone distribution plants, and pipelines. |
| 20-year | 25 or more years; e.g., municipal sewers. |

## Depreciation Method

The Code goes on to prescribe certain depreciation methods and accounting conventions for each class of property. Specifically, properties in the 3, 5, 7, and 10-year classes are eligible to be depreciated using the 200 percent declining-balance depreciation method, switching to the straight-line method in the year in which the latter method would give a larger deduction than would the former method. This ordinarily occurs in the third year with 3-year properties; the fourth year with 5-year properties; the fifth year with 7-year properties; and the seventh year with 10-year properties. Properties in the 15 and 20-year classes are eligible to be depreciated using a 150 percent declining-balance method with a switch to the straight-line method in the seventh and ninth years, respectively. (Taxpayers may also elect to use the straight-line method and/or longer lives for all properties.)

In using a declining-balance method, the taxpayer must first determine the straight-line depreciation rate, as follows:

$$\frac{1}{\text{Number of years class life}} = \text{Straight-line rate.}$$

Thus a property in the 5-year class would have a 20 percent (i.e., $\frac{1}{5}$) straight-line rate; one in the 10-year class, a 10 percent rate. Having determined the straight-line rate, the taxpayer adjusts that rate as implied in the name given the depreciation method. That is, a 200 percent method is simply one that doubles the straight-line rate; a 150 percent method uses a rate exactly 1.5 times the straight-line rate. Some examples follow:

| Class Life | Straight-Line Rate | 200 Percent Rate | 150 Percent Rate |
|---|---|---|---|
| 5-year | 20% | 40% | 30% |
| 10-year | 10 | 20 | 15 |
| 20-year | 5 | 10 | 7.5 |
| 25-year | 4 | 8 | 6 |

Finally the taxpayer multiplies the prescribed rate times the previously un-recovered cost each year.

To illustrate, assume that a taxpayer purchased $100,000 of property in the 10-year class. Using the 200 percent or double declining-balance depreciation method (DDB) would yield the following results *if there were no special ccounting conventions and the asset were placed in service on the first day of the year:*

| Year | Depreciation per "Pure" DDB Method |
|------|-----------------------------------|
| 1 | $20,000 (i.e., 20% × $100,000) |
| 2 | $16,000 (20% × [$100,000 − $20,000] ) |
| 3 | $12,800 (20% × [$100,000 − $36,000] ) |
| 4 | $10,240 (20% × [$100,000 − $48,800] ) |
| 5 | $ 8,192 (20% × [$100,000 − $59,040] ) |
| 6 | $ 6,554 (20% × [$100,000 − $67,232] ) |
| 7 | $ 5,243 (20% × [$100,000 − $73,786] ) |
| 8 | $ 4,194 (20% × [$100,000 − $79,029] ) |
| 9 | $ 3,355 (20% × [$100,000 − $83,223] ) |
| 10 | $ 2,684 (20% × [$100,000 − $86,578] ) |

Using a declining-balance method will, obviously, always yield some constantly smaller and smaller depreciation deduction. To avoid this problem in perpetuity, and to allow the taxpayer to recover slightly larger amounts in the last few years, the tax law permits taxpayers to switch to a straight-line method in the year it becomes beneficial to do so. Using the unrecovered cost figures in the previous example, we can compute the straight-line depreciation that would result from a switch in years 2 through 10, as follows:

| Year | Unrecovered Cost | ÷ | Years Left | = | Straight-Line Deduction |
|------|-----------------|---|-----------|---|------------------------|
| 2 | $80,000 | ÷ | 9 | = | $ 8,889 |
| 3 | 64,000 | ÷ | 8 | = | 8,000 |
| 4 | 51,200 | ÷ | 7 | = | 7,314 |
| 5 | 40,960 | ÷ | 6 | = | 6,827 |
| 6 | 32,768 | ÷ | 5 | = | 6,554 |
| 7 | 26,214 | ÷ | 4 | = | 6,554 |
| 8 | 20,971 | ÷ | 3 | = | 6,991 |
| 9 | 16,777 | ÷ | 2 | = | 8,389 |
| 10 | 13,422 | ÷ | 1 | = | 13,422 |

Then, by comparing the deduction in the far-right column, above, with the depreciation determined in the earlier DDB schedule, we can see that in year

7 the switch to a straight-line method would yield a larger deduction—i.e., $6,554 versus $5,243—hence that is the year that this change would be made for tax purposes. In years 7 through 10, claiming a constant depreciation deduction of $6,554 would cause the aggregate unrecovered cost ($26,214 at the end of year 6) to be fully deducted by the end of the 10-year period.

## Accounting Conventions for Personal Property

In order to minimize record keeping, the tax law simply assumes, in most cases, that a taxpayer both acquires and disposes of any tangible personal property in the middle of the year. This assumption is called the half-year convention. In effect it allows the taxpayer to claim one-half a year's depreciation in both the year of acquisition and disposition. This also means, of course, that property classified in the three-year class, and retained for its full life, is actually depreciated over four tax years, not three. That is, the total depreciation is divided among the years, as follows:

Year 1: one-half year's depreciation

Year 2: full year's depreciation

Year 3: full year's depreciation

Year 4: one-half year's depreciation

The actual write-off periods for all properties classified in the 5, 7, 10, 15, and 20-year classes are similarly extended for this one year. While this convention does simplify one aspect of depreciation, it also complicates matters somewhat because, for example, in year 2 the taxpayer is entitled to one-half of the first full year's depreciation plus one half of the second full year's depreciation; a somewhat cumbersome calculation. To facilitate the computational aspects of this somewhat cumbersome cost allocation system, the IRS published a series of tables in Rev. Proc. 87-57 that make compliance with these rules relatively simple. Table 1 of Rev. Proc. 87-57, reproduced here as Table 10-1, sets out the one composite depreciation rate that can be used in each year, for the six different classes or categories of depreciable personal property, and for calculating the modified ACRS deduction generally allowed for personal properties placed in service after 1986.

To illustrate the usefulness of the IRS table, assume that a taxpayer acquired a new computer for $100,000 in 1987. Assuming that this computer was used exclusively in an active trade or business—and knowing from information given earlier in this chapter that computers are classified as 5-year properties—we can determine the correct ACRS deduction for 1989 and 1990 (or any other years) very easily; that is—

$$1989: \$100,000 \times 32\% = \$32,000$$
$$1990: \$100,000 \times 19.2\% = \$19,200$$

**TABLE 10-1**   General Depreciation System

| If the Recovery Year Is: | and the Recovery Period Is: | | | | | |
|---|---|---|---|---|---|---|
| | 3-Year | 5-Year | 7-Year | 10-Year | 15-Year | 20-Year |
| | | | the Depreciation Rate Is: | | | |
| 1 | 33.33 | 20.00 | 14.29 | 10.00 | 5.00 | 3.750 |
| 2 | 44.45 | 32.00 | 24.49 | 18.00 | 9.50 | 7.219 |
| 3 | 14.81 | 19.20 | 17.49 | 14.40 | 8.55 | 6.677 |
| 4 | 7.41 | 11.52 | 12.49 | 11.52 | 7.70 | 6.177 |
| 5 | | 11.52 | 8.93 | 9.22 | 6.93 | 5.713 |
| 6 | | 5.76 | 8.92 | 7.37 | 6.23 | 5.285 |
| 7 | | | 8.93 | 6.55 | 5.90 | 4.888 |
| 8 | | | 4.46 | 6.55 | 5.90 | 4.522 |
| 9 | | | | 6.56 | 5.91 | 4.462 |
| 10 | | | | 6.55 | 5.90 | 4.461 |
| 11 | | | | 3.28 | 5.91 | 4.462 |
| 12 | | | | | 5.90 | 4.461 |
| 13 | | | | | 5.91 | 4.462 |
| 14 | | | | | 5.90 | 4.461 |
| 15 | | | | | 5.91 | 4.462 |
| 16 | | | | | 2.95 | 4.461 |
| 17 | | | | | | 4.462 |
| 18 | | | | | | 4.461 |
| 19 | | | | | | 4.462 |
| 20 | | | | | | 4.461 |
| 21 | | | | | | 2.231 |

Applicable depreciation method: 200 or 150 percent
Declining balance switching to straight line
Applicable recovery periods: 3, 5, 7, 10, 15, 20 years
Applicable convention: half-year

The depreciation rates given in Table 10–1 can *not* be used, however, if a taxpayer purchases too many assets late in any year.

The half-year convention previously described will not apply if a taxpayer places in service during the last quarter of the year more than 40 percent of the cost of all depreciable personal property put into service during the year. In that event the Code requires the taxpayer to use a midquarter convention for all additions during the year. Under a midquarter convention the taxpayer would claim:

1. 87.5 percent of the full first-year depreciation for assets placed in service during the first three months of the year;
2. 62.5 percent of the full first-year depreciation for assets placed in service during the second quarter of the year;

3. 37.5 percent of the full first-year depreciation for assets placed in service during the third quarter of the year; and

4. 12.5 percent of the full first-year depreciation for assets placed in service during the last quarter of the year.

The midquarter convention is a real tax trap in that ordinarily it both (1) decreases the amount of depreciation otherwise allowed and (2) complicates the depreciation calculations required. In some unusual situations—for example, in situations where a taxpayer makes 60 percent of all additions in the first quarter, and 40 percent in the fourth quarter—it will actually increase the depreciation deduction. Taxpayers are advised, therefore, to watch carefully the timing of all fixed-asset acquisitions, especially those made during the last three months of each year.

Rev. Proc. 87–57 also includes four different tables (reproduced as Tables 10–4, 10–5, 10–6, and 10–7) that should be used to calculate the modified ACRS deduction if a taxpayer falls into this special case. Table 10–4 should be used to determine the deduction for any properties placed in service during the first three months of the year; Table 10–5, for properties placed in service during the second quarter; Table 10–6, the third quarter; and Table 10–7, the final quarter. These four tables are reproduced in an appendix at the end of this chapter. Using those four tables we can confirm a somewhat surprising conclusion noted earlier. That is, this apparent tax trap can sometimes be fortuitous. To illustrate, assume that a taxpayer acquired a total of $100,000 worth of 10-year equipment in 1989, buying $60,000 worth in January and $40,000 in December. Using the "normal" Table 10–1 the ACRS deduction would be $10,000. Using the correct tables (10–4 and 10–5), however, the proper ACRS deduction would be $11,500 (i.e., $60,000 × 17.5% plus $40,000 × 2.5%) or $1,500 more than it would have been following the generally applicable rules.

### Optional Depreciation Methods for Personal Property

A taxpayer may always elect to depreciate personal property under either one of two alternative depreciation methods. First, the taxpayer may use the same ACRS-recovery period but use the straight-line rather than a declining balance depreciation method. Second, the taxpayer may use something called the "alternative depreciation system." In general this method also uses a straight-line method and either the same or longer useful lives than under the regular ACRS method. Because of the time preference value of money, it is not likely that many taxpayers will elect this option.

In a few cases the alternative depreciation system is actually required. For example, it must be applied to property used primarily outside the U.S.; to property leased by a tax-exempt entity; and to property financed from tax-exempt bond proceeds. It is also required when calculating the alternative minimum tax as noted in Chapter 6. Because these options are of little general interest, we will not consider them further here. Incidentally Rev. Proc. 87-57 also includes tables to make these calculations easy.

## Small Business Election

In lieu of claiming the usual ACRS deduction (using either the regular or an optional method) some taxpayers are given one additional option for a limited amount of qualifying personal property. That option allows a taxpayer the right to expense (i.e., to deduct immediately) the cost of personal property not in excess of $10,000 per year. This maximum, however, is reduced dollar-for-dollar if the aggregate cost of qualifying property exceeds $200,000 in any one year. Thus a taxpayer cannot elect to expense any amount if qualifying property placed in service during the year exceeds $210,000. Hence the reason for calling this option a small business election is obvious.

Incidentally this election is also subject to other limits. For example, the amount expensed cannot exceed the taxable income for the year derived from the trade or business in which the property is used. If this limit applies, disallowed amounts can be carried forward and used to increase the $10,000 maximum in the next year.

## Classification of Real Property

Most depreciable real property is classified as either residential rental property or nonresidential real property. The Code prescribes a 27.5-year life for the former real properties; a 31.5-year life, for the latter. Both types of real property must be depreciated using the straight-line depreciation method. Incidentally these same rules apply to leasehold improvements built on leased property even if the remaining term of the lease is shorter than this estimated life.

Although the current rules are generally realistic, they are in stark contrast to those in effect between 1981 and 1986. In those five years real properties could be written off using an accelerated depreciation method over—

1. 15 years, if acquired between January 1, 1981, and March 15, 1984;

2. 18 years, if acquired between March 16, 1984, and May 8, 1985; or

3. 19 years, if acquired between May 9, 1985, and December 31, 1986.

Under prior tax law, real estate was given a tremendous tax advantage over many other forms of investment. It is readily understandable, therefore, why so many U.S. cities have excess building space available today. A major part of the blame in this instance lies clearly with the administration and Congress who recommended and passed such dramatically divergent depreciation provisions in such a short period of time.

## Accounting Conventions for Real Property

All real property is subject to a midmonth convention. This means, of course, that for tax purposes it will be assumed that all transactions in real estate took place exactly in the middle of the month in which the transaction actually occurred. It applies to both acquisition and dispositions.

To facilitate the computations, the IRS has once again prepared tables that can be used to make the necessary calculation. The two most frequently used realty tables are those numbered 6 and 7 in Re. Proc. 87-57, reproduced in the appendix to this chapter. Table 6 is for residential realty; Table 7 for nonresidential real estate. Because the prescribed depreciation method is the straight-line method, however, these tables are of limited benefit in any year other than the year of acquisition or disposition. In all other years the straight-line depreciation can be determined by dividing the cost of the asset by 27.5 (if the property is a residential rental property) or by 31.5 (if it is a nonresidential real property).

## Optional Depreciation Methods for Real Estate

A taxpayer may always elect to depreciate real property over a 40-year life (still using the straight-line method and a midmonth convention). Because of the time-preference value of money, however, it is doubtful that many taxpayers will make this election.

## Depletion Methods

As minerals are extracted from the ground and sold, a taxpayer owning an economic interest in the mineral rights is entitled to recover his or her investment through a depletion deduction. Except for the critical difference that an extracted mineral cannot be restored by human action, from an accounting standpoint a depletion deduction provides for replacement capital in the same manner that the depreciation deduction does. In an operational sense, however, depletion and depreciation may be radically different because, in some situations, the code authorizes a method of depletion, called *statutory depletion,* which may continue to provide a tax deduction even though the adjusted basis of the investment has been wholly recovered in prior periods. The alternative method, called *cost depletion,* does *not* provide that same opportunity.

**Cost Depletion.**    Cost depletion effectively guarantees the right of a taxpayer to recover an original capital investment in a mineral property, assuming production. To illustrate this cost recovery technique, we will consider the tax factors associated with a $500,000 investment in a mineral venture. If the intangible drilling and development costs (IDC) approximate 80 percent of the investment, and the taxpayer is not an integrated producer, the taxpayer will deduct $400,000 of the initial $500,000 investment in the first year. The remaining $100,000 investment is deducted as production proceeds. If the engineers estimate that the mineral deposit contains 500,000 barrels of oil (or cubic feet of gas), the taxpayer can deduct 20 cents for each barrel of oil extracted and sold. The $100,000 unrecovered tax basis is divided by the 500,000 estimated barrels of oil to determine a cost depletion allowance of 20 cents per barrel. When the well is exhausted, the taxpayer will have deducted an amount equal to the original investment: $400,000 as an immediate deduction for intangible drilling and development costs, and $100,000 as cost depletion over the productive life of the well. If the initial estimates of the mineral deposit prove erroneous, an appropriate adjustment must be made to the cost depletion allowance. Under all circumstances, however, the effect of *cost* depletion is to guarantee the taxpayer's right to deduct only the initial investment, and not a dollar more.

**Percentage Depletion.**    The tax magic of the percentage depletion deduction is that it is *not* restricted to the unrecovered cost of an investment in a mineral deposit in terms of the total dollar amounts that can be deducted. Percentage depletion may go on and on, thus providing a lucky taxpayer with a tax deduction that is many multiples of the initial investment if the well continues to produce. This tax distinction of percentage depletion is of major economic significance to potential investors. Prior to 1976, percentage depletion was equally available to large integrated oil companies, small independent producers, and the landlords who owned the land on which the well was located. Since 1975, however, only *independent* producers and royalty owners have been able to claim percentage depletion. Furthermore, even those taxpayers have been eligible for smaller amounts of percentage depletion each year. Since 1980 the maximum production limit has been 1,000 barrels of oil per day; the statutory rate is now 15 percent.

Technically, the percentage depletion deduction is determined by multiplying (1) a statutory rate by (2) the gross income from the mineral property. The statutory rate varies from one mineral to the next. The code currently authorizes a rate of 22 percent for molybdenum, sulfur, and uranium deposits; a rate of 15 percent for gold, silver, iron ore, and copper; a rate of 5 percent for gravel, sand, and certain other minerals; and many other statutory rates for many other minerals. Because we are interested only in the principle of percentage depletion, we will utilize a 22 percent rate in the remaining illustrations, even though the 22 percent historically associated with oil and gas wells has decreased to 15 percent. The "gross income from the property" is usually an estimated value or a posted price of a mineral in its crude state, before transportation and refining have increased its value. Thus, if a sulfur mine produced $50,000 in gross income in a particular year, a taxpayer with the rights to that production might be entitled to claim a percentage depletion deduction of $11,000 (22 percent of $50,000). Incidentally, any taxpayer can always claim cost depletion if it is larger than percentage depletion or if that taxpayer is not eligible for percentage depletion.

Percentage depletion is always limited, however, in that it can never exceed 50 percent of the *net* income from the property in any particular year. This rule effectively sets a ceiling on statutory depletion, which comes into play in high-cost operations. If, for example, the $50,000 gross income produced for the taxpayer in the previous illustration required a $40,000 expense to obtain it, percentage depletion would be reduced from the apparent $11,000 determined earlier to $5,000—that is, to 50 percent of ($50,000 − $40,000). For years after 1975, percentage depletion on oil and gas properties is further limited in that it cannot exceed 65 percent of any taxpayer's net taxable income from all sources, computed without a depletion or net operating loss deduction.

Because of the 50 percent net income limitation, a complex series of rules is brought into consideration in some circumstances. Note that both percentage depletion and the net income limitation are based upon the gross or net income *from the property.* Exactly what are the definitional boundaries of "the property"? Is each mine or well a "separate property"? Are all mines or wells on a single lease "a property"? Must all mines or wells on one lease be combined, or can they be treated separately? If contiguous leases are obtained at the same time, can mines or wells on different leases be combined? Must they be combined? Is the date of the lease significant? The answers to these and many related questions are much too complex to state here. The reader should simply observe that, when allowed, certain combinations may prove to be very valuable with regard to taxes. The two illustrations in Tables 10–2 and 10–3 amply demonstrate this conclusion, which, like so many other tax opportunities, turns on definitional considerations.

In summary, the tax advantages associated with the *use* of an investment in mineral properties (that is, during the production period) stem from the fact that the taxpayer may be able to claim percentage depletion in excess of the unrecovered tax basis. Before this opportunity is meaningful, however, the taxpayer must (1) have invested in a producing well or mine, (2) operate it commercially at a reasonable cost so that the net income limitation does

**TABLE 10–2**  Two Sulfur Mines that Should Be Combined and Treated as One Property, if Possible

| Mine No. | Gross Income | Net Income | Percentage Depletion If Separate | Percentage Depletion If Combined |
|---|---|---|---|---|
| 1 | $100,000 | $10,000 | $ 5,000 | |
| 2 | 100,000 | 80,000 | 22,000 | |
| 1 + 2 | $200,000 | $90,000 | $27,000 | $44,000 |

**TABLE 10–3**    Two Sulfur Mines that Should Not Be Combined and Treated as One Property, if Possible

| Mine No. | Gross Income | Net Income (loss) | Percentage Depletion If Separate | If Combined |
|---|---|---|---|---|
| 1 | $100,000 | ($20,000) | $    0 | |
| 2 | 100,000 | 30,000 | 15,000 | |
| | $200,000 | $10,000 | $15,000 | $5,000 |

not come into play, and (3) be eligible for statutory depletion—that is, be either an independent producer or a royalty owner in the case of oil and gas properties. The final tax factors pertinent to such an investment involve disposition considerations. Before we turn to these considerations, we must examine briefly one remaining tax problem associated with the use of fixed assets.

### Expenditures during Use—Repair or Improvement?

Typically, after a taxpayer begins to use a fixed asset, a number of expenditures that present additional tax difficulties will be incurred. Expenditures for routine repairs are quite properly deducted immediately; expenditures for capital improvements are added to an asset account and recovered through subsequent cost allocation provisions. At the extreme, the difference between such expenditures is easy to illustrate for an individual taxpayer. For example, the gasoline used in an automobile on a business trip is, quite obviously, a deductible expense. A major overhaul of a "business" automobile is an equally obvious capital expenditure. The problem, of course, lies with intermediate expenditures, such as new tires, paint jobs, and minor overhauls. Are these expenditures immediately deductible, or must they be capitalized and recovered through depreciation? The classification problem is greater with buildings than with automobiles because of the major differences in estimated lives, potential changes in use, dollar amounts involved, and related values. Yet the need to distinguish between an expense and a capital expenditure is common to the use of all fixed assets.

In this problem area, as in the area of depreciation, the taxpayer may want to make one election for tax purposes and another for financial accounting purposes. The usual answer, naturally, is to expense as much as possible for tax purposes, but to capitalize as much as possible for accounting purposes. To a limited extent, a different treatment is possible, although the right of the taxpayer to differentiate here is not as clear-cut as it is in the case of depreciation.

## TAX FACTORS PERTINENT TO THE DISPOSITION OF FIXED ASSETS

The tax factors associated with the disposition of a fixed asset can be classified into three basic areas. The first factor is classification of the gain or loss realized on disposition as a capital gain or loss or as an ordinary gain or loss. The second factor involves the potential recapture of an earlier investment tax credit. The third factor relates to each of the first two in that it considers alternative ways of disposing of a fixed asset so that the taxpayer might influence the character of the gain or loss or the need to recapture the investment credit. Fortunately we have considered each of these problems earlier in this book; only a brief review is necessary here.

### Capital Gain or Ordinary Income?

Chapter 7 includes a discussion of the definitional problems associated with capital gains and losses. Table 7–1 adequately summarizes the most probable tax treatment of the gains and losses typically realized on the sale or exchange of a fixed asset used in a trade or business. The likelihood of a capital gain or loss is common to the following assets:

1. All "pure" capital assets according to the statutory definition.
2. Any depreciable *real* properties used in a trade or business *if*—
   a. The *gain* is attributed to the land.
   b. The *gain* is attributed to a nonresidential building or building component *and* that building was depreciated on a straight-line method.
   c. The *gain* is attributed to a residential rental property and that property was owned for 18 years or longer. (Note: if the property was held for more than one year, but less than 18 years, some portion of the gain will be ordinary income; some, capital gain.)
3. Part of the gain associated with a mineral right, *if* the disposition is complete, the transaction is so worded, and the gain is greater than the amount of any intangible drilling cost that is recaptured on a pro rata basis with the recovery of the minerals.

Most other dispositions of fixed assets will produce ordinary income. In addition, special rules may convert an additional part of the gain realized by corporate taxpayers on the disposition of Section 1250 (i.e., real) property from capital gain into ordinary income.

### Investment Credit Recapture

If a taxpayer disposes of a five-year property acquired prior to 1986 before the end of five years, some part or all of any investment credit claimed when that property was acquired will have to be recaptured in the year of the disposition. The exact amount to be added to the taxpayer's gross tax liability in the year of disposition depends on how early the disposition is made and the amount of credit originally claimed. In general, the investment credit is "earned" ratably at 2 percentage points per full year that the property is held.

To illustrate, assume that a taxpayer purchased on May 1, 1985, a five-year property that qualified for the 10 percent investment credit at a cost of $600,000. That taxpayer would have claimed an investment credit of $60,000 in 1985. If this taxpayer subsequently disposed of that same property sometime during 1989—that is, after only three full years of use—then 40 percent of the original $60,000 investment credit, or $24,000, would have to be added to the taxpayer's gross tax liability in 1989. If this disposition could be delayed until early in 1990, only 20 percent, or $12,000, would have to be recaptured.

In a few instances, a taxpayer might be able to delay a disposition for a very brief period and thereby avoid the need to recapture any investment credit. The need for detailed records is obvious. Finally, the reader should observe that the term *disposition* covers many events in addition to the obvious sale or exchange.

### Form of Disposition

Just as a taxpayer can change the tax consequences associated with the acquisition of a fixed asset by changing the form of the acquisition, so too the tax consequences associated with a disposition can be changed. Unintended dispositions, through casualty or theft, initially create the usual tax problems associated with all other dispositions. However, special rules often apply to alleviate the tax burdens that might attach to an unintended disposition if the taxpayer makes certain elections on a timely basis. Some of these options will be considered in Chapter 11. Finally, the reader should observe that it may be desirable to modify intended disposition plans at least temporarily to achieve certain desirable tax consequences. For example, instead of selling a fixed asset, a taxpayer may be able to modify it to another use and thereby modify the holding period or change the year of reporting so that a tax benefit can be maximized. The number of alternatives is large, and a good imagination combined with some knowledge of the tax rules (directly or through an adviser) can occasionally pay limited dividends.

## PROBLEMS AND ASSIGNMENTS

1. Define each of the following words or phrases as they are used in matters related to federal income taxation.
   a. Three-year property.
   b. Five-year property.
   c. Residential real property.
   d. Cost depletion.

    e. Percentage depletion.
    f. ACRS deduction.
    g. Cost recovery.
    h. Straight-line method.
    i. Recapture—depreciation.
    j. Recapture—investment credit.
    k. Amortization.

2. Stable Corporation has been in business for many years and consistently reports a taxable income of somewhere between $1 million and $1.4 million per year. Struggle Corporation, on the other hand, is a new business. Because of heavy start-up costs, Struggle anticipates that it will incur net operating losses or, at best, very small profits for the next five to seven years. Fortunately, Struggle has a strong financial base and it can reasonably anticipate a period of substantial profits in later years.
   a. How might these differences in financial circumstances affect the depreciation policies of each corporation? Explain briefly.
   b. What good *tax* reasons might Struggle Corporation have for leasing some or all of its equipment? Explain briefly.

3. Dan Wright purchased some new farm equipment in 1989 for $100,000. Dan knows that this equipment is properly classified as five-year property; he elects *not* to make the small business election.
   a. How much of the $100,000 investment can Dan deduct on his 1989 tax return if he uses the ACRS method and he purchased this equipment on January 1, 1989? On December 31, 1989? Assume the midquarter convention does *not* apply.
   b. How much of the $100,000 investment can Dan deduct on his 1989 tax return if he elects to recover the cost of this equipment using the five-year, straight-line, cost-recovery method and he purchased this equipment on January 1, 1989? On December 31, 1989? Assume the midquarter convention does *not* apply.
   c. If Dan uses the ACRS method, how much of the $100,000 investment may he deduct in 1990?
   d. If Dan uses the five-year, straight-line method, how much of the $100,000 investment may he deduct in 1990?
   e. Would the election to use the straight-line cost-recovery method increase the chance that Dan will report capital gain rather than ordinary income whenever he sells this property? Explain briefly.

4. Dee Stone purchased $300,000 of five-year property in 1989; $100,000 was purchased in March; $60,000, in May; and $140,000, in October. These were the only equipment purchases that Dee made in 1989. Compute Dee's depreciation expense on these purchases.

5. Sally Wright purchased a new barn for $100,000. Sally knows that this barn is properly classified as a nonresidential real property. Sally purchased the barn in 1989.

    a. How much of the $100,000 investment can Sally deduct on her 1989 tax return if she uses the ACRS method and purchased this barn on January 1, 1989? On December 31, 1989?

    b. How much of the $100,000 investment can Sally deduct on her 1989 tax return if she elects to recover the cost of this barn using the 40-year, optional straight-line, cost-recovery method and she purchased this barn on January 1, 1989? On December 31, 1989?

    c. If Sally uses the ACRS method, how much of the $100,000 investment may she deduct in 1990 if she purchased the barn on January 1, 1989? On December 31, 1989?

    d. If Sally uses the 40-year straight-line method, how much of the $100,000 investment may she deduct in 1990?

    e. Would the election to use the straight-line method increase the chance that Sally may report capital gain rather than ordinary income whenever she sells this property? Explain briefly.

6. ACME Products, Inc. is constructing its corporate headquarters. ACME is paying a contractor $10,000,000 to build the headquarters; the project is being financed with an $8,000,000 mortgage and $2,000,000 of the company's own funds. Construction began on 1/1/89. ACME had $2,400,000 working capital loans outstanding throughout 1989. ACME paid $1,200,000 in interest expense on the mortgage and $300,000 in interest expense on the working capital loans during 1989. The headquarters was opened on July 1, 1989.

    a. How much of the 1989 interest costs of $1,500,000 must ACME capitalize?

    b. What is ACME's 1989 depreciation expense on their new building?

7. In January 1989, Sherri Baker placed in service $9,000 of five-year property and $8,000 of seven-year property. What is Sherry's 1989 cost-recovery deduction, assuming that she wants to minimize her 1989 taxable income?

8. Dale Long, a limited partner in an oil and gas drilling partnership, was allocated the following expenses in 1989:

| | |
|---|---|
| Oil sales | $10,000 |
| Intangible drilling costs | 7,000 |
| Depreciation expense | 2,000 |
| Operating expenses | 3,000 |
| Cost depletion | 500 |

    a. Compute the effect on Dale's income tax from these transactions, without regard to any limitations. Assume that Dale is in the 28 percent marginal tax bracket.

    b. What limitations or restrictions could reduce or defer Dale's tax reduction computed in a?

9. In what fundamental way does percentage depletion differ from every other cost recovery method? Explain briefly.

# Case 10–1

Shopping Centers, Inc. owns and operates a shopping mall. In 1988, it began constructing a second mall at a cost of $10 million. One half of the cost of construction is being financed by debt and one half by equity. Construction is expected to be completed in 1990. The company has no other debt.

It is January, 1989. The management of SCI is considering borrowing $150,000 to fund an advertising campaign. Management expects the campaign to generate $170,000 additional revenues for the mall this year. Interest costs on the money borrowed will be $18,000. SCI will repay the loan in January of next year with proceeds of sales of other investments.

Should SCI borrow the money and engage in the advertising campaign? Assume that SCI is in the 34 percent marginal tax bracket and uses a discount rate of 8 percent.

# Case 10–2

Dewey Cheetum runs a construction equipment rental yard. He has some aging light-duty trucks which are costing him $2,000 each per year to maintain. These trucks have been fully depreciated for tax purposes, but will last for at least six more years with $4,000 of annual maintenance each. He could sell these trucks for $4,000 each and buy five new trucks for $22,000 each. Maintenance on the new trucks would be only $1,000 per year. He has decided he needs to have five trucks available for rent throughout the next six years. Both the new and old trucks would generate the same amount of revenue.

Dewey operates his business as a proprietorship with a 28 percent marginal tax bracket. His alternative rate of return on tax-free investments is six percent. In the current year he is not considering any other equipment acquisitions besides the trucks. He will utilize the small business election and the 200 percent declining balance with the mid-year convention. Assume that at the end of the six years the new trucks and the used trucks would have the same value. Disregard financing costs.

Dewey has calculated that both options will cost him $120,000 in pretax dollars. What is the aftertax present value of his options?

# Appendix to Chapter 10

**Table 10–4**   General Depreciation System

| If the Recovery Year Is: | and the Recovery Period Is: | | | | | |
|---|---|---|---|---|---|---|
| | 3-Year | 5-Year | 7-Year | 10-Year | 15-Year | 20-Year |
| | the Depreciation Rate Is: | | | | | |
| 1 | 58.33 | 35.00 | 25.00 | 17.50 | 8.75 | 6.563 |
| 2 | 27.78 | 26.00 | 21.43 | 16.50 | 9.13 | 7.000 |
| 3 | 12.35 | 15.60 | 15.31 | 13.20 | 8.21 | 6.482 |
| 4 | 1.54 | 11.01 | 10.93 | 10.56 | 7.39 | 5.996 |
| 5 | | 11.01 | 8.75 | 8.45 | 6.65 | 5.546 |
| 6 | | 1.38 | 8.74 | 6.76 | 5.99 | 5.130 |
| 7 | | | 8.75 | 6.55 | 5.90 | 4.746 |
| 8 | | | 1.09 | 6.55 | 5.91 | 4.459 |
| 9 | | | | 6.56 | 5.90 | 4.459 |
| 10 | | | | 6.55 | 5.91 | 4.459 |
| 11 | | | | 0.82 | 5.90 | 4.459 |
| 12 | | | | | 5.91 | 4.460 |
| 13 | | | | | 5.90 | 4.459 |
| 14 | | | | | 5.91 | 4.460 |
| 15 | | | | | 5.90 | 4.459 |
| 16 | | | | | 0.74 | 4.460 |
| 17 | | | | | | 4.459 |
| 18 | | | | | | 4.460 |
| 19 | | | | | | 4.459 |
| 20 | | | | | | 4.460 |
| 21 | | | | | | 0.557 |

Applicable depreciation method: 200 or 150 percent
Declining balance switching to Straight line
Applicable recovery periods: 3, 5, 7, 10, 15, 20 years
Applicable convention: Mid-quarter (property placed in service in first quarter)

**Table 10–5**   General Depreciation System

| If the Recovery Year Is: | and the Recovery Period Is: | | | | | |
|---|---|---|---|---|---|---|
| | 3-Year | 5-Year | 7-Year | 10-Year | 15-Year | 20-Year |
| | the Depreciation Rate Is: | | | | | |
| 1 | 41.67 | 25.00 | 17.85 | 12.50 | 6.25 | 4.688 |
| 2 | 38.89 | 30.00 | 23.47 | 17.50 | 9.38 | 7.148 |
| 3 | 14.14 | 18.00 | 16.76 | 14.00 | 8.44 | 6.612 |
| 4 | 5.30 | 11.37 | 11.97 | 11.20 | 7.59 | 6.116 |
| 5 | | 11.37 | 8.87 | 8.96 | 6.83 | 5.658 |
| 6 | | 4.26 | 8.87 | 7.17 | 6.15 | 5.233 |
| 7 | | | 8.87 | 6.55 | 5.91 | 4.841 |
| 8 | | | 3.33 | 6.55 | 5.90 | 4.478 |
| 9 | | | | 6.56 | 5.91 | 4.463 |
| 10 | | | | 6.55 | 5.90 | 4.463 |
| 11 | | | | 2.46 | 5.91 | 4.463 |
| 12 | | | | | 5.90 | 4.463 |
| 13 | | | | | 5.91 | 4.463 |
| 14 | | | | | 5.90 | 4.463 |
| 15 | | | | | 5.91 | 4.462 |
| 16 | | | | | 2.21 | 4.463 |
| 17 | | | | | | 4.462 |
| 18 | | | | | | 4.463 |
| 19 | | | | | | 4.462 |
| 20 | | | | | | 4.463 |
| 21 | | | | | | 1.673 |

Applicable depreciation method: 200 or 150 percent
Declining balance switching to straight line
Applicable recovery periods: 3, 5, 7, 10, 15, 20 years
Applicable convention: Mid-quarter (property placed in service in second quarter)

**Table 10-6**   General Depreciation System

| If the Recovery Year Is: | and the Recovery Period Is: | | | | | |
|:---:|:---:|:---:|:---:|:---:|:---:|:---:|
| | 3-Year | 5-Year | 7-Year | 10-Year | 15-Year | 20-Year |
| | the Depreciation Rate Is: | | | | | |
| 1 | 25.00 | 15.00 | 10.71 | 7.50 | 3.75 | 2.813 |
| 2 | 50.00 | 34.00 | 25.51 | 18.50 | 9.63 | 7.289 |
| 3 | 16.67 | 20.40 | 18.22 | 14.80 | 8.66 | 6.742 |
| 4 | 8.33 | 12.24 | 13.02 | 11.84 | 7.80 | 6.237 |
| 5 | | 11.30 | 9.30 | 9.47 | 7.02 | 5.769 |
| 6 | | 7.06 | 8.85 | 7.58 | 6.31 | 5.336 |
| 7 | | | 8.86 | 6.55 | 5.90 | 4.936 |
| 8 | | | 5.53 | 6.55 | 5.90 | 4.566 |
| 9 | | | | 6.56 | 5.91 | 4.460 |
| 10 | | | | 6.55 | 5.90 | 4.460 |
| 11 | | | | 4.10 | 5.91 | 4.460 |
| 12 | | | | | 5.90 | 4.460 |
| 13 | | | | | 5.91 | 4.461 |
| 14 | | | | | 5.90 | 4.460 |
| 15 | | | | | 5.91 | 4.461 |
| 16 | | | | | 3.69 | 4.460 |
| 17 | | | | | | 4.461 |
| 18 | | | | | | 4.460 |
| 19 | | | | | | 4.461 |
| 20 | | | | | | 4.460 |
| 21 | | | | | | 2.788 |

Applicable depreciation method: 200 or 150 percent
Declining balance switching to straight line
Applicable recovery periods: 3, 5, 7, 10, 15, 20 years
Applicable convention: Mid-quarter (property placed in service in third quarter)

**Table 10–7**   General Depreciation System

| If the Recovery Year Is: | and the Recovery Period Is: | | | | | |
|:---:|:---:|:---:|:---:|:---:|:---:|:---:|
| | 3-Year | 5-Year | 7-Year | 10-Year | 15-Year | 20-Year |
| | | | the Depreciation Rate Is: | | | |
| 1 | 8.33 | 5.00 | 3.57 | 2.50 | 1.25 | 0.938 |
| 2 | 61.11 | 38.00 | 27.55 | 19.50 | 9.88 | 7.430 |
| 3 | 20.37 | 22.80 | 19.68 | 15.60 | 8.89 | 6.872 |
| 4 | 10.19 | 13.68 | 14.06 | 12.48 | 8.00 | 6.357 |
| 5 | | 10.94 | 10.04 | 9.98 | 7.20 | 5.880 |
| 6 | | 9.58 | 8.73 | 7.99 | 6.48 | 5.439 |
| 7 | | | 8.73 | 6.55 | 5.90 | 5.031 |
| 8 | | | 7.64 | 6.55 | 5.90 | 4.654 |
| 9 | | | | 6.56 | 5.90 | 4.458 |
| 10 | | | | 6.55 | 5.91 | 4.458 |
| 11 | | | | 5.74 | 5.90 | 4.458 |
| 12 | | | | | 5.91 | 4.458 |
| 13 | | | | | 5.90 | 4.458 |
| 14 | | | | | 5.91 | 4.458 |
| 15 | | | | | 5.90 | 4.458 |
| 16 | | | | | 5.17 | 4.458 |
| 17 | | | | | | 4.458 |
| 18 | | | | | | 4.459 |
| 19 | | | | | | 4.458 |
| 20 | | | | | | 4.459 |
| 21 | | | | | | 3.901 |

Applicable depreciation method: 200 or 150 percent
Declining balance switching to straight line
Applicable recovery periods: 3, 5, 7, 10, 15, 20 years
Applicable convention: Mid-quarter (property placed in service in fourth quarter)

**Table 10–8**    General Depreciation System

| If the Recovery Year Is | And the Month in the First Recovery Year the Property Is Placed in Service Is: | | | | | | | | | | | |
|---|---|---|---|---|---|---|---|---|---|---|---|---|
| | 1 | 2 | 3 | 4 | 5 | 6 | 7 | 8 | 9 | 10 | 11 | 12 |
| | the Depreciation Rate Is: | | | | | | | | | | | |
| 1 | 3.485 | 3.182 | 2.879 | 2.576 | 2.273 | 1.970 | 1.667 | 1.364 | 1.061 | 0.758 | 0.455 | 0.152 |
| 2 | 3.636 | 3.636 | 3.636 | 3.636 | 3.636 | 3.636 | 3.636 | 3.636 | 3.636 | 3.636 | 3.636 | 3.636 |
| 3 | 3.636 | 3.636 | 3.636 | 3.636 | 3.636 | 3.636 | 3.636 | 3.636 | 3.636 | 3.636 | 3.636 | 3.636 |
| 4 | 3.636 | 3.636 | 3.636 | 3.636 | 3.636 | 3.636 | 3.636 | 3.636 | 3.636 | 3.636 | 3.636 | 3.636 |
| 5 | 3.636 | 3.636 | 3.636 | 3.636 | 3.636 | 3.636 | 3.636 | 3.636 | 3.636 | 3.636 | 3.636 | 3.636 |
| 6 | 3.636 | 3.636 | 3.636 | 3.636 | 3.636 | 3.636 | 3.636 | 3.636 | 3.636 | 3.636 | 3.636 | 3.636 |
| 7 | 3.636 | 3.636 | 3.636 | 3.636 | 3.636 | 3.636 | 3.636 | 3.636 | 3.636 | 3.636 | 3.636 | 3.636 |
| 8 | 3.636 | 3.636 | 3.636 | 3.636 | 3.636 | 3.636 | 3.636 | 3.636 | 3.636 | 3.636 | 3.636 | 3.636 |
| 9 | 3.636 | 3.636 | 3.636 | 3.636 | 3.636 | 3.636 | 3.636 | 3.636 | 3.636 | 3.636 | 3.636 | 3.636 |
| 10 | 3.637 | 3.637 | 3.637 | 3.637 | 3.637 | 3.637 | 3.636 | 3.636 | 3.636 | 3.636 | 3.636 | 3.636 |
| 11 | 3.636 | 3.636 | 3.636 | 3.636 | 3.636 | 3.636 | 3.637 | 3.637 | 3.637 | 3.637 | 3.637 | 3.637 |
| 12 | 3.637 | 3.637 | 3.637 | 3.637 | 3.637 | 3.637 | 3.636 | 3.636 | 3.636 | 3.636 | 3.636 | 3.636 |
| 13 | 3.636 | 3.636 | 3.636 | 3.636 | 3.636 | 3.636 | 3.637 | 3.637 | 3.637 | 3.637 | 3.637 | 3.637 |
| 14 | 3.637 | 3.637 | 3.637 | 3.637 | 3.637 | 3.637 | 3.636 | 3.636 | 3.636 | 3.636 | 3.636 | 3.636 |
| 15 | 3.636 | 3.636 | 3.636 | 3.636 | 3.636 | 3.636 | 3.637 | 3.637 | 3.637 | 3.637 | 3.637 | 3.637 |
| 16 | 3.637 | 3.637 | 3.637 | 3.637 | 3.637 | 3.637 | 3.636 | 3.636 | 3.636 | 3.636 | 3.636 | 3.636 |
| 17 | 3.636 | 3.636 | 3.636 | 3.636 | 3.636 | 3.636 | 3.637 | 3.637 | 3.637 | 3.637 | 3.637 | 3.637 |
| 18 | 3.637 | 3.637 | 3.637 | 3.637 | 3.637 | 3.637 | 3.636 | 3.636 | 3.636 | 3.636 | 3.636 | 3.636 |
| 19 | 3.636 | 3.636 | 3.636 | 3.636 | 3.636 | 3.636 | 3.637 | 3.637 | 3.637 | 3.637 | 3.637 | 3.637 |
| 20 | 3.637 | 3.637 | 3.637 | 3.637 | 3.637 | 3.637 | 3.636 | 3.636 | 3.636 | 3.636 | 3.636 | 3.636 |
| 21 | 3.636 | 3.636 | 3.636 | 3.636 | 3.636 | 3.636 | 3.637 | 3.637 | 3.637 | 3.637 | 3.637 | 3.637 |
| 22 | 3.637 | 3.637 | 3.637 | 3.637 | 3.637 | 3.637 | 3.636 | 3.636 | 3.636 | 3.636 | 3.636 | 3.636 |
| 23 | 3.636 | 3.636 | 3.636 | 3.636 | 3.636 | 3.636 | 3.637 | 3.637 | 3.637 | 3.637 | 3.637 | 3.637 |
| 24 | 3.637 | 3.637 | 3.637 | 3.637 | 3.637 | 3.637 | 3.636 | 3.636 | 3.636 | 3.636 | 3.636 | 3.636 |
| 25 | 3.636 | 3.636 | 3.636 | 3.636 | 3.636 | 3.636 | 3.637 | 3.637 | 3.637 | 3.637 | 3.637 | 3.637 |
| 26 | 3.637 | 3.637 | 3.637 | 3.637 | 3.637 | 3.637 | 3.636 | 3.636 | 3.636 | 3.636 | 3.636 | 3.636 |
| 27 | 3.636 | 3.636 | 3.636 | 3.636 | 3.636 | 3.636 | 3.637 | 3.637 | 3.637 | 3.637 | 3.637 | 3.637 |
| 28 | 1.970 | 2.273 | 2.576 | 2.879 | 3.182 | 3.485 | 3.636 | 3.636 | 3.636 | 3.636 | 3.636 | 3.636 |
| 29 | 0.000 | 0.000 | 0.000 | 0.000 | 0.000 | 0.000 | 0.152 | 0.455 | 0.758 | 1.061 | 1.364 | 1.667 |

Applicable depreciation method: Straight Line
Applicable recovery period: 27.5 years
Applicable convention: Mid-month

**Table 10–9**   General Depreciation System

| If the Recovery Year Is | \multicolumn{12}{c}{And the Month in the First Recovery Year the Property Is Placed in Service Is:} |
|---|

| If the Recovery Year Is | 1 | 2 | 3 | 4 | 5 | 6 | 7 | 8 | 9 | 10 | 11 | 12 |
|---|---|---|---|---|---|---|---|---|---|---|---|---|
| | \multicolumn{12}{c}{the Depreciation Rate Is:} |
| 1 | 3.042 | 2.778 | 2.513 | 2.249 | 1.984 | 1.720 | 1.455 | 1.190 | 0.926 | 0.661 | 0.397 | 0.132 |
| 2 | 3.175 | 3.175 | 3.175 | 3.175 | 3.175 | 3.175 | 3.175 | 3.175 | 3.175 | 3.175 | 3.175 | 3.175 |
| 3 | 3.175 | 3.175 | 3.175 | 3.175 | 3.175 | 3.175 | 3.175 | 3.175 | 3.175 | 3.175 | 3.175 | 3.175 |
| 4 | 3.175 | 3.175 | 3.175 | 3.175 | 3.175 | 3.175 | 3.175 | 3.175 | 3.175 | 3.175 | 3.175 | 3.175 |
| 5 | 3.175 | 3.175 | 3.175 | 3.175 | 3.175 | 3.175 | 3.175 | 3.175 | 3.175 | 3.175 | 3.175 | 3.175 |
| 6 | 3.175 | 3.175 | 3.175 | 3.175 | 3.175 | 3.175 | 3.175 | 3.175 | 3.175 | 3.175 | 3.175 | 3.175 |
| 7 | 3.175 | 3.175 | 3.175 | 3.175 | 3.175 | 3.175 | 3.175 | 3.175 | 3.175 | 3.175 | 3.175 | 3.175 |
| 8 | 3.175 | 3.174 | 3.175 | 3.174 | 3.175 | 3.174 | 3.175 | 3.175 | 3.175 | 3.175 | 3.175 | 3.175 |
| 9 | 3.174 | 3.175 | 3.174 | 3.175 | 3.174 | 3.175 | 3.174 | 3.175 | 3.174 | 3.175 | 3.174 | 3.175 |
| 10 | 3.175 | 3.174 | 3.175 | 3.174 | 3.175 | 3.174 | 3.175 | 3.174 | 3.175 | 3.174 | 3.175 | 3.174 |
| 11 | 3.174 | 3.175 | 3.174 | 3.175 | 3.174 | 3.175 | 3.174 | 3.175 | 3.174 | 3.175 | 3.174 | 3.175 |
| 12 | 3.175 | 3.174 | 3.175 | 3.174 | 3.175 | 3.174 | 3.175 | 3.174 | 3.175 | 3.174 | 3.175 | 3.174 |
| 13 | 3.174 | 3.175 | 3.174 | 3.175 | 3.174 | 3.175 | 3.174 | 3.175 | 3.174 | 3.175 | 3.174 | 3.175 |
| 14 | 3.175 | 3.174 | 3.175 | 3.174 | 3.175 | 3.174 | 3.175 | 3.174 | 3.175 | 3.174 | 3.175 | 3.174 |
| 15 | 3.174 | 3.175 | 3.174 | 3.175 | 3.174 | 3.175 | 3.174 | 3.175 | 3.174 | 3.175 | 3.174 | 3.175 |
| 16 | 3.175 | 3.174 | 3.175 | 3.174 | 3.175 | 3.174 | 3.175 | 3.174 | 3.175 | 3.174 | 3.175 | 3.174 |
| 17 | 3.174 | 3.175 | 3.174 | 3.175 | 3.174 | 3.175 | 3.174 | 3.175 | 3.174 | 3.175 | 3.174 | 3.175 |
| 18 | 3.175 | 3.174 | 3.175 | 3.174 | 3.175 | 3.174 | 3.175 | 3.174 | 3.175 | 3.174 | 3.175 | 3.174 |
| 19 | 3.174 | 3.175 | 3.174 | 3.175 | 3.174 | 3.175 | 3.174 | 3.175 | 3.174 | 3.175 | 3.174 | 3.175 |
| 20 | 3.175 | 3.174 | 3.175 | 3.174 | 3.175 | 3.174 | 3.175 | 3.174 | 3.175 | 3.174 | 3.175 | 3.174 |
| 21 | 3.174 | 3.175 | 3.174 | 3.175 | 3.174 | 3.175 | 3.174 | 3.175 | 3.174 | 3.175 | 3.174 | 3.175 |
| 22 | 3.175 | 3.174 | 3.175 | 3.174 | 3.175 | 3.174 | 3.175 | 3.174 | 3.175 | 3.174 | 3.175 | 3.174 |
| 23 | 3.174 | 3.175 | 3.174 | 3.175 | 3.174 | 3.175 | 3.174 | 3.175 | 3.174 | 3.175 | 3.174 | 3.175 |
| 24 | 3.175 | 3.174 | 3.175 | 3.174 | 3.175 | 3.174 | 3.175 | 3.174 | 3.175 | 3.174 | 3.175 | 3.174 |
| 25 | 3.174 | 3.175 | 3.174 | 3.175 | 3.174 | 3.175 | 3.174 | 3.175 | 3.174 | 3.175 | 3.174 | 3.175 |
| 26 | 3.175 | 3.174 | 3.175 | 3.174 | 3.175 | 3.174 | 3.175 | 3.174 | 3.175 | 3.174 | 3.175 | 3.174 |
| 27 | 3.174 | 3.175 | 3.174 | 3.175 | 3.174 | 3.175 | 3.174 | 3.175 | 3.174 | 3.175 | 3.174 | 3.175 |
| 28 | 3.175 | 3.174 | 3.175 | 3.174 | 3.175 | 3.174 | 3.175 | 3.174 | 3.175 | 3.174 | 3.175 | 3.174 |
| 29 | 3.174 | 3.175 | 3.174 | 3.175 | 3.174 | 3.175 | 3.174 | 3.175 | 3.174 | 3.175 | 3.174 | 3.175 |
| 30 | 3.175 | 3.174 | 3.175 | 3.174 | 3.175 | 3.174 | 3.175 | 3.174 | 3.175 | 3.174 | 3.175 | 3.174 |
| 31 | 3.174 | 3.175 | 3.174 | 3.175 | 3.174 | 3.175 | 3.174 | 3.175 | 3.174 | 3.175 | 3.174 | 3.175 |
| 32 | 1.720 | 1.984 | 2.249 | 2.513 | 2.778 | 3.042 | 3.175 | 3.174 | 3.175 | 3.174 | 3.175 | 3.174 |
| 33 | 0.000 | 0.000 | 0.000 | 0.000 | 0.000 | 0.000 | 0.132 | 0.397 | 0.661 | 0.926 | 1.190 | 1.455 |

Applicable depreciation method: Straight Line
Applicable recovery period: 31.5 years
Applicable convention: Mid-month

# CHAPTER 11

# The Nontaxable Transactions

In Chapter 2, we noted that realization is almost always a necessary condition to the recognition of a profit for income tax purposes. In addition, we observed that virtually any change in the form or the substance of a property or property right may be sufficient to constitute realization as far as the tax laws are concerned. This chapter examines a number of special statutory exceptions to the general rule that income must be recognized for tax purposes as soon as it has been realized. These special exceptions are commonly referred to as the nontaxable transactions.

The importance of the nontaxable transaction to business management derives from the fact that postponement of the date on which a tax is due allows a taxpayer to keep a larger amount of capital at work for a longer period of time. Other things being equal, this increases the absolute amount of capital that an entrepreneur can accumulate and manage over a lifetime. For example, if a taxpayer invested in a particular property that has substantially increased in value, the taxpayer may be reluctant to dispose of that investment, even if its present financial performance is unsatisfactory, and even if several better investment opportunities can be identified right now. If this taxpayer were to dispose of the initial investment, an immediate income tax would be payable on the entire unrealized gain, and only the aftertax proceeds would be available for reinvestment in the new opportunity.

To illustrate the importance of the tax factors to an investment decision, consider the situation in which an investor has a tax basis of $10,000 in an asset presently worth $110,000 and generating an annual $6,600 income (that is, a 6 percent return based on present worth). If the taxpayer is in a 33 percent marginal tax bracket, an income tax of approximately $33,000 would be payable if this asset were to be sold. After paying the tax, the investor would have only $77,000 to reinvest in a new property. Accordingly, the new investment would have to provide an annual return of more than 8.6 percent before it could be considered preferable to the initial investment (that is, $6,600 divided by $77,000 equals .0857). Investment opportunities that would yield a return of 7 or 8 percent would have to be rejected in favor of the extant 6 percent return simply because of the tax consequences. The increase required in the new return depends importantly on: (1) the absolute amount of the unrealized (or "paper") gain; (2) the marginal tax rate that would be applied to that gain; and (3) the present return on the investment. In general, the larger the amount of the paper gain, the higher the marginal tax rate, and the higher the present return, the greater the increase in the return that will be required to make the change.

If one understands how important these tax factors are to investment decisions, it is easy to see why knowledgeable business managers and investors are interested in the nontaxable exchange provisions of the Code. Before we begin to examine any of the specifics of the several statutory provisions, however, we need to consider a few characteristics common to all of the nontaxable transactions.

## COMMON CHARACTERISTICS OF NONTAXABLE TRANSACTIONS

The detailed requirements of each of the several statutory provisions that authorize a nontaxable transaction vary substantially. Some of the provisions are mandatory if the prescribed conditions are met, whereas others are elective under all circumstances. Some apply to gains only; others apply equally to gains and losses. Some demand a direct exchange—that is, a barter transaction involving no cash—whereas others allow a taxpayer to pass through a temporary cash position, provided that reinvestment is completed within a prescribed period. In spite of the many differences, all nontaxable transactions commonly share a "boot" requirement, a transfer of tax basis, and a time constraint. In this first section of Chapter 11, we will consider these common characteristics so that the subsequent discussions of specific provisions can proceed with minimal attention to the general characteristics.

### The Potential Need to Recognize Some Gain

The term *nontaxable transaction* is commonly used to refer both to partially taxable transactions and to transactions that are wholly free from any immediate income tax. To be entirely free of any income tax, a taxpayer involved in a nontaxable transaction generally cannot *receive* anything except *qualified property.* Observe that a taxpayer *may* be able to *give* nonqualifying property and still not be subject to tax; he or she simply cannot receive such property. Exactly which property will pass as a qualifying property varies from one nontaxable exchange to the next; in all nontaxable exchanges, however, it is common to refer to any nonqualified property as boot. Cash is, of course, the most frequently encountered form of boot. Finally, observe that the tax consequences to one party to a transaction need not be determined by the tax consequences to the other party to that transaction. In other words, a single transaction may create wholly taxable ordinary income for one party and be a wholly nontaxable transaction for the other party.

The fundamental concepts common to nontaxable exchanges that have been stated thus far can be illustrated by use of a simple diagram, as in Figure 11–1. Knowing nothing further about the transaction than what is shown in that illustration, we can safely make the following tax conclusions:

1. The transaction generally *cannot* be wholly tax-free to B because she received boot.
2. The transaction *may be* wholly tax-free to A, even though he gave boot.
3. A's tax consequences are not necessarily affected by B's.
4. B's tax consequences are not necessarily affected by A's.

The need to recognize taxable income in any transaction is always dependent upon the presence of a gain. To determine whether or not a gain is present, we must apply the tax rules stated beginning on page 138. Although the rules stated there were worded in terms of capital assets, they are equally applicable to all assets. A taxable profit is simply the difference between (a) the fair market value (FMV) of everything received in a transaction and (b) the adjusted tax basis of everything given up in that same transaction. No taxpayer ever needs to recognize for income tax purposes more gain than that realized. To give meaning to these sentences, let us return to our simple diagram and add some assumed values to that illustration, as shown in Figure 11–2. In this modified illustration, A's gain realized is $6,000; that is, $20,000 in value was received (we call this the "amount realized") and $14,000 in tax basis was given up ($10,000 in qualifying property and $4,000 in cash); hence, $20,000 − $14,000 = $6,000. By applying the same formula, we find that B's realized gain is $12,000 (that is, $20,000 − $8,000). If this particular transaction qualifies under one of the special statutory provisions that will be examined later in this chapter, it means that A mould *not have to recognize any of the $6,000 gain that he had realized.* If the same transaction also qualifies as a nontaxable exchange for B, it means that B *must recognize $4,000 of the $12,000 gain that she realized* because she received boot.

**FIGURE 11–1**

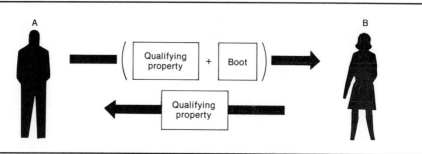

**FIGURE 11–2**

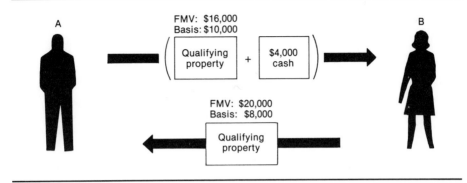

Observe again, however, that a taxpayer need never recognize more gain than that realized. In other words, if in this transaction, B's adjusted tax basis in the property given to A had been $18,000 instead of $8,000, then B's realized and recognized gain is reduced to $2,000 notwithstanding the fact that B received $4,000 cash. Although this rule is often confusing to the uninitiated taxpayer first encountering the nontaxable exchange rules, the problem is really one of being caught up in words rather than in complexity. Note what would have happened if B had simply sold her qualifying property to someone for $20,000 cash. If her basis were $18,000, she would report only a $2,000 taxable income. Why, then, should the tax answer be different if, instead of selling the property for cash, a taxpayer trades it for another property plus cash? Obviously it should not be different—and that is what the rule stated accomplishes. The fact that more cash than gain may be realized in an exchange simply menas that the taxpayer is getting a partial return of capital as well as realizing a profit on the exchange.

### Transfer of Basis

The apparent intent of the law in all nontaxable exchanges is to provide for only a postponement of an income tax rather than a permanent forgiveness of that tax. The postponement is accomplished through related provisions, which require that a taxpayer assume a "carry-over" tax basis in any property acquired in a nontaxable exchange. The law assumes that sooner or later the taxpayer will dispose of any property in a taxable transaction and will, at that time, report as taxable income the difference between the value received and the basis carried over from the prior property. In the case of an individual taxpayer, this may be an invalid assumption since individuals often die with appreciated property, and neither they nor their heirs would have to recognize the deferred gain. Thus, if a taxpayer can exchange properties in only qualified nontaxable exchanges until the time of death, everyone will effectively escape income taxation on predeath appreciation in value. The fresh-start basis rules for inherited property cause the "old" gain to disappear if the property is sold by the deceased taxpayer's executor, heir, or devisee immediately after the decedant's death. If a taxable disposition is made before the taxpayer's death, the carry-over basis rule of the nontaxable exchange ensures the recognition of the "correct" amount of gain or loss on the several transactions combined.

To demonstrate the effect of the carry-over basis rules, let us return to the facts assumed in connection with Figure 11–2. If this transaction qualifies under one of the nontaxable exchange provisions of the Code for both A and B, we can determine that A's tax basis in the property received would be $14,000. That is, A would take as his tax basis the basis he had in the property given up in this nontaxable transaction. Because he had $10,000 adjusted basis in the qualifying property given to B, and because he gave B an additional $4,000 in cash (and cash almost always has a tax basis equal to its face value), A's adjusted basis in the property received is deemed to be $14,000. B's tax basis is somewhat more difficult to determine.

Remember that, as the problem was originally worded, B was required to recognize $4,000 of the $12,000 gain realized in this exchange. This means that B must report on her next tax return an additional taxable income of $4,000 and that she must pay an income tax on that amount. Because B has to recognize that income and pay that tax, she also obtains the right to increase her tax basis in the property received by that same amount. In other words, B can increase her tax basis from $8,000 to $12,000. However, B must also divide the new larger tax basis between the boot (cash) and the qualifying asset received in the transaction. The law assumes that cash has a basis equal to its face value; hence B must allocate $4,000 in basis to the cash, leaving her with a continuing $8,000 basis in the new property acquired in the exchange.

The reasonableness of the carry-over basis rules can be demonstrated by further assuming that each taxpayer sold the newly acquired property shortly after completing the exchange. If there were no further change in the value of any properties, this would mean that A could sell this property for $20,000. Since A's carry-over basis is $14,000, he would have to recognize income of $6,000 at the time of the sale. Because A did not recognize any of the $6,000 gain realized at the time of the initial exchange, this carry-over of basis yields a correct result, considering the two transactions together. If there were no further changes in value, B would have to recognize $8,000 on any subsequent sale. This again is a correct solution, considering both exchanges, since B initially recognized $4,000 of the $12,000 gain realized at the time of the first exchange and no further change in values transpired before the second sale.

In some circumstances, it becomes rather difficult to determine the adjusted basis of property acquired in a nontaxable exchange, especially if a single exchange involves both qualified and nonqualified property and the nonqualified property is something other than cash. In general, however, a taxpayer can most easily determine a correct adjusted tax basis for property acquired in a nontaxable transaction by use of the following formula:

Fair market value of noncash property received

− Gain realized but *not* recognized on the exchange

= Adjusted basis of the property received.

Returning to our earlier illustration and applying the above formula to each taxpayer, we can confirm our prior calculations as follows:

|  | Taxpayer A | Taxpayer B |
|---|---|---|
| Fair market value of noncash property received | $20,000 | $16,000 |
| Less gain not recognized on the exchange | 6,000 | 8,000 |
| Adjusted basis of property received | $14,000 | $ 8,000 |

These results are consistent with the determinations made earlier.

### Time Constraints

Most of the nontaxable exchange provisions require that a taxpayer go directly from one investment into a second investment in a barter transaction. A few nontaxable exchange provisions, however, allow a taxpayer to move indirectly from one investment, through a temporary cash state, into a second investment, and still avoid the recognition of gain in the interim. In these provisions, the code stipulates a maximum period for the reinvestment. If the taxpayer does not meet the time requirements, the gain or loss following the traditional rules must then be recognized. The exact time requirements stipulated for each provision will be noted, along with other details, in the next section of this chapter.

## SPECIFIC NONTAXABLE EXCHANGE PROVISIONS

The most important nontaxable exchange provisions in the Code, in terms of their impact on business behavior, are those dealing with transactions between corporations and corporate shareholders. These are among the most complex provisions in the entire tax law. Consequently, the discussion that follows must be superficial in coverage. Hopefully, this brief discussion will permit the reader to appreciate the general constraints that are operative, as well as the golden opportunities that are available. In addition to examining several corporation–corporate shareholder transactions, we will examine the nontaxable exchange provisions covering productive-use and investment properties; involuntary conversions from condemnation proceedings, fire, storm, shipwreck, and other casualties; sales of the taxpayer's primary residence; and investments in low-income housing.

## Exchange of Productive-Use or Investment Properties

Code Section 1031 provides that a taxpayer will not recognize taxable gain or loss on the exchange of property held for productive use in a trade or business or for investment solely for property of a like kind. Another part of this section, however, specifically excludes from its effect the exchange of inventory, assets held primarily for resale, stocks, bonds, etc. The reader should observe that this provision (1) requires a direct exchange before it is operative, (2) applies equally to gains and losses, and (3) is mandatory, not elective. In other words, if a taxpayer trades one qualifying property for another, the tax law provides that he or she cannot recognize gain or loss following the usual rules and that the carry-over basis rules will automatically apply. This observation is often important in loss situations: If a taxpayer desires to recognize a tax-deductible ("paper") loss on a productive-use or investment property, it is imperative that he or she sell the property in one transaction and purchase the desired property in a second transaction. If the taxpayer directly trades for the second property, any loss will go unrecognized and the higher tax basis of the old property will be carried forward in the new property.

Words and phrases such as *productive use, investment, trade or business, held primarily for sale, solely,* and *like kind* create obvious definitional problems in applying this code section. Perhaps our first critical observation should be to note that, even though the section purports to deal with investment properties, the most common forms of investment properties are specifically ruled out of consideration. That is, stocks, bonds, notes, and securities cannot be treated as investment properties for purposes of this section. If an investor were to directly exchange 100 shares of General Motors common stock for shares with an equivalent value in another corporation Section 1031 would *not* be authority to defer the income tax recognition of any paper gain or loss that had accumulated between the date of purchase and the date of the exchange. Indeed, under these circumstances, the taxpayer would have to report the gain or loss realized just as if the GMC shares had been sold for cash and the other corporation's stock was subsequently purchased for cash.

Section 1031 does apply to almost all real and depreciable properties used in a trade or business, as well as to other investments. It applies, for example, to such assets as machinery and equipment, factory buildings, warehouses, and parking lots used in a trade or business, as well as to farmlands and speculative investments in apartment houses, oil wells, and art objects. The section would not be applicable to an exchange of a personal residence or a private automobile because these are neither investment nor productive-use properties. Even though a quick reading of the Code would seem to require that there be no boot in a qualifying Section 1031 exchange—that is, the Code first states that a tax-free exchange be *solely* for property of a like kind—other subsections of Section 1031 modify the apparent stringency of this rule and provide that the recipient of boot must report as taxable income the lesser of the gain realized or the boot received.

The most troublesome qualification in Section 1031 has proved to be the like-kind requirement. At present, a taxpayer can exchange almost any form of productive-use or investment property for any other form of productive-use or investment property and still qualify the exchange as a nontaxable transaction so long as either both properties are real properties or both are personal (nonreal) properties. It does not seem to change the tax consequences if one property is developed real estate and the other is undeveloped, or if one property is used in a business and the other is held as an investment. Thus, the exchange of undeveloped ranchland for a midtown apartment building would qualify as a nontaxable transaction (realty for realty), whereas the exchange of an airplane for an apartment building would not qualify (personalty for realty). The exchange of an airplane for apartment furnishings (personalty for personalty) could qualify so long as both were either used in a trade or business or held as an investment. One major statutory exception to the general rule just stated specifically disallows the exchange of livestock of different sexes from like-kind treatment under Section 1031.

In many Section 1031 exchanges, only one party to the exchange is affected by the existence of the nontaxable exchange rules. For example, if a car used entirely for business is traded for a new model through an automobile dealer, only the taxpayer giving up the old car and acquiring a new one is affected by the nontaxable exchange provisions. Both the used and the new car would constitute inventory (or "stock-in-trade") for the auto dealer, and therefore the exchange could not be even partially nontaxable for the dealer. On the other hand, if a dentist and a farmer were to exchange a city duplex (which the dentist had owned as an investment) for some farmland (which the farmer had been tilling), the nontaxable exchange provisions would apply to both taxpayers involved in the exchange. Incidentally, this provision is equally applicable to individual, corporate, and fiduciary taxpayers.

To illustrate how this section might apply to an actual situation, let us review the tax results that would accompany an exchange of 100 acres of mountainous timberland owned by ABC Corporation for a large corner lot in Silver City owned as an investment by Tom Jones, a local attorney. Assume that both ABC and Jones agree that the fair market value of the timber tract is $200 per acre and that the city lot is worth $30,000. To complicate matters a little more, let us also assume that Jones has an outstanding mortgage of $18,000 on his lot and that ABC Corporation agrees to assume that mortgage. Under these assumptions, Jones's interest in the city lot is currently worth only $12,000, whereas the timberland is worth the full $20,000; thus, Jones would be expected to give ABC Corporation $8,000 boot. Before we can proceed to determine the tax results, we must know what adjusted basis each taxpayer has in the property traded. Let us assume that Jones's basis in the city lot is $21,000 and that ABC Corporation's basis in the timberland is $3,000.

The determination of the tax consequences in nontaxable exchanges is often facilitated by a simple visual presentation of all critical facts. In order to restate the facts of this illustration, let us utilize Figure 11–3, a diagram

**FIGURE 11–3**

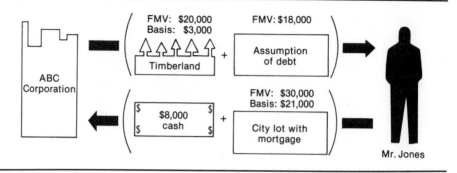

similar to the one introduced earlier in this chapter. The introduction of a mortgage is the only new addition to the former diagram. For purposes of a like-kind exchange, the assumption of a mortgage is tantamount to giving the debt-relieved taxpayer an equivalent sum of cash. In this illustration, therefore, ABC's assumption of Jones's $18,000 mortgage will be treated just as if ABC Corporation had paid Jones $18,000 cash.

The pertinent tax results are summarized in the accompanying table. Because the transfer of the $18,000 mortgage from Jones to ABC is treated just like an equivalent amount of cash, Jones must recognize his entire $9,000 gain in the year he makes this exchange. Since Jones must recognize his entire gain realized, his basis in the property received becomes its fair market value, or $20,000.

*For ABC Corporation*

| | |
|---|---:|
| Amount realized ($30,000 lot plus $8,000 cash) | $38,000 |
| Less adjusted basis given ($3,000 in land plus $18,000 in debt) | 21,000 |
| Gain realized on the exchange | $17,000 |
| Less gain recognized (due to receipt of $8,000 cash boot) | 8,000 |
| Gain realized but not recognized | $ 9,000 |
| | |
| Fair market value of noncash property received | $30,000 |
| Less gain realized but not recognized | 9,000 |
| Adjusted tax basis in city lot received | $21,000 |

*For Tom Jones*

| | |
|---|---:|
| Amount realized ($20,000 land plus $18,000 debt transferred) | $38,000 |
| Less adjusted basis given ($21,000 lot plus $8,000 cash) | 29,000 |
| Gain realized on the exchange | $ 9,000 |

Regardless of any uncertainty about several of the calculations, the reader should understand the few really basic tax results demonstrated in this illustration: first, that the transfer of a mortgage or other debt is treated as if the debtor had received an equivalent sum of cash in the exchange and used that sum to pay any prior obligation; second, that even though both taxpayers in this transaction exchanged qualifying property, the effect of Section 1031 applied to only one party because the amount of boot received by the other party was larger than the gain realized; third, that a taxpayer receiving a partial tax deferral because of a nontaxable exchange provision has a substitute (or carry-over) basis in the property received. In this illustration, ABC's tax basis in the city lot becomes $21,000, which represents a carry-over of the former basis ABC had in the timberland plus an additional $18,000 in basis, which it obtained by assuming the mortgage against the city lot. As this illustration demonstrates, the economic importance of the right to engage in a nontaxable exchange varies from one situation to the next. Other things being equal, the greater the amount of the unrealized gain, the more important it is for a taxpayer to arrange a nontaxable transaction.

The use of the word exchange in Section 1031 seems to demand a *simultaneous* giving and taking of property if a transaction is to be a nontaxable transaction. As a matter of fact the Code is not quite that demanding. In general it allows a taxpayer up to 45 days, after giving up one qualifying property, to identify the other property that he or she desires to receive in exchange. Furthermore, the taxpayer also has up to 180 days, after relinquishing one property, to receive the other qualifying property. This short term delay in completing a taxfree exchange can be especially helpful in real estate deals. For example, a would-be seller might: (1) give up title to a parcel of realty on May 1, 19x1; (2) first identify another piece of land, as the one he desires to receive in exchange, on June 9, 19x1; and (3) complete the deal by October 25, 19x1, and still report the transaction as one nontaxable exchange.

## Nontaxable Transactions between a Corporation and Its Shareholders

Transactions between a closely held corporation and its stockholders are often of more significance in terms of legal form than they are in terms of economic substance. For example, when a taxpayer incorporates a business that has been operated for a number of years as a sole proprietorship, the act of incorporation is of very little economic importance to anyone so long as all of the new corporation's stock is issued to the former proprietor. Under these circumstances, it seems entirely reasonable to suspend the usual rules requiring that any unrealized gains or losses be recognized for income tax purposes on the date of incorporation. The rationale for extending nontaxable exchange benefits to transactions between giant corporations and minority shareholders is much more difficult to explain. Nevertheless, under the proper circumstances, both classes of transactions can be brought within the purview of the nontaxable transaction rules.

**Forming a Corporation.**   Code Section 351 provides that no gain or loss shall be recognized for income tax purposes if one or more persons transfer property to a corporation solely in exchange for the stock or securities of that corporation *and* the person or persons transferring the property own 80 percent or more of the voting control of the corporation after the transfer. The importance of this provision is that it allows taxpayers to create new corporations without immediate tax consequences as long as those who transfer property to the new corporation own 80 percent of the corporation's stock after the transfer and receive no boot. Once again, if all the conditions are satisfied, this tax result will follow whether the taxpayer wants it to or not. If a taxpayer desires to engage in a taxable transaction, there are three options: (1) the taxpayer can make certain that the transaction is arranged as a sale rather than as an exchange of property for stock and/or securities; (2) the taxpayer can make certain that sufficient boot is received to guarantee the right to recognize a gain that he or she desires to recognize; or (3) the taxpayer can make certain that the transferors of property own less than 80 percent of the transferee corporation's stock.

In any exchange to which Section 351 applies, the usual carry-over basis rules also apply. Observe, however, that the effect of a nontaxable transfer to a corporation is to double the aggregate tax basis existing in the world without incurring any tax. The transferors of property in a wholly nontaxable Section 351 transaction will transfer their former tax basis in the property transferred to the new stock or securities received; at the same time, the corporate transferee also acquires that same tax basis in the properties that it receives. This doubling of basis can be illustrated simply, as in Figure 11–4, in a before-and-after comparison.

Under some circumstances, a taxpayer is well advised to attempt a nontaxable incorporation; under other circumstances, a taxable one might be preferred. In the previous illustration, for example, taxpayer Z might prefer to purchase stock in corporation A for cash if asset 1 were a plot of undeveloped land with a tax basis of $100,000 and a fair market value of $10,000. After taxpayer Z purchases the stock for cash, corporation A might subsequently purchase taxpayer Z's land for $10,000. If the form of these two transactions can be sustained, taxpayer Z may assure the right to report a $90,000 loss on the sale of the land (unless such a loss is precluded by a related-party sale rule).

**Reorganizing a Corporation.**   The officers of an extant corporation sometimes decide that the corporation can achieve its objectives better if it can be reorganized in some way. For example, the corporate officers may decide to divide one corporation into two or more corporate entities in order to allow

**FIGURE 11–4**

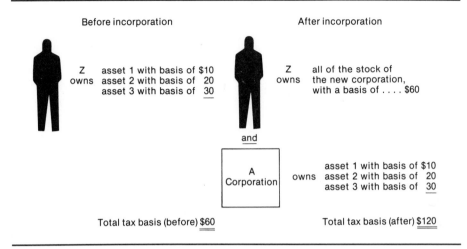

| Before incorporation | After incorporation |
|---|---|
| Z owns  asset 1 with basis of $10<br>asset 2 with basis of  20<br>asset 3 with basis of  30 | Z owns  all of the stock of the new corporation, with a basis of . . . . $60 |

and

| A Corporation | owns  asset 1 with basis of $10<br>asset 2 with basis of  20<br>asset 3 with basis of  30 |

Total tax basis (before) $60      Total tax basis (after) $120

each to pursue a different business. Alternatively, the corporate officers may try to add economic strength to a financially distressed corporate organization by arranging a reorganization that would decrease the amount of outstanding debt and increase the amount of the stockholders' equity by the same amount. Under still other circumstances, the officers of one corporation may desire to acquire another corporate organization or all of its assets. Such a corporate acquisition can be accomplished in any of several ways—by merger, by consolidation, by acquisition of all of the second corporation's operating assets, or by acquisition of sufficient stock of the second corporation to make that corporation a subsidiary of the acquiring corporation. Each of these corporate reorganizations can be accomplished as a nontaxable transaction if all parties to the transaction fully comply with the intricate rules of Subchapter C of the Internal Revenue Code.

The general requirements of the corporate reorganization provisions follow the characteristics common to all nontaxable exchanges described earlier in this chapter, except for the fact that the corporate reorganization provisions usually apply to both parties to the transaction if they apply to either one. If the reorganization is to be accomplished wholly tax-free, the parties to the reorganization usually can exchange only qualifying property. A limited amount of boot is allowed in certain corporate reorganizations, but not in all of them. In some nontaxable reorganizations, the only form of qualifying property is stock or securities in corporations that are party to the reorganization.

To demonstrate the importance of the corporate reorganization provisions, let us consider the case of an assumed Adam Smith, who owns 100 percent of the stock of Smith Industries, Incorporated. Smith, who is approaching retirement age, has decided to dispose of his interest in Smith

Industries. Initially, Smith thought that he might sell his entire interest to a local investor group, which had expressed an interest in his company. Smith discovered, however, that such a sale would be almost prohibitively expensive in terms of the income tax. He had formed his corporation many years ago with invested capital of $100,000. During the intervening years, this small corporation had grown, until today it is worth in excess of $5 million. If Smith were to sell his stock, he would trigger an immediate income tax of something like $1.5 million, leaving him with $3.5 million to reinvest. Instead of selling, therefore, Smith agrees to exchange all of his stock in Smith Industries for stock in Giant Conglomerate Corporation of America. If everything is properly arranged, this means that the exchange will proceed without tax consequences to Adam Smith, Smith Industries, or Giant Conglomerate Corporation. This result will be possible even if Smith ends up owning only, say, 1 or 2 percent of the outstanding stock of Giant, and even if Smith Industries constitutes only a small part of Giant Conglomerate Corporation. In this situation, the economic transformation achieved by Adam Smith is much more than one of legal form alone. Before the nontaxable exchange, Smith owned and operated his own business; after the exchange, he owns a small interest in a giant enterprise engaged in a multitude of diverse economic endeavors. Even though the realization of economic gain in this illustration is as complete as it can ever possibly be, the tax laws authorize the total deferral of any income tax if all of the Code requirements are met. In this area even the tax experts fear to tread alone. Before a corporate reorganization is finalized, most tax experts and corporate officers will insist upon an advance ruling on all tax consequences by the Internal Revenue Service. If the IRS issues an adverse ruling, or if it will issue no ruling, the original reorganization plans are almost invariably called back and modified or dropped. The tax consequences are often so substantial for so many people that no corporate officers or tax advisers are willing to risk the potential liability of proceeding in the face of an adverse ruling, even if they are of the opinion that the ruling is incorrect and would not be upheld by a court.

The fact that corporate reorganizations can proceed as nontaxable exchanges has had a tremendous impact on our economy. In the 1960s, and again in the 1980s, corporate stocks and securities almost became a second form of money. Stocks and securities were as good as money only because they could, under the right circumstances, be exchanged tax-free. Empires were built, and often lost, through corporate mergers and acquisitions alone. Very little of this merger activity would have been possible had the tax laws not provided nontaxable exchange opportunities. If a corporation or its shareholders had to recognize all prior appreciation in value for income tax purposes before proceeding with a corporate reorganization, reorganizations would be economically impractical.

The reader should now be in a position to understand why the author could state earlier that the double tax often was not a major consideration for the closely held corporation. Prior to the 1986 Act, in most closely held corporations, the owners would extract (with only a personal income tax) whatever amount of income they needed for personal consumption in the form of salaries, interest, and rents during their years of active interest in corporate affairs. All corporate income in excess of the owners' personal needs was accumulated within the corporate shell, where it was expanded through new and larger business investments. If the owner did not die sooner, and if he or she did not desire the control of the corporation to pass to another member of the family, the owner typically allowed the firm to be reorganized as part of a larger venture in a nontaxable transaction. Finally, then, the stock of either the original company or of the merged organization was passed to heirs or devisees who inherited the property with a basis equal to the stock's value on the date of the decendent's death. Thus the accumulated income originally recognized by the corporation was never "realized" by the family; instead, the personal income tax was permanently deferred. Because corporate (business) reorganizations are still of major importance, the next chapter will consider the pertinent tax factors in detail.

**Liquidating a Corporation.** The liquidation of a corporation is typically a taxable transaction as far as the corporate entity is concerned. Under most circumstances, a liquidation also necessitates the recognition of taxable gain (or loss) on the part of the recipient shareholders. The need for both the corporation and the shareholder to recognize some gain on the liquidation of a corporation means, quite obviously, that it is often much more expensive with regard to taxes to get out of a corporate form of business organization than it is to get into it. For this reason, a taxpayer should never take lightly a decision to incorporate. The inconsistency of the tax rules can be demonstrated simply, as in Figure 11–5. The gain or loss realized by the stockholders on the liquidation of the corporation can be classified either as ordinary income or capital gain. If the corporation is not a collapsible corporation, the gain realized by the shareholders will generally be classified as a capital gain. The corporation being liquidated will determine the ordinary or capital nature of the gain it must recognize on an asset-by-asset basis.

## Involuntary Conversions

If a taxpayer's property is involuntarily converted into cash or other property by action of a condemnation proceeding, a casualty, or a theft, the taxpayer is usually free to treat the involuntary conversion as a nontaxable transaction as long as it resulted in a gain *and* the taxpayer reinvests the proceeds received in a similar property within a prescribed period. The proceeds received in an involuntary conversion are typically either a condemnation award or insurance proceeds, both of which are commonly paid in cash. Section 1033 gives the taxpayer an option: He or she is free to report the gain realized on an involuntary conversion under the usual tax rules if it is desirable to do so; if not, the gain may be treated as the gain realized on

**FIGURE 11–5**

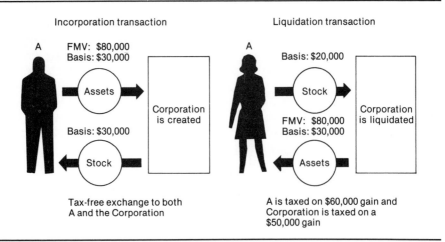

Incorporation transaction

A    FMV: $80,000
     Basis: $30,000

Assets → Corporation is created

Basis: $30,000

Stock

Tax-free exchange to both
A and the Corporation

Liquidation transaction

A    Basis: $20,000

Stock →  Corporation is liquidated

FMV: $80,000
Basis: $30,000

Assets

A is taxed on $60,000 gain and
Corporation is taxed on a
$50,000 gain

a nontaxable exchange if the destroyed property is replaced with a similar property within two years after the end of the year in which the gain was realized. If the taypayer does not reinvest the entire proceeds in a similar property, the amount retained is treated as boot. Interestingly, the option of treating an involuntary conversion as a nontaxable transaction does not extend to losses; they must be reported and deducted in the year realized.

To illustrate the tax rules applicable to involuntary conversions, assume that a taxpayer had the four assets, listed in the accompanying table, destroyed by fire, that the insurance company made reimbursements in the amounts indicated, and that the taxpayer reinvested the amounts shown in a similar property within the prescribed period.

| Asset | Adjusted Basis | Insurance Proceeds | Amount Reinvested |
|-------|----------------|--------------------|--------------------|
| 1 | $10,000 | $15,000 | $17,000 |
| 2 | 20,000 | 26,000 | 24,000 |
| 3 | 30,000 | 37,000 | 28,000 |
| 4 | 40,000 | 30,000 | n.a. |

The gain realized on asset 1 is, of course, $5,000 ($15,000 − $10,000). If the taxpayer elects, however, there is no need to recognize any of the $5,000 gain realized because all of the insurance proceeds, and more, were reinvested in a similar property. Assuming that the taxpayer elects not to recognize the gain realized, the basis in the replacement property will be $12,000—that is, a carry-over basis of $10,000 from old asset 1 plus the *extra* $2,000 cash ($17,000 reinvested minus $15,000 insurance proceeds) invested in the similar property.

The gain realized on asset 2 is $6,000 ($26,000 − $20,000). Because the taxpayer retained $2,000 of the insurance proceeds ($26,000 received − $24,000 reinvested), $2,000 of the $6,000 gain realized must be recognized. The taxpayer may, however, elect to defer recognition of the remaining $4,000 gain realized. Assuming that the taxpayer does elect to defer recognition of that $4,000, the basis in the replacement property will be $20,000 ($24,000 fair market value of the new property less $4,000 gain not recognized).

The gain realized on asset 3 is $7,000 ($37,000 − $30,000). Because the taxpayer invested only $28,000 in the replacement property—that is, $9,000 in cash was retained—the entire gain of $7,000 must be recognized. The basis of the new property then becomes its cost, $28,000.

The involuntary conversion of asset 4 resulted in a $10,000 loss. The taxpayer has no option but to report that loss in the year of the involuntary conversion. It is immaterial whether the taxpayer reinvests any or all of the insurance proceeds from asset 4; the loss must be recognized immediately. If replacement is made, the basis of any new property will be its cost.

Surprisingly, perhaps, a most difficult aspect of applying Section 1033 has been in the determination of what constitutes a qualifying replacement property. The code requires only that it be "similar or related in service or use" to the property destroyed. The IRS and the courts have interpreted the statutory requirement very narrowly. If the taxpayer desires to exercise the right to treat any gain from an involuntary conversion as a deferred gain, great caution must be taken in selecting replacement properties. Because the law is constantly changing is this regard, no attempt will be made to summarize the kinds of replacements that will satisfy each of the many courts in the various jurisdictions. The need for expert assistance in making replacement investments is obvious.

### Residence Sales

If a taxpayer sells a primary residence at a gain, the usual rules would require that the gain realized be reported immediately as a capital gain. If a taxpayer sells a primary residence at a loss, the usual rules deny the right to any deduction since the residence is a purely personal property. Section 1034 of the code provides some relief from the usual rules, but only if the taxpayer sells a primary residence at a gain.

Section 1034 in effect allows a taxpayer 24 months (before or after a sale) during which a former primary residence must be replaced with another one if the recognition of any gain realized on the sale of a former home is to be deferred. Within the prescribed period, a taxpayer may replace any form of primary residence with any other form and still avoid recognition of gain. For example, if both were in fact the taxpayer's primary residence, he or she could move from a ketch-rigged sailboat to a mobile home, or from a condominium to a country estate, and avoid the recognition of any gain on the sale of the former home. This provision is also worded to be mandatory if the conditions are satisfied. A taxpayer who desires to recognize the gain realized on the sale of a former home must either reinvest a sufficiently small amount in the new home or remain without a purchased home for longer than the prescribed time period.

If the taxpayer does not reinvest the entire cash proceeds from the sale of the former residence in a new home, any excess cash retained is again treated like boot. In this regard, the rules applicable to involuntary conversions are very much like the rules applicable to sales of a primary residence. To demonstrate their comparability, let us assume numbers with residence sales that are identical to the numbers assumed earlier for involuntary conversions, and then compare the tax results of the two situations. (Obviously, these dollar amounts are not realistic, but the principle would not change just because larger numbers were used.)

| Case | Adjusted Basis of Old Home | Amount Realized on Sale of Old Home | Cost of New Residence |
|---|---|---|---|
| 1 | $10,000 | $15,000 | $17,000 |
| 2 | 20,000 | 26,000 | 24,000 |
| 3 | 30,000 | 37,000 | 28,000 |
| 4 | 40,000 | 30,000 | n.a. |

Because the analysis of the tax results is so similar to that of the earlier discussion, it will not be repeated here. In summary form, the critical tax results of each of the above "cases," assuming that all time requirements are satisfied, are shown in the table below.

| Case | Gain (or loss) Realized on Sale of Old Home | Gain (or loss) Recognized on Sale of Old Home | Adjusted Tax Basis of New Home |
|---|---|---|---|
| 1 | $ 5,000 | $    0 | $12,000 |
| 2 | 6,000 | 2,000 | 20,000 |
| 3 | 7,000 | 7,000 | 28,000 |
| 4 | (10,000) | 0 | n.a. |

The only difference between the tax results for involuntary conversions and for residence sales concerns case 4. There, because the loss realized on the sale of a personal asset is not deductible, the tax result differs from the case of the involuntary conversion—in which instance a tax deduction may be authorized.

Special rules are applicable to residence sales made by taxpayers who are 55 years of age or older. The special rules grant the senior citizen the right to *exclude* the first $125,000 of gain realized on the sale of a primary residence, in addition to the more general right to treat the sale of a residence as a nontaxable transaction if gain is realized and a replacement is made on a timely basis. For tax-planning purposes, it is important that every taxpayer realize that he or she may be entitled to a special $125,000 *exclusion* if the primary residence is not sold until after the taxpayer's 55th birthday. It would be especially unfortunate if a taxpayer sold a primary residence at a sizable gain shortly before becoming eligible for that special exclusion. Because it is of limited applicability, however, we will not discuss the details of that special provision here. Readers who are approaching 55 years of age, and who own homes that have appreciated in value, should be especially careful in timing their home sales wisely.

Individuals of any age who sell their primary residence at a gain should understand that the general rules described above are subject to additional and sometimes confusing detail. For example, in determining the "amount realized" a homeowner is allowed to deduct all "selling expenses" from the sales price of the home. In many instances the broker's commission is the largest single selling expense but that term may also include substantial advertising expenses and the cost of legal services. In addition, the amount that the homeowner must reinvest in their next primary residence is not simply the "cash proceeds", as suggested earlier, but an amount technically known as the "adjusted sales price." This term is equal to the amount realized less "fixing-up expenses." The latter term includes the cost of such expenditures as painting and papering a former home but only if (*a*) incurred for work performed in the 90-day period ending on the day a contract to sell is entered into and (*b*) paid on or before the 30th day after the date of sale.

To illustrate a few of the many possible additional details, assume that Mary and John Howe, age 45 and 47, sold their old home for $195,000. At closing, the Howes paid a realtor's commission of $11,700 and $3,000 in legal fees for preparing the deed. They also incurred and paid $2,500 to a handyman, within the prescribed time periods, for various fixing-up expenses. In this example the "amount realized" by the Howes is $180,300, not $195,000. If they do not want to recognize any gain on the sale of their old home, the Howes must acquire a new primary residence costing $177,800 or more—i.e., $180,300 less $2,500—within the 24-month period.

## Other Nontaxable Exchanges

This discussion does not exhaust all of the nontaxable exchange provisions in the code. Section 1035, for example, authorizes a tax-free exchange of insurance policies under prescribed conditions. Section 1036 authorizes a nontaxable exchange of stock for other stock in the same corporation (which guarantees the tax-free character of most stock splits). Section 1037 authorizes the reacquisition of real property on a tax-free basis under certain circumstances and Section 1039 allows the tax-free rollover of any gain on investments in "low-income housing." These and other nontaxable exchange provisions will not be discussed here, either because they are of limited applicability or because they are of minimal importance to most tax-planning opportunities. In the few remaining pages of this chapter, we will consider briefly several planning considerations of more general importance.

## PLANNING CONSIDERATIONS IN NONTAXABLE TRANSACTIONS

Many taxpayers seem to be remotely aware of the nontaxable exchange provisions, and yet they seem to take inadequate advantage of them. Perhaps their reluctance is attributable to some misunderstanding of the more practical aspects of completing a nontaxable exchange successfully. For example, the taxpayer may believe that he or she must personally locate another investor who is willing to trade properties before it is possible to successfully engage in a tax-free rollover of a productive use or investment property. If that belief were factually correct, there would indeed be few meaningful tax opportunities available. Fortunately, many tax-free exchanges can be arranged through the use of a property broker in what is known as a three-cornered exchange.

### Three-Cornered Exchanges

A taxpayer who owns a substantially appreciated productive-use or investment property should generally spend more time and effort locating a desirable replacement property, and less time and effort locating a potential buyer for the property to be exchanged, if he or she wants to maximize the tax opportunity available. After the taxpayer has located an appropriate replacement property, the taxpayer should proceed to contact a property broker to play the necessary intermediary role in a tax-free exchange. That is, the taxpayer requests the broker to purchase the property that the taxpayer wants to acquire, and following such a purchase by the broker, the taxpayer and the broker exchange properties. This, of course, leaves the broker with the appreciated property that the taxpayer wanted to sell. Because selling such properties constitutes their business, brokers are quite willing to make such arrangements if they can see a reasonable profit in the deal for themselves. The seller may be willing to pass along to the broker a small portion of any profit because this allows the seller to achieve investment objectives at a minimal tax cost. The sequential steps of the three-cornered exchange can be diagramed as in Figure 11–6. If all parties take sufficient care in arranging the details of these separate transactions, taxpayer A can achieve her investment objectives tax-free. The arrangements between A and B are especially

**FIGURE 11–6**

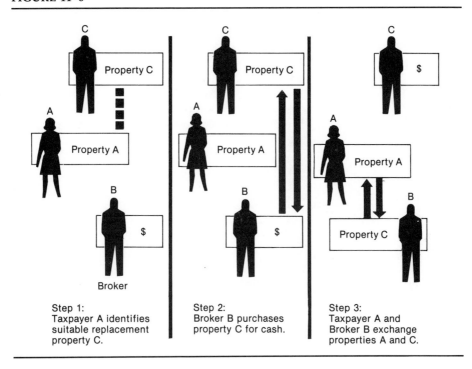

Step 1:
Taxpayer A identifies
suitable replacement
property C.

Step 2:
Broker B purchases
property C for cash.

Step 3:
Taxpayer A and
Broker B exchange
properties A and C.

critical. If the tax authorities can determine that B only acted as an agent of A, the plan will fail and A will be treated as if she personally purchased property C for cash. Taxpayer A also must be careful in her dealings with C. If A proceeds too far into the negotiations with C, so that the sale is all but finalized before the broker is introduced into the deal, some courts will conclude that A actually purchased property C, even though the legal papers show that technically the sale by party C was made to B rather than to A. For those who know the rules and who document their way carefully, however, the three-cornered exchange can be a useful technique in minimizing the tax consequences of semiroutine business transactions.

## Mortgaged Properties

Taxpayers sometimes reject the use of a tax-free exchange, believing that the existence of a mortgage on a property will in effect be treated as boot and therefore, for all practical purposes, convert an apparently tax-free transaction into a wholly taxable one. This danger was adequately demonstrated in Figure 11–3. What was not explained there, however, is that the tax authorities will not treat the transfer of a mortgage as an equivalent of cash to the extent that two mortgages offset each other.

If the two taxpayers in Figure 11–3 had understood the tax rules, they would have arranged a slightly different transaction from the one proposed there. Specifically, ABC Corporation might first arrange to borrow $18,000 against 150 acres of its timberland. This would, of course, give ABC $18,000 cash tax-free since borrowing money is not deemed to constitute realization, even if property is mortgaged in the process. Then ABC Corporation and Attorney Jones might proceed to exchange the city lot, with its $18,000 mortgage, for the 150 acres of timberland, which also carries an $18,000 mortgage. Under these revised conditions, neither party would have to recognize any taxable income on the exchange because the two mortgages exactly cancel each other out. Thus, Mr. Jones ends up with 150 acres of timberland (rather than 100 acres) and an $18,000 mortgage, but he need not pay any income tax on the $9,000 gain, which now remains entirely unrecognized. Jones's tax basis in the 150 acres would be $21,000—a carry-over basis from his old city lot. ABC Corporation, under the revised circumstances, ends up with $10,000 more cash than it had before, 50 acres less timberland, and the right to ignore $8,000 in taxable income that had to be recognized in the previous arrangement. ABC Corporation's basis in the city lot would be $4,500, a carry-over basis from the 150 acres of timberland. (Since ABC's tax basis in 100 acres was $3,000, it is assumed that its basis in 50 contiguous acres would be another $1,500.)

## The Role of Intent

Each of the nontaxable exchange provisions contains potential tax traps for the unwary taxpayer. For example, before a taxpayer can properly defer the recognition of a gain realized on the sale of his or her home, the taxpayer must be able to establish that the home sold was in fact his or her *primary residence*. If the taxpayer were to try to apply that provision to the gain realized on the sale of a summer cottage on the coast, this would probably not be sustained. If a taxpayer has more than one home, determining which home constitutes the primary residence turns largely upon the role of intent. The number of days spent at each location may be indicative of intent, but such a simplistic criterion need not control in any particular disposition. The point is that a taxpayer must sometimes take great care in documenting intent if he or she wishes to retain the right to claim that a particular transaction is a nontaxable one.

One case history in this regard seems especially instructive. A California taxpayer decided to dispose of a particular investment property. At the moment he could not identify a satisfactory replacement property, but a buyer was anxious to purchase the property that he wished to sell. In order not to lose the sale, the taxpayer agreed to make an exchange with a broker that would allow the anxious buyer to acquire his property. The property accepted in return was not what the California taxpayer really wanted, and this fact was adequately documented in correspondence between the taxpayer and the broker. Everyone wanted it well understood that, as soon as an appropriate property could be located, the broker was to acquire that property and trade for the one temporarily accepted by the California taxpayer. Before long, the taxpayer found his desired investment property and the second exchange was promptly completed. Much to everyone's surprise, however, the tax authorities found that the series of exchanges did not satisfy the requirements of Section 1031. The IRS argued that the California taxpayer never intended to hold the intermediate property as either a productive-use or an investment property. It was held only as an expedient to attain certain tax results. The taxpayer's own letters proved his intent, and the IRS position was sustained by the courts. As this case demonstrates, a nontaxable transaction can very easily be converted into a taxable transaction by taxpayers who proceed without giving sufficient attention to every detail.

## PROBLEMS AND ASSIGNMENTS

1. Dick Primer and Jane Kinder will soon combine their two sole proprietorships into a new corporation—Dick and Jane, Inc. Dick agrees to transfer property 1 (value, $20,000; basis, $14,000) and his own valuable professional services (value $10,000) to Dick and Jane, Inc., in exchange for 3,000 shares of common stock. Jane agrees to transfer cash of $15,000 and property 2 (value, $15,000; basis, $17,000) to the corporation in exchange for another 3,000 shares of common stock.

   a. Will Dick have to recognize any gain or loss on this incorporation transaction? Explain briefly.

   b. Will Jane have to recognize any gain or loss on this incorporation transaction? Explain briefly.

   c. Is it likely that either Dick or Jane, or both, would prefer a taxable to a nontaxable transaction? Explain briefly.

   d. What is Dick's basis in the 3,000 shares of stock he receives?

   e. What is Jane's basis in the 3,000 shares of stock she receives?

   f. What is Dick and Jane, Inc.'s basis in property 1? Property 2?

2. Alpha and Omega would like to exchange real estate properties.

|          | *Alpha*   | *Omega*   |
|----------|-----------|-----------|
| FMV      | $200,000  | $180,000  |
| Mortgage | 120,000   | 50,000    |
| Basis    | 140,000   | 60,000    |

   a. How much boot should be paid (and by whom) in order for this transaction to make sense economically?

b. If the cash in part a is paid, what will be Alpha's realized gain, recognized gain, and basis of new property?

c. If the cash in part a is paid, what will be Omega's realized gain, recognized gain, and basis of new property?

d. What tax-planning advice could you give Omega to reduce the recognized gain?

3. David Hoffman owns an apartment house in Chapel Hill, North Carolina. This property has an adjusted basis of $48,000 and a fair market value of $100,000. David plans to exchange it for a seaside condominium on Hilton Head Island, South Carolina, that he will rent to unrelated persons. The condo has a fair market value of $85,000 and is subject to an outstanding mortgage of $30,000. David's apartment house is subject to a mortgage of $45,000. David has agreed to assume the $30,000 mortgage, and the other party agrees to assume David's $45,000 mortgage. Thus, they will be able to complete the exchange without involving any cash.

a. What amount of income must David recognize if he proceeds with the exchange as planned? Explain fully.

b. If this can be arranged as a nontaxable exchange (or a partially taxable exchange), what will David's basis be in the condominium?

c. Could David exchange the apartment house for a ketch (sailboat) tax-free if the boat were valued at $55,000 and no boot was involved? Explain briefly.

4. Mary Jenkins is the president of Jenkins Press and is a noted scholar of old books and rare manuscripts. It is not surprising, therefore, that Mary frequently causes Jenkins Press, a corporation, to purchase various books and manuscripts, which it holds as an investment. In fact, during the past five years, Jenkins Press has made approximately 200 such purchases. Over half these items have subsequently been traded for other books and manuscripts on a tax-free basis under Section 1031. Recently, Mary has become convinced that rare manuscripts are overpriced and that original art works, especially oils, are underpriced. She has, therefore, caused Jenkins Press to make four recent exchanges involving rare manuscripts for original oil paintings. Will these exchanges be tax-free under the authority of Section 1031? Explain.

5. Curt Johnson recently exchanged his old primary residence (basis, $30,000; value, $55,000) and a one-acre building lot located in another city (basis, $7,000; value, $15,000) for a new primary residence (value, $70,000). Since Curt owned his old home completely free of debt, no cash changed hands on this exchange.

a. What amount of gain or loss, if any, must Curt recognize because of this exchange? (Assume that Curt is under 55 years of age.)

b. What is Curt's basis in his new primary residence?

6. Cotton Candy Company lost two of its warehouses in a recent fire. Warehouse 1 had a basis of $150,000 but was insured for $200,000, its fair

market value. Warehouse 2 had a basis of $120,000 and was insured for $100,000, its fair market value. The insurance company paid the face amount of insurance on both properties. Cotton Candy Company replaced warehouse 1 with warehouse 3, costing $190,000; it replaced warehouse 2 with warehouse 4, costing $70,000.

   a. What amount of gain or loss, if any, must Cotton Candy Company recognize on warehouse 1? Does it have any election to make? Explain briefly.

   b. What is Cotton Candy Company's basis in warehouse 3?

   c. What amount of gain or loss, if any, must Cotton Candy Company recognize on warehouse 2? Does it have any election to make? Explain briefly.

   d. What is Cotton Candy Company's basis in warehouse 4?

7. Rudolph Sommers is 87 years old and in failing health. He owns three major properties, the important tax aspects of which can be detailed as follows:

| Property | Basis | Value |
|---|---|---|
| Family residence (for 50 years) | $ 40,000 | $200,000 |
| Stock in New Company | 700,000 | 300,000 |
| Stock in Old Company | 200,000 | 2.2 million |

Rudolph plans to leave his entire estate to his two daughters, Clara and Matilda, neither of whom has any business experience. Several individuals have recently tried to buy Rudolph's home, since he now lives in a private retirement facility and the house sits empty. Other companies have also approached him about the possibility of acquiring his interest in either or both the Old Company and the New Company. Considering his age and poor health, what would you recommend that Rudolph do so far as the following are concerned?

   a. The family residence. Should he sell it? Explain briefly the tax consequences of such a sale.

   b. His stock in New Company. Should he sell it, or would it be better to arrange a nontaxable exchange of this interest if he no longer desires to hold it? Explain briefly.

   c. His stock in Old Company. Should he sell it, or would it be better to arrange a nontaxable exchange of this interest if he no longer desires to hold it? Explain briefly.

8. Joe Izod exchanged 100 shares of Chrysler common stock (basis, $1,400; value, $500) for 23 shares of Ford common stock (value, $500). Can Joe

recognize a $900 loss? What will Joe's basis be in the 23 shares of Ford common?

9. Beth Williams owns 100 percent of Amalgamated Stopsigns, Inc., a regular C corporation. The stock is worth $100,000 and has a tax basis of $40,000. The assets and liabilities of Amalgamated Stopsigns are worth $100,000 and have a tax basis of $30,000. Beth is in the 28 percent marginal tax bracket, and Amalgamated Stopsigns is in the 34 percent marginal tax bracket. What are the consequences if Beth:

a. Sells her stock for $100,000?

b. Liquidates the corporation and sells the business for $100,000?

c. Exchanges her stock for 1 percent of the stock of Three Initial Corporation; the TIC stock is worth $100,000?

## Case 11–1

We Be Toys (WBT) is a regular C-corporation owned by Joe Parker. WBT has two divisions, a toy division and a game division. The company has prospered in the past five years, but Joe now wishes to sell the business and retire. Joe has received three offers for the business. He can:

1. Sell his stock to Amalgamated Toys for $100,000.

2. Sell the assets and liabilities of the toy division to the Toy Box for $70,000; sell the assets and liabilities of the game division to The Avalon Hill Company for $60,000; and liquidate the corporation.

3. Exchange 100 percent of his stock for 1 percent of the stock of Three Initial Corporation. The TIC stock is worth $87,500, on which Joe expects to receive regular dividends of $8,750 per year.

Joe is in the 28 percent marginal tax bracket and WBT is in the 34 percent marginal tax bracket. Joe can invest his proceeds in securities that yield a 10 percent return. Which alternative should Joe choose if—

a. Joe's basis in the stock is $70,000; WBT's basis in its assets is $50,000?

b. Joe's basis in the stock is $60,000; WBT's basis in its assets is $40,000?

c. Joe's basis in the stock is $50,000; WBT's basis in its assets is $30,000?

## CASE 11–2

Fred Flatstone has been farming Flatstone Fields ever since he inherited it from his father 30 years ago. Shopping centers and residential developments are being built near the farm. When Fred inherited the land from his father, the estate tax return gave the land an estate value of $30,000. Fred has made permanent capitalized improvements to the land of $15,000. In addition Fred owns common stock in Dinosaur, Inc. with a value of $100,000 and a basis to Fred of $15,000. Fred expects to live many more years and to become actively involved in owning and managing commercial properties.

Cliff Barnes, a local developer and real estate broker, is eager to acquire Flatstone Fields for a new development. He is willing to give Fred $900,000 in cash for the land. Alternatively, Cliff will give Fred the Barnes Shopping Plaza, consisting of land and buildings, for Flatstone Fields and the Dinosasur, Inc. stock. The basis of the Plaza is $500,000 to Cliff. Cliff buys and resells this type of property frequently. There is no reason to believe that either of Cliff's offers is not fair.

a.  What amount and type of taxable income must Fred recognize if he exchanges his farm and stock for the shopping center? What would Fred's basis in the Plaza be?

b.  Is there some reason why Fred might want to structure the exchange differently?

c.  What amount and type of taxable income must Cliff recognize if he exchanges the shopping center for the farm and stock? What would Cliff's basis in Flatstone Fields be?

# CHAPTER 12

# Corporate Reorganizations

For reasons explained in Chapter 11, the tax rules authorizing a tax-free corporate reorganization are among the more important provisions in the Internal Revenue Code. They are also, unfortunately, among the most complex provisions in the tax law. What follows in this chapter is an introduction to this important and fascinating aspect of the American way of taxation. Just enough information is provided here to enable the typical business executive to begin to understand the major tax opportunities and problems that must be given detailed attention in the actual acquisition or disposition of any corporate business venture. Related problems of securities regulations and financial accounting requirements must remain outside the scope of this book.

This chapter is divided into three major sections. The first section is devoted to definitional distinctions among the several forms or types of corporate reorganizations. The second section investigates the most important code sections that come into operation whenever any type of corporate reorganization is found to exist. The third section includes a brief discussion of five of the more common problem areas often associated with corporate reorganizations.

## BASIC DEFINITIONS

Section 368 (*a*)(1) of the Internal Revenue Code defines seven different types of corporate reorganization. Other sections provide the operative consequences. If any particular business rearrangement cannot be fit into one of these definitions, the reshuffling of corporate ownership and/or corporate properties will generally be treated like any other transaction and thus be subject to the usual tax rules explained in Chapter 2. On the other hand, reorganizations that can be definitionally fit into one of these technical provisions can be treated as a nontaxable transaction even if the real economic consequence is essentially that of realization.

In the financial press, the seven types of corporate reorganization are commonly known as types A, B, C, D, E, F, and G—a derivation of their tax heritage. Subparagraph A of Section 368(*a*)(1) defines the type A reorganization; Section 368(*a*)(1)(B) defines the type B reorganization; and so on. Because this terminology has been generally accepted, and because it facilitates reference to some otherwise cumbersome descriptive phrases, we shall utilize it throughout the chapter.

## The Type A Reorganization

The type A reorganization involves the merger or consolidation of two or more corporate entities under state law. If one of the old entities survives the reorganization, it is known as a merger; if neither of the old entities survives and a new entity is born, the reorganization is referred to as a consolidation. In skeletal form, the typical merger can be depicted as in Figure 12–1. The specific merger transaction involves the exchange by Group II of all their B stock for A stock and, possibly, other property; the transfer of all assets from corporation B to corporation A; and the dissolution of corporation B. The type A reorganization is popular in part because the Code imposes no restrictions on the form or amount of compensation other than stock of the acquiring corporation that can be used by corporation A to effect the merger. The acquiring corporation can, for example, purchase for cash the shares of B owned by dissident stockholders, or it can issue its own bonds or preferred stocks rather than its own common stock to other former shareholders of corporation B. Only judicial doctrines of uncertain scope are applied to distinguish between a routine sale and a type A reorganization in borderline cases. The critical test is that enough of the old Group II (i.e., the former shareholders of B) elect to receive stock in A corporation to satisfy a "continuity of ownership" test.

Although the type A reorganization has minimal restrictions on the amount and form of consideration other than stock that can be utilized, it is sometimes rendered ineffective by the fact that it generally requires the approval of a stipulated majority of both corporations' shareholders before it can be accomplished. In addition, the acquiring corporation generally inherits all of the acquired corporation's potential problems as well as its possible benefits. Consequently, if contingent liabilities, for example, are of major significance in a given situation, a type A reorganization may be quickly ruled out of contention for wholly nontax reasons.

## The Type B Reorganization

The type B reorganization is defined as the acquisition of control (meaning 80 percent of the voting stock and 80 percent of the number of shares of all other classes of stock) by one corporation over another corporation, with acquisition achieved *solely* by the exchange of voting stock for voting stock. A reorganization in which any consideration other than voting stock of the acquiring corporation (or its parent) is used to effect the transfer cannot be a type B reorganization. Nevertheless, a "creeping" type B acquisition—that is, one spread over a reasonable period and involving *unrelated* transactions, some of which may have included cash—is possible under the proper cir-

**FIGURE 12–1**    Type A Reorganization

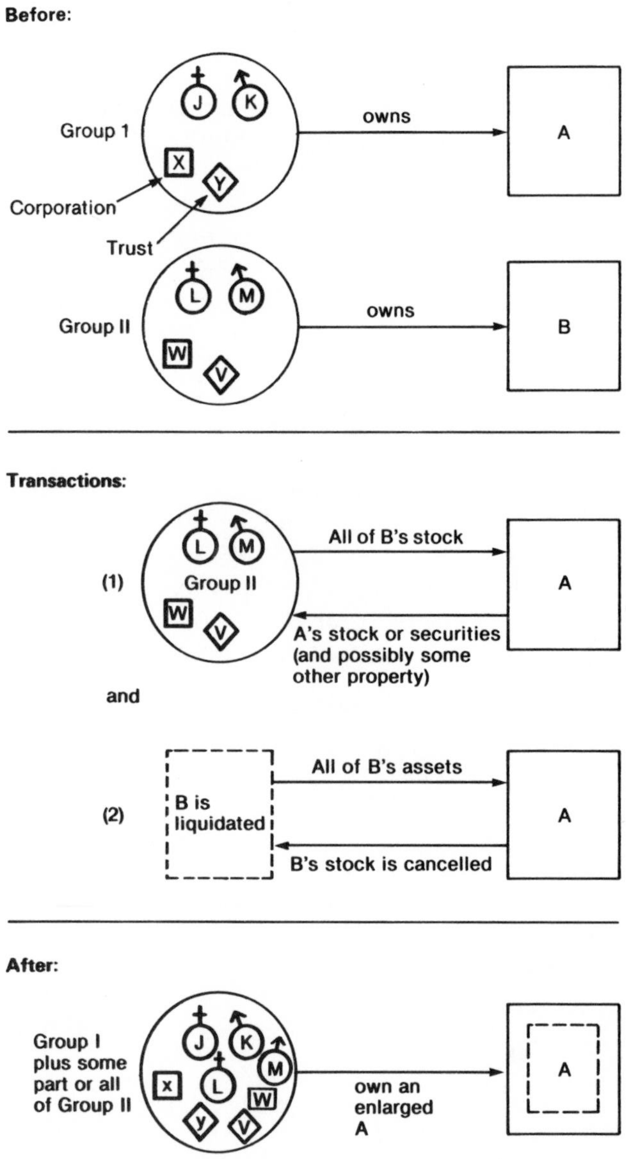

cumstances. In other words, it is not mandatory that the 80 percent control be achieved in a single stock-for-stock transaction, but if control is not achieved by the exchange of voting stock for voting stock, the classification of the final acquisition as a tax-free reorganization will be open to challenge. If the acquiring corporation obtains less than an 80 percent control over the acquired corporation, the transaction cannot be a type B reorganization under any circumstances. The net result of a type B reorganization is the acquisition of a subsidiary corporation by a parent corporation. In skeletal form, the acquisition can be diagramed as in Figure 12–2. The specific transaction in a type B reorganization involves only the exchange of B stock for A stock by part or all of Group II.

A comparison of Figures 12–1 and 12–2 emphasizes one very important difference between type A and type B reorganizations. In the latter, both

**FIGURE 12–2**   Type B Reorganization

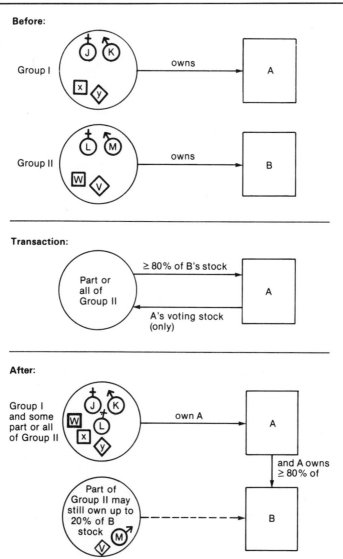

corporations are kept alive. This means, of course, that any liabilities of corporation B generally do not extend to the assets of corporation A. It also means that any unique value that corporation B may have—such as a well-known name, customer goodwill, a scarce franchise, or any other privilege—can be permanently retained by corporation A through its control over corporation B. Type B reorganizations may also be preferred over other types because of lesser appraisal rights given dissenting shareholders, or because the shareholders of the acquiring corporation may not have to be consulted before such reorganizations can be effected. These specific rules are part of our securities laws.

The major restricting condition of the type B reorganization is the voting-stock-for-voting-stock requirement. Even apparently routine concomitants of a normal reorganization—such as fractional shareholder's rights, reorganization legal and accounting expenses, debt assumptions, and contingent exchanges—have sometimes raised havoc with this one requirement. In general, the IRS and the courts have taken a narrow interpretation of the restricting Code provision, and all tax planners must exercise extreme caution in this area.

Finally, the reader should note that it is entirely possible for the acquiring corporation to liquidate its new subsidiary shortly after a type B reorganization. In that event, the economic effect is, for all practical purposes, the same as a statutory merger. The form and the sequence of the events that transpire, however, will determine which (if any) form of reorganization has occurred. A type B reorganization will always create a parent-subsidiary relationship, at least temporarily. If an acquisition fails to satisfy at least one of the definitions contained in Section 368(a), the transaction generally becomes wholly taxable.

### The Type C Reorganization

The type C reorganization is one in which the acquiring corporation obtains *substantially all* of the properties of another corporation in exchange for its own, or its parent corporation's, voting stock and possibly a limited amount (not more than 20 percent in value) of other consideration. In skeletal form, the assets-for-stock merger contemplated in a type C reorganization can be depicted as shown in Figure 12–3. The specific transaction in this situation involves the transfer of assets, and very often of liabilities as well, from corporation B to Corporation A in exchange for corporation A's voting stock and, possibly, a limited amount of cash or other property.

The most troublesome requirement of the type C reorganization has proved to be the "substantially all" requirement. If corporation B initially owns some assets that corporation A does not wish to acquire, great care must be taken in the manner and the timing of the disposition of the unwanted assets if the subsequent asset-for-stock exchange is to withstand an IRS challenge as a valid type C reorganization. If a corporation is nearly insolvent, a type C reorganization may also prove difficult to arrange because the acquired corporation has few assets that can be acquired. In this situation, most of the assets belong to the corporation's creditors, and therefore the acquiring corporation will find it nearly impossible to acquire "substantially all" of the insolvent corporation's properties.

The boot relaxation rule—that is, the provision authorizing up to 20 percent of the consideration in some form other than voting stock of the

**FIGURE 12–3**   Type C Reorganization

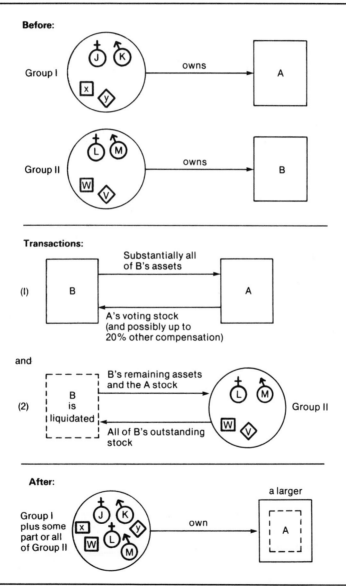

acquiring corporation or its parent corporation—can also be troublesome in certain circumstances. If any consideration other than voting stock is utilized in a type C reorganization, then the liabilities assumed by the acquiring corporation must also be treated as part of the boot. Because such liabilities often exceed 20 percent of the value of the assets in a reorganization exchange, the opportunity to utilize any consideration other than voting stock is severely limited. An error in the valuation of properties might also prove fatal to a type C reorganization that attempted to take advantage of the boot relaxation rule. If the original valuation of the properties transferred for voting stock proved to be in excess of their real fair market value, and the value of the properties transferred for other consideration proved to be greater than that originally estimated, then the 20 percent limitation might be exceeded and the exchange fail to qualify under the type C requirements.

As is emphasized in the skeletal diagram of the classic type C reorganization (Figure 12–3), the essential result of a type A and type C reorganization is virtually identical. (To emphasize this fact, compare the "after" diagram in Figure 12–1 with that in Figure 12–3.) The critical difference between the two is found in how the parties got to that result. In the type A reorganization the acquiring corporation exchanges its stock—and, possibly, other assets— directly with Group II and then, after it has control over B corporation, A proceeds with the liquidation of B. In the type C reorganization, on the other hand, A corporation effectively "guts" B corporation by exchanging its own stock—and, perhaps a limited amount of other property—for substantially all of the assets B had. Then, once B is reduced to nothing more than a shell (holding stock in corporation A), the old B shareholders (i.e., Group II) proceed to liquidate B corporation. (To emphasize these important distinctions, compare carefully the "Transactions" portion of Figure 12–1 with that in Figure 12–3.) As a consequence of these deceptively simple distinctions, corporation A was never a shareholder of B; hence A never acquires any risk that can derive from ownership of B corporation. Those potential liabilities remain with B corporation and, possibly, its former stockholders (i.e., with Group II). In short, if the acquiring corporation wants to make a stock-for-assets acquisition, it must follow the C form of the reorganization, not the A form. Obviously, in this area of tax law, form appears to control over substance, at least from an economic point of view.

### The Type D Reorganization

The type D reorganization encompasses two essentially dissimilar business rearrangements. It can apply to the transfer of substantially all of the assets of a corporation to *its own* subsidiary corporation if this transfer is followed by the liquidation of the transferor (parent) corporation. The net effect of this form of the type D reorganization is to put a new corporate shell around an old corporate body, which is essentially the equivalent of a type E or type F arrangement. Alternatively, a type D reorganization may apply to the division of an existing corporation into two or more corporations. Because the latter alternative is by far the more important and common variety of the type D reorganization, we will restrict our attention to the divisive form. In skeletal form, the simplest divisive type D reorganization can be illustrated as in Figure 12–4. The specific transactions in this divisive type D reorganization involve the transfer of some part of corporation A's assets to a new *or* existing corporation B in exchange for B's stock and the distribution

**FIGURE 12–4**    Type D Reorganization (spin-off form)

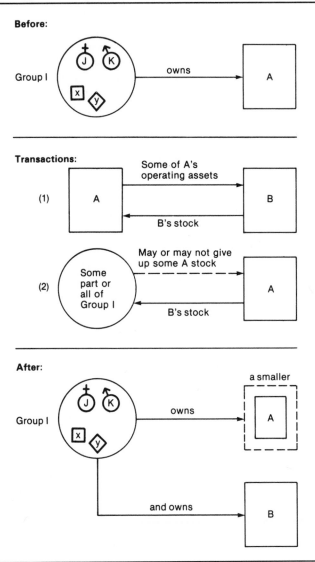

of this stock by corporation A to all or some portion of its shareholders (that is, to Group I, but not necessarily pro rata to all members of that group). If the distribution of the B stock is made to only some part of Group I, and if this distribution is made in exchange for all of those shareholders' shares in corporation A, then the "after" diagram would have to be modified to look like that in Figure 12–5.

Before a corporate division can be effected as tax-free type D reorganization, other code requirements must also be satisfied. Among the most important collateral requirements is the one in Section 355 which stipulates that both surviving corporations must be engaged in an active trade or business that had been conducted by the now-divided corporation (or corporation A in our diagram) for no less than five years preceding the division. Suffice it to say here that both the meaning of the phrase *trade or business* and the outer boundaries of the "five-year rule" have been the source of many disputes between taxpayers and the IRS. Litigation in this area is commonplace, and only the bravest or most foolish entrepreneur would attempt to draw his or her own conclusions as to the meaning of the requirements without competent advice.

The requirement that the shares of the second entity be distributed in a divisive type D reorganization can be satisfied in one of three ways. Returning to our earlier diagram (Figure 12–4), if the old Group I shareholders surrender no stock in corporation A when they receive the B shares, the division is properly called a *spin-off*. If some part or all of some owner's shares in corporation A are surrendered on the receipt of the B stock, the division is known as a *split-off* (Figure 12–5). Finally, if the original corporation transfers all of

**FIGURE 12–5** A Split-Off

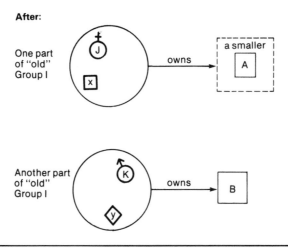

its assets to two or more corporations (say, for example, to corporations B and C) and is itself liquidated, the division is called a *split-up*.

The type D reorganization is very useful in separating warring factions of stockholders of a single enterprise. It may also be useful in isolating the riskier trades or businesses in separate corporate shells. This can also be accomplished, of course, by the easier creation of a subsidiary corporation under Section 351 if the stock of the riskier entity is not to be distributed. Historically, the divisive type D reorganization was also of importance in dividing what was essentially one business into two or more corporations to gain the added advantage of another corporate surtax exemption, an idea explained in Chapter 3.

## The Type E and Type G Reorganizations

The type E reorganization encompasses the recapitalization of an existing corporation. The precise definitional boundaries of a "recapitalization" are admittedly elusive. In general, the expression refers to a reshuffling of the outstanding stocks and bonds of a single corporation in terms of their amounts, priorities, maturity dates, or other features. The exact transaction involved in a type E reorganization may involve the exchange of (1) "old" stocks for "new" stocks, (2) "old" bonds for "new" bonds, (3) "old" bonds for "new" stocks, or (4) "old" stocks for "new" bonds. Each of these alternatives presents slightly different tax possibilities. In general, only the movement *from* an equity (or stock) interest *to* a creditor (or bond) interest creates major tax problems. The stock-for-bonds exchange may be treated as essentially equivalent to a dividend and taxed accordingly.

The type G reorganization, which closely resembles the type E reorganization, is commonly associated with a corporate insolvency. Corporations in financial difficulties are often reorganized in a way that it is hoped will shore up their financial structure and stave off bankruptcy. In terms of tax-planning opportunities, the type G reorganization is of limited importance.

## The Type F Reorganization

A mere change in identity, form, or place of organization is a type F reorganization. Like the type G reorganization, it has little tax-planning importance. To say that a code provision is not of much importance for tax-planning purposes is certainly not to suggest that the provision is void of tax importance. Note, for example, that, if it were not for the type F reorganization, a stockholder could be taxed on the difference between the present fair market value and the tax basis in shares of stock in a corporation that decided for good business reasons to reincorporate in another state.

As noted earlier, if a particular business reorganization satisfies any one of the seven definitions of Section 368(*a*)(1), the usual tax result is a nontaxable transaction and a carry-over tax basis. The seller of a business that has increased significantly in value over the years generally has a strong preference for a nontaxable disposition. The buyer, on the other hand, often prefers to make a business acquisition in a taxable manner. Tender offers and prices paid, therefore, may vary substantially, depending on how the details of the transaction are arranged.

## TAX CONSEQUENCES

Code Sections 354 and 361 are the provisions that guarantee nontax treatment to the various parties to a corporate reorganization. Sections 356 and 357 make an otherwise nontaxable transaction partially or wholly taxable in the event that boot is involved in the transaction. Finally, Sections 358 and 362 demand a carry-over tax basis in the event of a nontaxable reorganization. In general, the effect of these several separate code sections is comparable to those detailed in Chapter 11 for less complex nontaxable transactions.

### The Recognition of Gain or Loss

Stockholders and security holders are granted immunity from the usual tax rules by Section 354 only to the extent that they exchange stock and securities of one corporation that is a party to a reorganization for stock and securities of another corporation that is also party to that same reorganization. (For purpose of this section, the word *securities* refers to long-term debt.) If a stockholder receives shares in a corporation that is not a party to that reorganization, he or she will be treated as receiving boot in an amount equal to the fair market value of those shares. Furthermore, the dollar value of securities that can be received tax-free is usually limited to the dollar value of securities surrendered. In other words, even in a corporate reorganization, a taxpayer typically cannot move upstream from an equity interest to a creditor interest without imposition of an income tax. A few years ago, the hybrid securities issued in some of the more glamorous corporate acquisitions caused major problems with tax definitions.

Corporations frequently transfer operating assets and other properties in types A, C, and D reorganization transactions. Such corporate transferors are protected by Section 361 from the need to recognize any gain in the transaction so long as those assets are transferred pursuant to a plan of reorganization and to another corporation that is a party to the reorganization, and so long as the transferor receives in return only the stock or securities of the other corporation. If property other than qualifying stock or securities is received, the transferring corporation may generally avoid paying a corporate income tax on such boot if, in pursuance of the plan of reorganization, it distributes such boot to its shareholders. Incidentally, Section 361 also denies the transferring corporation the right to recognize (that is, to deduct) any loss realized in a reorganization-related transfer of properties.

**The Treatment of Liabilities.**    Corporate reorganizations frequently include the transfer of liabilities as well as assets. Generally Section 357 provides that the assumption of a liability will not be treated as boot or money received by the party being relieved of the debt if the transaction would otherwise be tax-free. Two exceptions to this general rule should, however, be noted. In the event of (1) a transfer of liabilities created either to avoid the federal income tax or to accomplish nonbusiness objectives, or (2) an assumption of liabilities in excess of the basis of properties transferred, the debt-relieved corporation must treat the assumed liabilities as the equivalent of cash boot. No ready operational definition of the several critical words and phrases can be stated briefly. Suffice it to say that this is one aspect of a planned business acquisition or disposition that a qualified tax adviser will investigate carefully before recommending action to a client.

**The Treatment of Boot.**    If any party to a corporate reorganization receives additional consideration—that is, if the transaction involves any property other than that authorized to be received tax-free by Section 354 or Section 355—the recipient taxpayer must recognize taxable income equal in amount to the lesser of (a) the boot received or (b) the gain realized. For a review of the meaning of the phrase *gain realized,* the reader should return to Chapter 7; in broad terms, gain realized is the difference in amount between the "amount realized" and the "adjusted basis" of the assets surrendered. If taxable income must be recognized, it can be classified as either ordinary income or capital gain, depending upon all the facts and circumstances surrounding the transaction. Loss cannot be recognized even if boot is received.

### Basis Rules

Taxpayers involved in wholly nontaxable corporate reorganizations usually take a carry-over tax basis in any assets received by operation of Section 358 or Section 362. Returning to our earlier diagram of a type A statutory merger (Figure 12–1), for example, the Group II stockholders would simply transfer whatever tax basis they had in their "old" corporation B stock to their "new" corporation A stock. In the type C reorganization diagram (Figure 12–3), corporation A would simply assume whatever tax basis corporation B had previously had in the assets transferred and corporation B would take that same tax basis in the corporation A stock it received.

As noted in Chapter 11, the idea of the carry-over basis is to achieve a temporary postponement rather than a permanent forgiveness of the pending income tax. The temporarily deferred gains and losses will be realized *and recognized* whenever the newly acquired properties are later disposed of in a more "normal" (taxable) transaction.

If boot is received and gain must be recognized in an otherwise nontaxable transaction, the parties to the reorganization may be able to increase their tax basis by the amount of the gain recognized. The taxpayer receiving boot, however, must also decrease the tax basis by the amount of boot received. Because the amount of gain recognized is often equal to the amount of boot received, the increase authorized by the gain recognized is often exactly offset by the amount of boot received, and the net effect of the two rules just stated is (for the recipient of boot) a return to the prior basis. For the party giving the boot, however, an increase in the basis usually results. Fortunately, business managers can let their tax advisers worry about the many details associated with the actual application of these tax basis rules. The good manager should always remember that a proper allocation of tax basis among the assets received may spell the difference between a profitable and an unprofitable exchange. In most circumstances, the buying taxpayer wants to allocate so as to maximize future tax deductions in as short a period as possible.

## SPECIAL PROBLEMS

Corporate reorganizations often involve hundreds of taxpayers and millions of dollars' worth of properties. It is little wonder, therefore, that the tax rules in this area are complex and the problems legendary. To close this brief review of reorganizations, we will examine six of the more common special problems very briefly.

### Unwanted Assets

An acquisition-minded corporation may desire to obtain something less than all of the assets of a business being offered for sale. As a consequence, the overly anxious seller may be tempted to make a hasty disposition of unwanted assets. Any seller must exercise great care to make such a disposition at a minimal tax cost. If, for example, the officers of the selling corporation were to distribute the unwanted assets to the corporation's shareholders to facilitate a subsequent merger, the likely result would be an ordinary dividend for the recipient stockholders. The distributing corporation might also discover that it too had to recognize a taxable income because of this distribution of property to the shareholders. A sale of unwanted assets to a third party could be equally costly if not prearranged properly. Under some circumstances, a corporation may be able to separate "wanted" and "unwanted" properties in two or more corporations via a tax-free type D reorganization before consummating a merger of the wanted-property corporation. In this event, however, a type C reorganization probably could not be arranged, even for the desired-asset corporation, because of the "substantially all" requirement. A type A or type B reorganization, however, might be successfully arranged under these circumstances. Both competent advice and an advance ruling from the Internal Revenue Service would be warranted under these conditions.

## Net Operating Losses

Profitable corporations at one time sought to acquire essentially worthless corporate shells solely because, by acquiring such corporate shells, they could also acquire the right to claim the acquired corporations' accumulated net operating loss deductions against their own taxable income. Consequently, Congress enacted provisions that substantially restricted the ability of corporations to use another corporation's tax attributes. Generally speaking, any greater than 50 percentage-point change in ownership (caused either by a purchase or a tax-free rearrangement) of a corporation with an NOL carry-over will limit the extent to which the loss corporation's carry-overs can offset taxable income in future years. The annual limit is the federal long-term tax-exempt rate (as determined by the IRS) multiplied by the value of the corporation immediately prior to the ownership change. Furthermore, the acquired corporation must either continue operating its prior business or retain at least one-third of its assets for two years after the ownership change; otherwise, the NOL carry-overs will be completely eliminated. There are other limitations which can apply which are beyond the scope of this text. Although buying and selling corporate tax attributes is not impossible, it is not a game for amateurs, and the day of buying and selling corporate NOLs may well be over.

## Contingent Acquisitions

Buy-sell agreements are sometimes drawn up as conditional contracts. For example, the number of shares of stock to be issued to the selling corporation or to its stockholders may be made contingent upon the profit performance of the acquired business for the next several years. Contingencies commonly raise numerous and difficult tax problems. For one, contingent consideration may create the possibility of boot. If the only additional consideration that can be received is more shares of qualifying stock, if the portion of the shares held in reserve is reasonable in relation to the total number of shares to be transferred, and if the entire transaction must be finalized within a reasonable number of years, then such a contingency usually will not constitute boot. Determining a tax basis for any shares disposed of during the period of the contingency, however, is less easily resolved. If the acquiring corporation retains the right to back out of an acquisition, or if it retains the right to rescind the transaction under specified circumstances, the tax problems multiply rapidly. Fortunately, the tax stakes in such arrangements are typically so great that they are usually given proper attention before it is too late to correct any problems inherent in the arrangements.

## Debt-Financed Acquisitions

Many business managers have sold their corporations for the long-term debt of an acquiring corporation. Because such a sale is ordinarily a taxable transaction, the seller may be able to negotiate a better price for any of several reasons. One factor increasing the price in a debt-financed acquisition is that the buyer can often deduct part of the purchase price as interest during years of payment for the new property. In addition, the buyer frequently gets a new and higher basis in the assets purchased, and thus a larger tax deduction in the future years than would have occurred had the sale been arranged in a nontaxable manner. Such a sale is often tolerable for the seller because the tax recognition of any gain realized may be deferred by virtue of the install-ment sale provisions of the Code. (See Chapter 5 for a discussion of the installment sale.) In many cases, the tax recognition can be deferred for 20 years or longer by the terms of the debt. If the seller discovers a need for additional funds in the interim years, he or she is always free to sell some portion of the acquiring corporation's debt and to pay tax on only the portion of the bonds sold.

Congress reduced the popularity of the debt-financed acquisition by en-acting two important provisions several years ago. First, the installment sale provisions were modified so as to preclude the deferral of the recognition of gain if the seller receives demand notes, coupon bonds, or any other security that is readily tradable in an established market. Second, the acquiring cor-poration may be denied the right to deduct interest on debt obligations issued to acquire another business directly or indirectly. This limitation is applicable only for interest in excess of $5 million, and then only under specified cir-cumstances. Needless to say, the few readers of this book who engage in such hefty acquisitions can also obtain ready reference to the other pertinent details. For smaller acquisitions dealing with unlisted securities, debt-financed ac-quisitions remain one of the several options available.

## Built-In Losses

When one corporation acquires the assets of a second corporation in a nontaxable reorganization, the adjusted tax basis of the assets acquired gen-erally carries over from the prior owner to the new owner. In the event that the adjusted basis of some assets exceed their fair market values, the new owner will in effect be acquiring the asset and the legal right to sell it and recognize the loss equal in amount to the excess of the asset's basis over its fair market value. This is, of course, very much like the opportunity noted earlier with regard to net operating losses of the acquired corporation. In order to discourage corporate acquisitions made for such dubious tax oppor-tunities, the law includes provisions intended to limit the amount of any "built-in loss deduction" that may be claimed subsequent to a reorganization by the acquiring corporation. This special rule will apply only if (*a*) the built-in losses are substantial in amount (i.e., if they are greater than 25 percent of the gross value of the non-cash assets acquired) and (b) the loss is recognized within the first five years after the corporate reorganization. The limitation applicable to these losses is essentially the same as that described earlier for NOL deductions. Incidentally, this limitation may also apply to depreciation deductions claimed by the acquiring corporation on assets obtained via a reorganization if the basis of those assets exceeds their fair market value by a sufficient amount.

### Greenmail Payments

Corporate acquisitions can generally be classified as either friendly or hostile. Friendly acquisitions are those supported by the owners of the target company; hostile reorganizations as those opposed by the target company. Since 1986 a growing number of corporate reorganizations have fallen into the hostile category. To avoid a hostile takeover the target corporation may offer to redeem a hostile "raider's" stock at a favorable price. These financial arrangements are popularly known as greenmail payments. To discourage hostile reorganizations Congress in 1987 imposed a 50 percent nondeductible excise tax on any gain realized from a greenmail payment. In general those payments are defined as payments in redemption of stock owned for less than two years by a shareholder who has made or threatened to make an offer for the stock of the redeeming corporation within the prior two years. Whether or not this new excise tax will decrease the recent flurry of hostile takeovers remains to be seen.

## PROBLEMS AND ASSIGNMENTS

1. Tad and Bit Successful started their corporate business in 1947 with an investment of $80,000. Although their tax basis in the stock of TABS Corporation remains at only $80,000 today, the value of that entity has increased to approximately $6 million. Because Tad and Bit would like to retire in order to enjoy the fruits of their financial fortune while they are still young and healthy enough to do so, they have told various people that their corporation is "available." In reaction to that "leak," they have received three different offers:

   a. Green Corporation has offered to buy their 100 percent interest in TABS Corporation for $6 million cash.

   b. Grey Coporation has offered to buy their 100 percent interest in TABS Corporation for $1 million cash plus $4.5 million in Grey Corporation's long-term debt. The latter, which carries a 9 percent interest rate, is *not* traded on any securities market.

   c. Gold Corporation has offered to exchange 400,000 shares of its common stock plus 100,000 shares of its 15 percent preferred stock for all of Tad and Bit's stock in TABS Corporation. Gold common stock is currently trading at $10 per share; Gold preferred, at $14 per share. Gold Corporation's stocks are regularly traded on the New York Stock Exchange and have a sound financial reputation.

Discuss the tax consequences of each proposal that Tad and Bit have received. Which would you recommend that they accept? Why?

2. The officers of Acquisition Ink have approached Paper Company with an offer to acquire those assets of Paper Company that are used in the production of newsprint; they do not, however, want any of Paper Company's assets used in the production of commercial paper bags. The officers of Acquisition have offered to exchange 350,000 shares of its own common stock for the newsprint assets it desires. Acquisition common is currently selling for $50 per share. Both because they believe that this a very "good" offer, and because they find it increasingly difficult to get an adequate supply of wood pulp to make paper, all the officers (and most of the stockholders) of Paper Company are inclined to accept the offer. One minority group of shareholders dissents from this conclusion; they have, however, indicated their willingness to allow Paper Company to redeem 100 percent of their stock for the commercial-paper-bag assets. In other words, they will return to Paper Company all their stock if Paper Company will give them the assets it uses to manufacture paper bags, as well as the right to manufacture those bags in the future. If the officers of Paper Company proceed with all the proposed plans, what (in general) will be the tax consequences for the following groups?
   a. The minority interest whose stock was totally redeemed.
   b. Paper Company, regarding the exchange of the newsprint assets for 350,000 shares of Acquisition Ink common stock.
   c. The remaining (majority) stockholders in Paper Company.

3. As part of a type E reorganization, Arthur Itis exchanged his 100 shares of Alpher common stock (basis, $10,000; value, $4,000) for 50 shares of Alpher 12 percent preferred stock (value, $2,500) and three Alpher securities (i.e., long-term notes carrying 15 percent interest) (value, $1,500). Assume Alpher Corporation has a substantial amount of accumulated earnings and profits at the time of this exchange, even though its recent history has been most disappointing.
   a. What amount of taxable income or loss will Arthur recognize because of this exchange?
   b. What tax basis will Arthur have in his 50 shares of Alpher preferred stock? In his three Alpher securities?

4. Kim and Dan Rosebud each inherited 50 percent of the stock in Thorn Corporation when their parents were killed in an airplane crash. Although this sister-brother duo tried to get along for three years after their parents' death, it became increasingly obvious to everyone that their strong disagreements over company policy would soon ruin what had been a fi-

nancially successful enterprise. Although the value of the stock in Thorn Corporation was estimated to be $1 million on the date Mr. and Mrs. Rosebud died, it is worth no more than $750,000 today. Because of their constant disagreements, Kim and Dan have decided to split the old family corporation into two new corporations—one owned by each of them. Would you recommend that they proceed to arrange this corporate split-up as a type D reorganization or as a taxable transaction? Explain briefly.

5. In each of the following situations, indicate whether (1) the acquired corporation's NOL carries over without limitation, (2) the acquired corporation's NOL carries over, but is limited, or (3) the acquired corporation's NOL is eliminated.
   a. 90 percent of XYZ is acquired in a taxable transaction (stock purchase).
   b. 48 percent of XYZ is acquired in a taxable transaction.
   c. 74 percent of XYZ is acquired in a nontaxable transaction (reorganization).
   d. 35 percent of XYZ is acquired in a nontaxable transaction.
   e. 45 percent of XYZ is acquired in a taxable transaction, after which 90 percent of XYZ's assets are sold.
   f. 55 percent of XYZ is acquired in a nontaxable transaction, after which 75 percent of XYZ's assets are sold.

6. Delores Fullapepper has owned all the stock of Tripartate Corporation since she divorced Billy Eversloe six years ago. Now, however, because her two children—Dana and Daniel—are responsible adults sharing her business responsibilities, Delores would like to divide some of Tripartate's assets among four new corporations: Tri, Par, Tate, and Tri-tate. After the intended division, Delores would continue to own 100 percent of the (now much smaller) Tripartate Corporation; she would split her ownership in Tri and Par Corporations on a 50–50 basis with Dana and Daniel respectively; and she would give complete ownership of Tate Corporation to Dana and complete ownership of Tri-tate to Daniel. Delores explains that this division of responsibilities would significantly reduce her own managerial responsibilities, allow each of the children to develop managerial talents to the maximum extent, and yet not risk the possible financial loss of their total business.
   a. Is it possible for such a major reorganization of Tripartate Corporation to take place on a tax-free basis? That is, can this be done without any federal income tax consequences to either the corporation or to Delores individually? Explain *briefly.*
   b. Although Delores's concerns may indeed center on the maximum development of managerial talent in her children at minimum financial risk, does there appear to be any "behind the scenes" federal income tax reason for the proposed reorganization? Explain briefly.

7. Anxious Corporation desires to acquire an exclusive beer distributorship held by Head Corporation. The contract between Head and the brewery

provides that the distributorship agreement is nontransferable. The officers of Anxious Corporation made a tender offer of four shares of its common stock for each share of Head stock outstanding. Generally, this was considered to be a very favorable exchange. However, two minority Head stockholders disagreed; neither I. M. Trouble (who owns 12 percent of Head Corporation) nor C. Mee (who owns 10 percent) was interested in exchanging his stock in Head for Anxious Corporation stock. Ted Anxious, the CEO of Anxious Corporation, is personally about to purchase C. Mee's 10 percent interest in Head for cash. If that sale transaction is completed, it is anticipated that the four-for-one stock exchange could be made with those owning 88 percent of Head Corporation.

   a. What type of reorganization are the officers of Anxious Corporation trying to arrange? Why is the form apparently so important; that is, why don't they simply rearrange the proposed reorganization into a simple type A merger? Explain briefly.

   b. Is the proposed deal likely to result in a tax-free reorganization? Explain briefly.

8. Pure X Corporation would very much like to acquire ownership of Bloody Corporation. The officers of Pure X fear, however, that there may be major undisclosed liabilities associated with Bloody. The owners of Bloody have made it clear that they are willing to dispose of their corporation, but only if that can be arranged as a tax-free transaction. Which type of reorganization seems to be required in this situation? Explain briefly.

9. In 1990, Three Initial Corporation was acquired in a transaction to which the NOL limitation rules apply. TIC has an NOL carry-over of $25,000. One hundred percent of TIC's stock was acquired for $100,000. The long-term tax-exempt interest rate is 8 percent. Determine TIC's taxable income for 1991, 1992, and 1993 if its taxable income before NOL carry-over was $20,000 in 1991, $6,000 in 1992, and $15,000 in 1993.

---

# Case 12–1

On January 1, 1988, Phil Phailure opened a grocery store, Phailing Phoods. The store was owned by Phil's wholly owned corporation, Phailing Phoods, Inc. Phil invested his life savings of $200,000 to purchase the $63,000 building and provide the store with adequate working capital.

By his incredibly poor management, Phil ran his business into the ground. Out of money, out of inventory (spoiled), and out of customers, Phil closed his doors in late 1990.

The location on which Phil had built his store had become very valuable due to the construction of a new shopping mall across the street. Knowing this, Phil sought out the management of Megafoods, Inc. to see if they wanted to purchase his company. Relying on his brother's appraisal and tax advice, Phil asked either $252,000 for the building or $240,000 worth of Megafoods common stock for 100 percent of his stock. Phailing Phoods, Inc. had an NOL carry-over of $57,600.

The Megafoods management knew that the store location was valuable, and felt that with proper management, they could immediately make the store very profitable, and decided to accept one of Phil's offers.

Which offer should they accept? Assume that the adjusted tax basis of the building is $59,000. Use a 34 percent marginal tax rate and an 8 percent discount rate in your calculations. Assume that the long-term tax-exempt interest rate is 8 percent.

# CHAPTER 13

# Common Tax Traps

Tax traps are often as ruinous to tax planning as sand traps are to shooting par. In the game of golf, the traps are equally visible to all players. In the tax game, unfortunately, the traps may be hidden from the view of all but the most erudite players. These tax traps can be of economic, judicial, or statutory origin.

Economic traps are not unique to transactions characterized by unusual tax consequences. Nevertheless, transactions embodying special tax advantages seem to be especially prone to chicanery. A few years ago one expert, whose only business was the investigation of potential tax-sheltered investments, reported that no more than 5 percent of the proposals he investigated were economically sound. Obviously, more than 5 percent of such investments were being sold to unwary customers. A possible thesis that might explain the apparent attraction of some investments is that prospective buyers get so involved in trying to understand the tax impact of the proposals that they fail to scrutinize the more mundane economic projections associated with them.

In this chapter, we will investigate some of the major tax traps that are of judicial or statutory origin. Any result that does not prove to be the most desirable possible result because of a special tax rule may be classified as a tax trap. For example, recognizing net capital losses in excess of $3,000 in a year may be considered a tax trap—so can claiming 20-year straight-line depreciation when a more rapid ACRS deduction is authorized. However, such a broad definition of tax traps proves to be unwieldly; it is, in fact, bounded only by the generous limits of human ignorance. In order to make our task more manageable, we shall define tax traps to include only those judicial doctrines and statutory provisions that have been designed to limit, defeat, or destroy tax-planning ideas that would otherwise be viable.

## JUDICIAL TAX TRAPS

Judicial tax traps may best be described as the few scattered black clouds dotting the generally clear horizon on a perfect summer day. Even the most experienced tax practitioner cannot predict with 100 percent certainty just when and where those black clouds will wreak disaster on an unsuspecting taxpayer. Although it leaves much to be desired in terms of academic precision, perhaps the safest generalization in tax planning can be expressed in the terms of the *pig theory*. As explained earlier, that theory suggests that you can make money being a bull and that you can make money being a bear, but that you can never make money being a pig. Judicial tax traps have an uncanny way of striking the "tax pig." The most common judicial tax traps have been conveniently labeled the *substance-over-form*, the *business purpose*, the *step transaction*, and the *assignment of income* doctrines.

## Substance over Form

The judicial notion that legal consequences should depend upon the substance of a transaction rather than upon its form is not unique to problems of income taxation. In tax matters, however, the consequences are very often critically different, depending upon what one assumes to constitute the substance of the transaction. Furthermore, the form of a transaction is usually deemed to be indicative of its intended substance. In a closely held corporation, we know that the owner has good reasons for preferring to make all corporate distributions to owners as salaries, rather than as dividends. What, then, is to prevent the owner-operating stockholder from declaring a particular corporate distribution to be the more tax-favored one? In other words, can the owner-manager transform a potential corporate dividend into a salary simply by declaring that intention and recording it properly in the corporate records? One court decision seemed for a few years to suggest that a portion of any assets distributed by a closely held corporation to the owner-manager could be considered to constitute a dividend, *even if the aggregate payment to the owner-manager did not exceed a reasonable compensation for the services rendered to the corporation.* That conclusion of the Claims Court was subsequently restricted to this one case by later court decisions. Until it was thus limited this decision constituted a radical extension of the substance-over-form concept. Certainly there never was a statutory basis for this decision; if there were any authority for it, that authority derived from judicial doctrines such as substance over form.

In Chapter 11, we learned that an *exchange* of one investment property for another investment property of "like kind" *must* be treated as a nontaxable transaction. If a taxpayer owned an investment property with a basis of $250,000, but a fair market value of only $200,000, could that taxpayer avoid the nonrecognition rule of Section 1031 (and thus deduct a $50,000 loss) by first selling the "loss property" to another taxpayer and then, a few days later, purchasing the second (like-kind) property from that same person? In other words, would the IRS and the courts recognize the form of these two apparently separate transactions—i.e., the alleged "sale" of the first investment property, and the alleged "purchase" of the second like-kind property—or would they treat the two apparently separate transactions as, in substance, merely one direct exchange? Obviously the substance-over-form doctrine is sufficiently broad to encompass the latter holding. The fact that the second transaction came only a few days after the first, and that both transactions were carried out with the same person, would certainly make the exchange conclusion a reasonable one.

We have considered here only two specific illustrations of the judicial substance-over-form doctrine. The doctrine can, however, appear in relation to almost any tax problem. The more a taxpayer stretches the boundaries of reasonableness in applying tax rules, the more likely he or she is to encounter this judicial tax trap. On rare occasions, taxpayers may attempt to utilize this judicial doctrine as an equity argument in their own interest. If, for example, a taxpayer clearly intended to do something, but failed to complete each and every technical detail required by the statute to achieve the intended objective, he or she may try to convince the court that the substance of the actions should prevail over any minor oversight in form. Although there is nothing to preclude such an argument, the business manager ought to be aware that most judicial tax doctrines seem to be the exclusive property of the IRS. In other words, as they are actually applied in tax cases, the judicial doctrines we are reviewing here seem to constitute a one-way street leading into a tax trap, not a two-way street that also provides a convenient way for the taxpayer to correct an unfortunate error.

### Business Purpose

The judicial doctrine of business purpose says that a transaction will not be given any effect for tax purposes unless it also achieves a valid business purpose. Incidentally, saving taxes alone is not deemed to constitute a valid business purpose. This doctrine stems from the case of *Gregory* v. *Helvering*, which was first tried in 1932. In that case, the taxpayer, Mrs. Gregory, fully complied with the letter of the tax law. Within a few days' time, she arranged a spin-off of some portion of her corporation's assets into a new, second corporation, a dissolution of this new corporation, a distribution of the assets held by the new corporation to her as sole owner, and a sale of the same assets to a third party. According to the law then in effect, the Revenue Act of 1924, the spin-off should have been a nontaxable transaction; the liquidation plus distribution of assets, a taxable transaction that would produce a capital gain for Mrs. Gregory; and the sale of assets, a taxable transaction, but one that would produce no taxable income. The absence of any taxable income in the final transaction could be attributed to the fact that the assets had received a tax basis equal to their fair market value in the liquidating distribution (which had just been taxed as a capital gain) a day or two prior to their sale. The trial court, the Board of Tax Appeals in this case, agreed with the taxpayer's conclusion, saying, in effect, that it had no authority to do anything but interpret literally the tax laws Congress had passed. The Circuit Court of Appeals for the Second Circuit and the Supreme Court disagreed with the trial court and thereby created the business purpose doctrine. Translated freely, their decisions said that literal compliance with the tax law may not be sufficient; if a transaction has no valid business purpose other than saving taxes, it does not satisfy the intent of Congress, and therefore should be given no effect. The critical result for Mrs. Gregory was that the court found that there had been a dividend distribution by the original corporation, to be taxed as ordinary income, rather than a liquidating distribution by the new corporation, to be taxed as a capital gain. The overlap between the judicial doctrines of substance over form and business purpose is apparent in this case.

Perhaps one of the most intriguing aspects of all judicial tax traps is that one is never certain just when the courts will elect to apply them. In 1956, the Circuit Court of Appeals for the Tenth Circuit, in the case of *Diamond A. Cattle Company* v. *Commissioner*, reached a decision in which it said: "when Congress passes an act in language that is clear and unambiguous, and construed and read in itself can mean but one thing, the act must be judged by what Congress did and not by what it intended to do." Here the taxpayer was allowed to claim a tax privilege that Congress did not intend, notwithstanding the potential application of contrary judicial doctrines that were already well established.

## Step Transactions

A third judicial concept sometimes utilized by the courts to destroy what would otherwise be effective tax-saving schemes concocted by taxpayers and their advisers is known as the step transaction doctrine. The effect of this judicial tax trap is to collapse a series of carefully arranged intermediate transactions into a single transaction and to look only at the substance of the net result to determine tax consequences. Although this judicial concept was not specifically mentioned in the *Gregory* decision, it could have been applied there as effectively as was the business purpose test. Any tax-planning idea that relies upon the recognition of each and every step of a complicated scheme that could be carried out in a much more direct manner, and that involves a minimal time span for its completion, runs a high risk of judicial intervention under one doctrine or another. The step transaction doctrine has been applied most frequently in corporate reorganizations. Again, however, it has not been applied consistently. On some occasions, the courts have given full recognition to each carefully arranged movement in a grand tax minuet; on other occasions, the courts have refused to see the beauty of it all. Even the seasoned opinion of the best legal counsel available may be uncertain of the outer boundaries of any judicial tax trap. In a social sense, the elusive quality of the traps may be their most redeeming feature.

## Assignment of Income

The final judicial doctrine that we will consider in this chapter, commonly known as the assignment-of-income doctrine, is perhaps the oldest and most pervasive of all. Its history dates back to an apparently tax-innocent agreement made between a husband and wife in 1901, a year well after the last of the Civil War income tax acts—passed between 1861 and 1894—and well before the Sixteenth Amendment and the 1913 Act. This apparently tax-innocent agreement provided that one Mr. and Mrs. Earl would, during the years of their marriage, divide all property and income equally, regardless of how acquired or earned. When, several years later, the Earls divided their taxable income equally, per the terms of their 1901 agreement, and each paid the tax on one half of their combined incomes, the IRS objected and the courts sustained the objection. The decision is reported in *Lucas* v. *Earl*, a case that reached the Supreme Court in 1930. There the Court held, in general terms, that income from services could not be assigned for tax purposes to anyone other than the person who rendered the service and that income from property could not be assigned to anyone other than the person who owned the property. In the decision, the Court analogized income to the fruit of a tree and suggested that a fruit could not be attributed to a tree different from the one on which it grew. Consequently the assignment of income doctrine has also come to be known as the fruit and tree doctrine.

The judicial concept articulated in *Lucas* v. *Earl* has been cited frequently since 1930 in a widely diverse set of circumstances. For example, taxpayers (like Eleanor Roosevelt) who have refused to accept compensation for services that they have rendered, even those who requested that their compensation be given to charity, have sometimes run aground on the assignment of income doctrine. Parents who have employed their children in a family business at generous salaries have also run headlong into this same judicial doctrine. And many others, who have attempted to give away a less than total interest in an income-producing property, in order to split that income in a most tax advantageous way, have come to understand clearly the fruit and tree analogy. At the same time, however, other families with competent advisers have been able to escape the apparent intent of this judicial tax trap by using carefully designed S corporations, partnerships, and trusts.

## STATUTORY TAX TRAPS

The life cycle of most unintended tax loopholes is characterized by four phases of development: (1) discovery, (2) successful application, (3) administrative, and sometimes judicial, intervention, and (4) legislative elimination. For the purposes of this book, we will define statutory tax traps to include only those code provisions that have been enacted as the fourth and final phase of this life cycle. One might think of this collection of code sections as the long fingers of Congress plugging the many holes in a dike that is intended to redirect resources from the private to the public sector. Today the most significant single statutory tax trap must be the limitation on passive activity losses. That trap was explained in some detail in Chapter 8. Among the additional sections that we shall consider here are the following:

*Sec. 532.* Corporations Subject to Accumulated Earnings Tax.

*Sec. 542.* Definition of Personal Holding Company.

*Sec. 318.* Constructive Ownership of Stock.

*Sec. 482.* Allocation of Income and Deductions among Taxpayers.

The code contains numerous other provisions that could properly be included within our limited definition of statutory tax traps. The preceding, however, are some of the more important sections for tax planning generally, as well as illustrative of the other sections. Tax practitioners are well acquainted with the details of most of these statutory tax traps. We will consider only their broad outlines for the benefit of the general manager.

### The Accumulated Earnings Tax

Prior to 1987 the top marginal corporate tax rate had been lower than the top personal rate on equivalent incomes for most wealthy individuals. Consequently the corporation was often used as a primary tax shelter by many taxpayers. Congress was aware of the potential abuse of the corporate rate shelter when it passed the initial income tax act in 1913, and therefore included provisions for an accumulated earnings tax in that act. The original idea was to ignore the corporate entity and tax the shareholder on a ratable share of the corporate income, whether distributed or not, if there was evidence of an accumulation of earnings beyond the reasonable needs of the business. That initial idea was dropped in 1921, when Congress enacted the present rules, which provide a wholly separate penalty tax imposed directly on the corporate entity under circumstances similar to those identified in the original bill. Even though the real reason for this tax largely disappeared with the passage of the 1986 act, the pertinent provisions were, for unexplained reasons, *not* deleted from the Code.

**Basic Provisions.** The major features of the present provisions, contained in Sections 531 through 537, are the imposition of a special tax at the rate of either 27.5 percent or 38.5 percent on unreasonably accumulated taxable income. The latter quantity is an adjusted version of the corporation's taxable income. The code does include an accumulated earnings tax credit of $250,000 (or $150,000 for personal service corporations) but this is an adjusted credit that must be reduced for accumulations of earnings in prior years. The 27.5 percent rate is applicable to the first $100,000 of unreasonably accumulated taxable income in any year; thereafter the rate is 38.5 percent. Because the real effective personal marginal tax rates rarely exceed 33 percent, the use of a corporate entity to accumulate income is never advisable if the accumulated earnings tax will be applied, because the total tax of 61.5 percent (34 percent ordinary corporate tax plus a 27.5 percent accumulated earnings tax) will be significantly greater than the worst possible tax that would be applicable if the income were received directly by the owners without the imposition of an intermediate corporate entity.

Before the IRS can impose the accumulated earnings tax, a court must find that the corporation has been formed or availed of for the purpose of avoiding the personal income tax of the shareholders. Whether or not this is even theoretically possible in the post-1986 world remains to be seen. In the past, as a practical matter, that meant that the business manager had to give primary consideration to recognizing those bits of evidence that could lead a court to find that the forbidden purpose existed, rather than worrying about the details of the actual tax calculation.

**Unreasonable Accumulations of Earnings.**   Most authorities in the past found that there was no unreasonable accumulation of earnings within a corporation unless one or more of the following factors were present:

1. Substantial loans from the corporation to major stockholders.
2. Corporate ownership of personal-benefit assets used exclusively by major stockholders.
3. An unusually high current ratio—that is, a ratio of current assets to current liabilities much higher than that common to the industry—and either large cash balances or large investments in relatively risk-free assets.
4. A minimal record of dividend payments.
5. Closely held corporate stock.

The reader should understand that these are general observations, not hard-and-fast rules. The imposition of the accumulated earnings tax has always turned on the facts of each individual case. The best defense in such situations was usually a good offense. It will be interesting to see if the IRS will continue to impose this tax today. If so, the following planning considerations may still be viable.

**Planning Considerations.**   If a taxpayer can prove by the preponderance of evidence that the accumulation of earnings is attributable to a valid business reason, this penalty tax can be avoided. Courts have found that the following constitute valid reasons for accumulating corporate earnings: the intent to expand a business or a plant without the dilution of the present owners' interest and without borrowing; the need to acquire a new business, especially if that business is directly related to the existing business of the accumulating corporation; the need to increase inventories; the intent to retire outstanding debt; the need to provide loans to suppliers or customers; the need to fund pension plans; and the desire to substitute a self-insurance reserve for commercial coverage. Each of these needs and intentions must be adequately documented in the corporate records if it is to be given much weight by an examining agent or the court. If a taxpayer anticipates a potentially dangerous accumulated earnings tax problem in sufficient time, it is usually not terribly difficult to find and document some valid reason for the accumulations made. The greater danger of this statutory tax trap seems to be its application in situations that should have been adequately diagnosed and prevented by anticipatory actions.

If the IRS should instigate an accumulated earnings tax case for any year after 1987, the taxpayer could easily prove that the existence of the corporate entity could no longer serve the purpose of "avoiding the personal income tax." That is, under virtually all circumstances, the taxpayer would now be better off, from a tax point of view, if the income had never been earned by the corporation in the first place. Hence, in order to sustain its case, the government will have to prove that simply because the income was earned by a corporation, Congress intends that that income should automatically be subject to *both the corporate and the personal income taxes.* In the opinion of this author, that would be akin to the pig theory on the part of the government. Hopefully, therefore, the IRS would be soundly defeated should it attempt to impose this anachronistic tax. Until that issue is judicially settled, however, every taxpayer must be aware of the existence of this penalty tax.

### The Personal Holding Company Tax

The accumulated earnings tax proved historically to be an inadequate weapon for the IRS against the use of the corporate rate shelter by wealthy individuals. In 1934, therefore, Congress enacted a second penalty tax in a further attempt to eliminate the use of this tax shelter. The new provisions were worded to provide somewhat more objective standards than the "unreasonable accumulation" criterion of prior law. Specific provisions were included to snare "incorporated pocketbooks" (that is, corporations whose only business consisted of buying, selling, and holding other stocks and securities), "incorporated talents" (that is, corporations whose only business consisted of the disposition of the owner's peculiar talent as an actor, athlete, or other star performer), and "incorporated pleasure facilities" (that is, corporations whose only business consisted of the leasing of a hunting lodge, island estate, or yacht to their owners). In each of these situations, the owner was trying to achieve through the corporate entity tax savings that the owner could not achieve directly as an individual. The incorporated pocketbooks provided the major advantage of the corporate dividend-received deduction plus the lower corporate tax rate. The incorporated talent provided an opportunity to accumulate and reinvest personal compensation beyond consumption needs at a minimum tax cost. The incorporated pleasure facility provided a way to convert a nondeductible personal (pleasure) expenditure into a tax-deductible business.

Today the first and third of the historical reasons for the personal holding company provisions still have vitality. That is, because of the dividend-received deduction, wealthy individuals could still attempt to create an incorporated pocketbook. And, because many pleasure facilities are still not deemed to create deductible expenses, incorporated pleasure facilities also retain their vitality. The concept of incorporating personal talent, however, no longer makes common sense.

In spite of the fundamental change brought about by the 1986 Tax Reform Act, Congress once again failed to modify the old personal holding company provisions. In this instance, however, they clearly have remaining vitality in some circumstances. It is, therefore, important for every taxpayer to understand the general outline of these provisions.

**Basic Provisions.** The present statutory provisions, contained in Sections 541 through 547, impose a special 28 percent penalty tax on any personal holding company that has undistributed personal holding company income at the end of a year. Thus, this penalty tax may be avoided in either of two ways. First, a corporation can make certain that it is not classified as a personal holding company. Second, the corporation can make certain that it does not retain personal holding company income at the end of the year. The objective of this penalty tax is to force distributions and to make the retention of certain kinds of income in a corporate entity an impractical alternative, not to collect revenues for the government. Thus, the Code authorizes a taxpayer to make a retroactive dividend distribution any time that the personal holding company tax would otherwise apply. If such a distribution is made, the tax base automatically disappears. Since the penalty tax rate is high (28 percent), the individual owner will virtually always prefer a dividend distribution, even if it is taxed at the highest marginal rate for individual taxpayers, to a retention coupled with this penalty tax.

Before a corporation is deemed to be a personal holding company, it must "fail" two tests. They are (1) a stock ownership test and (2) an income test. A corporation will not be considered a personal holding company if the five largest stockholders own less than 50 percent of the value of the corporation's outstanding stock. This means that any corporation with 10 or fewer owners automatically fails the ownership test, since some 5 of those owners would have to own no less than 50 percent of the stock. On the other hand, 11 or more unrelated and *equal* owners would automatically avoid any danger of this statutory tax trap.

If less than 60 percent of any corporation's adjusted ordinary gross income is personal holding company income, that corporation will not be deemed to be a personal holding company. For purposes of this book, we can define personal holding company income as either (1) "unearned" income or (2) income from personal talent. Unearned income includes income from dividends, interest, rents (under specified conditions), royalties, annuities, and payments by shareholders for their use of corporate properties. In general, unearned income is distinguished from earned income—that is, income collected more or less automatically through ownership is distinguished from income earned by entrepreneurial effort.

**Planning Considerations.** The shrewd manager will realize that the task is to combine earned and unearned income streams in such a way as to avoid the personal holding company tax and then to prepare a record that will substantiate a finding that all accumulations of earnings are reasonable. To illustrate this possibility, let us assume that an unmarried taxpayer commands an annual income stream of $100,000 from an active business venture and another $60,000 from dividends. If this taxpayer requires an annual income of about $60,000 before taxes for personal consumption needs, $100,000 (before taxes) remains available for reinvestment. If the taxpayer did not incorporate the two income streams in a single business, the tax liability would be in the vicinity of $45,000 per year. With incorporation and an annual salary of $60,000, the taxpayer's annual tax liability would drop to something like $24,800, determined as follows:

| | | |
|---|---:|---:|
| Gross corporate income | $160,000 | |
| Less salary paid to owner | (60,000) | |
| Less dividend-received deduction (70%) | (42,000) | |
| Corporate taxable income | $ 58,000 | |
| | | |
| Corporate income tax on $58,000 | | $ 9,500 |
| Individual income tax on salary (approximate) | | 15,300 |
| Total annual tax liability | | $24,800 |

The mixing of dividend-producing stocks with an active business serves to avoid the danger of a personal holding company tax as long as the income from the active business exceeds 40 percent of the total corporate income. The problem of unreasonable accumulations of earnings can best be handled by well-documented plans for corporate expansion, debt retirement, pension plans, and similar programs.

Individuals with nothing but unearned income might consider the creation of a corporation owned equally by 11 taxpayers. The group can then enjoy the benefits of the corporate rates on taxable income of $75,000 or less and the dividend-received deduction, even though the owners could not achieve the same advantages individually, because such a corporation would not be a personal holding company.

## Constructive Ownership of Stock

Many tax consequences can be determined only after one knows what percentage of a corporation's outstanding stock is owned by the shareholder who is involved in a particular transaction. For some purposes, it is desirable for the owner to reach as large a percentage ownership as possible; in other circumstances, the taxpayer may desire to minimize the percentage of his or her interest. A taxpayer, for example, must own more than 80 percent of a corporation's stock if an individual transfer of property to a corporation is to pass as a nontaxable transaction under Section 351. On the other hand, it was noted above why a taxpayer might desire to be deemed to own as little stock as possible when the personal holding company tax is in question.

In order to achieve a smaller percentage ownership, a taxpayer may be tempted to give or sell some shares to a related person. As a practical matter, such evasive tactics are seldom of any use because of the constructive ownership rules. The code contains several slightly different sets of constructive ownership rules for different purposes. For example, Section 318 contains one set of rules for use in most questions arising under Subchapter C of the Code; Section 544 contains another set of constructive ownership rules for use in connection with personal holding company problems; and Section 1563(e), yet another set for use in defining a controlled group of corporations. Although there are important differences in each of the several sets of constructive ownership rules, we need only observe that their common result when determining tax consequences is to find that a taxpayer is deemed to own many shares in addition to those he or she owns personally and directly. Usually, a stockholder must include as his or her own shares any shares owned by a spouse, parents, children, and grandchildren, as well as shares owned by partnerships, corporations, and trusts in which the stockholder has a beneficial interest. Finally, the stockholder must also include as shares owned any shares that he or she has an option to acquire. The net result of these imputations is, of course, to give many taxpayers a larger interest than they would prefer to have for many tax determinations.

### The "At Risk" Rules

During the heyday of tax-sheltered investments, taxpayers were often able to reduce their federal income tax liability by some multiple of the amount they invested. Advertisements promised investors tax savings equal to three, four, or five times the amount of cash payment required. The apparent magic behind many of these investment schemes was debt in one form or another.

The tax benefits of many investments derived directly from the large depreciation deductions and/or investment tax credits they provided. Those two items were, in turn, dependent upon the taxpayer's basis in the investment property; and, as we learned in Chapter 10, basis generally is determined by the amount of cash expended *plus* the amount of debt assumed. Several years ago it made no difference for federal income tax purposes whether a taxpayer's liability was an ordinary recourse debt or a nonrecourse obligation.

In the typical debt a debtor is personally liable for the entire amount owed. This means that, if the debtor defaults on the note and the creditor (a) forecloses the loan, (b) causes the pledged property to be sold, and (c) still has not satisfied the entire debt, the debtor will have to pay any remaining balance from personal assets. With a nonrecourse loan, however, a creditor can look only to the pledged property to satisfy the debt. If the value of the pledged property is less than the amount of remaining debt, a creditor cannot force a debtor to pay the balance from other (personal) assets.

An investment status roughly comparable to that of a nonrecourse debtor could also be achieved in many tax-sheltered deals via a limited partnership arrangement. In the ordinary partnership, every partner is fully liable for all debts incurred by the partnership. Thus if a partnership goes bankrupt, creditors will first force the sale of the partnership assets to settle claims; thereafter they will demand payment on any remaining debt from the partners. In a limited partnership, creditors cannot force limited partners to make additional capital contributions to settle partnership obligations. In the event of default, creditors can force the sale of partnership assets and can look to general partners for additional cash; they simply cannot look to limited partners for additional payments. Hence a limited partner has achieved an economic status roughly comparable to that of a nonrecourse debtor.

Section 465 was added to the Code to disallow tax benefits in excess of the amount the taxpayer was "at risk." In general this means that a taxpayer cannot claim tax benefits in excess of the sum of the cash invested plus the amount of recourse debt owed. Nonrecourse debts and limited partnership investments, therefore, sometimes create a real tax trap for unwary investors. To illustrate, assume that a taxpayer acquired a 10 percent interest in a limited partnership for $20,000. Assume also that this partnership reports a $250,000 loss. As a 10 percent partner the investor would expect to deduct a $25,000 loss. If the investor were a limited partner, however, the tax deduction would be restricted to $20,000; i.e., to the amount the partner was "at risk." The $5,000 disallowed loss would go into suspense and be deducted if and when the taxpayer either contributed additional capital, assumed additional debt, or reported later profits from the investment.

Prior to 1987 real estate investments were generally exempt from the at-risk rules. The 1986 Tax Reform Act initially extended these rules to real estate, but, at the same time, established a new and potentially broad exception for certain "qualified nonrecourse financing." That new term now refers to debt (1) secured by real property, (2) for which *no-one* is personally liable, (3) that is not convertible into an equity interest, and (4) is provided by either (*a*) an unrelated person or an entity regularly engaged in the business of lending money or (*b*) a related person on commercially reasonable terms. In a limited number of instances, therefore, a taxpayer may still be able to deduct losses in excess of the amount for which they are at risk. In general, however, that is no longer permissable.

## Allocation of Income and Deductions

The explicit rules of the statutory tax traps that we have examined thus far tend to be aimed at specific abuses, which were revealed by prior practical experience. The only exception is that relating to the accumulated earnings tax, and in that instance Congress needed no prior experience to predict accurately what would happen in the absence of a statutory prohibition. Although Section 482 has a specific history similar to that of the other statutory tax traps, this provision has been applied in several ways never contemplated when Congress first enacted it. For this reason it is more difficult to determine the limits of this potential statutory tax trap.

In general, Section 482 gives the IRS the authority to distribute, apportion, or allocate any item of gross income, any deduction, or any tax credit between or among two or more controlled businesses if it determines that such an adjustment is necessary to prevent the evasion of income taxes or to reflect income clearly. It is this code section that the IRS has cited as authority for its enforcement of more realistic pricing policies in sales transactions between related persons, especially between domestic parent corporations and their foreign subsidiaries. The same section has been cited as the authority for requiring interest on loans made between related taxpayers and for charging out managerial services rendered by one corporation's employees for a related corporation.

Although we do not know the limits of the commissioner's authority under this statutory provision, we do know that business managers must give more careful consideration in the future than they have in the past to the tax consequences that might attach to transactions between related taxpayers. If a taxpayer desires to keep all of these transactions free of any tax consequences, that usually can be done satisfactorily, either by merging the two businesses or by filing consolidated corporate tax returns. If these alternatives are not satisfactory, the business manager should become aware of the potential tax implications of Section 482. The danger of this tax trap is that it may trigger the recognition of taxable income at an undesirable time and that it may allocate that income to the least desirable entity.

In summary, a taxpayer should always be aware of the fact that the commissioner of the Internal Revenue Service has an arsenal of weapons to defeat a taxpayer's desire to capitalize on a questionable tax privilege. Tax-saving provisions deliberately written into the Code by Congress are not at issue here. For example, the tax advantages that attach to ACRS allowances, to viable corporate business ventures, and to percentage depletion are well established and beyond question by the IRS. When the taxpayer or a tax adviser extends these special provisions to a new or unusual case, however, he or she may discover that an objective will be challenged by the IRS on the authority of an elusive judicial doctrine or on the basis of prior statutory action of Congress in somewhat analogous situations. In taxation as in love, however, it is often better to try and to fail than never to have tried at all.

## PROBLEMS AND ASSIGNMENTS

1. If you were an IRS agent trying to determine whether or not a particular corporate taxpayer should be accused of unreasonable accumulation of

earnings, which traditional financial statement—the income statement, balance sheet, or funds flow statement—would you be most interested in reviewing carefully? Explain briefly. How can this question be related to positive tax planning? Again, explain briefly.

2. Translated very loosely, the Internal Revenue Code provides that a corporation will *not* be considered to be a personal holding company if (among other things) more than 40 percent of its "gross income" is derived from an active trade or business. For federal income tax purposes, the cost of goods sold is considered a direct reduction of gross income, not a tax deduction. For example, a retail store with a $750,000 sales revenue and a $700,000 cost of goods sold would be deemed to have a $50,000 gross income. Of what significance is the latter tax convention (or "tradition") to the taxpayer who wants to utilize a corporate entity to shelter a substantial income from dividends? Explain briefly.

3. Suppose that taxpayer I, who owned 100 percent of corporations A and B, "sold" 50 of his shares in corporation A to corporation B. The essential facts might be diagramed as follows:

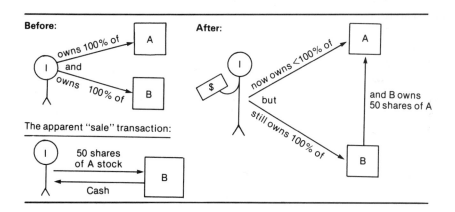

If I's tax basis in the 50 shares of A stock "sold" was $1,000, and if corporation B paid $1,500 for those shares, how should that transaction be reported—
a. Using the "normal" rules previously explained in this text? Explain briefly.
b. Using common sense? That is, looking realistically at what has taken place, how would you personally suspect that this transaction is likely to be taxed either using a judicial rule or applying some Code provision not mentioned in this text? Explain briefly.

4. Suppose that taxpayer H, who owned 100 percent of corporation X, "sold" 50 of his shares in corporation X to corporation Y, which was 100 percent

owned by taxpayer W, who is H's wife. The essential facts might be diagramed as follows:

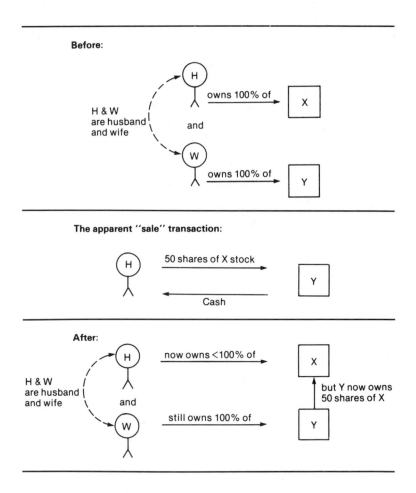

**Before:**

H

owns 100% of → X

H & W are husband and wife

and

W

owns 100% of → Y

**The apparent "sale" transaction:**

H

50 shares of X stock →

Y

← Cash

**After:**

H

now owns <100% of → X

H & W are husband and wife

and

but Y now owns 50 shares of X

W

still owns 100% of → Y

If H's tax basis in the 50 shares of X stock "sold" was $1,000, and if corporation B paid $3,500 for those shares, how should that transaction be reported—

a. Using the "normal" rules previously explained in this text? Explain briefly.
b. Using common sense? That is, looking realistically at what has taken place, how would you suspect that this transaction is likely to be taxed either using one of the judicial rules discussed in your text or applying some statutory provision not mentioned? Explain briefly.
c. What, if anything, would the constructive ownership rules have to do with this transaction? Explain briefly.

5. Assume that taxpayer I, who owned 100 percent of the outstanding stock of PLC Corporation received assets valued at $810,000 in a partial liquidation from PLC. Assume further that the $810,000 in assets distributed represents exactly one fourth of PLC's total assets. Finally, assume that a partial liquidation is generally treated as a sale of stock by the shareholder. If I's total ownership in PLC is represented by 2 million shares of common stock with a tax basis of $1 per share, how should the partial liquidation distribution be reported if—
   a. Taxpayer I surrenders back (in the partial liquidation) half of his total shares in PLC *and* the "normal" rules previously explained in this text control the transaction? Explain briefly.
   b. Taxpayer I surrenders back (in the partial liquidation) half of his total shares in PLC *and* common sense controls this transaction? That is, looking realistically at what has taken place—but still accepting the statutory provision that partial liquidation will generally be treated as a sale—how would you suspect that this transaction will be taxed? Explain briefly.
   c. Draw a three-part diagram of this partial liquidation similar to the diagrams in Problems 3 and 4. Part 1 should depict the facts before the partial liquidation; part 2, the partial liquidation transaction; and part 3, the facts after the partial liquidation.

6. Assume that two unrelated individual taxpayers—J and K—form a new corporation, J & K, Inc. Section 351 provides that no gain or loss shall be recognized on the transfer of property to a corporation so long as those who transfer property own 80 percent or more of the corporation immediately after the transfer. Assume that, in the initial incorporation transaction, J transfers a property (basis, $13,000; value, $10,000) to J & K in exchange for 5,000 shares of J & K common stock, and that K transfers—
   a. Only her services, worth $10,000, in exchange for 5,000 shares of J & K common stock. Based solely on the "normal" rules previously explained in this text, may taxpayer J recognize any loss on the incorporation transaction? Explain briefly.
   b. Her services, worth $9,999, plus $1 (in cash) in exchange for 5,000 shares of J & K common stock. Looking realistically at what has taken place and using common sense, would you suspect that taxpayer J will be allowed to recognize any loss on the incorporation transaction? Explain briefly.

7. Suppose that the Zee family has very carefully arranged its ownership of five family corporations to avoid the statutory definition of a controlled group; that is, they arranged the ownership in a manner suggested in your text on page 58. On audit, the IRS agent discovered that one family corporation was selling to a second family corporation various merchandise at approximately half the price that it sold the same merchandise to others.

    a. What tax reasons might the family corporations have for their unusual pricing policy? Explain briefly.

    b. What statutory provision might the IRS agent apply to disallow the half-price sales and to impute other costs (or sales prices) to these same sales?

8. On relatively rare occasions, the courts have held that a corporation was a mere sham and refused to recognize its existence for federal income tax purposes. Without doing any research, and basing your answer solely on common sense, what facts do you suppose contributed to the courts' decision in these cases? In other words, what facts might explain such an unusual decision by a court?

9. Billy C. is engaged in a dispute with an IRS agent over a $200,000 loan from his wholly owned Nut corporation. Billy contends that it is a true loan; the agent insists that it is a dividend. If this disagreement proceeds to trial, what facts do you think will contribute significantly to the court's resolution of the issue?

10. Passive Investments, Inc. (PII) is wholly owned by Helen and Joe Morris who file a joint return. PII earned $50,000 in dividend income from investments in domestic stocks. Assume PII earned no other income; hence its undistributed personal holding company income is $47,750 (i.e., $50,000 less $2,250 in regular corporate income tax). Should PII make a retroactive dividend distribution if the Morrises' taxable income from other sources is—

    a. $10,000?

    b. $80,000?

    c. $200,000?

# Case 13–1

    Joe and Evelyn Demski are a married couple with two children. They own and operate a manufacturing business that generates gross income of about $1 million and expenses of about $800,000 each year. The Demskis claim a standard deduction of $5,000 in lieu of itemizing deductions and have no other sources of income. (Assume personal exemptions are $2,000 each.)

    a. If the Demskis chose to incorporate their business, how much salary would you expect them to be paid annually?

    b. If the Demskis also owned a stock portfolio that generated $50,000 each year in dividend income, should they transfer those stocks to the corporation? Explain briefly.

# Case 13–2

Dr. Phil N. Pullem earns a substantial amount of income from his dental business. He owns only the following two investments:

|  | Alpha Investment | Beta Investment |
|---|---|---|
| 19x1 purchase price | $15,000 | $20,000 |
| 19x1 income/(loss) | (12,000) | 10,000 |
| 19x2 income/(loss) | (10,000) | 3,000 |
| 19x3 income/(loss) | 7,000 | 2,000 |

Neither investment will make any distributions nor require any additional investment during these three years.

a. Assume Alpha and Beta are two separate partnerships in which Pullem participates on a material basis. What is the net effect on Dr. Pullem's taxable income for 19x1, 19x2, and 19x3?

b. Assume Alpha and Beta are two separate limited partnerships and that Dr. Pullem is a passive investor in both of them. What is the net effect on Dr. Pullem's taxable income for 19x1, 19x2, and 19x3? (Hint: You may need to review the treatment of passive activity losses in Chapter 8.)

c. Assume that Alpha and Beta are combined into a single limited partnership, Alphabet, and that Alphabet generates only portfolio income and loss. Alphabet will require a $35,000 investment in year 19x1, and generate a $2,000 capital loss in 19x1, a $7,000 capital loss in 19x2, and $9,000 of capital gain) in 19x3. What is the net effect on Dr. Pullem's taxable income for 19x1, 19x2, and 19x3?

# CHAPTER 14

# Family Tax Planning

Family tax planning centers on the taxation of gifts and estates. Although many states also impose inheritance taxes, the federal estate and gift taxes are dominant. Historically, the federal gift and estate taxes were two entirely separate taxes; since 1976, however, they technically are both a part of one tax—the donative transfers tax. Nevertheless, for pedagogical reasons, we will generally treat them as two separate taxes. The two were first enacted many years ago (a) to raise federal government revenues and (b) to achieve at least a limited amount of wealth redistribution in the United States. For all practical purposes, the two failed to achieve either objective. In 1988, federal gift and estate tax collections are estimated to be approximately $5.8 billion, less than one percent of total tax revenues. All empirical studies attempting to determine the effect of the two taxes on wealth redistribution conclude that they have had a very limited impact. Although neither tax ever was a real success in terms of the original objectives, the effect of many years of inflation was to make the old provisions, which had not been modified in a significant manner since 1942, even less satisfactory than they had been when they were originally adopted. In 1969, estate tax returns were required in only 7 percent of all deaths; by 1972 this had increased to 9 percent; and by 1976 it was estimated at 11 percent. Most of the increase was, of course, attributable to small estates—that is, to estates valued at just over $60,000, the minimum point at which the estate could take effect under pre-1977 rules. Consequently, when President Ford, in 1976, called for a substantial increase in the basic estate tax exemption, his proposal received widespread support. President Reagan found similar support in 1981 when the basic exemption was again dramatically increased (to $600,000 for 1987 and thereafter). Today it is estimated that only one half of one percent of all persons are subject to the federal estate tax. Once Congress began to tamper with the estate tax provisions, it did not stop with an increase in the basic exemption. Instead, Congress proceeded to enact massive changes in the area of gift and estate taxation, which will be important to family tax planning for years to come.

In this chapter, we will review in a general way the current provisions that determine the tax liability imposed by the federal gift and estate tax, as well as possible methods of minimizing that tax. The chapter is divided into three sections. The first section deals with the tax on gifts; the second deals with the tax on estates; the final section attempts to integrate a few ideas on income, estate, and gift taxes into relatively simple family tax planning.

## FEDERAL TAXATION OF GIFTS

The federal gift tax is an excise tax imposed on certain gratuitous transfers of property. The tax is a liability of the donor, the person making the gift, not of the donee, the person receiving the gift. Incidentally, unlike the situation with our income tax, joint gift tax returns by a husband and wife are not possible. The tax applies equally to all forms of property: real and personal property; business, nonbusiness, and purely personal-use property; tangible and intangible property; and to both present and future interests in property. In other words, if a taxpayer today makes an irrevocable transfer of a future interest in a property to a person not yet born, the transfer may be subject to an immediate gift tax, even though the full economic impact of the transfer of property rights may not be realized for many years. The problems encountered in valuing a future interest in property are sometimes substantial. Suffice it to note here that valuation may involve the need to determine a discounted present value of an estimated earnings stream based on the life expectancy of several parties to a gift.

Note also that a transfer must be irrevocable before the gift tax will apply. If a person prepares a last will and testament, or names a beneficiary to a life insurance policy, such action does not constitute a gift so long as the taxpayer retains the right to modify a present intention at any time in the future. Finally, the reader should understand clearly that the gift tax has essentially nothing to do with the income tax. For example, the interest on state and local government bonds is exempt from the federal income tax. A gift of either a state bond or the interest from such a bond, however, would be wholly subject to the federal gift tax. Similarly, a gift paid from a salary already reduced by the income tax may be further reduced by the gift tax.

### Basic Provisions

A determination of the gift tax liability proceeds conceptually in a manner very similar to that used to determine an income tax liability. The broad outline of the gift tax calculation can be stated as follows:

*Gross* value of all *gifts* made minus *exempt gifts* and *deductions* equals *taxable gifts*.

*Taxable gifts* multiplied by *tax rate* equals *gross tax liability*.

*Gross tax liability* minus *tax credits* equals *net tax payable*.

Translating real-world events into such a simplistic formula is subject to the usual number of definitional and calculational problems. We shall examine only a few of the more common problems and opportunities.

**Gross Gifts.** The determination of a dollar value to represent the "gross value of all gifts made" typically involves two major kinds of problems. One set of problems involves the specification of exactly which transfers will be deemed to constitute gifts (as opposed to nongratuitous transfers); the second set of problems involves the determination of the fair market value of those transfers found to be gratuitous. The former problem is generally resolved by the intent of the taxpayer.

The Internal Revenue Code provides that any transfer of property for less than an adequate and full consideration in money or money's worth shall be included in computing the amount of gifts made. The intent of this provision is apparent, but its application is sometimes difficult. If a person makes a foolish deal—if the person, for instance, unwittingly sells a property worth $500,000 for $300,000—the code would seem to require that a gift tax be paid on the miscalculation (in this instance, on $200,000). In practice, the IRS is not that cruel. Instead of trying to apply the Code literally, the IRS usually tries to determine the intent of the taxpayer. If he or she entered into an arm's-length transaction in the ordinary course of business, the transaction will not be subject to a gift tax. If the transaction is one between related parties, or if the IRS has any other reason to suspect that the transaction is not a bona fide sale or exchange, it may attempt to tax as a gift the difference between the fair market value given and the consideration received.

In unusual circumstances, a gift tax may also become payable through the inadvertent or unintended action of a taxpayer. In these circumstances, a taxpayer may not have given any conscious thought to making a gift, but the taxpayer's actions may in fact accomplish such a result. Suppose, for example, that a father and his adult son began raising a herd of cattle in a joint venture. Under these circumstances, it would not be unusual for the father to create, solely from his personal funds, a joint bank account for the use by both his son and himself in the cattle venture. Without formalizing their agreement, the two men may generally understand that the proceeds of the venture will be split equally and that both are free to draw upon the bank account for personal as well as business needs. The potential gift element in such an arrangement is easiest to see if we assume that (1) both men contribute an equal amount of effort to the operation, (2) after 10 years of operation, the business breaks exactly even, (3) neither party ever uses the bank account for personal needs, and (4) the two finally split the balance in the account when they terminate their joint venture. Under these extreme assumptions, it is clear that the father effectively made a gift to his son of one half of the amount he initially placed in the joint bank account. When the simplifying assumptions are removed and the venture is allowed to make a profit or a loss in various years, when the relative contributions of the two men are unequal in terms of personal effort as well as capital, and when the account is used for both personal and business needs, the determination of the amount of any gratuitous transfer is much more difficult to establish. Theoretically, however, it is necessary that the gratuitous transfer be separated from any nongratuitous transfer in this arrangement and that the former quantity be made subject to the federal gift tax. The latter quantity might also be subject to the income tax.

After a taxpayer has identified a gratuitous transfer, it is necessary to determine its fair market value on the date of the gift. If the transfer is one of a total present interest—that is, the donee receives an immediate rather than a deferred value of an entire property—only the normal problems of valuation are present. Even "normal" problems of valuation are substantial for all properties not regularly traded on an open market, and occasionally they are substantial even for widely traded properties. In settling disputed values, the courts commonly refer to such ephemeral criteria as a willing buyer, a willing seller, a free market, and full knowledge—assumed conditions that do not exist even in the most active markets of an economic world more accurately characterized by substantial ignorance than by full knowledge. Nevertheless, the valuation process must go on, and when taxpayers and government authorities cannot agree, the parties can only turn to the judicial system for an arbitrated settlement of their differences.

If a taxpayer transfers less than a total interest in a property, new and even more difficult problems of valuation are encountered. For example, a taxpayer may make a gift of the income from a property to person A for her lifetime, a gift of the same income stream to person B for his lifetime, but to take effect only after the life of person A, and finally a gift of the remainder interest in the property to person C. Before the gift tax consequences can be determined, we must know the value of the gifts made to persons A, B, and C. Obviously, such valuations can only be made with certain presumptions about the size of the income stream over a period of years, a discount rate, and a mortality table of expected human lives. In these instances, the Code specifies the use of designated actuarial tables. Any attempt to investigate problems of valuation would lead us far afield of the objectives of this book. We will therefore assume that such valuation problems can somehow be solved, and proceed with the more direct tax consequences.

**Exempt Gifts and Deductions.**   The taxpayer may subtract "exempt gifts and deductions" from the gross value of all gifts to determine taxable gifts. Exempt gifts and deductions fall into three categories: (1) a $10,000 exclusion per donee each year; (2) all gifts to nonprofit religious, charitable, literary, scientific, or educational organizations, and to the U.S. government and its political subdivisions; and (3) an unlimited deduction for property given the taxpayer's spouse.

The $10,000 individual exclusion is an annual exclusion that makes the vast majority of gifts nontaxable events. Note that any individual can give an unlimited amount of property away without a gift tax if he or she is willing to give it to enough different people. Also note that, over a lifetime, a rather large sum can be given tax-free to any one individual if the donor will begin early to take advantage of the annual exclusion. Over 50 years, for example, a person could transfer $500,000 to one child without incurring a gift tax, if the taxpayer would but make the maximum $10,000 tax-free gift each year. If a husband and wife each make gifts in that amount, the total that can be transferred tax-free is doubled. Gifts of future interests are generally not eligible for the annual exclusion; an exception exists for gifts to minors.

Although gifts to religious, charitable, literary, scientific, and educational institutions are generally exempt from the gift tax, such gifts must be reported and then deducted on the gift tax return if they exceed $10,000 to any one donee in any one year. A taxpayer may desire to retain a property for as long as he or she lives, but wish to guarantee the passing of the property to a charity at death (or the death of a spouse). In these circumstances, the taxpayer can either make an appropriate provision in a will or make an immediate and irrevocable gift of the remainder interest to charity. Alternatively, a taxpayer can currently transfer property to a "charitable lead trust"; immediately deduct for income tax purposes some of the value of the property put into trust; and yet transfer the title to the remaining property (i.e., the "remainder interest") to a family member or friend. Only the latter interest is subject to the gift tax.

Finally, since 1981, any taxpayer can give his or her spouse an unlimited amount of property without incurring any gift tax because of the "marital deduction." This provision in the gift tax law was responsible for the revision of many wills and other property distributions within families. Its impact will be felt for years to come. Additional details and planning suggestions related to the marital deduction are explained later in this chapter.

**Tax Rates.**   The apparent tax rates applied to all taxable gifts is determined according to a progressive rate schedule specified in the code. The present gift tax rates are stated in Table 14–1. These donative transfer tax rates—like the income tax rates explained in Chapter 3—are, for a wealthy few, only the "apparent" tax rates because the lower marginal rates (and the unified credit, which is explained later in this chapter) are phased out via a 5 percent surtax on taxable donative transfers in excess of $10 million. As a result of this surtax all taxable transfers in excess of $21.04 million are now taxed at a flat (or proportional) rate of 55 percent. The reader should observe that this one usually progressive rate schedule is applicable to the total taxable gifts made during a person's lifetime. Thus, the gift tax liability for gifts made during any one year depends upon the aggregate value of all taxable gifts made during the taxpayer's life, not just upon the gifts made in that year. This is a striking difference between the gift tax and the income tax. For the income tax, every taxpayer starts over at the lowest possible marginal rate each year; therefore, spreading taxable income equally over time serves to minimize the aggregate income tax liability. Except for the annual $10,000 exclusion provision, spreading gifts over time is of no benefit for gift tax purposes.

**TABLE 14–1**   Unified Estate and Gift Tax Rates

| (1)<br>For Taxable Transfer<br>Equal to or<br>More than— | (2)<br>But Less<br>than— | (3)<br>The Tax Is<br>Equal to— | (4)<br>PLUS the Following<br>Rate Times<br>Any Amount in<br>Excess of that in<br>Column 1: |
|---|---|---|---|
| $       0 | $    10,000 | $       0 | 18% |
| 10,000 | 20,000 | 1,800 | 20 |
| 20,000 | 40,000 | 3,800 | 22 |
| 40,000 | 60,000 | 8,200 | 24 |
| 60,000 | 80,000 | 13,000 | 26 |
| 80,000 | 100,000 | 18,200 | 28 |
| 100,000 | 150,000 | 23,800 | 30 |
| 150,000 | 250,000 | 38,800 | 32 |
| 250,000 | 500,000 | 70,800 | 34 |
| 500,000 | 750,000 | 155,800 | 37 |
| 750,000 | 1,000,000 | 248,300 | 39 |
| 1,000,000 | 1,250,000 | 345,800 | 41 |
| 1,250,000 | 1,500,000 | 448,300 | 43 |
| 1,500,000 | 2,000,000 | 555,800 | 45 |
| 2,000,000 | 2,500,000 | 780,800 | 49 |
| 2,500,000* | 3,000,000* | 1,025,800* | 53* |
| 3,000,000* | — | 1,298,000* | 55* |

*After 1992, any taxable transfer in excess of $2.5 million will be taxed at a marginal rate of 50 percent.

**Tax Credits.**   In order to determine the net gift tax liability for any single reporting period, a taxpayer must first determine a gross tax liability on all taxable gifts made during the taxpayer's life (as explained above), and then subtract from that gross tax liability the sum of all gift taxes paid in prior periods. The prior gift tax payments constitute a tax credit for the current period. (This credit is calculated using the current rate schedule, and that amount, rather than the amount actually paid, is utilized in determining the aggregate credit for prior taxes.) Only by utilizing this tax credit arrangement can a progressive tax be achieved over a lifetime with multiple reporting periods and without taxing gifts more than once.

In addition to the cumulative credit for all gift taxes paid in prior years, the new law also provides a one-time cumulative, unified gift and estate credit. The amount of the unified credit is $192,800. The effect of the unified credit is to allow a minimum amount, in addition to the annual $10,000 per donee exclusion, to wholly escape the federal gift and estate tax. The $192,800 credit is equivalent to a $600,000 exclusion.

## An Illustration

In order to illustrate the progressive nature of the federal gift tax, let us determine, *ignoring the unified credit* explained above, the gift tax liability for an imaginary single taxpayer who makes the gifts detailed below.

| Year | Gifts to Daughter | Gifts to Son | Gifts to Charity | Current Taxable Gifts |
|---|---|---|---|---|
| 19x1 | $20,000 | $13,000 | $15,000 | $13,000 |
| 19x2 | 20,000 | 27,000 | 20,000 | 27,000 |
| 19x3 | 30,000 | 30,000 | 20,000 | 40,000 |
| 19x4 | 20,000 | 20,000 | 40,000 | 20,000 |

The illustration assumes that the taxpayer had made no prior taxable gifts, and that all gifts are of present interests. If there were no unified credit, the taxpayer in this illustration would have to file a gift tax return and pay a gift tax in each of the years 19x1 through 19x4, because gifts in each year exceed the $10,000 annual exclusion per donee.

In terms of the general formula suggested earlier, this taxpayer's gift tax computation might be summarized as follows:

| Year | Gross Gifts, Current Year | Current Exemptions and Deductions | Current Taxable Gifts | Aggregate Taxable Gifts | Gross Tax Liability* | Tax of Prior Periods Taxable Gifts* | Current Net Tax Liability* |
|---|---|---|---|---|---|---|---|
| 19x1 | $48,000 | $35,000 | $13,000 | $13,000 | $ 2,400 | $     0 | $ 2,400 |
| 19x2 | 67,000 | 40,000 | 27,000 | 40,000 | 8,200 | 2,400 | 5,800 |
| 19x3 | 80,000 | 40,000 | 40,000 | 80,000 | 18,200 | 8,200 | 10,000 |
| 19x4 | 80,000 | 60,000 | 20,000 | 100,000 | 23,800 | 18,200 | 5,600 |

*Ignoring the unified gift and estate tax credit.

Aggregate taxable gifts are, of course, the sum of all taxable gifts in the current and prior years. The gross tax liability for any year is calculated on this base (aggregate taxable gifts), but a credit is granted for all gift taxes paid in prior years. For example, in the above illustration, the taxpayer in 19x4 would determine the gross tax liability based on aggregate gifts of $100,000 (even though in that year the taxpayer actually made taxable gifts totaling only $20,000). Based on gifts of $100,000, the gross tax liability is

$23,800 but this taxpayer would claim a credit of $18,200 for all of the gift taxes paid in 19x1–x3. Thus the actual tax liability for 19x4 would be only $5,600, ignoring the unified credit. Obviously a taxpayer must maintain a record of all gifts made throughout a lifetime if he or she is to complete the gift tax return correctly.

## Planning Considerations

The gift tax is exceedingly easy to avoid. A taxpayer who does not want to incur this tax merely has to refrain from making any gifts. In practice, therefore, tax planning relative to the gift tax usually relates to the determination of the lesser of two evils. The taxpayer will accept the need to pay a gift tax whenever doing so reduces some other tax by an amount greater than the gift tax incurred. The general constraints to be considered in making such a determination will be discussed in the final section of this chapter.

**Systematic Giving.** Taxpayers with substantial amounts of property should begin a systematic pattern of giving as early in life as possible if they want to minimize the aggregate tax they or their heirs must pay. In some situations, a taxpayer may believe that nontax considerations are more important than tax savings, and the actions of such a taxpayer should be guided accordingly. A taxpayer who believes that childhood wealth leads to laziness, unhappiness, or family strife, for example, would be well advised to forgo any tax savings in the interest of a better quality of human existence. For those who do not believe that early wealth contributes to a less meaningful existence, however, systematic giving can be beneficial.

Only systematic patterns of giving can assure a taxpayer that he or she has taken maximum advantage of the $10,000 annual exclusion. Observe that this tax-minimizing provision is applicable to every taxpayer. Thus, if a husband and wife want to maximize their gift tax opportunities, they should make all gifts jointly. If both parties consent to this special treatment, even if the property given belongs entirely to one spouse, the annual exclusion for the couple increases from $10,000 to $20,000 per donee. A consent to make gifts jointly must be in writing and filed on a timely basis with the IRS.

To demonstrate the importance of systematic giving, observe that if a couple has two married children, and if each child has two children, that couple can transfer more than $3 million tax-free to members of their family in just 20 years. That is, if each parent gives each child, child's spouse, and grandchild $10,000 per year, the total—$20,000 × 8 × 20—amounts to $3,200,000 in 20 years!

**Charitable Gifts.** A taxpayer may have many good reasons for making a gift to charity. Most important, charitable gifts allow personal support of those eleemosynary institutions and activities an individual believes to be most deserving. There are also at least four important tax reasons for making charitable gifts. Two tax reasons are related to the income tax, and a third is associated with the estate tax. Further aspects of these tax consequences will be discussed in the next two sections of this chapter. For the moment we need only note that a charitable gift can be made without incurring a gift tax.

**Cross Gifts.**    Several years ago one imaginative taxpayer tried to avoid the gift tax provisions in a unique way. He arranged an agreement with close friends whereby each of them would make gifts of $10,000 to designated persons. By pooling their individual rights to a $10,000 annual exclusion per donee, the taxpayer hoped to be able to increase effectively his own ability to give more to a limited number of people without a gift tax. The basic idea of cross gifts is illustrated simply in Figure 14–1. Under this plan, taxpayers A, B, and C would each designate three individuals to whom they wish to make tax-free gifts each year; in this illustration, the donees are designated a1, a2, a3, b1, b2, and so on. Each of the three donors would make the maximum tax-free gift to each of the nine donees. The effect of a three-person agreement is obviously to triple the maximum tax-free gift from $10,000 per donee to $30,000 per donee. If successful, the idea could be expanded with larger numbers of participants to the agreement. In this case, the court found, however, that the transfers were not gifts, since there was consideration exchanged by each party to the agreement—that is, the promise of the other

**FIGURE 14–1**

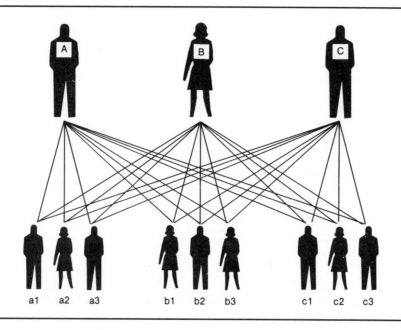

al    a2    a3        b1    b2    b3        c1    c2    c3

parties to make a reciprocal transfer. Although the rationale for the tax result is confusing, the court apparently decided that the extra amounts would not be eligible for the annual exclusion because they were *not* gifts, and that the same extra amounts would be subject to the gift tax because they were gifts! The theory of substance over form seems to be a more adequate explanation of the conclusion than does the definitional nuance suggested by the court.

**Serial Gifts.**    Under certain circumstances, a taxpayer may desire to transfer a particular property to a donee, but the transfer of the entire property at one time may be made expensive because of the gift tax rules. Suppose, for example, that, after exhausting their unified credit, a couple jointly desired to transfer a specific property worth $120,000 to their daughter. If they made the complete transfer in a single year, the transfer would be subject to a gift tax on $100,000. Instead of arranging the transfer as a gift, the couple might consider selling the property to the daughter, with the initial payment to be made in the form of six $20,000 promissory notes, with one note maturing in each of the next six years. Each year, the couple might forgive the daughter the $20,000 note due that year and thus avoid any gift tax on the transfer. This possibility raises several interesting tax questions for both the parents and the daughter. For example, the form of the initial transfer might be disregarded and the transfer treated as a gift rather than a sale under the substance-over-form rule. If the form of the transaction is sustained, it could create taxable income for the parents, even though they receive no cash. The tax basis of the property to the daughter, for income tax purposes, would depend upon how she is deemed to have acquired it; one set of basis rules applies to property acquired by gift and another set to purchased property. (See Chapter 6 for a statement of the different basis rules.) Although this serial gift notion creates several interesting tax problems, it has been used successfully in the minimization of gift taxes.

## FEDERAL TAXATION OF ESTATES

The federal estate tax is an excise tax that is imposed when an individual transfers property rights at death. The estate tax is *not* a tax on property as such, but a tax on the right to transfer property at death. In other words, the estate tax is a tax on *the transfer of ownership* occasioned by the death of a property owner. Note also that the estate tax is not an inheritance tax on the right to receive property. Although the estate tax may reduce the net size of an inheritance received, it is a tax liability paid by the executor of the deceased taxpayer, not a tax on the recipients' rights to receive. Because the federal estate tax is a tax on the transfer of property at death, the initial determination essentially must be an inventory process. That is, in order to determine the estate tax it is first necessary to determine exactly what properties a person owns at the time of his or her death.

## Basic Provisions

The final determination of an estate tax liability proceeds conceptually as follows:

Gross value of the estate
− Deductions
_____

= Taxable estate
+ Adjusted taxable gifts
_____

= Tax base
× Tax rate
_____

= Gross tax liability
− Tax credits
_____

= Net tax payable.

Once again, it is the translation of real-world phenomena into a simple formula that creates both problems of compliance and opportunities for tax avoidance. The estate and gift taxes share the major common problem of valuation; both taxes demand that an explicit dollar value be specified for certain property rights, whether or not the properties are ever sold or exchanged. If the tax collector and the taxpayer cannot agree on valuation, the courts must resolve all differences of opinion. We shall again assume that all necessary valuations can be made, in one way or another, so that we may concentrate our attention on the related estate tax problems and opportunities that may be subject to deliberate intervention.

**Gross Estate.** If we ignore the problems of valuation, the major problems remaining in the determination of the estate tax liability are those of discovery and identification. All property owned by a decedent at the moment of death must be included in the estate. This includes real and personal property, tangible and intangible property, and business as well as purely personal-use property. Code Section 2033 states it this way: "The value of the gross estate shall include the value of all property to the extent of the interest therein of the decedent at the time of his death."

One of the common definitional problems encountered in determining an estate tax involves property that is jointly owned. The law recognizes several different forms of joint ownership, including joint tenancy, tenancy in common, tenancy by the entirety, and community property. Since 1981 this problem has become less critical because of a provision that makes any property jointly owned by a husband and wife belong one-half to each spouse, regardless of who furnished the consideration to acquire the property. Another common definitional problem involves the need to determine whether or not the value of a gross estate must include property over which the deceased person held certain "powers of appointment." These and many other problems can only be noted in passing. Solution of them in any specific circumstance may require many hours of work by a qualified attorney.

More generally, we can observe safely that a gross estate typically does not include property that a taxpayer gave away prior to death. The major exception to this conclusion involves transfers of certain properties, such as life insurance, made within three years of death. In most circumstances, any value added back is based on the value of the property on the date of the gift; not on its value on the date of death. In addition, for deaths occurring after 1981, any gift tax paid on gifts made within three years of death must be added back to the gross estate.

If an "early" gift is made with the intent of reducing the size of an eventual estate, the would-be donor must take care to complete the gift in every respect. For example, a taxpayer, as explained earlier, does not make a gift simply by naming a beneficiary for an insurance policy; since the insured may change a designated beneficiary up to the moment of death, there is no gift and the value of the policy must be included in the deceased taxpayer's estate. It is possible, of course, for a person to make a gift of an insurance policy or of any other property prior to death, but this act requires more than good intentions. (Incidentally, completed gifts of insurance policies made within three years of death are valued for estate tax purposes—in the addback described above—as of date of death; not as of the date of the gift.)

Sometimes a donor will try to make a gift of less than a complete property in order to reduce the estate tax. Although a partial gift is always a possibility, special care must be exercised in these circumstances. For example, several years ago the Supreme Court ruled that the retention of voting rights of stocks otherwise transferred to another in trust was not sufficient to justify the inclusion of the value of those shares in the deceased donor's estate. The statutory law was later changed so that the full inclusion of value under those circumstances is now required. Thus, in making partial gifts, extreme caution is warranted.

A taxpayer's rights in an annuity, pension, or profit-sharing plan may also present unusual problems in estate tax determinations. Whether or not such rights must be included in the gross estate depends upon how the rights were acquired (by purchase or through employment), how the plan is worded, who the employer was, and what options were exercised prior to death. The number of possible alternatives is too large to permit a restatement of all possible results here. One major rule, however, should be noted: Retirement plans that can *only* be satisfied by a lump-sum payment on the death of the insured must be included in a decedent's estate; those providing for a non-lump-sum distribution may sometimes be excluded. Taxpayers with substantial estates should make certain long before their death that such contracts are arranged in the most favorable way.

After the executor or administrator of an estate has determined which properties must be included in a deceased taxpayer's gross estate, attention turns to problems of valuation. In the case of the federal estate tax, the executor can generally elect to value all properties at either the date of the decedent's death or six months afterward. Usually, the executor will select the value on the date that will yield the lower aggregate valuation and therefore the lower estate tax. Unless a special exception applies, the fair market value of any property is the selling price that would obtain in a free market, with a willing buyer, a willing seller, and full knowledge, assuming that the property will be put to its highest and best use. In the absence of an actual sale, of course, this theoretical value may be nearly impossible to determine. Furthermore, the general valuation rules may not apply to real estate used in a family farm or other closely held business.

In an attempt to minimize concern over the fact that an estate tax liability could force the disposition of a family farm or business, Congress wrote several special provisions into the law. Among those special provisions is one that allows an executor to reduce the value of land used in a family farm or other closely held business by as much as $750,000 if certain conditions are satisfied. Among those conditions are the following: (1) a family member must have been actively involved in the farm or business for at least five of the eight years immediately preceding the decedent's (*a*) becoming disabled, (*b*) receipt of social security benefits, or (*c*) death; (2) the real estate must represent at least 25 percent of the adjusted value of the decedent's estate; (3) the value of all property used in the family farm or business must represent at least 50 percent of the adjusted value of the decedent's estate; (4) the real estate must pass to a qualified heir (generally a family member or a close relative); and (5) a family member must continue to actively manage or operate the farm or business for 10 years after the decedent's death. If all of the conditions are fully satisfied, the executor may value qualifying real estate at its "special use value" rather than its "highest and best use value." For example, if a farm were located near a growing city's limits, the fair market value of the land as residential or commercial property might be considerably in excess of its value as farmland. Nevertheless, if the stipulated conditions were satisfied, the land could be valued as farmland and the estate tax determined on that lesser value. Other privileges—such as a deferred payment of the estate tax with a minimal interest rate—might also apply in this situation.

**Deductions.**   The estate tax, like every other tax, has a list of deductions that serve to reduce the size of the tax base. The most important deductions for estate tax purposes are (1) a deduction of all debts against the estate or against the deceased taxpayer, (2) all funeral expenses and the administrative expenses of settling the estate, (3) an unlimited marital deduction, and (4) most contributions to charitable organizations and/or certain governmental units. Each of these deductions is in turn subject to special interpretations and applications in particular circumstances. We can only note in passing the broad outlines of each item.

The authorized deduction of all debts against the gross estate in the determination of the taxable estate means, of course, that the federal estate tax is imposed on the *net* value of the taxpayer's property, not on its gross value. A taxpayer who purchases a $300,000 property on a contract requiring a $50,000 down payment and assumption of a $250,000 mortgage shortly before death would not be increasing the size of the taxable estate by making such an acquisition. This result is in direct contrast with the usual property tax based on gross values. As noted earlier, the estate tax is not a property tax, even though valuation of property owned is the first step in the tax determination process.

The deduction authorized for administrative expenses includes the executor's commission, attorneys' fees, court costs, and all costs associated with selling property and otherwise managing the estate after the taxpayer's death and prior to the property distribution. An executor cannot, however, get both an income tax deduction (on the decedent's final return) and an estate tax deduction for a single expenditure. For example, the cost of selling a property can only be deducted once, either in the income or the estate tax calculation. The right to deduct funeral expenses serves similarly to reduce the estate tax base to the net value of property that a deceased person could actually pass to family or other heirs.

As noted above, the current law also provides an unlimited estate-tax marital deduction. Suffice it to note here that the estate-tax marital deduction serves to remove most small estates from the federal estate tax so long as there is a surviving spouse. Under the law existing prior to 1982, only a complete transfer of all property rights could create a marital deduction. Since 1981, however, an executor may elect to treat a bequest of a mere life interest, left to a spouse, as qualifying for the marital deduction. For example, a husband can now leave a life interest in all his assets to a spouse, and pass all remainder interests to his children, and still have this bequest qualify for the unlimited marital deduction. In that event, however, the total value of the remainder interest must be included in the gross estate of the wife when she dies.

Finally, the law authorizes a deduction for property transferred to a nonprofit religious, charitable, scientific, literary, or educational organization, or to the U.S. government or one of its political subdivisions. In general this deduction is limited to present interests in property. A remainder interest—that is, an interest that will mature on the death of a designated person at some time in the future—may be deductible, however, if the charitable remainder is in a farm or personal residence. Special rules apply to the deduction of charitable gifts made in trust.

**The Addition of Taxable Gifts.** The fact that gifts and estates are really subject to a single, unified tax is implicit in the general formula suggested on page 304. Observe in that formula that adjusted taxable gifts are added back to the taxable estate to determine the total taxable estate. The adjusted taxable gifts are the total post-1976 taxable gifts made by the taxpayer.

**Tax Rates.** The tax rates applied to the total taxable estate to determine the gross estate tax liability are exactly the same tax rates as those applied to taxable gifts. Thus, as is evident in the heading, Table 14–1 is equally applicable to gifts and estates. Hence the gross tax liability is determined by multiplying the tax rate indicated in Table 14–1 times the amount of the total taxable estate.

**Tax Credits.** The federal estate tax authorizes tax credits for (1) any federal gift tax paid on values also included in the total taxable estate, (2) state inheritance taxes, subject to certain limits and adjustments, (3) prior federal estate taxes paid on properties included in more than one estate within a 10-year period, and (4) the unified gift and estate tax credit. Each of the first three tax credits, as well as a possible foreign death tax credit, is intended to reduce the multiple taxation of a single tax base. We noted earlier the need to include taxable gifts within the value of the taxable estate. This means, of course, that a single property transfer could be subject to both the federal gift tax and the federal estate tax. In order to avoid the multiple taxation of a single property transfer, the estate authorizes a tax credit for applicable gift taxes.

The tax credit allowed against the federal estate tax for taxes paid as state inheritance taxes serves to provide all states with a minimum revenue from inheritance taxes. If an individual state did not impose such a tax, its residents would obtain no personal benefit since the federal estate tax would be increased accordingly. On the other hand, if an individual state attempted to increase its own state inheritance tax substantially above the maximum federal tax credit, it would stand a real chance of losing its wealthier citizens to another state. The few states that have attempted to impose significantly higher inheritance taxes have found that state residency is often a mobile condition, especially for the wealthiest taxpayers.

The tax credit allowed for successive federal estate taxes on specific properties included as part of more than one taxable estate within a single 10-year period is intended to reduce the potential cumulative effect of the estate tax. The amount of this credit is directly related to the time interval that has elapsed between the deaths of the various owners. If 2 years or less have elapsed since the property was last passed through a taxable estate, the tax credit is 100 percent of the previous estate tax; if 2 to 4 years have elapsed, the credit is equal to 80 percent of the prior tax; if 4 to 6 years, it is 60 percent; if 6 to 8 years, 40 percent; and if 8 to 10 years, 20 percent. No tax credit is allowed if the property last passed through a taxable estate more than 10 years earlier. As a practical matter, this tax credit is of limited importance because most people with substantial property try to arrange their personal affairs to ensure that property will not pass through a taxable estate in such a short period under ordinary circumstances.

The unified gift and estate tax credit was explained earlier. As noted there, the effect of this credit is to exempt otherwise taxable gifts and/or estates from federal tax. If a taxpayer desires to maximize the amount of property to be left to his or her heirs, each taxpayer must fully utilize the maximum amount of this credit. Generally this means that wealthy taxpayers should not leave all of their assets to a surviving spouse.

## Planning Considerations

Since death is a certainty for everyone, the federal estate tax cannot be permanently avoided unless a taxpayer is willing to renounce U.S. citizenship and become a citizen and resident of a non–estate-taxing country. If a taxpayer dies intestate (that is, without a will), the laws of the state of residency will determine how property is divided among potential heirs. In general, a person's property will be divided between a surviving spouse and children, if any. If no child or spouse survives the taxpayer, the property will usually pass to any grandchildren. If there is no surviving spouse, child, or grandchild, the property will typically be divided among siblings. The exact rules are commonly referred to as the *laws of descent and distribution*, and they vary from one state to the next. If a taxpayer prepares a valid will prior to death, he or she may, within certain limits, distribute properties in any manner deemed appropriate. Prior to the Tax Reform Act of 1986, much of the sting of the federal estate tax could be avoided for many years by the simple expedient of a trust that skipped several generations. In other words, in arranging the disposition of his or her property, a taxpayer could create a testamentary trust giving a successive life interest (and possibly a limited right to invade corpus under specified conditions) to a surviving spouse or any children, grandchildren, and even great-grandchildren. A *life interest* is just what the words imply: A person receiving a life interest has only the right to income from certain property for so long as he or she lives. A life interest does not grant the recipient any right to decide who shall receive the trust corpus at the time of his or her death. Under prior law, when a person with a life interest died, there was nothing to be included in the decedent's estate for estate tax purposes. That was the tax beauty of a generation-skipping trust; a wealthy individual could "take care of" several successive generations without the imposition of the estate taxes. Only the recipient of the remainder interest—that is, the person who finally received the right to dispose of whatever was left when the intervening life interests had all been satisfied—received anything that could be subject to another round of estate taxation. And only the legal rule against perpetuities required the designation of a remainder interest somewhere down the line. The current rules are by no means as generous.

**Generation Skipping**    A generation-skipping tax will generally apply to any "taxable distribution," "taxable termination," or "direct skip" occurring after October 22, 1986. Although it is tempting to investigate the many nuances of the new generation-skipping tax, such an excursion would do little to accomplish the objectives of this book. Consequently we will satisfy ourselves with the broadest outline of current provisions.

In general terms, the 1986 act put an end to generation-skipping transfers. It achieved this result by (1) the definition of generations and (2) an operative provision that provides that any trust with two or more generations of beneficiaries who belong to a generation younger than that of the grantor will be a generation-skipping trust. Under current law, therefore, if a trust were created with a life interest for a spouse (deemed to be of the same generation as the grantor), with subsequent life interest for any children (deemed to be of the next younger generation), and with a remainder interest for any grandchildren (considered to be two generations younger than the grantor), it would be a generation-skipping trust. A trust with only a life interest for a surviving spouse and a remainder distribution to any great-grandchildren would be a direct skip and also subject to tax.

The new generation-skipping tax is, for all practical purposes, equivalent to the gift or estate tax that would be payable if the property were transferred from each generation to the next generation, regardless of how it actually is distributed. The new tax will be payable because of the death of a younger generation beneficiary who held only a life interest; because of a distribution of trust property to a younger generation beneficiary, from a trust that also benefited another younger generation beneficiary who is (was) a member of a generation older than that of the distributee; or because of a direct skip. The new tax may be paid from the assets of the trust, the assets received by a transferee, or from the assets of the transferor.

The new law has two major exemption provisions: (1) every person has a $2 million generation-skipping tax exemption per grandchild for transfers of property made before 1990; and (2) every person can make tax-free generation-skipping transfers after September 25, 1985, of up to another $1 million either during life or at death. Because both of these exemptions are allowed to every person, married couples can effectively double the available exemptions by electing to make joint gifts. (That is, they may treat their transfers as having been made one half by each spouse.)

Transfers subject to the generation-skipping transfer tax are taxed at the top marginal rate in the donative transfers tax rate schedule. That rate is 55 percent today; it is scheduled to drop to 50 percent in 1993.

The potential impact of the new generation-skipping tax can be illustrated as in Figure 14–2. Although that illustration ignores several possible modifications, which would be commonplace in most real-world circumstances—for example, it ignores all possible marital deductions, as well as the special $1 and $2 million exemptions—it serves to indicate the potential impact of

**FIGURE 14–2**

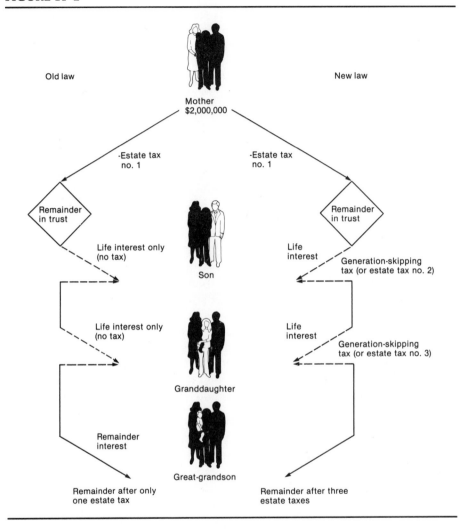

Old law

New law

Mother
$2,000,000

-Estate tax
no. 1

-Estate tax
no. 1

Remainder
in trust

Remainder
in trust

Life interest only
(no tax)

Life
interest

Generation-skipping
tax (or estate tax no. 2)

Son

Life interest only
(no tax)

Life
interest

Generation-skipping
tax (or estate tax no. 3)

Granddaughter

Remainder
interest

Great-grandson

Remainder after only
one estate tax

Remainder after three
estate taxes

the new provisions. In summary, it shows why a great-grandson might have received more under prior law. Under the old law, the only estate tax was that incurred at the death of the mother. Current law would impose a generation-skipping tax at the deaths of the son and the granddaughter. Both taxes would, of course, reduce the amount passing to the great-grandson.

**A Time to Give.** If a taxpayer desires to minimize both the gift and the estate tax, a careful selection of property and good predictive ability (possibly good luck) is now required. Note that the tax base for both the gift and the estate tax is the value of the property transferred on the date it is transferred. Any appreciation in value that takes place after a gift has been completed, and before the death of the donor, escapes both the gift and the estate tax so far as the donor is concerned. Thus a new tax minimization strategy has been created: The early gift of a property that will subsequently appreciate in value will minimize the federal gift and estate tax of the donor. Because of the basis rules for inherited property, however, that same gift may increase income taxes.

A full consideration of the possible tax impact of family tax planning must give further weight to the disposition plans of the recipient, the marginal tax rate of all possible donees, and the time-preference value of money. These and related considerations will be examined briefly in the remaining pages of this chapter.

## INTEGRATING THE INCOME, GIFT, AND ESTATE TAXES

In the final analysis, there are only two things that a person can do with any property that is not consumed: it can be retained or it can be given away. For tax purposes, the first alternative can be further broken down into three choices: (1) hold the property in its present form until death; (2) exchange the property for another property, in a nontaxable exchange, prior to death; or (3) dispose of the property in a taxable transaction before death and reinvest the proceeds. The second alternative can be broken down into two choices: (1) give the property to a charitable/literary/scientific/educational organization, or (2) give it to a "nonqualifying recipient" (e.g., a relative or friend). In summary, a propertied taxpayer seems to be faced with two basic questions: a "how much" question and a "what" question. That is, the taxpayer must decide (1) how much to give and how much to retain, and (2) what to give and what to retain. Even if the only decision criteria to be considered were tax factors, a decision model would be difficult to implement because there are so many unknown future variables in this model. In the real world, of course, nontax factors often govern these decisions. The taxpayer simply should be aware of the tax considerations before making a final decision.

The previous illustrations in this chapter imply that (beyond annual gifts of $10,000) there is little *tax incentive* to give property away to nonqualifying recipients prior to death. That conclusion is only valid, however, if you ignore both (1) predeath changes in value and (2) the fact that any gift tax paid more than three years prior to the decedent's death will reduce the remaining estate by the amount of the tax. (That gift tax, however, will be fully credited against the gross estate tax.) For very large estates, these two additional considerations create a bias in favor of giving property away, rather than retaining it. In other words, if the objective is to maximize the wealth passed to subsequent generations, the model will ordinarily favor gifts over retention, other things being equal. Unfortunately for the maximizing taxpayer, however, other things generally are not equal. One of the most important unequal factors has to do with the marginal tax rates that are pertinent to the various potential recipients.

## The Importance of the Marginal Tax Rate

The importance of the marginal tax rate to successful tax planning cannot be overemphasized. This conclusion is equally valid for any progressive tax, which includes the federal income and the federal donative transfers tax for all but a very few individuals who, because of the 5 percent surtax, pay one flat tax rate. In terms of successful family tax planning, this means that property ownership may have to be rearranged among family members before it is sold or exchanged outside the confines of the family unit. In Chapter 3 we observed how special entities, such as the trust and the corporation, might be used to help minimize the federal income tax. Let us now consider still other possibilities of minimizing the income tax by rearranging affairs within the family.

**Income Tax Considerations.**    The aggregate income tax on a family unit might be minimized when the family income is divided equally among all family members. For example, instead of having one married couple report the total family income of $400,000 per year, it *may* be possible to divide that income equally among eight family members and thereby reduce the annual income tax liability. The tax savings in this relatively simple yet extreme example would, however, be in the vicinity of only $12,000 to $15,000 annually—an amount almost certainly not worth the costs of achieving it. To illustrate the difficulties inherent in this tax plan consider the following complications:

To the extent that this family income derived from services rendered by either of the parents who originally reported the entire income, little or no equalizing could be achieved because the parents will be required to deduct and recognize a "reasonable salary" for their own services as explained in both Chapters 9 and 13.

To the extent that this family income derives from the ownership of capital, equalizing can be achieved but only if the transfer of property ownership is complete and then only at the probable cost of an immediate gift tax.

If any of the eight family members is under age 14 there would still be little or no advantage to the transfer of a capital interest because, as explained briefly in Chapter 3, those persons must pay the "kiddie tax" on passive income in excess of $1,000 per year—that is, they must pay income tax on passive income using their parents' top marginal tax rate.

If the parents attempt to utilize a reversionary trust or any other device to give others less than a complete interest in any property, that trust would, for reasons explained briefly in Chapter 3, be deemed a grantor trust; therefore, all of the income would still be taxed to the parents without regard for how the income was actually distributed.

For these and many other reasons, it is highly unlikely that any family would attempt to take advantage of marginal rate differences in this extreme manner. That does not mean, however, that no income tax planning remains viable for family units. In general it means that smaller steps will be more appropriate to achieve limited success for the same fundamental reason. The following examples illustrate the kind of family income tax planning opportunities that remain viable.

> Any family member can be employed by the family business, paid a reasonable salary for services rendered, and thereby achieve some tax savings because of the likely difference in the higher marginal tax rate applicable to the business paying the salary and the lower rate of the individual receiving it.

> Family members 14 years of age or older can also be given (or otherwise acquire) assets that will subsequently be leased to the family business and thereby once again achieve some tax savings because of the difference in the marginal tax rates of the business paying the lease rents and the individual receiving them.

> Children under age 14 can be given money to acquire Series E savings bonds, the interest from which can be deferred through a timely accounting election until the child is 14 years of age or older, and thus the family can once again utilize the difference in marginal rates to maximize tax savings on interest earned.

Another possibility involves the tax associated with the disposition of an appreciated asset. If a taxpayer decides to make a taxable disposition of any property that has significantly increased in value, that taxpayer should at least consider giving the property to another family member before completing the disposition. Obviously the taxable sale of an appreciated property might best be made by the family member in the lowest marginal income tax bracket. Typically this tax plan involves a gift of the appreciated property (about to be sold) from an older, high-marginal-bracket taxpayer to younger, low-marginal-bracket taxpayers. Giving the property may, of course, create an immediate gift tax, but that creates no additional gift or estate tax liability (except for the time-preference value of money) in the long run. Since most older family members intend to transfer their accumulated wealth to a younger generation at some time or other, they should always consider the possibility of making part of that transfer whenever they make a decision to dispose of any highly appreciated asset. To make such a gift on a timely basis will clearly add to the total asset values that can be passed to the younger generations.

On the other hand, observe that the tax plan just explained will not work with depreciated properties. A highly depreciated property—that is, a property with a tax basis that is substantially greater than its fair market value—cannot be transferred by gift to a taxpayer in the highest marginal tax bracket to obtain a greater tax savings. Because of the basis rules for property received as a gift, which were explained in Chapter 7, only the original owner can get the tax benefit of any predisposition decrease in the value of property. Also, a depreciated property should always be sold prior to death. If a taxpayer does not sell that property in a taxable transaction prior to death, the potential income tax deduction implicit in the decline in value will be lost forever because of the basis rules for inherited property.

**Estate Tax Considerations.**    The importance of giving full consideration to the marginal tax rate is just as applicable to estate planning as it is to income tax planning. Translated into plain English, the prior sentence appears to suggest that people should generally divide their family wealth equally among as many taxpayers as possible if they wish to minimize the donative transfers tax. That conclusion, however, is very often incorrect. To illustrate, suppose that a husband, H, has an accumulated taxable estate of $1 million and that his wife, W, has an accumulated taxable estate (of separate property) of $2 million. If H were to sign a will providing that all of his property should pass to W on the occasion of his death, and if H were to die before W, then H's executor would pay no estate tax because of the unlimited marital deduction. Although his will would clearly serve to minimize H's estate tax, on first blush it might appear that such a testamentary disposition of H's property would be foolish because H's property, upon the death of W, would be subject to higher marginal estate tax rates. Specifically, if H left his property to anyone other than W, it appears that H's estate would currently be subject to taxation at a *maximum* marginal rate of 39 percent. On the other hand, if H left all of his property to W, and if W's estate is thereby increased from $2 to $3 million, then what was originally H's property would now be subject to a marginal estate tax rate of about 50 percent. By increasing W's estate by $1 million, H effectively increased the maximum marginal rate on his own estate from 39 to 50 percent. Clearly such an increase in marginal tax rates could be avoided. But should it be avoided?

Observe that W would have all of H's property to invest from the date of his death until the date of her own death. If W made reasonably good investments, and if W lived for several years, this opportunity to invest all of H's assets could easily provide more assets than might be consumed by the differential in the marginal tax rates. Because the 37 percentage point difference between the lowest marginal estate tax rate (18 percent) and the highest marginal estate tax rate (55 percent) is relatively small, many taxpayers may discover that the time preference value of money is greater than the difference in marginal estate tax rates.

## The Importance of the Basis Rules

As explained in Chapter 7, inherited property ordinarily takes a basis equal to the fair market value of the property on the date of the decedent's death (or, possibly, six months after death). This rule is very important to family tax planning. If a taxpayer owns a property that has substantially increased in value since it was acquired, and if it is likely that the next recipient of that property will dispose of it before his or her death, there is a strong tax incentive to retain that property and allow it to pass through the taxpayer's estate. At the moment of death, the income tax potential implicit in the increase in value is permanently removed for the next owner. Theoretically, the heir or devisee could sell the property immediately after the decedent's death and recognize no taxable income because of this basis rule.

As previously explained in both this chapter and Chapter 7, the basis rules for property acquired by gift make depreciated properties—that is, those properties that have decreased in value since their acquisition—inappropriate for gifts to family members or friends. The ideal gift property for those donees is characterized by a fair market value that is approximately equal to basis. The exception to this rule, already noted in this chapter, is found in a situation in which (for economic reasons) a taxpayer desires to sell an appreciated property prior to death. In that case, a gift of the appreciated property to a family member in a low marginal tax bracket can make good tax sense.

In very large estates it is common to find that a majority of the decedent's assets have values greater than basis. Because of the dominant position of these assets, plus the apparently normal tendency for most people to want to keep much of their estate until death, a simple table can be prepared to give rule-of-thumb answers to the "what to keep" and "what to give" questions. That table appears as follows:

| Recommended Action | FMV > Basis | FMV ≈ Basis | FMV < Basis |
|---|---|---|---|
| Sell or exchange in taxable transaction prior to death | No | OK | Always |
| Exchange only on nontaxable transactions | Yes | OK | No |
| Retain in present form | Yes | OK | No |
| Give to family or friends before death | No | Yes | No |
| Give to charity | Yes | OK | No |

The tax reasons for selecting only certain properties for gifts to charity will be explained shortly. The reader should understand, however, that the word *charity* is used here to mean any organization that would qualify the gift as a tax deduction—for federal income tax purposes, for federal gift and estate tax purposes, or for both. In general, this can be any charitable literary, scientific, or educational organization qualified under Section 501(c).

## Charitable Gifts

The combined effect of several tax rules is to allow a wealthy taxpayer to support favorite eleemosynary institutions and activities at a minimum economic cost. Before we can determine the actual cost of charitable giving, it is necessary to introduce the income tax provisions pertinent to the charitable contribution deduction. In general, the Code authorizes an individual taxpayer to deduct, for income tax purposes, contributions made to charitable organizations up to a maximum of either 50 percent or 30 percent of the taxpayer's adjusted gross income. The 50 percent limit applies to contributions of cash made to public charities; the 30 percent limit applies to contributions of capital gain properties to public charities. Contributions made in excess of these limits in any one year can be carried forward and deducted in subsequent years. Contributions made to private charitable foundations are subject to more stringent rules. None of those rules will be discussed here even though a private foundation may be an excellent idea for the wealthy taxpayer interested in minimizing taxes.

The act of making a gift is *not* deemed to constitute realization for income tax purposes, except in the case of properties that may involve a liability greater than the tax basis. This means that a taxpayer with an appreciated property can generally avoid any income tax by giving away the property. (This conclusion will not be true, however, for individuals subject to the alternative minimum tax because this difference between the basis and the value of contributed property is a tax preference item.) If the gift is made to a charitable organization, the charity can sell the property and avoid any recognition of gain because of its general exemption from the income tax. A charitable gift thus usually serves to avoid for everyone concerned the income tax implicit in an appreciated property. As noted earlier in this chapter, charitable gifts are also authorized deductions in the computation of the gift and estate tax. Thus the act of making a charitable gift of an appreciated property serves to reduce both a taxpayer's income tax and estate tax without increasing the gift tax.

The measure of a charitable contribution deduction depends upon the class of property given. Contributions made in cash are simply measured by the amount of cash given. Contributions of property that, if sold, would produce a long-term capital gain are measured by the fair market value of the property on the date of the contribution. Contributions of property that, if sold, would produce ordinary income (including short-term capital gains) are measured by the basis of the property given unless the fair market value is lower than basis, in which case the fair market value becomes the measure of the deduction.

A translation into practical advice of the many tax rules that apply to charitable contributions is: a taxpayer who is not subject to the alternative minimum tax should give *only* appreciated long-term capital gain properties to favorite charities. The correctness of this conclusion can be demonstrated by a comparative analysis. The following comparison is based on the assumptions that the contributing taxpayer is in a 28 percent marginal tax bracket, does not exceed the annual limits for the charitable contribution deduction, makes all gifts to public charities, *and would have sold the same properties in a taxable transaction had he or she not given them to the charities.* Because of the assumptions implicit in these calculations— that is, the assumptions that the taxpayer is in the highest marginal tax bracket and that the donated property was a highly appreciated property—we can determine that, under certain conditions, a taxpayer can give a very valuable long-term capital gain property to charity at a relatively small after-tax cost. In this 1989 illustration, the taxpayer would be able to keep only $82,000 of the proceeds if he or she had sold the capital gain property on the open market. That is, the $110,000 received on the sale minus the $28,000 income tax would leave the taxpayer with $82,000. If the taxpayer gave the same property to a charity, the income tax liability would be reduced by $30,800, that is 28 percent of $110,000, plus $28,000 or 28 percent of $100,000. Thus the real economic cost of this generous gift is really $51,200, not $110,000.

| Form of Gift | Amount to Be Given (FMV) | Tax Basis of Property Given | Income Tax Saved due to Contribution Deduction | Income Tax Saved due to Nonrecognition of Gain | Net Real Economic Cost |
|---|---|---|---|---|---|
| Cash | $110,000 | $110,000 | $30,800 | $ 0 | $79,200 |
| LTCG property | 110,000 | 10,000 | 30,800 | 28,000 | 51,200 |
| Ordinary income property | 110,000 | 10,000 | 2,800 | 28,000 | 79,200 |

This illustration actually overstates the real economic cost of making a charitable contribution because the act of making the gift also serves to reduce the size of the donor's taxable estate and thus the estate tax. In some states it also reduces the state income tax. Any refinement of the illustration to include a measure of these additional tax savings would have to be based upon too many assumptions to have much practical value. The important conclusion, however, is that a substantial charitable gift may sometimes be made at a relatively low real aftertax cost to the donor. Whether or not a large gift to charity is possible, nearly all taxpayers give some thought to their retirement income.

### Retirement Income Funds

The proper disposition of assets accumulated over a lifetime of work to provide a possible source of retirement funds presents one of the most complex of all problems in family tax planning. As explained briefly in Chapter 9, the assets accumulated in a qualified pension, profit-sharing, or stock bonus plan may be taxed under any one of several options at the time those funds are distributed from the employee trust fund to the primary beneficiary and/ or the primary beneficiary's heirs. Lump-sum distributions create the most problems and present the most opportunities. Generally speaking, a taxpayer can elect to tax one lump-sum distribution as a special kind of income, subject to a five-year-forward income-averaging calculation. If a taxpayer does not make an election to receive the funds before death, the entire amount accumulated will be subject to the estate tax unless the contract provides for a distribution other than a lump-sum distribution to named beneficiaries. If paid as an annuity to the beneficiaries, any receipts will represent ordinary income, subject to no special provisions.

The many special rules necessary to make a wise decision concerning the preferred method of disposing of assets accumulated in a qualified pension, profit-sharing, or stock bonus plan must remain beyond the confines of this short book. Unfortunately, the rules are so complex that any attempt to describe them briefly would probably lead to more misinformation than information.

Successful family tax planning obviously involves the careful consideration of personal objectives as well as income, gift, and estate tax provisions. Most successful tax plans involve a substantial lead time if they are to be implemented properly. The use of life estates, placed in trust prior to a taxpayer's death, may in some instances still serve to decrease the family income tax liability as well as the donor's gift and estate tax liabilities. The careful integration of the many pertinent considerations involves full cooperation on the part of all parties. Any individual who has accumulated over $600,000 worth of property should give serious consideration to discussing his or her personal situation with a qualified tax adviser. The author's personal experience suggests that first-generation wealth is typically least interested in tax consequences. In other words, "the man or woman who made it" is least concerned about what taxes might do to an accumulated estate. Possessors of second-, third-, and fourth-generation wealth are often much more willing to modify personal fortunes to minimize the tax cost for everyone.

## PROBLEMS AND ASSIGNMENTS

1. Mr. and Mrs. Retired have a net worth of $6 million, most of which is invested in securities yielding 9 percent. Although they live very comfortably, they do not spend all of their earnings from their investments. They have four children, ages 15 to 30, who are all in school and have low incomes.

a. If Mr. and Mrs. Retired live for 10 more years, how much estate tax will they have saved if they give each of their children $20,000 this year?

b. What are some other tax-motivated reasons for making such gifts?

2. Laura Wealthy desires to give common stock to charity; the stock she wishes to give has a tax basis of $10,000 and a fair market value of $60,000.

a. If Laura is in the 28 percent marginal tax bracket, what is the amount of her (regular) income tax savings?

b. If Laura pays the alternative minimum tax, what is the amount of her income tax savings?

3. In 1991, John Phillips transferred stock worth $1 million to a trust in which his son receives a life estate and his grandson receives a remainder interest. His son died in 2025, when the stock was worth $3 million. If Phillips elects the $1 million exclusion, how much of a generation-skipping tax will be paid in 2025?

4. Compare the gift, estate, and generation-skipping transfer tax consequences of the following transactions, ignoring the various exclusions.

a. Joan gives stock to her daughter, June. When June died, the stock passed to June's daughter, Janet, by will.

b. Joan gives stock to a trust in which her son is the life beneficiary and her granddaughter is the remainderman.

c. Joan gives stock directly to her granddaughter.

5. Grandmother Ewing owns a large ranch in West Texas (basis, $75,000). Although people say the ranch is worth $1 million, it provides Mrs. Ewing with an income of only $60,000 (more or less) each year. Since Mrs. Ewing has adequate income from other sources, this low rate of return on the ranch does not bother her at all. She loves the family ranch and hopes that it will stay in her family for many years to come, remaining in essentially the same undeveloped condition that it is in today. Mrs. Ewing has already decided to pass title to the ranch to her son, R.J., but she is uncertain whether to do it now (before she dies) or to wait, letting the ranch be part of her estate. Mrs. Ewing fully understands that she could guarantee that the ranch would remain in the family for many years if she would place the property in trust, with appropriate instructions to the trustee not to sell the land. She also knows that trustees charge management fees and that financial conditions sometimes change so that ideas that seem good now turn out to be unsatisfactory in the future. Anyway, because of her strong feelings on these matters, she has clearly ruled out the use of a trust as far as the ranch is concerned. Her only remaining decision is whether to give it away now or let it pass through her estate. Given the strength of Mrs. Ewing's nontax feelings on this matter, what do you recommend that she do? Explain.

6. Mr. and Mrs. Rhyme would like to make a sizable gift to their alma mater, The University of Exes. The Rhymes own property worth several million

dollars, so their only real problem is deciding what to give the university. Among the options they are considering are the following:
(1) Cash of $100,000.
(2) A beautiful diamond (basis, $60,000; value, $100,000), which Mr. Rhyme purchased as an investment eight years ago.
(3) Part of this year's bumper cotton crop (basis, $0; value, $100,000). (One of the Rhymes' many trades and businesses is raising cotton. The cotton has no basis because, like all other farmers and ranchers, the Rhymes immediately deduct the cost of seed, fertilizers, etc.

a. From the income tax point of view, which of these properties would make the best gift, assuming that the Rhymes are in the 28 percent marginal tax bracket? Explain briefly. (Ignore AMT possibilities.)
b. From the gift tax point of view, which of these properties would make the best gift? Explain.

7. Martin Harvard strongly believes that three properties he owns will increase significantly in value within the next 24 to 36 months. Those three properties can be described as follows:

EFG stock: basis, $160,000; current value, $162,000.

FGH stock: basis, $2,000; current value, $162,000.

GHI stock: basis, $260,000; current value, $162,000.

Mr. Harvard is thinking seriously about making a gift of one of these three properties to his only child, Mervin. Given his premonition about the next two or three years, which property do you recommend that he give? (Assume that Martin and Mervin are in approximately the same marginal tax brackets.) Explain briefly.

8. A wealthy couple made the following gifts in years 19x1 through 19x4.

| Year | Gifts to Daughter | Gifts to Son | Gifts to Charity |
|------|------|------|------|
| 19x1 | $ 80,000 | $ 50,000 | $55,000 |
| 19x2 | 100,000 | 120,000 | 60,000 |
| 19x3 | 120,000 | 100,000 | 60,000 |
| 19x4 | 200,000 | 230,000 | 90,000 |

Assuming that these were the first taxable gifts ever made by this couple, that they elected to use the unified credit immediately to the maximum extent possible, and that all gifts were considered to be made jointly by husband and wife, determine the following.
a. The current taxable gifts in each year, 19x1 through 19x4.
b. The current net gift tax liability in each year, 19x1 through 19x4.

9. When Relson Nockafellar died this year, the title to all of his property passed to the Nockafellar Trust under the terms of a will giving Mrs. Nockafellar a mere "life interest" in the property. Relson's will further

stipulated that, upon the death of Mrs. N., the remainder interest in any Trust property should pass to their two children, Suzzie and Brad Nockafellar.

a. Describe in simple terms what is meant by Mrs. Nockafeller's "life interest" in the property previously owned by her deceased husband.
b. Would the terminable interest left by Relson to his former wife qualify for the marital deduction?
c. What valid nontax reasons might Relson have for leaving his property "in trust" rather than leaving it directly to his former wife and/or their children?
d. What good tax reasons might Relson have had for leaving all of his property in trust even if Mrs. Nockafellar owned a substantial amount of property in her own name and clearly had no need for additional assets during her remaining lifetime?

# Case 14–1

Amy Davis has built her printing business up from a small, hand-operated machine to a multimillion dollar publishing empire. Amy is nearing retirement age and is planning to let her son, Bobby Davis, take over the company in a few years. Amy expects the company to keep growing rapidly under her ambitious son's leadership. Amy has reinvested her profits in the company for years, and is consequently wealthy but illiquid. Amy's goals are to:

1. Retire in three to five years and receive a steady income stream from her holdings.

2. Transfer at least partial ownership of the company to her son when she retires.

3. Minimize and/or postpone her eventual gift/estate tax liability.

Amy recognizes that an outright gift of the business to her son would trigger a gift tax that she could not pay; on the other hand, if she retains ownership, the value of the rapidly appreciating company would be included in her estate. What should Amy do?

# Case 14–2

Sam Brown, age 55, has a horse farm near a rapidly growing city in northern California. His son, Robert, age 25, has been helping to manage the farm for the past five years. Sam and Robert are both interested in keeping the family in the horse farm business for the next several years. The farmland is presently worth $2 million and increasing in value by 15 percent each year. The horses and equipment are worth $500,000 and increasing in value by 5 percent each year.

Sam is very concerned that estate taxes could drive Robert out of farming.

a. What can you tell Sam about estate taxes to relieve him?

b. Is there something that Sam could do now that would remove the problems caused by the growing city and be likely to keep Robert in the farming business?

# CHAPTER 15

# The Taxing Process

Actual participation in the taxing process is quite different from reading about the myriad existing tax rules. Books on taxation usually describe it as a series of apparently sterile rules of the "if A, then B" variety. The reader is tempted to conclude that taxation consists only of learning and impartially applying all of the many rules. Any reasonable exposure to the real process of taxation will quickly dispel that notion. Taxation is in fact a very dynamic process of interaction among people. *Tax rules are made, interpreted, and administered in minutely different situations by unique humans who work with a very imprecise language.* Because the taxing process is an entirely human one, distinct opportunities and problems are created. First, this means that the tax rules are in a constant state of flux, and that, under the proper circumstances, they can actually be rewritten or reinterpreted to the distinct advantage (or disadvantage) of one or a few taxpayers. Second, it means that a knowledgeable taxpayer can often prearrange events so that only the most favorable tax results will be applicable. Third, it means that even when a taxpayer fails to exercise any preliminary caution, he or she may be able to argue successfully that a particular situation is (or is not) within the meaning of certain statutory words and that, therefore, rule A rather than rule B ought to apply.

Our income, estate, and gift taxes are all self-compliance taxes. Theoretically, the individual determines the tax liability and reports that determination with the proper remittance to the government on a timely basis. As a practical matter, the tax rules have become so complex that a majority of the taxpayers believe that they are individually incapable of self-compliance, and therefore they turn to ostensible tax experts for assistance. Although an expert can help a taxpayer meet an obligation, the taxpayer alone bears the brunt of the liability for complying with the law.

In practice, the taxing process seems to take place at three different levels: first, at the legislative level, where the initial rules are hammered out in a political process called government; second, at the planning and compliance levels, where the taxpayer works with an adviser and the two attempt to satisfy the legal and financial requirements placed upon the taxpayer; and third, at the level where disagreements are resolved between the government and the taxpayer. At the last level especially, the taxpayer tends to stand on the sidelines watching the experts spar over his or her fate. The taxpayer plays the role of an innocent bystander who must ultimately pay the consequence of battle.

In this chapter, we shall consider only the second and third levels of the taxing process. The first level can be dismissed because so few taxpayers ever attempt to influence tax legislation directly for their individual benefit. Those few who take this narrow route to legal tax avoidance usually have a sophistication far beyond that envisioned for the readers of this book. Virtually every taxpayer, on the other hand, is faced with problems of planning and compliance. A lesser but still significant number face the problems of resolving disagreements with the IRS. The chapter is divided into three major sections. The first section contains a description of tax compliance procedure from the filing of a tax return through the litigation of potential differences of opinion. The second section consists of a brief discussion of the tax experts who offer their assistance on a commercial basis to taxpayers seeking help. The third section consists of a very brief forecast of what may lie ahead in the area of federal taxation.

## COMPLIANCE CONSIDERATIONS

The first official step in the compliance process generally consists of the filing of a tax return on a timely basis. Long before the reporting date arrives, of course, the taxpayer may have made an investigation into the available alternatives and so arranged matters that a given result is almost certain. This preparation for the filing of a return may even have included a request for an advance ruling on a technical point by the IRS. Whether or not preliminary tax planning has taken place, every taxpayer must eventually report to the IRS the tax result of the events that have actually transpired. The date on which any tax return is due will depend upon many different considerations, including the tax involved (for example, the income, estate, or gift tax) and the kind of taxpayer involved (for example, an individual, a corporation, or a fiduciary). Several hundred forms and instructional booklets have been prepared and distributed by the IRS to facilitate this reporting process. In some circumstances, the IRS may accept the taxpayer's computer tapes and individual computer printouts in lieu of the more typical forms. However it may be accomplished, the act of reporting is generally the first step in the taxing process.

### Filing Tax Returns

In a recent year, approximately 110 million income tax returns were filed with the IRS by individual, corporate, and fiduciary taxpayers. An additional 28 million employment tax returns and 166,000 estate and gift tax returns were also filed in that year. On the whole, the income, estate, and gift tax returns represent the greatest challenge in terms of compliance considerations. At present, most tax returns are filed with one of the 10 IRS service centers located in various sections of the country. These service centers are largely information processing facilities. They do perform a check of the arithmetic accuracy of virtually all returns received, and a very limited review of obvious errors, but this check should not be confused with an actual audit, which will be discussed shortly. Having confirmed the arithmetic, and determined the general correctness of a return, a service center clerk will prepare a computer record of the documents received. The computer record is forwarded to Martinsburg, West Virginia, for storage and further reference. If the return indicates that a refund is due the taxpayer, the service center personnel will also initiate the action required for the preparation of a refund check. If a remittance is included with a return, service center personnel will separate the check from the tax return and deposit the tax paid to the government's account.

Many taxpayers place unjustified significance upon the fact that they receive a refund check from the government or that the government cashed their check as submitted. As just explained, this means little more than that their return has passed a simple check of arithmetic accuracy and that it has been logged into the government computer for possible retrieval at a later date. It does not mean the tax return has been accepted as filed. For most purposes, the IRS has at least three years during which it may raise questions concerning the accuracy of any return. If a return contains a material error—for example, an omission of more than 25 percent of the gross income—the assessment period is extended to six years. If fraud is involved, the assessment period remains open indefinitely. As a practical matter, much of the routine work being done by IRS agents involves tax returns that are two to three years old. Thus every taxpayer should keep all supporting records for at least three years; certain records are best retained for a lifetime.

### Returns Selected for Audit

Several years ago, the actual audit selection process was a special task assigned to some of the most experienced employees of the IRS. Since then, that task has been largely delegated to the computer. Based upon a highly classified discriminate function analysis, the computer scores each tax return received by the IRS. The return with the highest score is supposedly the one most deserving of an audit; the return with the second highest score, the next most deserving of an audit; and so on. Although the computer program utilized by the IRS must remain secret for obvious reasons, it seems reasonable to speculate that it gives special attention to, among other things, deductions that are larger than normal for a taxpayer in any given income bracket, deductions that are especially prone to abuse (travel and entertainment expenses, for example), returns reporting a substantial gross income but little or no taxable income, and returns reporting a very large income from any source. Some returns are also selected for audit each year on a purely random basis to determine the general compliance standards of taxpayers as a whole.

The audit of a tax return is conducted by IRS personnel assigned to a district office, not by service-center personnel. At present there are 63 district offices scattered throughout the United States. To facilitate compliance the IRS maintains resident audit personnel in each major city, whether or not there is a district office in the city. The audit staff is generally divided between revenue agents and special agents, who perform rather different functions. The revenue agent conducts more or less routine investigations into the adequacy of the returns selected for audit; the special agent is assigned to more investigatory work in cases where fraud is suspected. Routine audits may be conducted either at an IRS office (which audit is classified as an "office audit") or at the taxpayer's place of business (which audit is referred to as a "field audit"). The decision on where the audit should take place is largely a matter of logistics. If a large number of bulky records must be examined, the IRS agents usually will agree to a field audit; otherwise, the taxpayer can expect to report to an IRS facility for completion of an audit.

### Settling Disputes

A taxpayer receiving a first notice of an IRS examination may panic unnecessarily. However, unless the taxpayer has reason to suspect that an audit is something more than a routine investigation, he or she usually has nothing to fear. The agent will request that substantiating records be produced for examination. If the taxpayer has maintained good records and the information was reported correctly, the audit may be closed promptly with little or no adjustment. If the records are questionable, or if the agent disagrees with the taxpayer's interpretation of the tax rules, a more detailed administrative review procedure is set into motion. In order to make the contest one between equals, a taxpayer should be represented in any administrative hearing by a knowledgeable tax expert if the proceeding involves anything other than a simple and direct verification of fact. In other words, it would not be necessary or helpful for a taxpayer to engage a tax expert if all that is asked is proof of 10 dependent children or of a charitable deduction *and* the taxpayer has adequate proof of the facts in question. On the other hand, if the taxpayer is trying to substantiate the conclusion that an aged grandmother really is a dependent, or if a taxpayer is trying to prove weekly cash contributions to an open church offering, an adviser may be most helpful. In more complicated business situations (such as situations involving corporate formations, pension plans, and similar circumstances), a tax adviser is virtually mandatory. Generally speaking, the taxpayer should contact an adviser as soon as he or she receives a notice of examination, not after meeting with the IRS representative. The way a case is initially presented may have something to do with its ultimate resolution.

**Administrative Reviews.**    If the original auditor, an IRS supervisor, and the taxpayer cannot agree upon the correct resolution of a particular issue, the code authorizes an additional administrative consultation before the taxpayer needs to consider the possibility of litigating the dispute in a court of law. The administrative review procedure authorizes a conference with a specially trained agent, called a conferee, who is assigned to the chief counsel's office and is entirely independent of the agent who conducted the original audit. Whether or not a taxpayer should utilize the possible administrative review procedure depends largely upon the question under consideration and the professional opinion of the expert handling the case. A visual presentation of the audit procedure is contained in Figure 15–1.

**Judicial Reviews.**    If the taxpayer and the representatives of the IRS simply cannot settle their differences of opinion in any administrative proceeding, the debate can proceed to trial in a court of law. In tax matters, any one of three courts may have initial jurisdiction. A taxpayer will end up in the Tax Court if he or she refuses to pay a tax deficiency assessed by the IRS and the dispute is then litigated. If the taxpayer pays the deficiency assessed by the IRS, that taxpayer may then turn around and sue the government in either a federal district court or the Claims Court for a recovery of money believed to be wrongfully collected. The selection of the most appropriate judicial forum should, quite naturally, be heavily influenced by the taxpayer's legal counsel. Each of the courts is quite different in its methods of operation, and each may be preferred under particular circumstances. Generally, the Tax Court has the better grasp of technical issues because it is a court whose jurisdiction is restricted to tax controversy. The federal district court is expected to try cases in all aspects of the law, and therefore its judges cannot be equally expert in every technical detail of the tax law. On the other hand, there is no provision for a jury trial in the Tax Court. If the question to be established is one of fact rather than law, counsel may prefer the district court route, believing that a jury may be more sympathetic to a taxpayer's point of view. If, for example, a taxpayer is trying to establish the fair market value of a painting donated to an art museum, there may be good reason to prefer a federal district court to the Tax Court. On the other hand, if the taxpayer is trying to prove that a $500,000 salary is reasonable, there may be good reason to avoid a jury. An appeal from either of these two courts must go to the circuit court of appeals for the taxpayer's place of residence.

An appellate court will generally not review findings of fact. The appellate courts tend to accept the lower court's determination of fact and to consider only errors in the application of the law. The losing party can usually force a disagreement before a court of appeals. Once that body has rendered an opinion, however, the only remaining appeal is to the U.S. Supreme Court.

FIGURE 15-1 Income Tax Audit Procedure—Internal Revenue Service

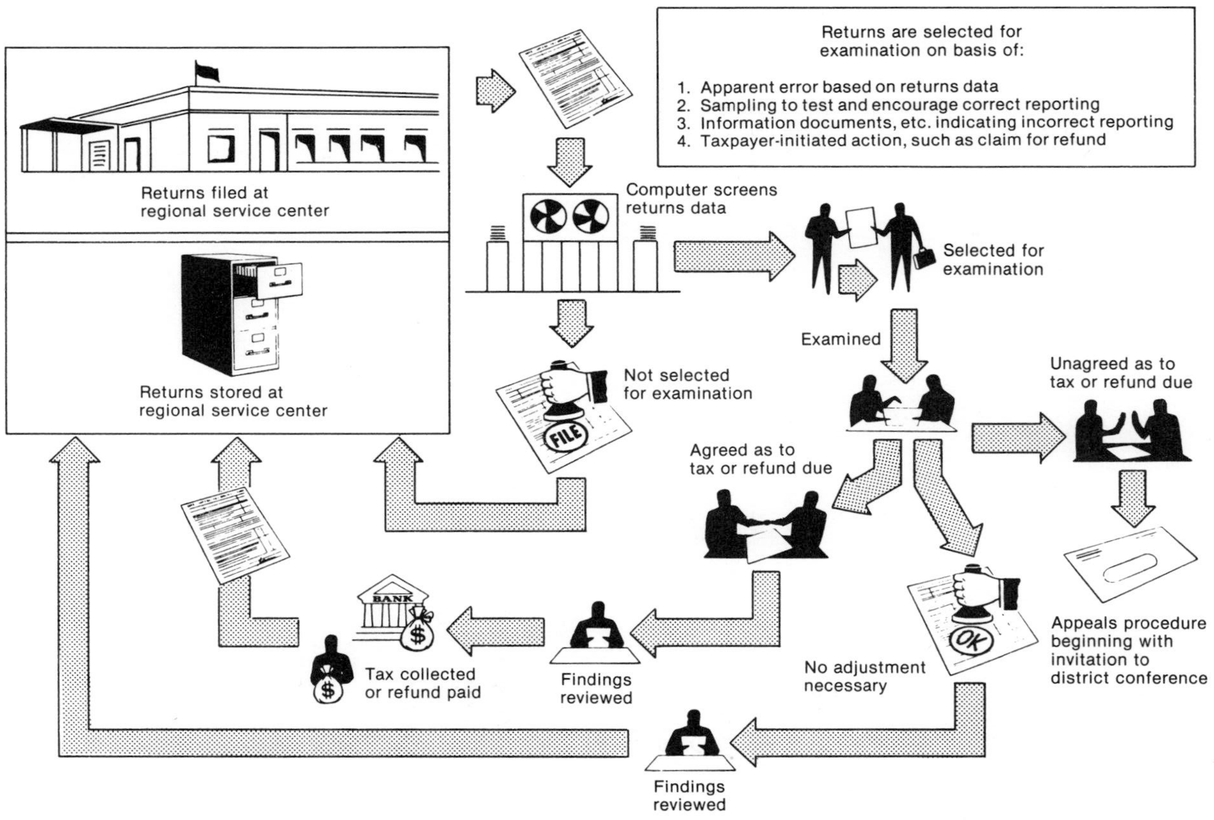

Returns are selected for
examination on basis of:

1. Apparent error based on returns data
2. Sampling to test and encourage correct reporting
3. Information documents, etc. indicating incorrect reporting
4. Taxpayer-initiated action, such as claim for refund

Returns filed at
regional service center

Returns stored at
regional service center

Computer screens
returns data

Not selected
for examination

Selected for
examination

Examined

Agreed as to
tax or refund due

Unagreed as to
tax or refund due

No adjustment
necessary

Findings
reviewed

Findings
reviewed

Tax collected
or refund paid

Appeals procedure
beginning with
invitation to
district conference

During an average year, the Supreme Court will agree to hear no more than five to eight tax cases. These cases are selected either because the Court believes that they contain some important tax principle requiring clarification or because two or more courts of appeal are in disagreement about how essentially identical questions should be answered. Appeals from the Claims Court go through the U.S. Court of Appeals for the Federal Circuit en route to the Supreme Court. A visual presentation of the income tax appeal procedure, including both administrative and judicial elements, is contained in Figure 15–2.

## A Summary Observation

In evaluating the IRS procedures, the reader should understand that the chance of any individual taxpayer's tax return being selected for audit is statistically about 1 in 100. The reason for this low probability of an audit is that the IRS does not have sufficient personnel to do more, not that all of the unaudited returns are deemed to be correct as filed. In one recent year, the IRS audited about 1.3 million tax returns. Of the returns audited, the vast majority were either accepted as filed or all differences were settled by agreement between the agent and the taxpayer. Relatively few cases went beyond the initial auditor to a conference procedure. Nearly 85 percent of those going to conference were settled without judicial proceedings. During that year, the IRS conceded about 30 percent of the tax deficiency initially assessed. Considering only the agreed cases that were settled without trial, the IRS conceded an even larger percentage of the initial deficiency assessment. The result of judicial proceedings in tax matters at the trial court level during 1987 have been summarized in Table 15–1.

The point of these statistics is simply to impress upon the reader the following important conclusions:

1. The chances that any particular tax return will be selected for audit are something like 1 in 100.
2. The chances that any error in a tax return will be discovered are even less than 1 in 100 because the IRS agents obviously cannot detect every error on every return examined.
3. If a return is audited, the overwhelming odds are that the taxpayer and the IRS will be able to settle any dispute without a judicial hearing.
4. If the IRS and the taxpayer do resolve a disputed item without a judicial hearing, the probabilities are that the IRS will agree to accept less than the amount of the initial deficiency assessed.
5. If a dispute proceeds to trial, the chances are about 3 out of 10 that the taxpayer will win at least some portion of his or her case.

These conclusions are important for several reasons. First, they should explain why a competent tax adviser may not be impressed by the argument that

**FIGURE 15–2**

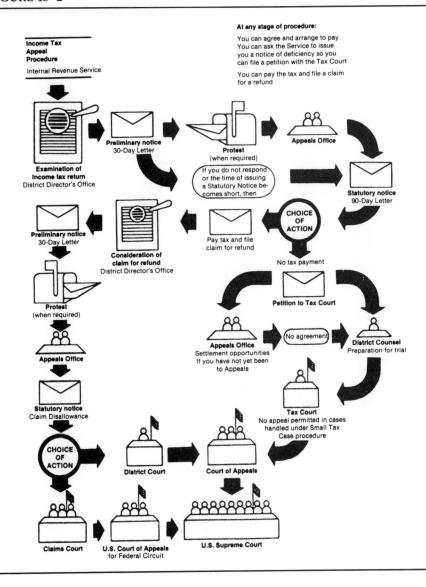

At any stage of procedure:

You can agree and arrange to pay
You can ask the Service to issue
you a notice of deficiency so you
can file a petition with the Tax Court

You can pay the tax and file a claim
for a refund

**Income Tax
Appeal
Procedure**
Internal Revenue Service

**Examination of
Income tax return**
District Director's Office

**Preliminary notice**
30-Day Letter

**Protest**
(when required)

If you do not respond
or the time of issuing
a Statutory Notice be-
comes short, then

**Appeals Office**

**Statutory notice**
90-Day Letter

**Preliminary notice**
30-Day Letter

**Consideration of
claim for refund**
District Director's Office

Pay tax and file
claim for refund

**CHOICE
OF
ACTION**

No tax payment

**Petition to Tax Court**

**Protest**
(when required)

**Appeals Office**

**Statutory notice**
Claim Disallowance

**Appeals Office**
Settlement opportunities
If you have not yet been
to Appeals

No agreement

**District Counsel**
Preparation for trial

**Tax Court**
No appeal permitted in cases
handled under Small Tax
Case procedure

**CHOICE
OF
ACTION**

**District Court**

**Court of Appeals**

**Claims Court**

**U.S. Court of Appeals**
for Federal Circuit

**U.S. Supreme Court**

something must be right just because a taxpayer has always done it that way and the IRS has never objected. Second, the statistics should explain why there is no real reason to panic when a taxpayer first learns that he or she is being audited. Third, the statistics should explain why the level of taxpayer assistance may be substantially less than ideal without the taxpayer ever being aware of this. Critics have often suggested that a surgeon's worst mistakes are buried, undiscovered. There can be little doubt that that observation holds true for many a tax adviser.

TABLE 15–1

| | Complete Taxpayer Victory (percent) | Split Decisions (percent) | Complete IRS Victory (percent) |
|---|---|---|---|
| Tax courts | 5 | 57 | 38 |
| District courts | 16 | 4 | 80 |
| Claims courts | 11 | 4 | 85 |

## TAXPAYER ASSISTANCE

Taxpayer advisory services have become a big business in the United States. It is estimated that there are currently more than 300,000 people offering their services to the public as tax advisers. Surprising as it may seem to many readers, most of these experts remain largely unregulated. In a world in which those who cut hair and fingernails can operate only by government license and regulation, it is surprising indeed that tax advisory services remain an open frontier.

### Questions of Competence

Most alleged tax experts can be divided between "regulated agents" and "unenrolled practitioners." The regulated agents can be further subdivided into (a) attorneys, (b) certified public accountants, and (c) "enrolled agents," or persons who are neither attorneys nor CPAs, but who have passed a special tax examination given by the Treasury Department. Attorneys and certified public accountants are automatically admitted to practice before the IRS, based upon their regular professional examinations and license. Of the estimated 300,000 people offering tax advisory services, approximately 120,000 are regulated and 180,000 are unenrolled practitioners. The 120,000 are regulated by Treasury Circular 230, as well as by the codes of ethics of the professions involved; the 180,000 are free to operate without risk of sanction other than the normal risk of civil and criminal liability, to which everyone is subject, and some preparer penalties that have been imposed since 1976. Although the latter group is free to claim almost anything that it wishes, the IRS will not allow an unenrolled practitioner to represent a taxpayer in an administrative conference.

Until the last few years, neither CPAs nor attorneys could advertise at all. This meant, of course, that those who were most likely to be capable of providing a valid tax advisory service were precluded from claiming their expertness, whereas those who had little or no special knowledge were entirely free to proclaim publicly anything that they wished. Under these conditions, the taxpayer might safely conclude only that anyone who could advertise or who could list himself as a tax expert in the Yellow Pages was probably not highly qualified as a tax expert, whereas anyone who could not make such claims just might be so qualified. The necessary "probably" and "might be" in the preceding sentence do little to add to a taxpayer's confidence in selecting a qualified tax adviser. Obviously, some unenrolled agents have reasonable skills in tax matters, while some who have proved their right to be licensed as attorneys or as certified public accountants are totally inept in matters of taxation. During the past few years, several states have granted attorneys with special expertise in selected areas, including taxation, the right to proclaim their special abilities to the world. It is hoped that the accounting profession will someday grant this same opportunity to its members. And, when that does happen, let us hope that certification will be by examination, not by self-proclamation, as it is with some attorneys. Until then, the buyer of tax advice must be wary of the service he or she receives.

**A Common Misconception.**    Most people erroneously believe that the formal education required of an attorney and a CPA includes a heavy background in taxation, especially federal income taxation. As a matter of fact, most colleges and universities offering a major in accounting require only one three-semester-hour course in taxation and most schools of law require no minimal study of taxation. Between 20 and 25 percent of the time devoted to the practice portion (which but one of three parts) of the nationally administered CPA examination is usually devoted to income tax questions. Although some state bar examinations include tax questions, other states have removed all tax questions from the bar examinations. Notwithstanding the minimal standards for formal tax education, a substantial number of certified public accountants and attorneys have become extremely competent in matters of taxation. Their general education in related subjects has been combined either with special graduate education in taxation or with heavy practical experience in tax problems. These professionals are, beyond any doubt, those best qualified to advise others on all matters of taxation. The major problem for the taxpayer seeking competent assistance is the fact that in most states there is no easy way to distinguish between highly qualified advisers and poorly qualified advisers. Someday, it is hoped in the near future, all of the state and federal professional associations in law and accountancy will recognize the need to certify tax specialists for the benefit of everyone concerned.

**A Worthless Guarantee.**    Some tax experts guarantee a taxpayer that they will pay for any technical errors made in their preparation of a tax return. The reader should observe that these guarantees extend only to the correct reporting of the facts as they are related to the preparer of the tax return. If the facts are erroneously reported, the preparer obviously cannot be held responsible for any additional tax imposed in a subsequent audit. More important, however, there may be a tendency of the "guaranteed" preparer to resolve all questionable items in favor of the government. To the extent that such a tendency exists, the guarantee becomes less than worthless. The guarantee actually may cost the taxpayer more than it saves. A real tax expert would explain all questionable issues to the taxpayer and allow the taxpayer to make the final decision on how those items will be reported. The taxpayer is, of course, entitled to know the expert's opinion of what he or she would do in the same circumstance, before reaching a conclusion. Given that kind of tax advisory service, a taxpayer cannot hold the expert responsible for an incorrect decision. Nevertheless, this would be the author's preferred way of resolving all doubtful issues. Even though a true tax expert may not be able to guarantee that the IRS and/or the courts will agree with a professional opinion on a difficult tax issue, an expert is very sensitive to the need to give consistently good tax advice and charges accordingly. The time required to reach a sound conclusion is the basis for the fee.

**What Is a Taxpayer to Do?**    The reader may well wonder how to find and recognize qualified taxpayer assistance if advertisements cannot be trusted and if it is not safe to assume that each and every CPA and attorney is knowledgeable in tax matters. The only certain method of locating qualified tax assistance known to the author is through personal reference. In other words, the only safe way to locate your first qualified tax adviser is to ask another taxpayer who has found out. Individuals who have been in business for a considerable period of time have encountered the need for qualified taxpayer assistance on a number of occasions, and they are usually willing to share their experiences with a fellow sufferer. Sometimes, on the basis of bitter personal experience, they will tell you who is not qualified, as well as suggest tax advisers whom they deem competent.

Once a taxpayer has made an initial contact with a qualified tax adviser, the taxpayer must decide what kind of service is needed and desired. Assuming that the taxpayer is engaged in a continuing business, it is the author's opinion that a taxpayer cannot be getting adequate service unless the taxpayer and the adviser are engaged in frequent communication with each other. The taxpayer must understand that an adviser will have to know *all* of the details of every proposed transaction at the *earliest possible* moment if he or she is to perform satisfactorily. Really qualified tax experts maintain the highest possible ethical standards and keep all client communications and records confidential. Therefore, the taxpayer has nothing to lose and everything to gain from sharing detailed plans with a tax adviser. A tax adviser who does nothing more than file tax returns on a timely basis is not rendering an adequate service to a continuing business. A good adviser will make numerous suggestions for change, as well as answer all of the taxpayer's inquiries. Such an adviser will also expect to be paid a reasonable fee for the work done.

## Questions of Cost

Most individuals have a natural reluctance to seek the advice of a competent tax adviser until long after the need for assistance has first been observed. The apparent reason for this reluctance is the belief that the fees charged by such advisers are exorbitant. Although it is true that good tax advisory service is expensive, it is seldom exorbitant, for several reasons. First, in many instances, a competent tax adviser will save the client substantially more in taxes than the charges for advice. Thus the taxpayer may come out ahead, not behind, in dollars. Second, the tax adviser's fees are usually deductible as a legal or accounting expense if business related or (subject to the 2 percent of AGI limitation) as a miscellaneous itemized deduction for individual taxpayers not engaged in a business. To the extent deductible, the cost of the service is shared by the government on a ratio determined by the taxpayer's marginal tax bracket. The higher the marginal tax bracket, the lower the real cost of the tax adviser's service. Third, most tax advisers bill their clients on a basis of hourly rates. These rates may range from \$30 to \$300 per hour for a qualified tax adviser. The taxpayer, however, generally need not fear that the adviser will be anxious to bill for the largest possible number of hours at the highest possible billing rate. Good tax advisers are so scarce that they cannot begin to handle the work that naturally gravitates to them. Consequently, the more competent the adviser (and very often the higher the billing rate), the more likely it is that he or she will either refer a problem to another firm or to a less experienced individual within a firm if a problem really does not warrant personal attention. Far from trying to acquire more clients, many of the qualified tax advisers known to the author are trying to reduce the number of clients they advise. Some charge a minimum fee to discourage the taxpayer with too small a problem. Fortunately, however, a competent adviser will always advise a client of any minimum fee before beginning work on a project. In summary, therefore, the author's advice to the reader is to aim too high rather than too low. Taking too simple a problem to an overly qualified tax adviser has a way of correcting itself in most cases; taking too complex a problem to an underqualified tax adviser has a way of becoming very costly in the long run, even though the real cost may not be discovered for several years.

## THE TAX FUTURE

No one, including the author, has a particularly clear view of what the future holds with regard to taxes. Successful tax planning must nevertheless take possible future tax changes into consideration. If the tax rates are going to increase significantly next year, we should all accelerate taxable income into this year and defer all possible tax deductions until next year. If the investment credit is to be reinstated anytime soon, taxpayers should consider the possibility of deferring orders for certain equipment. The prescriptions come easily if only we know the prognosis.

The Tax Reform Act of 1986 was a truly major piece of tax legislation; possibly the most significant single tax act since 1913. Because of the breadth of change and the sheer length of that public law, a follow-on technical corrections act is needed; it should have been passed in 1987 but, for largely political reasons, it remains in limbo in the fall of 1988. Although our politicians in Washington will inevitably stray beyond a narrow definition of technical correction when they finally do enact this bill, few people anticipate much further tax change of major importance before 1989.

What happens next will most likely depend upon the accuracy of the revenue projections that accompanied the 1986 Act. It was intended to be a revenue neutral bill. To achieve both revenue neutrality and a major reduction in the marginal tax rates on individual taxpayers, it was necessary to increase corporate income taxes by approximately $120 billion even though the corporate tax rates were also reduced. Early evidence suggests that the original revenue projections were unduly optimistic. If it were not for rather large surpluses in the social security trust funds, the current federal deficit would be well beyond the maximum spending limits of the Gramm–Rudman law. Exactly how the new Administration and Congress—to be elected in November 1988—will handle this problem is very uncertain.

Should a call for increased taxes become politically acceptable, there will, in all probability, be a major ideological fight over how the additional tax revenues could best be obtained. Some will argue strongly for simply increasing the present marginal income tax rates—either directly or via a surtax mechanism—while others will argue with equal force that the time has come for the federal government to find a new tax source for the additional revenues required. If the former opinion prevails, it is also predictable that many of the special provisions—most particularly the capital gain advantages—will return. If the latter opinion prevails, it is entirely possible that Congress will turn to the value-added tax (or VAT) for help. This variation of a national sales tax is one of relatively few tax bases capable of raising very large sums with minimal objection from the average taxpayer. Admittedly, several powerful political organizations would fight the introduction of VAT but, once enacted, there would be minimal objection to this tax from the voting public. Comparable revenue increases derived from alternative revenue sources—including major increases in the individual income tax—would be much more likely to generate major political dissent. State and local governments would likely oppose the entry of the federal government into any form of sales taxation because that has traditionally been their exclusive domain.

This is, therefore, a particularly difficult time to do much long-range tax planning. Models and projections that compound the presently low income tax rates into managerial recommendations are particularly suspect. Although it is entirely possible that the income tax rates will remain low (especially if the VAT advocates win), both historical perspective and international comparisons make that prediction a somewhat risky one.

Most major tax revisions enacted into law have been made retroactive to the date on which they were first discussed publicly in a congressional committee. The reader should therefore make a habit of following proposed tax legislation through daily newspaper accounts and weekly magazine reports. Any proposal that appears to harbor potential tax consequences for the reader or a business should be called to the immediate attention of a tax adviser. A really good tax adviser will take it from there.

## PROBLEMS AND ASSIGNMENTS

1. Businessperson A is pleased with tax adviser T because T always answers A's questions promptly, T always files A's tax returns on a timely basis, and none of A's tax returns have ever been questioned by the IRS. Would you agree with A that T is an excellent tax adviser? Discuss briefly.

2. The education and examination required of all lawyers and certified public accountants engaged in public practice are sufficient to justify the conclusion that these professionals are real tax experts. True or false? Explain briefly.

3. IRS agent I has just displayed his official credentials before taxpayer T in the course of a tax investigation. T observes that I's government identification badge states that I is an IRS special agent. T has no reason to be alarmed and should cooperate with I. True or false? Explain briefly.

4. Taxpayer T is the founder of the City Service Exchange Club. This club encourages its members to do things for each other; for example, T (a tax adviser) frequently prepares tax returns for other club members in exchange for their babysitting services, lawn-mowing services, auto repair services, etc. T has never reported the value of any of these services as taxable income, and the IRS has never questioned T's tax return in 20 years of filing. These facts properly support the conclusion that utilization of an exchange club membership does not create taxable income. True or false? Explain briefly.

5. In 1987, taxpayers won complete victories approximately 16 percent of the time in the district courts and 11 percent of the time in the Court of Claims; they won comparable victories only 5 percent of the time in the Tax Court. If your tax dispute cannot be settled short of litigation, these statistics are sufficient reason to avoid the Tax Court whenever possible. True or false? Explain.

6. Tax adviser T charges $100 per hour for professional services. Important details concerning two of T's clients are shown on the next page.

|                                                          | Taxpayer Little | Taxpayer Giant |
|----------------------------------------------------------|-----------------|----------------|
| Amount of tax in dispute                                 | $1,000          | $100,000       |
| Marginal tax rate (percent)                              | 15              | 34             |
| Changing of winning dispute (percent)                    | 50              | 50             |
| Number of tax adviser's hours required to handle dispute | 5               | 500            |

Both Little and Giant have an equal incentive to engage T to handle their dispute with the IRS. True or false? Explain.

7. If a taxpayer has sufficient funds, he or she can be assured that any dispute with the IRS can be continued until the Supreme Court has finally ruled on the issue. True or false? Explain.

8. Assuming that a taxpayer has not understated the gross income reported to the IRS by 25 percent or more, there is little reason to retain federal income tax returns for more than three years after the due date of the return. True or false? Explain.

9. What, in your opinion, are the prospects for massive tax reform in the near future? Contrast your personal opinion with that of the author.

10. Some tax policy experts suggest that people should be taxed according to what they take out of the economy, not what they put into it. Compare the income tax and the value-added tax according to this standard.

11. What is the aftertax cost of $10,000 worth of tax advice to an individual in the 28 percent marginal tax bracket who:
    a. Does not itemize deductions?
    b. Itemizes deductions, has $200,000 of AGI, and has no other "miscellaneous itemized deductions" (i.e., those that are subject to the 2 percent-of-AGI limitation)?
    c. Itemizes deductions, has $200,000 of AGI, and has $5,000 of "other itemized deductions"?
    d. Is subject to the alternative minimum tax?

# Case 15–1

Julie Smith is seeking a tax preparer to prepare her individual income tax return for the year just ended. Julie is a self-employed consultant with gross revenues of $50,000. In previous years she was able to do her own return, but this year she has questions about how to report some office equipment and a car she is leasing.

Acme Tax Service advertises that they have been in business for 15 years and that they will do a "basic return" for $100. Acme guarantees that they will pay the tax and penalty due for any error that is discovered by the IRS.

Bob Barker, CPA, has talked with Julie over the phone and said that he could do her return for $100. Bob has been a CPA for two years. Bob does not offer any guarantee about what he will do if an error is discovered.

    a. Is there likely to be any difference in the amount of Julie's tax liability calculated by these preparers?

    b. Is there likely to be a difference in the quality between these preparers?

# Index